D0709275

The Revenger's Madness

The Revenger's Madness
A STUDY OF REVENGE TRAGEDY MOTIFS

Charles A. Hallett and Elaine S. Hallett

L.C.C.C. LIBRARY

University of Nebraska Press / Lincoln and London

Publishers on the Plains

UNP

The publication of this book was assisted by a grant from the Andrew W. Mellon Foundation.

Copyright © 1980 by the University of Nebraska Press
All rights reserved
Manufactured in the United States of America

Library of Congress Cataloging in Publication Data

Hallett, Charles A
    The revenger's madness.

    Bibliography: p. 323
    Includes index.
    1. Revenge in literature.   2. English drama—Early modern and Elizabethan,
1500–1600—History and criticism.   3. English drama—17th century—History
and criticism.   4. English drama (Tragedy)—History and criticism.   I.   Hallett,
Elaine S., 1935–   joint author.   II.   Title.
PR658.R45H3   1980   822'.0512   80–13893
ISBN 0–8032–2309–9

To Ken Frost

Contents

Acknowledgments

WHEN ELAINE AND I set off on the journey through the realm of revenge tragedy, we felt ourselves entering an exciting and mysterious region of English drama. Little did we know how expansive a domain this was or how long it would be before we emerged again. In the course of our critical explorations we have constantly drawn on the labors and insights of others and have in various ways incurred obligations, so many, in fact, that we cannot hope to thank each person individually. We are extremely conscious, as anyone working in the field must be, of the debt we owe to Fredson Bowers. His pioneering study of the field laid the groundwork that made much of this book possible. But we also owe much to later studies, as we have acknowledged in our notes.

To those colleagues and friends without whose personal encouragement the present study would not exist, we wish to express particular gratitude. First we must thank Miriam Gilbert, Ray Heffner, and Bill Kupersmith of *Philological Quarterly*, whose enthusiastic reception of the theory inspired us to write the book. We are also indebted to Edward Partridge, who helped us to clarify our thoughts about the madness; to Roy Battenhouse, Mark Caldwell, Scott Colley, Alan Dessen, and Albrecht Strauss, all of whom read and commented on one or another of the chapters; to Charles Forker and Norman Rabkin, who made valuable suggestions on the whole manuscript; and to Susan O'Malley, who lent us extensive material on Thomas Goffe. We sincerely appreciate, too, the generosity of Fordham University, which provided funds in the form of a Faculty Fellowship to assist with expenses of writing and research.

There is another debt we take special pleasure in acknowledging. For many years now we have been able to boast that among our friends is a man dedicated to the life of the mind as few are. Anyone who knows Ken Frost can give witness to the endlessly stimulating quality of his conversation. Many of the ideas in this book were hammered out over coffee, over dinner, and over the telephone with Ken. For this, much thanks.

And, finally, to speak as individuals for a moment—from Chuck, a special thanks to Mark Caldwell and Bill Siebenschuh, who endeavored to keep him sane as he contemplated revenge at Fordham. And from Elaine, the deepest gratitude to Grace and Wallace Stewartson, for bearing her frenzies with infinite patience while this book was in production, and to June Schlueter, for enduring three years of lunatic chatter.

The following publishers have allowed us to reprint previously published material:

Chapter 1 appeared as "Andrea, Andrugio, and King Hamlet: The Ghost as Spirit of Revenge" in *Philological Quarterly,* volume 56, number 1, copyright 1977 by The University of Iowa. Used by permission.

Chapter 7 appeared as "*Antonio's Revenge* and the Integrity of Revenge Tragedy Motifs" in *Studies in Philology,* volume 76, number 4, October, 1979. © 1979 The University of North Caro-Press. Reprinted by permission of the publisher.

Quotations used throughout the text appeared as follows: From *Hamlet, Titus Andronicus, King Lear, As You Like It,* and *The Merchant of Venice* by William Shakespeare in *The Riverside Shakespeare,* edited by G. Blakemore Evans et al. Copyright 1974 by Houghton Mifflin Company. Reprinted by permission. From

Antonio's Revenge, The Broken Heart, The Spanish Tragedy, and *The Revenger's Tragedy.* Used by permission of University of Nebraska Press. From *The Plays and Poems of George Chapman.* Used by permission of Routledge & Kegan Paul Ltd. From *Horestes.* Used by permission of The Malone Society.

The Revenger's Madness

Editions used in quoting from
primary sources are identified in
the Selected Bibliography on
page 325.

Introduction

Let the poor girl go mad; we always have a mad scene
in a Revenge Play.

G. B. Harrison, *Shakespeare's Tragedies*

REVENGE TRAGEDY IS NOTED (or notorious) for its theatricality.
True, certain playwrights were assiduously grinding out revenge
plots to the proven formula. Henry Chettle is one. Thomas Goffe
is another. But there is increasing recognition that other playwrights, even John Marston, had higher aspirations. Fredson
Bowers reminds us that the Elizabethans were intensely interested in revenge "as a criminal passion," noting that the heroes of
Hamlet, The Spanish Tragedy, Antonio's Revenge, and *Titus Andronicus* are "normal persons caught up by demands often too strong
for their powers and forced into a course of action which warps
and twists their characters and may lead even to the disintegration of insanity." G. K. Hunter holds a similar view: "Hieronimo
and Titus (perhaps we should add Hamlet) are martyrs to their
own sense of duty and justice; their martyrdom carries them into
the area of passionate and evil behavior which lies waiting, even
for the virtuous man, at the very edge of his endurance, close to or

3

indistinguishable from madness." J. M. R. Margeson, too, had this insight:

> The demand for revenge, like love, is assumed to be a passion that it is impossible to resist once it is given sufficient cause to exist. Destiny imposes the necessity of revenge upon certain individuals, and when those individuals are innocent of any part in the original, crucial deed, revenge becomes an agonizing but inescapable burden. . . . It was the revenge play that first showed how a great character could be overcome by evil tides of feeling in the act of opposing them and be driven to breakdown or madness.[1]

But as frequently as this relationship between Elizabethan revenge tragedy and human experience is noted, its implications are rarely explored. Although commentators realize that the playwrights are struggling to analyze the emotion of revenge, most are content to state the fact and rush on to matters which interest them more. Scholarship on revenge tragedy has been confined, almost from the start, to two major preoccupations. Critics study either the history of the genre or audience attitudes toward it.

From the beginning there was an overwhelming interest in the history of the form. In short order the major conventions of the genre were isolated, the basic formula defined, the theatricality of the conventions explored. No sooner had the elements which held the genre together—a ghost, for example, and a madness—been successfully identified than scholars set out to determine the sources of those elements. Sweeping explorations are regularly made through any realm of early drama that might harbor clues to the origins of revenge tragedy. Some scholars trace the entire genre to Seneca, some to early Tudor drama. Others suspect the origins to be in the villain-hero play, still others in satire. These researchers seek out kinship as well as ancestry. They hope to identify the borrowings of Marston from Kyd, Shakespeare from Marston, Tourneur from Shakespeare. Questions of dating and influence become paramount. Such studies examine the conventional motifs more for the evidence they give that one playwright's work derives from another's than for what they tell us about the revenge experience.[2]

This first kind of revenge tragedy criticism handles the plays as documents of theatrical history. The alternative approach, even more common, reads them as enigmas to be understood only after detailed study of contemporary social custom. Pondering whether the Elizabethan audience considered the revenger justified or guilty, the critic concentrates upon the playgoer rather than the hero. He focuses upon audience attitudes. Ideas in manuals, sermons, and other texts replace his own emotional responses as the basis for judgment. This approach to revenge tragedy has a long and venerable tradition dating back before Bowers wrote his influential book. It has received fresh impetus from Eleanor Prosser's *Hamlet and Revenge*, which raises once more the question of whether the orthodox view or the popular countercode was definitive in governing audience responses to the revenger.[3]

Both of these approaches—in practice the two are often combined—have continuously dominated the scholarship. Even while commentators speak of the passion which triggered the playwrights' imagination, they regard it as incidental that that passion is revenge. Many critics assume that any passion—love, envy, jealousy, pride—could have served as the backbone of the action. And unfortunately, the entire thrust of this kind of scholarship precludes our ever discovering whether revenge tragedy has significance as a literary form.

This book tries to approach revenge tragedy through experience. It requests the reader to focus upon the passion of revenge. It argues that the dramatists, to describe that passion, ingeniously wove an intricate symbolism from the theatrical elements at hand. This symbolism was at once universal and personal—universal in its ability to illuminate the effects of the passion of revenge upon the human psyche and personal in its adaptability to the vision of the individual author who utilized it.

In searching for the significance of revenge tragedy, one must first determine why the passion of revenge could capture the imagination of three generations of playwrights—among them some of the greatest that the world has known—and inspire them to write their finest work. The appeal lay in two specific aspects of this particular passion which make it a natural subject for dramatic treatment. From the point of view of the larger, more universal perspective, the revenge situation provided an action that had the potential of raising the hero's story to tragic proportions. Here was a situation—the same situation used by Aeschylus in *The Eumenides*—where the hero was caught between two goods. Whichever way he turned, he was right—and yet wrong. The revenger, seeking to comprehend the meaning of his situation and frustrated by the seeming injustice of it, became for the playwrights an emblem of Man himself. Yet at the same time, at the level of the particular, the study of the effects of the passion of revenge upon the human psyche provided a foundation for character delineation which is probably insurpassable. Individual psychological reactions to stress are always material for drama, and given the revenge situation stress was both inevitable and accumulating. The emotional pressures generated by the strain were intriguing, and one playwright after another turned to the form as a means of probing the psychology of revenge.

A detailed analysis of the relationship between the revenge experience and the tragic mode will be attempted in chapter 5. Until then, we shall leave this aspect of the matter in abeyance. The intervening chapters, and indeed the bulk of this book, will be concerned with the passion rather than the tragic situation, that is, with the attempts of the dramatists to analyze the changes wrought upon the psyche by the emotions of revenge. Our subject is their collective and individual insights into the passion and the symbolic methods developed to dramatize these insights.

Thomas Kyd and those who followed him had basic insights about revenge, consciously understood or otherwise, which had profound effects both on the form and content of the plays. The first, that revenge is a deep-seated fundamental urge, as fundamental perhaps as love, is best studied in the villain-revenger. Although the revenger is most often portrayed in revenge tragedy as one who has a legitimate grievance, he is invariably coupled with the villain-revenger who does not. This dichotomy of hero-revenger versus villain-revenger has considerable symbolic importance for the genre. The hero-revenger is one who is led (one might almost say dragged) to revenge by forces outside himself. The villain-revenger is a man prompted to his actions by nothing more than his own cravings. As a symbol, he represents that aspect of revenge which originates in the psyche of the individual.

The authors of revenge tragedy saw that at the core of human nature there is a volcano of smoldering rage. Its presence is not normally acknowledged because, except in cases of dementia or in rare acts of gratuitous violence, this free-floating anger is never allowed to make its way to the surface. Although repressed, the fire is not extinguished. And occasionally, when it can disguise itself as something else, something more acceptable to the individual himself as well as to society, it finds release. Revenge is one of these self-justifications. Unconsciously, we continually scan the actions of others, like sensitive radar units, hoping to pick up a word or gesture to build on. We keep our nerve endings raw and our tempers short, and we grow ingenious in finding imagined offenses to be angry at and to seek revenge for.

The fact that the purely psychologically motivated revenger is invariably depicted as a villain-revenger highlights a fundamental truth about *this* kind of revenge: frequently, only the revenger himself is deceived into believing there is any justice in in the act. The dramatists are going beyond the questionable validity of any particular case. They have reached down and exposed the psychological foundations of revenge itself, which has nothing to do with the particular object that appears to have triggered the revenge but is actually a release for the floating rage within.

In most of the revenge tragedies, this aspect of revenge is simply touched on as a contrast to the more complex (because not wholly psychological) revenge of the protagonist. We must wait for John Webster in *The Duchess of Malfi* to bring the villain-revenger forward for closer psychological scrutiny in the character of Ferdinand.

Beyond this, the dramatists definitely understood revenge to be an emotion that could easily present itself as having a claim on the reasonable as well as the irrational, and on the moral as well as the evil. At times indeed, as in *Hamlet*, it seems the one necessary course of action. Yet no matter what the circumstances or who the individual, revenge will prove cataclysmic. And that is the second insight of the dramatists, that the revenger, whoever he is, whatever the moral quality of his intentions, has launched himself on a predictable course of action. It does not

matter in the least whether his philosophic point of view is
Christian, Humanist, Stoical, or Machiavellian, whether he is a
hero or a villain. The fact that he is a revenger determines his
fate.

From the conventional elements they found in the theater of
their day, the Elizabethan playwrights fashioned a form of
drama which gave expression to the archetypal shape of revenge. They took various of the stage conventions and by
embuing them with universal significance, raised them above the
realm of theatricality into the realm of symbol. These symbols
are in fact those conventional elements of the Elizabethan
stage—the ghost, the madness, the delay, the play-within-a-play,
the multiple murders, and the avenger's death—which have
been recognized as appearing with such surprising frequency in
the revenge tragedies as to be particularly characteristic of them.
The playwrights—Marston, Shakespeare, Tourneur, for example—inherited these devices as part of the paraphernalia of the
Elizabethan stage. But by the combination of their insight into
the nature of revenge and their innate dramatic sense they
transformed articles of common stagecraft and convention into
symbols and in doing so forged a configuration that has exercised immense power over the imagination for more than three
hundred years.

A study of the symbolic meaning of revenge tragedy might well
begin with the symbol which comes earliest in the plays, *the ghost.*
In analyzing any single symbol of the genre, one must remember,
of course, that meaningful images are never unequivocal and
always require interpretation. One must also bear in mind that
each of these plays blends themes from revenge tragedy with
themes arising independently from the playwright's personal
vision; because of their multiple functions, the symbolic motifs
must sometimes embrace a wide spectrum of meanings. Nevertheless, certain constant patterns can be discerned. The ghost,
obviously, represents the supernatural. It informs us that, in the
case of these hero-revengers, the impulse to revenge originates
outside of man, as a force in the universe resembling that force
which the Greeks personified in the Furies. Authoritative, but
hardly identifiable with the God of Christianity whose primary
attributes include mercy and forgiveness, it exerts irresistible
pressures upon the revenger to do a deed which it presents as

natural. But, with an ambiguity typical of all the motifs, this "spirit of revenge" also rises inside the avenger; its voice is as much the voice of the revenger's own passion as it is of his recognition of nature's demand that blood be paid for blood.

However justified his cause or noble his convictions, the revenger, once he surrenders himself to the entreaties of the ghost, is no longer rational. Were the murder he is to commit a rational act, no ghost would be needed to stir him to it. To act, he must pass beyond the rational world to dwell in the inner recesses of his own mind, where nothing takes precedence over his craving for revenge. Passion must consume his entire being. This is another way of saying that the ghost pushes the revenger into madness. Paradoxically, in obeying one natural order, the revenger is disregarding another. In the Christian scheme of things, it was natural to follow reason. To submit the rational soul to the dictates of the irascible was considered a distortion of the divine order and consequently a form of madness.

The madness universally found in revenge tragedy is not a crowd-pleasing spectacle, meant to send shivers up the spines of those in the galleries, but an integral part of the revenge theme. The Renaissance assumption that irrational emotions distract and craze the psyche allows the madness to function symbolically as well as literally and gives it supreme dramatic effectiveness. This motif becomes the central symbol that binds *all* of the motifs together. Not only is the madness initiated by the appearance of the ghost; it also initiates the motif of delay, which in turn culminates in the play-within-the-play. There, still another aspect of the madness of the revenger—the excess—climaxes the drama and drives it toward its conclusion in the tragic death of the avenger.

From one vantage point (and let us quickly put in a cautionary word—this is one of several views of the revenger that the alert reader or theatergoer must keep in his mind simultaneously), the whole structure of the revenge tragedy can be understood in terms of the revenger's efforts to free himself from the restraints that forbid the act of vengeance, a process that involves moving from sanity to madness. As these restraints are the very characteristics that mark him as a civilized rational man, the revenger, to achieve his end, must reject what is best in him. However, virtues deeply engrained are not easily removed. The change must be gradual. And it must include a radical shift in the way the psyche views the world. The process through which the revenger hardens himself to carry out the entreaties of the ghost is a process of reshaping the world. Since the objective world resists the changes the revenger would impose upon it, the world he alters is unfortunately the subjective world. This period of change is represented symbolically by the delay. The delay might be defined as the pause necessitated by the revenger's need to construct his world-within-a-world, that private, self-justifying world which will foster the act the external world would never sanction.

The delay leads to and ends at the play-within-the-play, for entrance into this self-created illusory world is what finally allows the revenger to act. Given the need for a symbol of the revenger's subjective world, the motif of the play-within-the-play is particularly appropriate. Any student of the drama knows well the commonplace that every play creates its own world and defines its own reality. How fitting, therefore, to represent the world of madness as a play-within-a-play. As such, it is a world-within-a-world, a reality-within-a-reality. The point is always made in revenge tragedy that the revenger is personally responsible for the play-within-the-play. Whether it be the *Soliman and Perseda* of Hieronimo, "The Mousetrap" of Hamlet, or the closing masque of *Antonio's Revenge,* this world-within-a-world is established by the revenger. The play-within-the-play is to be the arena in which he shall accomplish his own ends.

In most instances the delay is not the only element that ends in the play-within-the-play; the drama itself reaches its climax here. Having successfully established in the play-within-the-play a private world which is approbative of his desire for revenge, the revenger acts and, in so doing, draws the tragedy to a conclusion. By acting within the framework of the mock play, the revenger is symbolically confusing the real world with a world created out of his own psyche which he has projected upon it. Such confusion, followed by such dire consequences, must be expected to unleash those forces in the universe which maintain the balance and harmony so necessary for the continuance of life.

The fact that the revenger never kills only the man against

whom he has a grievance but indulges himself in a blood-bath before the final curtain is as integral a part of the experience as the madness. The act of revenge does not correct an imbalance and restore order, purely and simply, with the even exchange of eye for eye, tooth for tooth. Revenge is itself an act of excess. To give added emphasis to this point and to highlight the symbolic impact, the playwright renders the excess in terms of the multiple murders that the revenger commits. Again the symbol reflects the experience. The spirit of revenge is not economical of human life. Since the act of revenge is only one part an act of retaliation, with the other part being a savage desire to strike out against the frustrations of life itself, the fact that the revenger is not satisfied to kill only the party against whom the ghost has entreated revenge is quite realistic as well as symbolic. Like a child's tantrum, the rage of revenge has a tendency to become undifferentiating. The specific incident that triggers the emotion is like a fuse burning down through the levels of consciousness to a point where not only reason but even self-restraint gives way to that smoldering rage that seeks its expression through violence.

The passion that drives a man to hold human life cheap hardly makes a distinction between the lives of others and his own. This brings us to the final motif, the death of the avenger. From the outset it should be admitted that in several of the revenge tragedies the death of the avenger seems contrived. Even *Hamlet* may be faulted in this respect. Yet this is more a criticism of how the event is handled than a claim that the death is not felt to be inevitable, for by the end of most revenge tragedies, there seems to be no way the revenger could go on living. He has committed atrocities that equal and in some cases even surpass those of his antagonist, and if justice requires the villain's death, it also requires the revenger's.

The revenger's death follows closely upon the play-within-the-play, which his acts of vengeance have shattered. There is always in revenge tragedy a feeling that the action is truncated. In *Oedipus Rex*, the hero learns all there is to learn from the tragic action he has been caught in. In *The Spanish Tragedy* or *The Revenger's Tragedy*, the heroes do not learn nearly as much from their actions as do the spectators. They die victims of their own passions without fully realizing why. This, too, is part of the tragedy of revenge. The passion is ultimately blinding rather than illuminating.

The passion of revenge, then, is such that, once the mind is freed from the restraints that normally control that passion, a fatal chain of events is set in progress. Transformations take place within the avenger, which, though requiring a certain period of time, alter his perception of the world to an extent that will enable him to perform heinous deeds and make his own death in atonement for these deeds inevitable. The conventional motifs actually function as dramatic symbols for the various stages of this archetypal experience and are given their meaning by playwrights who, part consciously and part subconsciously, recognized the primordial significance of the pattern of the revenger's actions.

But if all of this is true, if revenge is in fact an archetypal experience and the revenge tragedies are actually about this experience, why has the archetype not been discovered before? Part of the answer lies in the fact that critics have consistently assumed that the function of the revenge motifs remains essentially theatrical. The conventions are habitually dismissed as gimmicks passed on from playwright to playwright simply because of their popularity with the groundlings. The ghost, for example, has been described as no more than "a serviceable piece of dramatic machinery" which "enabled the playwright to place his audience in possession of the preliminary data." The delay is widely viewed as a device to keep the plot from ending before the five acts have run their course. The mass murders are said to occur because playgoers liked their tragedies "richly coloured" with blood. In general, the motifs are considered "melodramatic touches that prevent us from taking the tragedy seriously."

Another part of the problem is that none of the plays are single-mindedly revenge tragedies in the sense that we have been speaking of revenge. The Jacobean dramatists were all highly individualistic artists. While it is true that they were at times in the grip of ideas that reached beyond themselves and their comprehension, it is also true that each stamped his work with an individual hallmark. The archetypal experience is there but it is not the totality. The Renaissance playwright, unlike his anonymous predecessors who shaped the great mystery cycles, is no longer willing to be solely the instrument through which the archetypes find expression. He has a personal vision which he wishes to express. And at times these personal preoccupations are only marginally related to the supposedly central theme of the work. So it is in *Hamlet*. Although the revenge structure is present there, Shakespeare's play is better approached as the study of a young man's dawning awareness of the existence of evil in the world (and to say this is not to begin to suggest the scope of Shakespeare's personal vision in *Hamlet*). In a similar way, the revenge motifs in *The Spanish Tragedy* are subordinated to Thomas Kyd's examination of the various levels of justice, in *The Revenge of Bussy D'Ambois* to George Chapman's interest in Stoicism, and so on. There is thus no such thing as a pure revenge tragedy, even among the earliest examples, to measure others against.

The necessity of adapting the motifs to the personal vision, moreover, means that the motifs themselves are constantly being subjected to shifting perspectives, with the result that in any cursory study the differences become further accentuated because the symbolism of the motifs, though suggested quite early by Kyd, is understood by his successors with varying degrees of clarity. Marston, at one end of the scale, fails to comprehend the full significance of certain conventions and thus violates their integrity, whereas Shakespeare, at the other end, so fully grasps their significance that he extends them far beyond their original range. The underlying functions of the motifs within the configuration consequently are unwittingly disguised.

Still another factor must be taken into account. While the individual playwrights recognize the appropriateness of the elements of the revenge tragedy, it always remains a form intuited and never codified; consequently, the prologues and epilogues from which we cull our knowledge of the critical attitudes of the period give us no hint of the important underpinnings of the revenge tragedy symbols. This silence, too, has allowed the significance of the motifs to go unheralded for so long.

For all of these reasons, the motifs which became traditional symbols for the various stages of the passion of revenge have never been explored for their fundamental experiential significance. It is to this task that we shall immediately set ourselves, in the hope first of convincing the reader that these motifs do carry for the playwrights the specific meanings attributed to them here and second of indicating the subtle ways in which the motifs are affected by their merger with the playwright's own personal preoccupations.

Because the goal of this study is more to prove that each motif has both an integrity of its own and a specific relationship to its fellows than to explain the historical development of the motifs, we have chosen to focus upon the four plays in which the original configuration remains most evident—Kyd's *The Spanish Tragedy*, Marston's *Antonio's Revenge,* Shakespeare's *Hamlet,* and Tourneur's *The Revenger's Tragedy*—with occasional references to less significant revenge plays where pertinent. The statements made here are true to some degree of other plays which belong to the genre, providing that the adaptations made as a result of the playwright's personal vision are taken into consideration; however, the theory is meant to be applied primarily to those plays where Kyd's influence remains the dominant one. Just as special emphasis will be placed upon the tragedies which are at the center of the genre, so preference will be given to the motif which stands at the heart of these plays—the madness. As the unifying motif through which all the others cohere, this motif is the first that should be fully understood, and, as the least understood at present, it needs the most attention.

Part I
The Experiential Basis of the Motifs

Chapter 1
The Ghost & Its Call to Excess

Three ghosts crying Vindicta.
Hearke Lords, as in a hollow place a farre,
The dreadfull shrikes and clamors that resound,
And sound reuenge vpon this traitors soule,
Traitor to kinne and kinde, to Gods and men.
Now Nemisis vpon her doubling drum,
Moude with this gastly mone, this sad complaint,
Larumes aloud into Alectos eares,
And with her thundering wakes whereas they lie,
In caue as darke as hell, and beds of steele,
The furies, iust impes of dire reuenge.

George Peele, *The Battle of Alcazar*

THREE REASONS WERE GIVEN in the introduction for the failure of contemporary scholars to detect the significance of the various revenge tragedy conventions: first, the natural inclination to overlook ideas that are never explicitly stated; second, the persistent habit of viewing the motifs as machinery employed for sensational effect; and third, the understandable tendency to ignore similarities in meaning because of more striking differences that arise as the artists impose their individual themes and styles upon the basic formula. In this chapter—focusing upon the ghost and its association with excess—all three of these notions will be shown to be in error; however, the last shall be foremost in our discussion. The changes wrought upon the ghost as this awesome figure is recast by one playwright after another to fit new molds are extremely instructive. In each of the plays in which the

17

ghost takes a significant role its position is unique. Yet underlying this seeming diversity there exists a remarkable unanimity
of purpose. The motif has a symbolic integrity that transcends the
personal vision. Analyzing in detail the successive reincarnations
of this "old truepenny," therefore, leads to a discovery of the
general way in which the universal and the particular are combined by the playwrights in *all* of the motifs.

I Preserved for us by the author of *A Warning for Fair
Women* (1590) is an amusing stage picture of the conventional Senecan ghost:

> A filthie whining ghost,
> Lapt in some fowle sheete, or a leather pelch,
> Comes skreaming like a pigge halfe stickt,
> And cries *Vindicta*, revenge, revenge:
> With that a little Rosen flasheth forth,
> Like smoke out of a Tabacco pipe, or a boyes squib.[1]

One can match this judgment, delivered derogatorily against a
character called Tragedie by another personifying Comedie,
with any number of commentaries from our own time:

> When Shakespeare wrote, the standard way to make a ghost com-
> prehensible was to imitate Seneca. The fact that most imitation Sene-
> can ghosts appeared first in hades and in a prologue fairly well fixed
> the understanding that the audience could have of them. As they were
> of hades they were genuinely antique shades of the dead; as they were
> of the prologue, they were machinery, decoration, signposts of an
> author's not very subtle intention. This kind of ghost was not only
> well-understood but well-worn on the Elizabethan stage. Few serious
> showings of the supernatural could be better insulation against any
> shock of life than the convention of the ghost with a mouthful of
> classical names and a yell for revenge.[2]

Like most judgments, these have elements of truth. Dramatically, the revenge tragedy ghost was never astonishingly successful. Of all the Senecan ghosts, including Gorlois, Abdelmunen, Albanact, Corineus, Andrea, Andrugio, Agamemnon,
and King Hamlet, only the latter escapes censure.[3] Yet the

melodramatic quality of such scenes has prevented us from seeing the ghost's value as a symbol.

Let us pay particular attention to the attributes assigned to
these "Senecan" ghosts. First, as Robert H. West declares, the
early ghosts were invariably "of hades": they cavorted with
Pluto, Proserpine, Minos, Aeacus, and Rhadamanthus, Hell's
judges, as well as with Cerberus, Sisyphus, Tantalus, and other
inhabitants of that nether region. Second, their arrival on the
earth spreads this lower kingdom's darkness over the human
world. In *The Battle of Alcazar* and *Antonio's Revenge,* as in *Locrine,*
"Hellish night, in cloudie charriot seated, / Casteth her mists on
shadie *Tellus* face, / VVith sable mantels couering all the earth,"
such darkness, of course, "foretelling some vnwonted miserie."[4]
Third, these frantic ghosts are filled with a particular desire, this
desire being expressed in the chilling cry, "*Vindicta,* revenge,
revenge." Finally, only through the spilling of blood can that
desire be satisfied. The call of blood for blood is as integral to the
conception of the Senecan ghost as are Hell and night:

> *Ghost of Albanact.* I traiterous *Humber,* thou shalt find it so.
> Yea to thy cost thou shalt the same behold,
> With anguish, sorrow, and with sad laments,
> The grassie plaines that now do please thine eies,
> Shall ere the night be coloured all with blood,
> The shadie groues which now inclose thy campe
> And yeeld sweet sauours to thy damned corps,
> Shall ere the night be figured all with blood,
> The profound streame that passeth by thy tents,
> And with his moisture serueth all thy campe,
> Shall ere the night conuerted be to blood,
> Yea with the blood of those thy stragling boyes,
> For now reuenge shall ease my lingring griefe,
> And now reuenge shall glut my longing soule.
> [*Locrine* 3.3.1099–112]

The hysteria communicated by the Senecan ghost was not new
in 1588, nor was it invented between A.D. 33 and 65 when Seneca
himself was writing. Throughout the history of Western society,
man seems to have recognized the existence of a mysterious and
inexplicable compulsion that presses itself upon the world as
soon as a deed of violence is perpetrated. The Greeks made
many attempts to express the concept and perhaps their efforts

help illuminate it. According to Jane Harrison, the most primitive attempt to deal with the experience led to the belief that blood spilled upon the earth caused a pollution which culminated in a curse upon the murderer, demanding blood for blood. At a later period, as reflected in a "tale of bygone days" quoted by Harrison from Plato's *Laws,* it was felt that the ghost of the murdered man was able to exert enough pressure upon the mind of the murderer to drive him to madness. It was perhaps a short step from this explanation of instinctual justice to the next—the vengeful ghost was named, and the Erinyes, the Angry Ones, came into being:

> The idea of Erinys as distinct from Ker is developed *out of a human relation intensely felt.* The Erinys primarily is the Ker of a human being unrighteously slain. Erinys is not death; it is the outraged soul of the dead man crying for vengeance; it is the Ker as Poine. In discussing the Keres it has been abundantly shown that ghost is a word too narrow: Keres denote a wider animism. With Erinys the case is otherwise: the Erinyes are primarily human ghosts, but all human ghosts are not Erinyes, only those ghosts that are angry, and that for a special reason, usually because they have been murdered. Other cases of angry ghosts are covered by the black Ker. It is the vengeful inhumanity of the Erinyes, arising as it does from their humanity, which marks them out from the Keres. . . . The Erinyes are primarily the vengeful souls of murdered men.[5]

By the time of Aeschylus, this sense of outrage which gives rise to the demand of blood for blood has been given solid form in the Erinyes of the *Oresteia.* In Greek thought, the compulsion emanating from the deed of violence directs itself against the murderer, making him an outcast and a renegade. In Elizabethan drama, it communicates itself to the revenger at the moment he learns of the wrong. But in both cases, its origin is external, mysterious, and somehow primeval. The anger that inspires this revenge is assumed to be more than a psychological phenomenon; it has a definite, if ineffable, objective reality.

But one need not go to Seneca or the Greeks to find a clarification of the ghost's purpose and function. George Peele in *The Battle of Alcazar* (1592) is quite explicit about the mythology of revenge and its significance. An "vnbeleeuing Moore," the murderer of the play, puts to death his uncle and two brothers, an act which disturbs the world order. Immediately the three slain men reappear as ghosts, giving testimony to the imbalance through their cries of "Vindicta." Their "dreadful shrikes and clamors" reach the ears of Nemesis, high mistress of revenge, who in turn "awakes the God of warre, / And cals the furies from Auernus crags." All of these forces combine to act upon the revenger Abdelmelec, who is thus moved to take action against the tyrant.[6]

Peele's reference to the *awakening* of Nemesis and the Furies is by no means merely decorative. The playwright implies the existence of natural forces that lie dormant until roused by atrocities too great for the world to bear. What these forces may be, where they come from, may remain mysterious; the orthodox theology of the Christian religion has given them no place in its mythology. But, say the playwrights, this element of the irrational cannot be excluded from any profile of justice that claims to be complete. The Senecan ghosts in all their shrillness are intermediaries between certain supernatural forces and mankind. They stress with an urgency that arises from man's most primitive instincts the need to right an imbalance resulting from some unnatural violation of human life.

II In the classic Kydian revenge tragedy (as distinct from the revenge chronicle), the ghost's role is slightly broader. The ghost speaks, in general, as the spirit of revenge—nearly, at times, as its allegorical representation. As the embodiment of the impulse for revenge, its demands are unambiguous, immoderate, and recognize no obligations in the direction of mercy or forgiveness. Its voice is the voice of passion. The effect on the avenger is to alter his perceptions and transform his relations with other characters. This spirit is both a reflection of the passion that is within the avenger, and a reminder that that passion is itself, at least in part, a response to a natural law that is external to the psyche in which it is aroused. The ghost, when it visits the revenger to prompt him to "remember me," consequently appears to bring with it the sanction and authority of another world, seemingly freeing the avenger from those mundane legal injunctions which would ordinarily forbid acts of vengeance. Because the ghost symbolizes natural law speaking directly to the passions, its power is at times irresistible, though not unlimited. The ghost itself is opposed by a higher power, one which prohibits the very actions which the ghost requires. This irreconcilable conflict between the forces that vie for the control of the individual indelibly marks the story of the revenger as tragedy rather than chronicle.

In Andrea, the ghost of *The Spanish Tragedy,* Kyd has embodied many of these attributes. Scholars have ignored this ghost's symbolic function, sometimes passing it by with the comment that Horatio rather than Andrea should have won the role, sometimes complaining that Andrea seems extraordinarily naïve. Certainly there is room for artistic improvement in both areas. Yet if we as readers are to understand the symbolism of this revenge-tragedy motif, we must study the ghost as Kyd offered it. Most crucial to this understanding is an awareness of the Ghost's relationship to its supernatural guide, Revenge, and, beyond that, a realization that the ultimate source of the Ghost's authority is not Heaven but Nature.

Let us consider first the relationship between the Ghost and Revenge. On the symbolic level, the Ghost of Andrea, as the returning spirit of a cruelly murdered man, embodies the sense of outrage which flares up in the face of such an act and therefore symbolizes the desire for vengeance. Andrea's will is solely that the man who killed him shall be punished for the deed ("I look'd that Balthazar should have been slain").[7] This remains his single-minded purpose throughout. Yet, as overwhelmed by desire as he is, Andrea has no idea how his goal will be realized; through the course of the play, he is learning right along with the audience about the consequences of a plea for revenge.

While the Ghost embodies the desire for vengeance, the figure of Revenge seems to symbolize the destined course of events set in motion by that desire. In contrast to Andrea, who is emotionally involved in the drama, Revenge appears almost bored. His ennui arises from the fact that, having prescience, he is left in no suspense as to the outcome of this affair. When Andrea asks why matters are proceeding in a direction opposite to his expectations, Revenge quietly remarks

> Thou talkest of harvest, when the corn is green;
> The end is crown of every work well done;
> The sickle comes not till the corn be ripe.
>
> [2.6.7–9]

So sure is Revenge that events can work out in only one way that he goes to sleep, leaving the anxiety entirely to Andrea.

Despite these obvious distinctions between the two characters, they function essentially as a unit. Kyd may appear to attribute only to Revenge the excessive destruction which occurs during the course of the play. The Ghost himself blames Revenge when, returning to earth from the nether regions, he finds Horatio slain and Bel-imperia abused (2.6.3–6). He had not looked for these effects. It seems to be Revenge who chooses to wreak havoc upon the world, he alone whose influence upon the court will

> . . . turn their friendship into fell despite,
> Their love to mortal hate, their day to night,
> Their hope into despair, their peace to war,
> Their joys to pain, their bliss to misery.
>
> [1.5.6–9]

It appears to be Revenge, not Andrea, who determines that Lorenzo, Bel-imperia, Hieronimo, and the innocent Duke of Castile will lose their lives along with Balthazar. Yet, for all his surprise and displeasure at the methods of Revenge, the Ghost is ultimately responsible for the carnage, for *his desire* first opened the door and ushered Revenge into the world. In this sense, Revenge stands in relation to the Ghost as the box of human ills did to Pandora. The Ghost, acting on impulse, introduces the passion of revenge into the affairs of man, only to find that, like any other passion, it is more easily conjured up than controlled or laid to rest. Events take the shape they do through his authorization.

Kyd, and everyone who follows him in the writing of revenge tragedy, postulates that the revenger believes he is acting on an authority that transcends the human order. The agency who grants him this authority is the ghost. Few critics dispute this fact. But they have debated long and hard over the exact source of the ghost's authority, that is, about where the ghosts come from. In *The Spanish Tragedy*, the inevitable march of events called into being by the desire of the Ghost and represented by Revenge is set in motion by the queen of the underworld, Proserpine (1.1.78–83). But is Proserpine to be taken as a metaphorical image of the Heaven whose support Hieronimo constantly seeks? Are the Ghost and Revenge actually figures of divine providence? Many critics assume some sort of identification between them:

> [Andrea] suggests the incomplete picture which mortals necessarily have of Providence and its workings.[8]

> Although this is ostensibly a human, not a divine revenge, it is in a sense raised to that level by the sanction of the Ghost, and the allocation, by whatever Gods may be, of appropriate punishments in Hades for the offenders.[9]

> In the final episode we return to the justice of Hell, where the characters of the play now supply the classical examples of sin and wickedness with which the play began ("Place *Don Lorenzo* on *Ixions* Wheele" [4.5.33]). A last judgment places everyone where he morally belongs. . . . Revenge has been completed; we have seen what Fulke Greville describes as the mode of modern tragedy: "God's revenging aspect upon every particular sin to the despair and confusion of mortality."[10]

All of these commentators equate the justice of Andrea's Hell with the justice of Hieronimo's Heaven.

If the Hades of the prologue is a metaphor for Providence, there are only two levels of justice in the play—heavenly justice and earthly justice. This is the customary division; critics of *The Spanish Tragedy* usually state that Hieronimo is maddened by the seeming failure of one system, the divine, to correct the wrongs resulting from the breakdown of the other, human law. And so, indeed, he is. Yet though Hieronimo looks for both heavenly justice and earthly justice at various times, he also appeals, not infrequently, to the judges of Hades—Minos, Aeacus, Rhadamanthus—and ultimately even to Pluto and Proserpine. He appeals in terms which make it clear that he himself sees this pagan or natural justice as a definite alternative to heavenly justice. Hieronimo's attitudes, far from suggesting that the pagan deities who encourage revenge signify "God's revenging aspect," warn us that revenge itself represents a third kind of justice: an irrepressible urge to return evil for evil which precedes and is probably the emotional stimulus for all codified forms of justice. A three-level hierarchy makes more sense of the play's symbolism.

Hieronimo, desiring revenge upon the murderers of his son, actually applies, in turn, to three separate ministers of justice. His initial appeal, occurring shortly after he has discovered the body of Horatio, is to God:

> Oh sacred heavens! if this unhallowed deed,
> If this inhuman, barbarous attempt,
> If this incomparable murder thus
> Of mine, but now no more my son,
> Shall unreveal'd and unrevenged pass,
> How should we term your dealings to be just,
> If you unjustly deal with those that in your justice trust?
>
> [3.2.5–11]

His sense of justice demands that Heaven punish so great an evil as was committed against Horatio; therefore, he persists (3.7.10–18) in his attempt to penetrate the seemingly impervious walls of Heaven with his cries.

In due course, Hieronimo receives evidence against the murderers in such a way as to convince him that Heaven will at least help to expose them. Having proof that Lorenzo and Balthazar are the guilty parties, firm proof that will stand up in court, Hieronimo makes his second appeal for justice, this time to earthly authorities:

> I will go plain me to my lord the king,
> And cry aloud for justice through the court.
>
> [3.7.69–70]

Though Heaven has not sent down lightning to blast his enemies, he might still hope to see them legally hanged.

Until the court rebuffs him, Hieronimo had been able to maintain suffient control to suppress in himself all but the rational course of action. Now, having failed to obtain satisfaction from the king, and, maddened by his frustrated desire for revenge, Hieronimo surrenders to his passion. He will forego the socially recognized channels of retribution and take matters into his own hands. It is here, where Hieronimo begins to function at

the level of instinct, that Kyd portrays him appealing to a third
minister of justice, Proserpine—from this point on, Hieronimo
seeks only the justice of Hades:

> Though on this earth justice will not be found,
> I'll down to hell, and in this passion
> Knock at the dismal gates of Pluto's court,
> Getting by force, as once Alcides did,
> A troop of Furies and tormenting hags
> To torture Don Lorenzo and the rest.
> Yet, lest the triple-headed porter should
> Deny my passage to the slimy strond,
> The Thracian poet thou shalt counterfeit.
> Come on, old father, be my Orpheus
> And if thou canst no notes upon the harp,
> Then sound the burden of thy sore hearts grief,
> Till we do gain that Proserpine may grant
> Revenge on them that murdered my son.
>
> [3.13.108–21]

Although this is not the first time that Hades has come into
Hieronimo's mind, such thoughts had on previous occasions
been firmly suppressed.[11] Only when the other two alternatives
have been abandoned, only when Hieronimo's passion for revenge has so maddened him that religious and social prohibitions fail, does he turn for solace to Proserpine. If this hypothe-
sis is acceptable, we may then take the justice of Hades as a
metaphor for the "wild justice" wrought by the passion of revenge when it is no longer controlled by the rational mind.

This justice of the passions belongs neither to the order of
God nor of man but to the order of nature.[12] Hieronimo is
certainly not the only character who has looked to it for support.
Shakespeare frequently has his villains appeal to the order of
nature for aid when their claims for justice are unfairly con-
cocted. Edmund in *King Lear*, seeking vengeance for his supposed injuries from both God and man, turns to that order of
being when he exclaims, "Thou, Nature, art my goddess." To
turn to nature for justice is, for Hieronimo as well as for Edmund, to deny the validity of the orders of both man and God
and to descend to the level of the animals.

Hieronimo's recourse to Hades, then, is identified with his
final and desperate recourse to his most primitive instincts.

When he can find satisfaction by no other means than personal violence upon the murderers, he seeks support from the same deities that encourage Andrea. Kyd has reinforced the association between Hieronimo and the realm of Hades in several ways. First, he indicates that the Ghost's state of mind is reflected in Hieronimo's—Hieronimo's desire for revenge mirrors that of Andrea. Second, Kyd provides a direct intermediary between Andrea and Hieronimo in the person of Bel-imperia, Andrea's former mistress, whose role it is to spur Hieronimo on to revenge. Third, he has Hieronimo mentally and symbolically travel Andrea's path to the "dismal gates of Pluto's court" (3.13.108–21). Finally, he permits Hieronimo, in his ravings, to imagine that he is prompted to revenge by a ghost come "from the depth, / to ask for justice in this upper earth" (3.13.133–34), a ghost whose desires prove identical to those of Andrea (3.13.133–43). Thus, though the Ghost of Andrea never formally comes in contact with the revenger in *The Spanish Tragedy*, Hieronimo's plight is shown to be a result of the events that began with the Ghost's application to Proserpine and the consequent unleashing of the spirit of Revenge.

What, though, of Hieronimo's conviction in act 4 that "heaven applies our drift, / And all the saints do sit soliciting / For vengeance on those cursed murderers" (4.1.31–33)? Critics have pointed out that this is the old man's final position; he sees himself as an agent of God. It is not surprising to find the revenger cloaking his actions in righteousness. Kyd's insight into the psychology of the revenger at this moment is telling. No matter what the evidence nor how sure the revenger is of his case, the actual act of revenge can only be undertaken in a state of madness, one aspect of which is to think of oneself not as a man committing murder but as a minister of God. What is surprising is to find critics taking the revenger at his word. After all, even in Aeschylus where there is ample recognition of the natural claims of blood revenge, there is also the realization that these natural impulses cannot be the foundation of a moral code. And surely if it is acknowledged that the Olympian gods of Aeschylus transcended the natural morality of blood for blood, it seems a crude interpretation of Christianity to attribute to it a morality more primitive and a godhead more indifferent.

Several facts militate against our accepting the revenger's in-

terpretation of events. For instance, the action of the play does
not support his claim. Hieronimo, maddened by his passion at
this point, can no longer make sound judgments. Moreover, the
"solicitations" which prompt his statement originate with the
less-than-saintly Bel-imperia (4.1.13–28), ever an advocate of
vengeance. And if the action of the play undermines Hieronimo's claim, so does the symbolism. Hieronimo has been
shown to be an instrument of Proserpine's Revenge—the excess
which results from the marshal's madness indicates that it is
"Hell's" deed he is about. All of this should warn us that Hieronimo is deceiving himself, as well as others, when he claims that
"heaven applies our drift."

When the evidence is analyzed, it becomes impossible to argue
that the Ghost, through its association with Revenge and Proserpine, has its authority from Heaven. Rather, Kyd made it a
symbol of the instinctual desire for vengeance which grips the
mind of Hieronimo when he learns of his son's death and which,
despite the resistance mustered by the more civilized levels of his
psyche, drives him into a state of madness. Similarly, Kyd used
the figure of Revenge to personify the "destiny" that the madness of revenge makes inescapable for the revenger, the destiny
that foresees Hieronimo's progression from grief to anger to
rage to madness to inhumanity—and finally even to suicide.

III Whether independently or under the influence of a lost
Hamlet play, Marston makes certain dramaturgical improvements in the ghost motif. He wisely combines the roles of
both Andrea and Revenge, and he has the ghost communicate
directly with the revenger. This latter alteration heightens the
dramatic impact and clarifies the authority of the ghost, who now
not only introduces the passion of revenge into the world but
plants it firmly in the bosom of the revenger. Marston's changes
necessarily had an impact on the ghost motif as well as on other
elements in his play. Interestingly, the changes by no means alter
Kyd's concept of the function of the ghost. Marston's achievement was to realize more fully the dramatic potential of the ghost
without altering the fundamental concept underlying its pres-

ence on stage. This fact indicates that Marston understood the symbolism of Kyd's ghost.

More than any other ghost in Elizabethan revenge tragedy, the Ghost of Andrugio is the embodiment of the anger that is released into the world at the moment a violent injustice is committed. All of the hatred and cruelty, the self-absorption and the excess of the passion of revenge is revealed in the attitude of Andrugio as he rises from his coffin to address his son:

> Thou vigor of my youth, juice of my love,
> Seize on revenge, grasp the stern-bended front
> Of frowning vengeance with impeised clutch.
> Alarum Nemesis, rouse up thy blood,
> Invent some strategem of vengeance
> Which, but to think on, may like lightning glide
> With horror through thy breast. Remember this:
> *Scelera non ulcisceris, nisi vincis.*
> [Injuries are not revenged except where they are exceeded.][13]

Particularly significant is the Ghost's demand for cruelty in excess of the crime. Andrugio cares not for any "strategem of vengeance" unless it be gruesome enough to make the normal mind recoil in horror. As the spirit of revenge, his passion for retaliation is so strong that no atrocity, not even the bloody murder of Piero's innocent son, seems harsh enough to quench it. This desire for excess inherent in the Ghost leads directly to the inhumanity which reaches its height during the play-within-the-play.

Marston makes an important connection between motifs here. What others implied, Marston makes explicit: excess is more than a firework exploding in the last act of the revenge play and showering the end with a spectacular display of blood. The excess of the revenge tragedies mirrors the excess in the psychology of revenge. Marston reveals this by having the Ghost cry out for both revenge and excess simultaneously and from the beginning. His handling of the theme of excess reveals just how closely the traditional motifs of revenge tragedy are integrated. The masque prepared by Antonio at the end of *Antonio's Revenge* dramatizes the excess which is the inevitable result of the passion for revenge now flowing pell-mell out of Antonio's mind. Piero is first served the flesh of his own son, then mutilated and tor-

tured, and at last violently murdered. Clearly this is excess and it
stems directly from the initial impulse of the Ghost; Andrugio
himself calls it into being. These recognizable interconnections,
constantly being made by the playwrights, are obvious indica-
tions that so long as the Kydian tradition remained, the vital
motifs were never strung together arbitrarily.

Thus attuned to excess, the Ghost of Andrugio communicates
every bit of its wrath to Antonio. Because the Ghost is brought
into direct contact with the revenger, we actually witness the
immediate and far-reaching change it effects in the revenger's
mind. Before his meeting with the Ghost, Antonio is reacting to
the fact of death. His dominant emotion is grief, the only outlet
for which, he feels, is suicide (3.1.13–15). The Ghost then makes
its appearance, bringing Antonio word that "I was empoison'd
by Piero's hand" (3.1.35). The passion of revenge thereupon
explodes in Antonio's psyche; he is catapulted by the Ghost to
the brink of madness. In the process of transforming Antonio,
the Ghost also persuades him to accept its authority as final.
Recognizing that the Ghost has its origins in a world beyond this
one, Antonio assumes that the Ghost has brought him the sanction of the supernatural for retaliation against Piero. Even more
than in *The Spanish Tragedy*, the Ghost legitimizes the deed of
revenge.

The danger of lifting the Ghost out of its choric role and
putting it onto the stage in close proximity with the revenger is
that the Ghost may strike the viewer as a figment of the revenger's
passion-crazed imagination. Marston has been careful to grant
this spirit of revenge an ontological existence by demonstrating
that other characters also see it. Here, as in *The Spanish Tragedy*,
the Ghost has a reality that goes beyond the psychological. Again,
therefore, we should be clear about the source of the Ghost's
power. The difficulties that confronted us in dealing with Kyd's
treatment of the same question do not present themselves in
Antonio's Revenge, at least not initially. The authority Andrugio
claims when he makes his first appearance is entirely of the order
of nature. He evokes no distant providence, only those forces in
the universe that are automatically aroused when an injustice has
been committed. Vengeance, Nemesis—these "deities" have been
neglecting their duty; Antonio himself must do their work
(3.1.45–48).

It is to the primitive law of revenge itself, personified as Vengeance or Vindicta, that the revenger makes obeisance immediately after the Ghost appears to him. He envisions Andrugio's tomb as the altar of Vengeance and offers young Julio's blood as a sacrifice to the Ghost:

> Sprite of Julio,
> Forget this was thy trunk. I live thy friend.
> Mayst thou be twined with the soft'st embrace
> Of clear eternity; but thy father's blood
> I thus make incense of, to Vengeance.
> 						 [*Sprinkles the tomb with blood*]
> Ghost of my poison'd sire, suck this fume;
> To sweet revenge, perfume thy circling air
> With smoke of blood. I sprinkle round his gore
> And dew thy hearse with these fresh-reeking drops.
> Lo, thus I heave my blood-dyed hands to heaven;
> Even like insatiate hell, still crying: "More!
> My heart hath thirsting dropsies after gore."
> Sound peace and rest to church, night-ghosts and graves;
> Blood cries for blood; and murder murder craves.
> 								 [3.1.202–15]

Throughout this portion of the play, Antonio is acting solely under the aegis of the spirit of revenge.

By the end of the play, however, we do run into problems in trying to assess the grounds of the Ghost's authority. Up to this point, the punishment of the murderer had been associated with immoderation and inhumanity. Andrugio, even here, is still insisting that Revenge is taking its destined course:

> The fist of strenuous vengeance is clutch'd
> And stern Vindicta tow'reth up aloft
> That she may fall with a more weighty peise
> And crush life's sap from out Piero's veins.
> 								 [5.1.3–6]

But as Andrugio continues we find him subtly and unexpectedly equating Vindicta with Providence:

> Now 'gins the leprous cores of ulcered sins
> Wheel to a head; now is his fate grown mellow,
> Instant to fall into the rotten jaws
> Of chapfall'n death. Now looks down providence

> T'attend the last act of my son's revenge.
>
> .   .   .   .
>
>   O, now triumphs my ghost,
> Exclaiming, "Heaven's just; for I shall see
> The scourge of murder and impiety."
>
>   [5.1.7–25]

The Ghost ends by suddenly suggesting that Heaven has orga-
nized the revenge. Antonio, as he kills Piero, takes the Ghost at its
word ("Thus the hand of heaven chokes / The throat of murder,"
[5.3.108–9]).

There is no point in arguing that Marston is mocking the
tradition; he is extremely serious in his defense of Antonio and
Pandulpho throughout act 5. He ennobles those who come forward to purge the evils of the state and contrives matters so that
society itself accepts Antonio as a minister of God. In the final
scene, senators are brought in to testify to the service done for
Venice, with one of them actually declaring that the revengers
have fulfilled a religious duty (5.3.127–28). Dignitaries from
neighboring states also lend the support of righteousness to Antonio and his friends. And the revengers themselves are invested
with a purity that sets them apart from—nay, above—the rest of
mankind.

In judging the claims to divine authority made by Andrugio, we
must proceed with caution, for, as Lawrence Ross warns us,
Marston's treatment of revenge seems at times "morally and
artistically incoherent."[14] Marston has fallen into a trap that Kyd,
Shakespeare, and Tourneur safely escape; he has tried to recon-
cile the Senecan tradition with the Christian. This, of course, is
what every revenger from Hieronimo to Vindice has longed to
do. But the author should know better. He must realize that the
intrinsic incompatibility of these two approaches to justice, each
with its own kind of validity, is exactly what makes the revenger's
plight tragic. If the incompatibility is removed, there is no tragedy. Not because some Elizabethan dramatists' guild stated in its
by-laws that all revenge tragedies would exhibit, as one of the
mysteries of the craft, a justice incompatible with itself. And not
because twentieth-century scholars have decreed that every revenge tragedy must have ambiguity and incompatibility as a
theme. What has guided both the Elizabethan dramatists and the
twentieth-century critics is what Marston failed to be guided by in

creating his ghost—the experience of the passion of revenge itself.

Modern commentators like Philip J. Ayres, who correctly notes that Antonio and the Ghost "assume a religious sanction to which they have no right," were not the first to recognize the violation of reality that such a claim involved.[15] Marston's contemporaries, too, understood that any ghost presenting itself as Heaven's agent must have qualities quite different from those possessed by Andrugio. Cyril Tourneur's *Atheist's Tragedy* offers a useful corrective to Marston.

In *The Atheist's Tragedy,* Tourneur has made his ghost a Christian and its authority is unquestionably that of Heaven. But unlike Marston, Tourneur is consistent. He realized that the ghost must change its nature before it could suitably speak for Providence. He purged the ghost of its former associations with Vindicta and put into its mouth the so-called orthodox view. Vastly different from the advice given by Andrugio to his son is the counsel of the Ghost of Montferrers to Charlemont:

> Return to France, for thy old father's dead
> And thou by murder disinherited.
> Attend with patience the success of things,
> But leave revenge unto the King of kings.[16]

Montferrers repeats the traditional Christian warning that vengeance belongs to God alone and that the proper human response to injustice is patience. How little this ghost resembles that of Andrugio, who sanctions murder, decries delay, and nevertheless (we are told) speaks with the authority of Heaven.

Marston's Andrugio is both a success and a failure. Insofar as Marston warped the ghost symbol to fit a theme that was foreign to it, Andrugio becomes a weak spot in the play. But insofar as the dramatist managed to convey through the Ghost the ferocity of the passion, the driving force with which it bears down upon the revenger, its ability to deflect any moral qualms in the revenger because of its authoritative appeal to natural justice, and its inevitable tendency to overrun its limits and rush blindly on to excess, Andrugio far more effectively embodies the spirit of revenge than did the simple-witted Ghost in *The Spanish Tragedy*. Marston's Ghost, for all its claims of divine support, remains a vivid and frightening personification of "frowning Vengeance."

IV Probably all great art combines the mythic, or what Carl Jung has called the "collective unconscious," with the individual imagination. Certainly in the drama of Elizabethan England, this bifocal quality was nearly everywhere present and nowhere more so than in the revenge tragedies. Not one of several plays of this type could be called a *pure* revenge tragedy. Each play is indelibly stamped with the imprint of an individual talent pursuing a unique vision. Now as the archetype and the personal vision must both find expression through the symbols and the actions of the play, the result is necessarily a degree of tension in the work as it attempts to render both. This is certainly true of the ghost symbol. In Kyd, the Ghost strongly reflects an aspect of the archetypal experience of revenge. In Marston the symbol still takes its essential form from the archetypal experience but the personal vision slightly distorts the convention. In later writers of revenge tragedy, the individual imagination overruns the archetype, and we find that the ghost motif becomes wrenched almost out of recognition. With Shakespeare, as is so often the case, it is otherwise. The personal vision is always markedly present, without distorting the relationship between the motif and the archetypal experience upon which it is based. Shakespeare's vision does not work against the motif, because he was obviously responding to his own intuition of its richness. While his vision in *Hamlet* goes vastly beyond the revenge theme, it nevertheless enriches the conventions as it pursues its own fulfillment.

Compared to *The Spanish Tragedy* and *Antonio's Revenge, Hamlet* exhibits a greater understanding and refinement of the symbolism. A certain heavy-handedness in *The Spanish Tragedy* reveals that the playwright is unsure of his symbols. Many problems beset Kyd in these first tentative attempts to describe in dramatic form how the spirit of revenge gains power over the soul of man. For his symbols, he went to Seneca and borrowed a ghost and to the medieval moralities for an allegorical figure. The continued use of the ghost by the men who followed Kyd is as much a tribute to his judgment as the fact that no one after him used the allegorical Revenge is a criticism. With Marston, we get the blending of the two. This is an obvious dramaturgical development. The playwright is now free from the ponderous allegorical figure whose appearances must halt the action. Furthermore, set loose from his tiresome companion, the ghost can now participate directly in the action of the play; it becomes more directly a motivating agent. As both the ghost of a murdered man and the embodiment of the spirit of revenge, the Ghost in *Antonio's Revenge* has a theatricality denied Kyd's figures, either singly or together. Unfortunately, everything Marston gained by combining these two transcendental figures is offset by the resulting shrillness in his characterization of the ghost, which makes it seem pathological—hence, less plausible—to the audience. The effect tends toward the melodramatic. In spite of their dramaturgical shortcomings, both Kyd and Marston had correctly intuited that one component of a revenge action must be the drive toward excess, and each felt the need to supply the revenger with some palpable motivation for his excess. Their solutions, to put the spirit of revenge on stage—in one form or another—indicates their perception that the excess stemmed directly from the impulse to revenge itself. But dramaturgically, both solutions leave much to be desired.

Shakespeare approaches the presentational problems inherent in the authorizing figure and the excess quite differently. In *Hamlet,* there is no attempt to render the motivation toward excess through a personification of the spirit of revenge. The Ghost of King Hamlet is, in a sense, a return to Kyd's Ghost. Like Andrea, the Ghost in *Hamlet* does not *seek* a blood bath; he merely desires to be revenged on the man who murdered him. But where Kyd felt the need to point the moral of the play with an allegorical figure, Shakespeare lets the action of the play itself render that excess that is so integral a part of revenge. With his superior dramaturgical instincts, Shakespeare saw that neither any allegorical figure nor any amount of shrillness on the part of the ghost could give sufficient dramatic motivation to what can only find justification by growing out of the action. The excess must be in the revenge action. If it is, the ghost need not "come skreaming like a pigge halfe stickt" and the emphasis can be placed upon his *authority.*

This change in approach makes Shakespeare's Ghost seem somewhat subdued, especially in comparison to Andrugio. The effect is increased by another adaptation of the convention made by Shakespeare. In *Hamlet,* a whole range of symbolism largely independent of revenge tragedy themes is imposed upon the ghost motif. As Mark Rose points out, Shakespeare has made the

elder Hamlet "an emblem of human dignity and worth." Or, to
quote Maynard Mack, Jr., he embodies "a true Renaissance ideal,
displaying a perfect balance of virtues."[17] The Ghost, in *Hamlet,* is
the spirit of a great and noble man whose like shall not be looked
upon again. Because of its new function, this ghost must possess a
dignity that ghosts in earlier revenge tragedies lack. It cannot be
the "ranting roisterous abstraction" which exists only at the level
of passion. It must display moderation and restraint, even a bit of
tenderness. Having given the Ghost a character, Shakespeare had
to make that character consistent.[18]

Yet for all its restraint, the function of Shakespeare's Ghost
remains the function which has been the hallmark of all of the
"classic" ghosts in revenge tragedy and which distinguishes them
from the host of other ghosts that populated the Elizabethan
stage. He comes, first and last, to demand and authorize the
killing of his murderer:

> List, list, O, list!
> If thou didst ever thy dear father love
>
> .   .   .   .
>
> Revenge his foul and most unnatural murther.[19]

The Ghost is still an angry ghost and one who desires to arouse a
similar passion in his son:

> Thus was I, sleeping, by a brother's hand,
> Of life, of crown, of queen at once dispatch'd,
> Cut off even in the blossoms of my sin,
> Unhous'led, disappointed, unanel'd,
> No reck'ning made, but sent to my account
> With all my imperfections on my head.
> O, horrible, O, horrible, most horrible!
> If thou hast nature in thee, bear it not.
>
> [1.5.74–81]

And though he seeks only the life of Claudius, through this very
desire he sets in motion a chain of catastrophic events that leaves
the stage strewn with corpses. Throughout *Hamlet,* the personal
and the archetypal are fused into an inseparable unit, and the
archetypal meaning remains essential to a complete understanding of the play.

Kyd had used the revenge form to analyze the psychological
processes of the mind of the individual placed under the stress

of the passion, and Marston had used it to portray the emotion itself. Shakespeare explores the interaction between the passion and the intellect. His revenger, therefore, after the first shock caused by the Ghost's revelation, responds by questioning the authority of the spirit which has visited him. Unlike Antonio, who assumes that the Ghost has its authority from the place from which he most wishes to receive support, Hamlet must know whether the Ghost can be trusted. Is it a "spirit of health"? Or simply a "goblin damn'd"? He will not act upon its demands until he is sure that the Ghost is "honest."

Since Hamlet himself seeks to discover the source of the Ghost's authority, commentators, too, have addressed themselves to this problem. It is widely observed that the Ghost of King Hamlet is more than a reflection of the revenger's psyche. As in *Antonio's Revenge,* the Ghost has an objective reality. Dover Wilson's statement can be taken as representative of opinion on this point. "Four appearances, three witnesses and one of them a sceptic," he says. "Why this minute detail, why this accumulation of circumstantial evidence, if not to assure us of the Ghost's objectivity, before it encounters Hamlet?" Or, to express it as John E. Hankins does, the Ghost "represents the direct intervention of another world in the affairs of living men."[20]

But what other world? Here the unanimity ends. The extent of the underlying disagreement is as wide as the nature of the subject will allow. Some commentators, Prosser being the most recent, are convinced that the Ghost has satanic propensities. Others view it as a spirit of health. Sister Miriam Joseph reminds us that the Ghost presents himself "as a saved Christian soul" newly ascended from Purgatory, "that a soul from Purgatory could not come without God's permission," and that souls in grace do not lie; then she asserts that "the command he brings can come only from God."[21] Can either of these theories be upheld?

Since Shakespeare apparently intends us to accept Hamlet's ultimate view of the Ghost, perhaps we had best ask how Hamlet resolves this problem. Hamlet assumes, after testing the Ghost, that it is not a demon come to tempt him to the loss of his soul. He takes it to be an "honest" ghost. Yet by *honest* Hamlet does not mean "saintly" or "angelic"; he never calls it a "good spirit" in the sense that Sister Miriam Joseph uses the term. He simply means that the Ghost *is* his father, or, what amounts to the same thing to him, that it has told the truth. His reasoning is that if the Ghost's story is true, he is bound to bring Claudius to justice. From Hamlet's point of view, the Ghost has not returned from the regions of the damned, but neither has it any position in the hierarchy of paradise.

What does the Ghost itself reveal of its origins? In setting limits to the punishment Hamlet may exact, calling for vengeance upon Claudius but referring Gertrude to a higher judge, the Ghost indicates that it is to be distinguished from rather than equated with Heaven. We certainly do not find it active at the end of the play when Hamlet begins to discover that Providence is at work in the affairs of Denmark (5.2.10–11). It troubles Hamlet, rather, in moments of emotional turmoil. In these early scenes, it seems to derive its authority from the order of nature. The emphasis which Roy Battenhouse has noted in the Ghost's speeches, though largely overlooked by subsequent critics, is forceful and convincing. The Ghost, says Battenhouse,

> seems to view its injuries as wrongs against Nature rather than against God. His complaint concerns a "most unnatural murder"; a wife's "decline Upon a wretch whose *natural* gifts were poor to those of mine"; a banishment from his natural right (so he evidently regards it) to the Christian sacraments. . . . There is indignation at the unnatural (because unkind) behavior of a brother in casting him off to suffer for the "foul crimes" done in his "days of nature." "If thou hast *nature* in thee bear it not." . . . The Ghost desires Hamlet to be "bound to revenge" and to himself. He wants morality re-established, but in obedience to the canons of human decency and natural conscience, and is silent as to invoking any specifically Christian canons.[22]

Although Shakespeare has taken the ghost out of the Senecan afterworld and set him in an Elizabethan one, his Ghost continues to associate itself with nature. The Ghost in *Hamlet* still symbolizes that justice which is naturally intuited by the individual psyche.

As the question of the Ghost's origins eventually dissolves for Hamlet, so it should for the audience. One of the themes of the play is stated in the rebuke that Hamlet makes to his friend who would have all things of heaven and earth explained and that

Shakespeare would himself make to critics who would reason away the mystery of the Ghost—there are questions in the universe that are unfathomable to the human mind. Hamlet cannot see beyond the bent knee and folded hands of the living man, Claudius, to the unrepentent thoughts inside the king's brain. How then can he comprehend and explain the ambiguities in the commands of his dead father? Or know what there is in the world beyond that lets one part of his psyche tell him he must punish Claudius while another warns him not to kill? All Hamlet can know, and all Shakespeare asks us to believe, is that the Ghost is real, that the Ghost *is* his father, and that his father's demands have an irresistable and natural claim upon him.

In writing about Elizabethan revenge tragedy, scholars often dismiss the ghost as "a stage thrill," a "messenger from the underworld variously compounded of Virgil and Seneca,"[23] popular in the London theaters because of its ability to incite feelings of horror in the groundlings. It can reasonably be argued that all three authors discussed here saw a greater potential in the figure of the ghost, that, despite individual differences arising from their own personal visions, all have utilized the ghost to symbolize that spirit of revenge which, while impelling the revenger on a course of passionate self-destruction, makes him believe that he is furthering the course of God's justice. All seem to concur that the essential—the archetypal—elements of the ghost-motif are: (1) an unappeasable anger which has been aroused by an injustice and which creates an imbalance in the universe; (2) the consequent unleashing of a force—always portrayed as objective and otherworldly but originating from the order of nature—which attempts to right that imbalance by eliminating the wrongdoer; (3) the attempt of that force to work through the psyche of the revenger, who accepts it as his authority to ignore the canons of civil and religious law; and (4) the tendency of that force to initiate an action which cannot be controlled and which will inevitably run to excess.

To oust the ghost from the celestial position critics have awarded it and return it to its place in an order that is often iconographically identified with Hell may seem to imply that the ghost should be understood solely in negative terms. Not at all. The ghost is destructive but not deliberately diabolic. Its author-

ity is *necessary* in raising the experience of revenge to tragic proportions. The ghost does have its positive aspects. We will speak
more of these in chapter 5.

Chapter 2
Madness as Dramatic Symbol in Jacobean Drama

The disease of madness ... in Elizabethan thinking meant either a temporary dethronement of reason in heightened passion, or the more permanent affliction, insanity, but a disease which, in either case was understood in terms of the principles operative in almost any perturbation. Madness is merely the extremity of distemperature, and as such, it may be studied with reference to theories of the passions.

　　Ruth Leila Anderson, *Elizabethan Psychology and Shakespeare's Plays*

I PERHAPS the most misunderstood revenge tragedy convention is the motif of madness. Since this is the central motif, important because it binds together the entire symbolic configuration, a particular effort to eradicate all confusion about it should be made.

Although madness is widely used as a symbol in the drama of the period, its symbolic functions have never attained a large degree of recognition. Some scholars insist on viewing every madness literally. They look only for clinical fact. When the facts do not point to a distinct phobia or psychosis which can be recognized and labeled with modern medical terminology, they consider the depiction a failure. In the single most comprehensive study of insanity in the plays of the era, Robert Reed uses realism as the basis for judgment. The result is predictable. He finds few madmen whom he can consider dramatically success-

41

ful. He denigrates the madman of sixteenth-century drama (i.e.,
Hieronimo, Orlando, Titus Andronicus) as "little more than a
mouthpiece for Elizabethan fustian." Though he feels happier
with the madman created by Jacobean playwrights, whose
greater objectivity "initiates a more genuine and pathologically
sound interpretation of mad folk," he is still constantly forced to
admit that many Jacobean representations of madness succeed
rather poorly—symptoms are sketchily presented and often
conflicting.[1]

The persistent refusal to look at the symbolic aspects of stage
madness leads many scholars to accuse the playwrights of a
dramatic naïveté as well as a scientific one.[2] These conclude, with
Reed, with that usual tiresome accusation: "theatricality seems
definitely to have been the primary motive behind the consistent
use of insanity."[3] This view is maintained by Louis B. Wright in
his presentation of certain madhouse scenes as "mere variety
show amusements." Wright is correct in arguing that "to an
Elizabethan, the antics of the madmen furnished comic entertainment" and that the comic elements of insanity were often
"exaggerated beyond dramatic necessity." But in asserting that
various *scenes* were extraneous, Wright conveys the impression
that madness itself had no organic purpose.[4] To say this of such
plays as *The Pilgrim, The Changeling,* and *The Duchess of Malfi* is to
overlook themes that are fundamental to their dramatic structure. The belief that, wherever it is employed, madness is
bogusly theatrical also turns up with annoying regularity in dis-
cussions of revenge tragedy. Manifested in remarks like G. B.
Harrison's "let the poor girl go mad; we always have a mad scene
in a Revenge Play," this attitude has so far prevented our fully
grasping the significance of the conventional madness of the
revenger.[5]

This is not to suggest that *all* madness in the drama is given
symbolic overtones—as Anselmo says in *The Honest Whore*, "there
are of mad men, as there are of tame, / all humourd not alike."[6]
Many depictions of madness fall well outside of the discussion
which is to follow. Nor do we claim that madness cannot look
beyond itself and be comic at the same time; it often does both.
Still less would we insist that all attempts to make the madness
symbolic are artistically successful (far from it!). We argue only

that the relationships implied in the drama between the sane and the insane should be more closely studied.

That lunacy is not generally thought of as having symbolic overtones is a minor worry: a problem more resistant to correction is that people no longer think of an inordinate passion as a lunacy.[7] Over the course of the past three centuries a rather violent alteration has occurred in the meaning of the word *madness*. Certain areas of meaning have become totally dissociated from the word. In addition, Freudian psychology has attached new connotations to it. Both developments hinder our getting back to the old conception.

The modern world makes a distinction that the Renaissance world did not make. The Doctor in August Strindberg's *The Father* is typical; he views temper and insanity as mutually exclusive categories:

> I am convinced that there has been an act of violence. But the question is—should that act of violence be regarded as an outbreak of temper or insanity?[8]

The same mechanical assumption that inordinate passion and madness are no more related than goats and grapes turns up in Prosser's analysis of the madness in *Hamlet:*

> If we want to know how Shakespeare and his audience conceived of real insanity, we can turn to Titus, Lear, and Ophelia. Each of them loses touch with reality. A better test is provided by Edgar. Since Edgar completely submerges his own identity in order to counterfeit madness, his behavior is good evidence of *what Shakespeare and his audience conceived real madness to be.* Edgar's imitation takes the form of totally incoherent raving and of complete disorientation. Hamlet, by contrast, never loses contact with reality. He always recognizes people (though he mockingly pretends not to do so); he always knows what he is doing. His speech is not even incoherent.[9]

Her concept of "what Shakespeare and his audience conceived real madness to be" is naïve in the extreme and leads her to find Hamlet incomprehensible when he speaks of his own madness to Laertes. Since many scholars (and most modern students) are similarly unaware that the most common kind of "madness," for Shakespeare's audience, was the one that coexists with clinical sanity, it seems necessary to begin with a detailed examination of this specific mental aberration.[10] The Renaissance sense of the word must be recovered. Once that task is accomplished, we may go on to examine madness in its specific relation to the revenge passion.

II What, exactly, *is* this aberration, by itself, before it is given expression through symbol? It is not, as Prosser suggests, demonic possession of the sort Edgar imitates in his role as Poor Tom. Nor is it the common lunacy of the scholar Stephano in *The Pilgrim,* who in rapt moments believes he is Neptune. It is not the retardation of the idiot, who is counted among the mad in most Jacobean stage asylums. These "clinical" madnesses have their symbolic functions, but we will talk of them later. What concerns us now is the doctrine, widely accepted throughout the Elizabethan and Jacobean periods but still being expressed by Thomas Hobbes, that

> to have stronger and more vehement passions for any thing, than is ordinarily seen in others, is that which men call MADNESS.
>
> Whereof there be almost as many kinds, as of the passions themselves. Sometimes the extraordinary and extravagant passion, proceedeth from the evil constitution of the organs of the body, or harm done them; and sometimes the hurt, and indisposition of the organs, is caused by the vehemence, or long continuance of the passion. But in both cases the madness is of one and the same nature. . . .
>
> In sum, all passions that produce strange and unusual behaviour, are called by the general name of madness.[11]

The idea goes back at least to Aristotle, who had said that "outbursts of anger and sexual appetites and some other such passions, it is evident, actually alter our bodily condition, and in some men even produce fits of madness."[12] The author of *The Court of Virtue* (1565) invokes an even earlier source:

> Socrates calles it a great poynt of madnes,
> To be without measure in ioy or in sadnes.[13]

Examples of the way the Renaissance mind automatically linked passion with madness abound in the literature. Robert Tofte proclaims that jealousy "sometimes bursteth out so farre, and exceedeth her bounds so much, as it turneth it selfe into extream Hatred, and from thence falleth into a Frensie, and Madnesse."[14] In *The Times' Whistle* (1614–16), Richard Corbet, before he is through, has reduced to a "bedlem fitt," each in its turn, the various excesses of grief, fear, and anger:

> Another, shuning comfort & reliefe,
> Suffers himselfe to be surchargde with griefe,
> And soe this passion doth his reason blinde
> That it begettes a frenzie in his minde.
> Another, if that fear doe him assaile,
> Doth suffer that affection to prevaile,
> And doth bring him [in] to such franticke fittes,
> As you would judge him to be out on's wittes.
>
> . . . .
>
> Mischiefe-procurer anger rules another,
> That knowes not friend from foe; stranger or brother,
> All's one to him; for in his bedlem fitt,
> Which quite deprives him of his little witt,
> He cares not whom he strikes.[15]

Because of its fierce intensity, anger is almost always described as lunatic. Joseph Hall writes that there is

> no difference between anger and madness, but continuance; for, raging anger is a short madnesse. What else argues the shaking of the hands and lips, paleness, or rednesse, or swelling of the face, glaring of the eyes, stammering of the tongue, stamping with the feet, unsteady motions of the whole body, rash actions we remember not to have done, distracted and wilde speeches? And madnesse again is nothing but a continued rage, yea some madnesse rageth not: such a milde madness is more tolerable, than frequent and furious anger.[16]

Obviously Renaissance theorists were convinced that passion, when carried to *extremes,* could excite all the fury of a lunacy.

The playwrights, like the theorists, viewed an excess of passion as a crippling disorder of the faculties. Almost every play of the period offers evidence of this fact. John Ford employs the word in a way that we hear it most often:

> Love is the tyrant of the heart; it darkens
> Reason, confounds discretion; deaf to counsel
> It runs a headlong course to desperate madness.
>
> [*The Lover's Melancholy* 3.3, p. 77]

Not only love but any of the seven *primary passions* might run this same headlong course. Ford is thinking in identical terms when he uses the word a few years later—this time not about love but about anger:

> Quiet
> These vain unruly passions, which will render ye
> Into a madness.
>
> [*The Broken Heart* 4.1.114–16]

Kyd, Marston, and Shakespeare allow their characters to define uncontrolled passion—be it anger or grief, hatred or desire—in a similar way:

> What madding fury did possess thy wits?
>
> [*The Spanish Tragedy* 3.10.33]

> Alas, my son's distraught! Sweet boy, appease
> Thy mutining affections.
>
> [*Antonio's Revenge* 3.1.74–75]

> How now! Has sorrow made thee dote already?
> Why, Marcus, no man should be mad but I.[17]
>
> [*Titus Andronicus* 3.2.23–24]

Our immediate reaction is to see these references to madness as metaphorical, yet the speakers display a serious and literal concern. Under different circumstances they might talk of madness lightly, as Shakespeare's Rosalind does when she coquettishly describes love as a state which "deserves as well a dark house and a whip as madmen do" (3.2.401). But here each is speaking with the conviction that the passion involved has somehow crazed the mind. The danger proposed by the playwrights is the same no matter what the affection: highly charged emotion, when permitted to tyrannize over the imagination, can overthrow the reason and so interfere with judgment that the individual cannot function normally. In him, all semblances of sanity disappear.

In the drama not only the primary passions such as love, hate, joy, grief, and anger but those derivable from them—*mixed passions* like envy, revenge, emulation, jealousy—may also run to excess; indeed, some are so prone to do so that they almost never exist in moderation. Every stage madhouse has an inmate who lost his wits in some fit of jealousy, and few stage revengers retain their sanity once they succumb to the desire for vengeance.

In depicting the jealous fury of Bassanes in *The Broken Heart,* Ford strives to demonstrate how jealousy can push the mind into a state of "unquiet" or "vexation" approaching insanity. The scene provides a useful illustration of the literal relationship assumed by Renaissance playwrights between passion and madness. In the scene, Bassanes' wife Penthea and her brother Ithocles meet on stage to discuss the latter's suit to Calantha. Because Bassanes has been excluded from the parley, he concludes that such privacy is required for the sexual intimacies of a love tryst and flips into a rage. He charges in upon Penthea and Ithocles, brandishing a dagger and making preposterous accusations about the "bestial incest" of the pair. Bassanes is clinically sane; this fit will pass and he will again reason normally. But it is clear from the judgments of the bystanders that, for as long as this irrational behavior lasts, Bassanes must be considered a madman:

Bassanes.	I can forbear no longer. More, I will not.
	Keep off your hands or fall upon my point.
	Patience is tir'd, for like a slow-pac'd ass
	Ye ride my easy nature, and proclaim
	My sloth to vengeance a reproach and property.
Ithocles.	The meaning of this rudeness?
Prophilus.	He's distracted.
Penthea.	O, my griev'd lord!
Grausis.	Sweet lady, come not near him;
	He holds his perilous weapon in his hand
	To prick 'a cares not whom nor where. —See, see, see!
Bassanes.	My birth is noble, though the popular blast
	Of vanity, as giddy as thy youth,
	Hath rear'd thy name up to bestride a cloud
	Or progress in the chariot of the sun.
	I am no clod of trade to lackey pride,
	Nor like your slave of expectation wait
	The bawdy hinges of your doors, or whistle
	For mystical conveyance to your bed sports.
Groneas.	Fine humors! They become him.
Hemophil.	How'a stares,
	Struts, puffs, and sweats. Most admirable lunacy!
Ithocles.	But that I may conceive the spirit of wine

	Has took possession of your soberer custom,
	I'd say you were unmannerly.
Penthea.	Dear brother —
Bassanes.	Unmannerly! Mew, kitling. Smooth formality
	Is usher to the rankness of the blood,
	But impudence bears up the train. Indeed, sir,
	Your fiery mettle, or your springal blaze
	Of huge renown, is no sufficient royalty
	To print upon my forehead the scorn "cuckold."
Ithocles.	His jealousy has robb'd him of his wits;
	'A talks 'a knows not what.
Bassanes.	Yes, and 'a knows
	To whom 'a talks: to one that franks his lust
	In swine-security of bestial incest.

[3.2.119–50]

The symptoms of Bassanes' madness differ radically from those of the monomaniacal Trouble-All in *Bartholomew Fair* whose fixation upon the warrant of Justice Overdo has rendered him mentally incompetent: Bassanes' madness is easily explainable in terms of the fears and suspicions of a jealous man. Yet the "stares, struts, puffs, and sweats," the appearance of drunkenness, the threats of violence, and the distorted vision of reality all point, for the onlookers and thus for the audience whose responses they are guiding, to an equally incapacitating mental derangement. "Excesses be madness" as much in the mixed passions as in the primary ones.

Strengthening the mode of thought that allowed inordinate passion to be viewed as a psychological madness was the corresponding belief that any failure to act in accordance with right reason was correspondingly a moral madness. We can appreciate the significance of this belief only if we are fully aware of the value placed upon reason in the era. Douglas Bush's description of "right reason" has been called "the most cogent and substantial statement of the concept" and is worth quoting again:

> Right reason is not merely reason in our sense of the word; it is not a dry light, a nonmoral instrument of inquiry. Neither is it simply the religious conscience. It is a kind of rational and philosophic conscience which distinguishes man from the beasts and which links man with man and with God. This faculty was implanted by God in all men, Christian and heathen alike, as a guide to truth and conduct.[18]

"A guide to truth and conduct"—this is the key. The role of the reason was to seek out knowledge of absolute truth, an inquiry requiring both the constant mental action of discriminating between good and evil and the subsequent application of that knowledge to daily life. Reason was raised to the level of wisdom only when, trained to choose the good, it manifested itself in virtuous action:

> And only wyt in speakyng well,
> Doth shewe his force and myght:
> But wysdome euer is exprest,
> In dealyng iust and ryght.[19]

This pursuit of the good was no matter of virtue for virtue's sake; the ultimate goal was not simply an ethical one but philosophic and religious. The more one knew of the good, the more one knew of God, and to perfect oneself was to make oneself over in His image. As Robert Hoopes concludes in a recent study of the subject,

> right reason may thus be thought of as a faculty which fuses in dynamic interactivity the functions of knowing and being, which stands finally as something more than a proximate means of rational discovery or "nonmoral instrument of inquiry," and which affirms that what a man knows depends upon what, as a moral being, he chooses to make himself.[20]

Because reason was the faculty through which a man "seeking truth, from cause to cause ascends, / And never rests till it the first attain," any mental aberration which deflected the reason from its natural course was deplored.[21] The man who deliberately chose to pursue a false good rather than the true was considered morally mad. Passion, which lacks the ability of the wit to "discourse to and fro, anticipating, and comparing things,"[22] which thus equates good with anything that promises pleasant sensations, and which consequently tends to frustrate the reason, even to work actively toward its overthrow, is deemed by the Elizabethans to be a moral madness as well as a physical one.

This is particularly true of those passions designated as vices—avarice, ambition, pride, lust. To the modern eye these "deadly sins" may seem unrelated to the passions. In essence, however, they are perversions of the passion of love, more specifically of desire (the love of a *future* good). As inordinate desires, they, too, are viewed in terms of mental disease and indiscriminately lumped with the numerous other madnesses which the age recognized:

> He is a rare man that hath not some kind of madness reigning in him: one, a dull madness of melancholy; another, *a conceited madness of pride;* another, a superstitious madness of false devotion; *a fourth, of ambition or covetousness;* a fifth, the furious madness of anger; a sixth, the laughing madness of extreme mirth; a seventh, a drunken madness; *an eighth, of outrageous lust;* a ninth, the learned madness of curiosity; a tenth, the worst madness of profaneness and atheism. It is as hard to reckon up all kinds of madnesses as of dispositions. Some are more noted and punished than others; so that the madman in one kind as much condemns another, as the sober man condemns him. Only that man is both good and wise and happy, that is free from all kinds of frenzy.[23]

Hall's catalog is typical in its failure to distinguish categories of madnesses. Physical madnesses like melancholy, theological madnesses like atheism, and temporary madnesses like drunkenness are thrown together with psychological madnesses like anger as sins against the reason. Prominent in the list are the moral madnesses—pride, ambition, covetousness, and lust.

The vices are treated as madnesses in the drama as well. Marston's Sir Edward Fortune considers it morally insane to harbor a desire for money so intense that in pursuit of it one violates the natural—that is the "sane"—relationship between man and his Creator:

> Oh madnes still to sweate in hotte pursuite
> Of cold abhorred sluttish nigardise,
> To exile ones fortunes from their native use,
> To entertaine a present povertie,
> A willing want, for Infidell mistrust
> Of gratious providence: Oh Lunacie.
>   [*Jack Drum's Entertainment*, act 1, pp. 183–84]

For Tourneur's Vindice also, to desire material comforts that will make one "miserably great, rich, [but] eternally wretched" is a "common madness" (*The Revenger's Tragedy* 4.4.73–75).[24] Such passages link the ungovernable fury of desire with the witless delusions of folly. As Sir Edward and Vindice attest, movement in these directions is movement away from man's natural goal. Since the proper object of love was the Divine, to channel the desires toward more transient goals was to risk damnation, a choice regarded as the ultimate form of irrationality affecting the clinically sane.

III This orientation should help us to understand how readily Jacobean playwrights choose the conduct of the insane to illuminate various indiscretions of the sane. The extravagant behavior of the true lunatic was a natural symbol for that ordinary everyday madness to which all men are subject. Demonic possession, monomania, lycanthropy—sometimes a whole consort of these lunacies—become playhouse mirrors to reflect the distortions of some chaotic passion.

In this era dramatists commonly used lunacy as an image for the inevitable outcome of a life spent in thralldom to the appetites. A character who has lived by the principle that rage or lust or jealousy is gloriously refreshing is suddenly inflicted with a real madness that mirrors on stage the interior of his mind and suggests the ultimate meaning of his life. During the course of the play he is, in a sense, making a pilgrimage into madness. In the final "lunatic" stage he is associated with the traditional medieval and Renaissance emblems of disorder—noise, frantic and unpatterned action, hatred, physical isolation, loss of identity, and (the ultimate chaos) Hell itself.

Such a character is Tangle in Thomas Middleton's *The Phoenix,* an argumentative rogue enamored of the law courts and dedicated to wrangling. Tangle is characterized throughout his career by that frenetic state of mind the Jacobeans called "mad"; he indulges his passion for peevish quarreling and finds pleasure in causing turmoil:

> *Tangle.* Still in law? I had not breathed else now; 'tis very marrow, very manna to me to be in law. I'd been dead ere this else. I have found such sweet pleasure in the vexation of others, that I could wish my years over and over again, to see that fellow a beggar, that bawling knave a gentleman, a matter brought e'en to a judgment to-day, as far as e'er 'twas to begin again to-morrow: O raptures! here a writ of demur, there a *procedendo*, here a *sur-*

surrara, there a *capiendo,* tricks, delays, money-
laws! . . . I'm old, yet have I at this present nine and
twenty suits in law. . . . I have so vexed and beggared the
whole parish with process, subpoenas, and such-like
molestations, they are not able to spare so much ready
money from a term, as would set up a new weather-
cock.[25]

In act 4 Prince Phoenix, the presenter, wonders aloud "how this
fellow keeps out madness" (4.1.73). The answer is that he does
not. At the end of the play, Tangle is transformed from a pug-
nacious but clinically sane fellow into a mindless lunatic. The
motivation is slight, the alteration swift and unexpected. But
Middleton, depending on his audience to make the connection
between passion and madness, had no qualms about employing
this dramatic shorthand. He merely gives to Prince Phoenix a
short speech indicating that the madness was to be viewed as the
right and inevitable end of a life so lived:

> The man's mad
> And privileg'd by the moon, if he say true:
> Less madness 'tis to speak sin than to do.
> This wretch, that lov'd before his food his strife,
> This punishment falls even with his life.
> His pleasure was vexation, all his bliss
> The torment of another;
> Their hurt his health, their starved hopes his store:
> Who so loves law dies either mad or poor.
>
> [4.1.139–47]

There is more than just satire involved in Middleton's handling
of this portrait. The playwright goes beyond the fault to specify
the remedy—Tangle, "one that has lov'd vexation so much / He
cannot now be rid on't" (5.1.271–72), is restored to sanity by the
ministrations of Quieto, a "quiet suffering, and unlawyer'd man;
/ An opposite, a very contrary / To the turbulent fellow"
(4.1.150–52)—the remedy, patience. With this resolution, Middleton indicates that true sanity lies in having the wisdom to
elevate the psyche to a state of rest.

Transformations of the Tangle type are standard. Charac-
terizations of the moneylender, whose desire for material gain
invariably reaches irrational levels, follow the same pattern. One
thinks of *Jack Drum's Entertainment,* where Marston uses lunacy to

symbolize the moral state of his usurer, Mamon. As in *The Phoenix*, a mad scene is employed to reveal the end toward which the character's perverse will has been driving him. Similarly, in *The Staple of News* Ben Jonson's usurer, Pennyboy Senior, cavorts through the play with the passions of a Shylock and finally goes mad during a fit of anger over the loss of his fortune. And in *A New Way to Pay Old Debts* Philip Massinger's Sir Giles Overreach, ruled not by "wisedome" but by hatred and ambition, falls into such a fury after discovering that he has been crossed by the forces of love that his "braine turnes."[26] His final speech (5.1.355–73) is that of a maniac; his imagination carries him into a grotesque world rivaling that of Hieronymus Bosch. Certainly Massinger's ending offers no dazzling display of dramatic genius. But it is not without purpose. The usurer's vision of Hell is, in a sense, the reflection of his state of mind.

At times the playwright, to make the point that a certain life style culminates in madness, will cause the characters surrounding the deviant to presume from his actions that he is mad; an actual lunacy need not develop. This variation emerges in Shakespeare's treatment of Malvolio, who, possessed by a passionate self-love, behaves so ridiculously that Olivia believes he is "tainted in's wits," and who, for our pleasure and his penance, is imprisoned as though he were indeed a lunatic. Though Malvolio never goes crazy, the symbolic effect is the same.

A lesser-known victim of this practice is Alphonso in John Fletcher's *The Pilgrim*. Alphonso is clinically sane, but he allows the passion of anger to dominate his personality and is led by it into a comic pilgrimage through a "wandering wood" to a madhouse.[27] As with the Athenian grove in Shakespeare's *Midsummer Night's Dream*, the forest in *The Pilgrim* is identified with error, and most who enter it are flustered by some distempering passion. Alphonso is the chief offender. Furious with his daughter Alinda, who has fled to the neighboring wood to avoid an unhappy marriage, he pursues the girl with unabated wrath. He is pursued himself by Alinda's maid Juletta, a gadfly of sorts. Juletta strives to vex and exhaust Alphonso, and she presents him to the audience as "this mad-man."[28] The mazes of the forest mirror the confusions of the mind; again, as in *Midsummer Night's Dream*, the characters fatigue themselves, get lost, travel in circles, and in general become more distraught than before.

Not surprisingly, Alphonso's quest leads him to a madhouse. By the time he arrives at the asylum his anger has subdued his reason so completely that the keeper takes him for a lunatic and has him committed. In reality, Alphonso is no more mad than Malvolio is. But the symbolic outcome of his journey informs us that, in giving rein to his anger, he too, is traveling the road to madness.

Whether the insanity is actual or implied, the playwright in each of these cases intimates that the particular desires of the character are desires that have their end in a chaotic "phrenzie." Just as the stage life of a Rosalind or a Viola ends in marriage, so that of a Ferdinand or an Alphonso, a Tangle or a Mamon, moves toward madness.

IV It is not always convenient to let an intemperate soul run mad, though his actions prove that he is so. The mode of symbolism may then be slightly altered—the madness is discreetly distanced from the offender but sends back signals about him. In this alternate form, the playwright brings in one or more madmen to act as a contrast to characters who are ruled by their affections. Although this method is less direct, its ramifications are broader. The contrast stresses that those outside of institutions behave as insanely as those within. The sentiment is implied by Middleton when he calls his play *A Mad World, My Masters* and is stated explicitly by Tourneur when he has Vindice observe, while meditating upon the lusts of mankind, that

> Surely we're all mad people, and they
> Whom we think are, are not: we mistake those;
> 'Tis we are mad in sense, they but in clothes.
> [*The Revenger's Tragedy* 3.5.79–81]

With the introduction of the madhouse, the comparisons between the mad and the supposedly sane made rhetorically by Middleton and Tourneur can be rendered in visual rather than metaphorical terms.

In drawing us into the precincts of Bedlam, the playwright introduces us to a diversified group of fools and madmen who, through their varied occupations or nationalities, make up a miniature world that reflects shrewdly upon the larger one. Reed notes the situation without perceiving its purpose. In the madhouse studies, he writes, "the satire, as popular satire should be, is almost invariably universalized." The individual lunatic brought on stage to perform

> serves only as the immediate butt of the satire; through him, whether he is Fletcher's Welshman, Dekker's merchant, or Webster's doctor, entire professions or classes of people are ridiculed. As a result, the satire, while first providing the Bedlamite with a degree of literary merit, also gave proportionally greater scope and emphasis to the spectacle; not one unfortunate individual, but a whole class of them was made the subject of a derisive display.[29]

Reed perceptively discerns that the satire widens the comic and theatrical potentials of the scenes. But he stops there, without noting that the madhouse is usually being presented as a microcosm of the stage world. The dramatists invite the audience to set the world of the madhouse against the world of the drama per se, ultimately against the real world itself, and to ask whether the clinically sane, having willfully overthrown the reason which alone separates them from the inmates, are not more mad than those they came to jeer at.

The madhouse in *The Pilgrim,* described briefly above as the goal of Alphonso's pilgrimage, is also used by Fletcher to call attention to the likenesses between certain modes of being. By employing a madhouse rather than individual lunacy as his symbol, Fletcher is able to contrast the involuntary derangements of the various inmates with the willed disorder which infects Alphonso, and to force a comparison between the confusion that reigns in the institution and the havoc that spreads throughout the household of the distracted Alphonso. The juxtaposition underscores the fact that Alphonso's fury has reduced the world under his purview to a state which approximates the chaos of the madhouse. Going a step further, Fletcher relates all of this, through certain observations made by the First Keeper, to the world outside of the playhouse; "Citizens," the keeper tells Alphonso, "have Bedlams of their own, Sir, / And are mad at their own charges" (4.3.25–26). We in the audience, creatures of passion ourselves, are thereby associated with both Alphonso and the mad folk, as the symbol of the sanitarium at the center of the play reverberates outward through the stage world into our own. The discords are resolved when, chastised by his imprisonment in the madhouse and abandoning his persecution of Alinda, Alphonso exchanges his anger for resignation and patience. In the final scenes of the play, the movement is from the asylum to the church at Segovia, from madness to marriage, from chaos to harmony.

The scenes set in the madhouse of Alibius in the subplot of *The Changeling* were also intended to be more than "a fine show on the stage."[30] They provide excellent insights into the relationships between the sane and the insane that playwrights and audiences alike took for granted. While the quality of the writing in the subplot is far inferior to that found in the better-known sequences of the play, the mad scenes are skillfully related to the main action. The juxtaposition of lovers and madmen in *The Changeling* is succinctly described by George Williams as "the powerful and spectacular device the dramatists use to say forcefully that sexual irregularities are madness and to represent through the symbol of the insane the bestiality of the sane."[31]

Middleton and Rowley themselves provide the customary hint, in an exchange that takes place between the caretakers of the institution, that the gap between the two states is not as broad as it might seem:

| Isabella. | Why, here's none but fools and madmen. |
| Lollio. | Very well; and where will you find any other, if you should go abroad? |

[3.3.14–16]

By allowing a pair of would-be lovers to infiltrate the asylum, disguised as lunatics in the hopes of seducing Alibius's wife Isabella, the dramatists establish two levels of madness in the world of this play. At the sanitarium we find the usual eccentrics and energumens. But we also discover there Franciscus and Antonio, ostensibly sane but "maddened" by desire. Franciscus and Antonio are changelings because, in succumbing to the dictates of their passions, they have transformed themselves from the rational beings they were into the lunatics they pretended to be (5.3.205–9). The link between Franciscus / Antonio and Beatrice is made at the end of the play when Vermandero, finding the two men missing from court, believes them guilty of Beatrice's crime

(they are accused of murdering Alonzo). Vermandero soon discovers that, on the contrary, Beatrice is guilty of their crime,
Beatrice, too, is a changeling. In engaging in the same tawdry
intrigue in order to enjoy the love of Alsemero, she, too, lowers
herself to the level of the addled beings housed by Alibius. What is
said of the legitimate inmates may be said of these three "sane"
characters—they "act their fantasies in any shapes / Suiting their
present thoughts" (3.3.190–91). The inmates are literally mad,
but Franciscus, Antonio, and Beatrice are symbolically so.

Isabella, through her unique ability to control her own affections, becomes a touchstone of sanity, against whom we are to
measure the self-indulgent Beatrice.The former is surrounded
by chaos and cacophony; she lives among fools and madmen,
demented creatures whose antic chanting of the refrain from
the game of barleybreak, "catch the last couple in hell," becomes
an ironic comment on the internal commotion of their minds.
Beatrice, on the other hand, belongs to the world of sanity. We
first meet her in a temple, where her beauties are loved "to the
holy purpose" and inspire thoughts of paradise, of perfection.
Each lady has two suitors. Isabella's admirers, Franciscus and
Antonio, are lawless; in rejecting their proposals of adultery, she
demonstrates her ability to make rational judgments as well as,
by implication, her sanity. Beatrice also has two suitors: she is
courted by Alonzo and Alsemero. And she has an initial advan-
tage over Isabella in that the intentions of both are honorable. In
her world, the potential exists to re-create a new Eden through
love and its sanctification in matrimony. But Beatrice lacks the
good sense of Isabella and judges with the eye of passion. She
hires DeFlores to murder the first suitor so she can be free to
wed the second, and thus turns the sane world she inhabits into a
madder world than that in which Isabella resides. As Beatrice
becomes involved in murder, blackmail, arson, adultery, and
perjury—all in the impossible hope of entering an earthly paradise through her marriage to Alsemero—she rapidly disrupts
the orderly round of life in Vermandero's castle. The potential
paradise becomes a chaotic hell. Meanwhile, Isabella continually
refuses to compromise with her surroundings. When she puts
on the "habit of a frantic" and pretends to be stricken with an
ardent love for Antonio, she does so only to poke fun at the
reality behind the appearance. By becoming what he asks her to

be, she reveals to him the madness of his request. Beatrice, on the contrary, violates the standards which were designed to maintain order, making one moral compromise after another, and her deviations symbolically permit the fools and madmen to penetrate into the sane world of the castle. They, too, as the visual representation of the inner soul of the corrupted Beatrice, reveal the reality behind the appearance; her union with Alsemero will be characterized by panicky judgments that reflect her own moral madness. Finally, in the last act of the tragedy, the two realms of insanity are clearly equated as Beatrice and DeFlores are caught in the madmen's game of barleybreak: she and her cynical lover, through their "madness," become "the last couple in hell." Time and again we find that when the contents of a madhouse are emptied onto the stage, the lunatics are brought in to indicate that one character or another is equally mad, if not madder, as a result of his blind submission to some distracting passion.

V The foregoing discussion dealt primarily with moral madnesses. The era also differentiated madnesses of passion that result when the individual is asked to bear too much. These are difficult to classify, but they are usually connected with grief and develop after a period of suffering. The symptoms, in dramatization, are frequently those of lunacy; the burdens of life become so great that the mind snaps.

Examples can be culled in abundance from the revenge plays or plays influenced by them. Isabella in *The Spanish Tragedy*, Lucibella in *Hoffman*, Cornelia in *The White Devil*, Penthea in *The Broken Heart* —all fall into this category, with Ophelia as its supreme achievement. Appearing in plays where evil and injustice oppress humanity, these softly feminine characters, unable to bear the tyranny of violence, sometimes function as mirrors or "reflectors" (this is Mack's term) of the revenger;[32] they reveal an aspect of *his* madness which it is inconvenient to make otherwise explicit. They invoke sympathy or pathos rather than moral indignation, and our response to them spills over onto the revenger, for he, too, suffers as they do.

This element of suffering is more widely present in madnesses of passion as one turns away from comedy toward tragedy. The revenger's madness itself partakes of it—most emphatically so in *Titus Andronicus* (where the cruelties of Aaron and Tamora are relentless and Titus is "wrung with wrongs more than our backs can bear"), but hinted at in relation to Hieronimo, Hamlet, and Orgilus as well. But its finest expression occurs in *King Lear*. Here, the passion combines with an intense suffering that turns the eye inward and eventually culminates in self-knowledge. Where the revengers experience the suffering but are doomed by their allegiance to the ghost and die before they achieve illumination, Lear descends into madness and comes out beyond it. No discussion of the uses of madness by the Elizabethan and Jacobean dramatists would be complete without a recognition of this ultimate power of madness to elevate and transform.

Enough has been said, we hope, to prove that when madness is imposed upon a character in Renaissance drama it is not always "for the purpose of climaxing the play with a highly spectacular episode" or simply to provide "cheap amusement to the groundlings." The madness may well be a manifestation of moral chaos.

Chapter 3

The Revenger's Madness
& Renaissance Psychological Theory

All the passions of the irascible rise from the passions of the concupiscible appetite and terminate in them. For instance, anger rises
from sadness, and, having wrought vengeance, terminates in joy.

St. Thomas Aquinas, *The Summa Theologica*

I "TAINT NOT THY MIND," says King Hamlet to his son,
"nor let thy soul contrive / Against thy mother aught"
(1.5.85–86).[1] He means quite specifically, "Taint not thy mind
. . . against thy mother," but by a deliberate manipulation of the
syntax and the inclusion of the parenthetical "nor let thy soul
contrive," Shakespeare so isolates the initial phrase from the
concluding one that the Ghost's meaning becomes ambiguous.
Standing thus alone, the phrase demands that attention be paid
to it. The words warn that the act authorized by the Ghost entails
a risk: to pursue a course of vengeance may indeed taint the
mind. Few of the heroes of revenge tragedy escape the danger.
Hieronimo, Titus, and Orestes go the full route to lunacy. Antonio, Hamlet, and Vindice are "tainted" to various though lesser degrees.

Since revenge is "a motion of the heart," an affection or a
perturbation like jealousy or love, the madness hinted at by
these ominous words of King Hamlet is, obligatorily, a madness
of inordinate passion. This chapter, with the help of evidence
found both in the plays and in psychological treatises of the day,
will trace the various stages through which this passion moves.

60

Because neither art nor life can be reduced to a formula, no single revenger will follow this pattern to the letter, but the idiosyncrasies of each will be better comprehended if the over-all pattern is acknowledged.

Current thinking about the madness motif in revenge tragedy demonstrates a certain fuzziness which should be cleared away before we go any farther. First, there is the matter of focus. When Harrison said "let the poor girl go mad; we always have a mad scene in a Revenge Play," he was referring, of course, to Ophelia.[2] But in supposing that the madness of Ophelia could ever qualify as the obligatory madness, Harrison makes a fundamental error. Those playwrights in touch with the tradition understood that not *any* madness would do; it was the madness of the revenger that was obligatory. Other mad folk may appear in a revenge play but only the protagonist's madness gives significance to all of the recurring motifs.

Second, there is the matter of development. Ophelia's condition is static. The audience is asked to pity her, not to analyze the mental processes which brought her to this state.[3] With the revenger, it is otherwise. In the classic revenge tragedy, the obligatory madness is a process, not a given. It begins as a result of the malfunctioning of the will which occurs when the passions obtain control over the rational powers. The eclipsing of reason is brief and sporadic at the beginning. As the passion increases, its effects are sustained for longer and longer periods of time, until madness becomes the dominant mode of behavior. When one speaks of the revenger's madness, therefore, one must remember that throughout the play this madness is always evolving.

Third, there is the matter of degree. The "poor girl's" madness is a lunacy in which the mind is totally gone. Having suffered a complete disintegration of the psyche, Ophelia is mentally unable to order the world. Though the chaos passion engenders in the mind of the revenger is symbolized by insanity, the madness never so far overtakes him that, were he to control this passion, he could not reason normally again. His mind remains capable of ordering the world. The kind of madness revealed in *The Spanish Tragedy, Titus Andronicus, Antonio's Revenge, Hamlet, The Revenger's Tragedy*—and even in *The Broken Heart*—is as capable of sharpening the mind as of dulling it. The revenger is always held responsible for the way he orders his world, as the lunatic is not.

Throughout this chapter the word *madness* will apply to (1) the madness of the *revenger*, (2) the mode of experience toward which his actions are driving him (a mode which he passes into and out of), and (3) a state of being in which the ordering powers of the mind never entirely cease to function.

II   Let us turn from these unproductive approaches to the madness to one that seems more fruitful. Since the madness under examination may be defined as *the overthrow of the reason by the passion of revenge,* we should be familiar with the psychological processes by which this feat is accomplished. What passions are integral to the experience of revenge, and how do these interact with the faculties of the mind involved in making judgments?

Renaissance psychologists saw man as a judgment-making animal, differentiated from other creatures by his ability to make conscious choices. Judging was for them the major activity of life. They were fascinated by the process of knowing, and studied the progress of an idea through the mind from its entry via the eye to its final destination in the brain, where all voluntary judgments were to be made. Borrowing here and there from their Greek and medieval predecessors, they formulated theories about the thought processes involved in decision-making that have far more sophistication than many of those around today.[4]

The acquiring of knowledge began in the sensible soul, which had two principle divisions, *apprehension* (the stage of becoming conscious of the outer world) and *motion* (the stage of doing something about it). Let us examine apprehension first. "Outward" apprehension, an inflated term for seeing, feeling, touching, tasting, smelling invented to place them in the theoretical context, need not concern us long, but as the first step in the process of knowing it cannot be overlooked. The knowledge that sparks the passion of revenge has its source in the senses:

Hieronimo *hears* Bel-imperia's cry, *sees* Horatio's body hanging from an arbor, *feels* his son's blood oozing from the corpse. These impressions from the outside world are taken into the mind individually and put together by the *common sense,* a synthesizing faculty of the "inward" apprehension. The resulting image of the perceived event gives Hieronimo a new awareness—his son Horatio has been murdered. The offense, in all its horror, has become known to him.[5]

The inward apprehension, of which the common sense is a part, has a second faculty, that of *imagination* (also called *fancy* or *phantasy),* and a third, *memory.* It is to the imagination that the common sense transfers the information it gains from the outer world. The imagination is, so to speak, the "distribution box" of the mind. It sorts out information presented to it and passes it along to the proper authorities for judging.

Information received by the imagination falls into three categories. Some, like "Richard Burbage played Hamlet in 1601," requires no action. This the imagination passes on to the memory for storage. Some, like "Derek Jacobi is playing Hamlet at the Old Vic this season," requires a decision in terms of pleasure or pain (shall I buy tickets?). This problem the imagination refers to the *voluntary appetites.* These are the judging faculties of the sensible soul, and, arriving here, we pass out of the realm of apprehension and into that of motion. The role of the appetites is to determine whether advancement or withdrawal is in order, and then to call upon the *passions* to take some physical action upon the decision (flagging a cab to the box office or posting a check). Other information received by the imagination requires decisions so complex that the sensible soul cannot handle them at all: "The role of Hamlet should have gone to me. Shall I seek revenge?" The sensible soul knows nothing of absolutes; hence, where moral decisions are required its judgments are notoriously unreliable. At this point the imagination must send the information directly to the *rational soul.*

As the appetites are to the passions in the sensible soul, so the *wit,* or *reason,* is to the *will* in the rational soul. Wit, "the mind's chief judge, which doth control / Of Fancy's court the judgments false and vain,"[6] has the power to determine of good and evil and is thus the ultimate authority in the brain. Here the data could be examined in the light of the *understanding* and an intellectual rather than an emotional judgment made as to the action to be taken. The will (the executive half of the rational soul) then acts upon that determination.

Cases of murder and injustice such as those perplexing Hieronimo and Hamlet so clearly raise problems of good and evil that only the third of these procedures would seem appropriate. To revenge or not to revenge? That is the question which the imagination of the incipient revenger must pose, and the reason should be called upon to answer it.

In a society like that which produced revenge tragedy, where values are derived from the Christian formulation of experience, reason's counsel would probably echo that of Pierre de la Primaudaye:

> Therefore wee may well conclude, that all priuate Reuenge proceeding of enuy, or of hatred, or of anger, is vicious and forbidden by God, who commaundeth vs to render good for euill, and not euill for euill. For hee hath ordained the meanes, whereby hee will haue vengeance executed among men. Therefore hee hath appointed Magistrates tò execute it according to his Lawe, and following his ordinaunce, not with any euill affection, but with iust indignation proceeding from loue, and from true zeale of iustice. . . . And as himselfe commeth in iudgement to take vengeance, so hee woulde haue them supplie his place among men, vnto whome hee hath committed the sworde for the defence of the good and punishment of euill doers, to followe his example.[7]

To contemplate an action of private revenge is to handle the problem on the level of the emotions; this "is vicious and forbidden by God." Rather, reason would urge, the wrong ought to be endured with patience.

The responsibilities of the wit do not end with its pronouncement of the right. It must also identify and counteract the tempting arguments that enable wrong to masquerade as right. Chief among these is the idea that patience is a cowardly, effeminate, and dishonorable response to an injury. To "beare vp his arme against his foe," to "reuenge to death the downe-disgrace," to scorn "al peace-content" as "too too cheap and base," and through such manliness to "vp-rise to *Ioues* benignities" —these are manly actions, and actions that falsely present themselves as good. Personifications of revenge come armed with such arguments in the literature of the age, and characters embodying reason must be prepared to deflect them.[8]

Tecnicus, the rational voice in *The Broken Heart*, approaches Ford's revenger, Orgilus, observing in him "a resolution / Of giddy rashness" that will "choke the breath of reason" (3.1.1–2), and attempts to alert Orgilus to the distinctions between these two kinds of manly honor:

Orgilus.   Could art
    Run through mine inmost thoughts, it should not sift
    An inclination there more than what suited
    With justice of mine honor.
Tecnicus.   I believe it.
    But know, then, Orgilus, what honor is:
    Honor consists not in a bare opinion
    By doing any act that feeds content,
    Brave in appearance 'cause we think it brave.
    Such honor comes by accident, not nature,
    Proceeding from the vices of our passion,
    Which makes our reason drunk. But real honor
    Is the reward of virtue, and acquir'd
    By justice or by valor, which for bases
    Hath justice to uphold it. He then fails
    In honor who for Lucre or revenge
    Commits thefts, murders, treasons, and adulteries,
    With suchlike, by intrenching on just laws,
    Whose sov'reignty is best preserv'd by justice.
    Thus as you see how honor must be grounded
    On knowledge, not opinion (for opinion
    Relies on probability and accident,
    But knowledge on necessity and truth),
    I leave thee to the fit consideration
    Of what becomes the grace of real honor.[9]

Tecnicus warns against the error of mistaking personal violence for manly honor. He would have found in Joseph Hall's description of the patient man a model for the revenger to emulate. The truly honorable man, says Hall, is

> a man made of metal not so hard as flexible. His shoulders are large, fit for a load of injuries; which he bears, not out of baseness and cowardliness, because he dare not revenge, but out of Christian fortitude, because he may not: he hath so conquered himself, that wrongs cannot conquer him; and herein alone finds that victory con-

sists in yielding. He is above nature, while he seems below himself.
The vilest creature knows how to turn again, but to command himself
not to resist, being urged, is more than heroical.[10]

Tourneur, in *The Atheist's Tragedy,* examines a situation where
the proper deference to reason is made. Charlemont, the Guyon
of revengers and the very image of Hall's patient man, responds
temperately to the knowledge that his father has been murdered, never vowing vengeance upon the murderer but stoically
enduring his trials. Not that Charlemont is without passion. At
moments his emotions tempt him to act precipitously, as when
he nearly slays Sebastian, the son of his father's murderer. But
Charlemont always regains control. His higher faculties inter-
pose themselves between the thought and the deed and restore
his perspective. Significantly, in *The Atheist's Tragedy* the revenger, fortified by reason, never goes mad.

The imagination, then, when apprehending the injury or offense, would ideally request a judgment from the wit, and the
wit would return advice to the imagination that would stave off
the terrifying madness.

III If this course were followed by every revenger, there
would be no tragedy. In revenge plays the imagination
is stirred by the knowledge of the offense to such an extent that
it ceases to operate normally.

One reason for this malfunction is that the pain caused by the
offense is unbearably severe. Something shocking has occurred,
something which knocks the world apart for the protagonist,
making him think that

> I feel the frame of nature shake.
> Cracks not the joints of earth to bear my woes?[11]

or that the world is

> no world, but mass of public wrongs,
> Confus'd and fill'd with murder and misdeeds.[12]

or

> an unweeded garden
> That grows to seed, things rank and gross in nature
> Possess it merely.[13]

So strong is the impression left by the injury that the order of the community, a former source of stability and protection, seems a blatant farce. The impact of the murder upon the revenger's imagination is overwhelming.

The faculties of motion, those powers of the sensible soul distinguished as the *concupiscible* and *irascible appetites* and responsible for calling particular passions into action to seek an end that promises pleasure or avoid one that threatens pain, have a certain kinship with the imagination and respond quickly to impressions from it. When the shock impresses itself upon the imagination, it also stimulates the appetites, which activate the forces that conduct the knowledge to the heart:

> To our imagination commeth by sense or memorie, some object to be knowne, conuenient or disconuenient to Nature, the which being knowne in the imagination which resideth in the former part of the braine . . . , presently the purer spirits, flocke from the brayne, by certain secret channels to the heart, where they pitch at the dore, signifying what an obiect was presented, conuenient or disconuenient for it. The heart immediately bendeth, either to prosecute it, or to eschew it: and the better to effect that affection, draweth other humours to helpe him.[14]

Messages from the heart, in the form of passions or *affections,* are then quickly sent back to the fancy. These passions combine with the original information, thus altering considerably the image that is ultimately presented to the reason.

Thomas Wright describes what happens when the passions enter the imagination and attach themselves to important knowledge before it is transferred to the wit:

> The gates of our imagination being preuented, yea, and welnie shut vp with the consideration of that obiect which feedeth the passion, and pleaseth the appetite; the vnderstanding looking into the imagination, findeth nothing almost but the mother & nurse of his passion for consideration, where you may well see how the imagination putteth greene spectacles before the eyes of our wit, to make it see nothing but greene, that is, seruing for the consideration of the Passion.
>
> Furthermore, the imagination representeth to the vnderstanding, not onely reasons that may fauour the passion, but also it sheweth them very intensiuely, with more shew and apparance than they are indeed; for as the Moone, when she riseth or setteth; seemeth greater vnto vs, than indeed she is, (because the vapours or clowdes are

interposed betwixt our eyes and her) euen so, the beauty and good-
nesse of the obiect represented to our vnderstanding, appeareth
fayrer and goodlier than it is, because a clowdy imagination inter-
poseth a mist.[15]

In other words, the information is distorted before the reason
has a chance to consider it. Where the object so seemingly beautiful is a woman, the interposing passion of love combining in
the imagination with her image would tend to magnify her
charms out of all proportion to the original and make the reason
deem it more desirable than it may be. The same holds true
when the perceived image is that of Claudius pouring poison
into King Hamlet's ear. The picture conveyed to the senses is
overlaid with emotion as the desire for revenge floods into the
imagination. Thereafter, the offense can scarcely be separated
again from the urge to destroy the offender. The reason, looking into an imagination thus infected, is hard put to distinguish
between the objective image and the subjective coloring—or
"mist"—which this furious affection of revenge has imposed
upon it. The effect is cyclical. The image of the offense stimulates the desire, which intensifies under the stimulus, while the
desire, thus magnified, blows up the image, throws it, as it were,
on a giant screen. So long as no mitigating information filters in
to halt this mutual magnification, the passion will continue to
intensify, darkening the senses and blinding the wit.

Despite the overwrought rhetoric of the "Oh eyes! no eyes"
soliloquy Kyd wrote for Hieronimo, the speech provides a mirror of the fermenting imagination. His poetry shows us a mind
as "confus'd and fill'd with murder and misdeeds" (3.2.4) as the
world outside it which Hieronimo rails against. The reason tries
to work, but the passion has so colored the event that all else is
obscured. The sense impressions made by the injury keep bat-
tering the mind, transforming what the eyes have seen into a
nightmare which the imagination continues to relive:

> The night, sad secretary to my moans,
> With direful visions wake my vexed soul,
> And with the wounds of my distressful son
> Solicit me for notice of his death.
> The ugly fiends do sally forth of hell,
> And frame my steps to unfrequented paths,

> And fear my heart with fierce inflamed thoughts.
> The cloudy day my discontents records,
> Early begins to register my dreams,
> And drive me forth to seek the murderer.
>
> [3.2.12–21]

The passions have stormed and occupied Hieronimo's imagination and like "ugly fiends" or Senecan Furies "drive" him in directions that reason would not have him go. Kyd strives to re-create that sense of the tortured imagination as Wright had described it, but vividly rendered through the poetic medium.

What are the passions that effect this conquest of the imagination? Revenge was classified as a compound passion, a mixture of several primary emotions. La Primaudaye's definition ranges across all of the primary passions involved:

> When the heart is wounded with griefe by any one, it desireth to returne the like to him that hath hurt it, and to rebite him of whome it is bitten. This affection is a desire of reuenge, which being put in execution, is reuenge accomplished: namely, when wee cause him that hath offended vs to suffer that punishment, which in our iudgement he hath deserued. This punishment is to damnifie him eyther in soule, or in body, or in his goodes, yea, sometimes by all the meanes that may bee. . . . Euery offence therefore that ingendereth hatred, anger, enuy or indignation bringeth with it a desire of reuenge, which is to render euill for euil, and to requite griefe received with the like againe.[16]

According to this definition, grief must be experienced first. The offense that arouses the grief also "ingendereth hatred, anger, enuy, or indignation"—all or singly. And growing out of that combination of affections is the desire "to render euill for euil," that is, the desire for revenge. Such are the individual "motions" involved in this compound passion.

At least three of these passions —grief, hatred, and anger —are emphasized in revenge tragedy.[17] Hieronimo is smitten by all three at once, because he gains in one scene the knowledge that later revengers receive gradually. Out of the realization that "my son is dead" grows Hieronimo's grief ("Ay me most wretched, that have lost my joy" [2.5.32]); from the knowledge that "my son has been murdered" stems that mixture of hatred and anger which is revenge. In Antonio and in Hamlet the emotions do not

arise together; they are presented in stages. From the separation
we perceive more clearly how the passions that make up revenge
are related.

Initially, only the concupiscible appetite is activated: the son
learns of his father's death and lapses into a deep-felt grief.
Marston attempts to render this emotion directly. His revenger,
learning that his father is dead and his fiancée "blurr'd with false
defames," succumbs immediately to the passion. It originates in
the heart, there initiating the appropriate physiological changes;
Antonio's "moist entrails are crumpled up with grief / Of
parching mischiefs," his heart "with punching anguish spurs his
galled ribs" (1.2.278–80). Surging then back to the brain, the
passion occupies the imagination, fortifying it against reason. To
Antonio the good advice of Alberto, that " 'Tis reason's glory to
command affects" (1.2.273), becomes "stale, ill-relish'd counsel"
(2.2.4), while the stoical precepts of Seneca's *De Providentia* are
eschewed as the "foamy bubbling of a fleamy brain" (2.2.55). His
grief has shut up the gates of his imagination against reason's
influence. And left to itself, the emotion whips itself up to
greater and greater proportions. The process of magnification
that is going on in the fancy forms the structural and rhetorical
bases for the development of Antonio's speeches:

> The chamber of my breast is even throng'd
> With firm attendance that forswears to flinch.
> I have a thing sits here; it is not grief,
> 'Tis not despair nor the most plague
> That the most wretched are infected with;
> But the most grief-full, despairing, wretched,
> Accursed, miserable —
>
> [2.2.11–17]

The process continually accelerates. His is a "giant grief" and
"will burst all covert" (2.2.5–6). In refusing to curb his "boundless woe," Antonio becomes the man Pandulpho refuses to be,
one who would "turn rank mad, / Or wrong my face with mimic
action / Stamp, curse, weep, rage, and then my bosom strike"
(1.2.313–15). He will "sigh and wring my hands, / Beat my poor
breast and wreathe my tender arms" (2.2.142–43) in sign of his
agony. Rapidly moving toward despair, Antonio goes to his father's tomb to end his misery in suicide.

In *Hamlet,* too, a period of grief is introduced. When we meet Hamlet, he is in mourning. But the grief is treated with greater dramatic decorum. Shakespeare does not compromise Hamlet's dignity by attempting to render the depth of the passion through tears and self-flagellation; he renders Hamlet's grief by having Claudius describe it. Claudius presents it as "obstinate condoliment," and through this reprimand Shakespeare alludes to the possibility of excess. Claudius is soon discredited, and what strikes the viewer instead is the sincerity of Hamlet's grief; it says much of deep sorrow and due respect. Yet the king's admonitions make the point: grief obviously possesses Hamlet's imagination.

For both Marston and Shakespeare, the period of grief seems designed to thrust the revenger into a frame of mind proper for the ghost to work on. This emotion temporarily clouds the imagination and weakens the reason, rendering the mind more highly susceptible to attacks by the stronger passions. The psyche becomes extremely vulnerable to the suggestions implanted in it by the ghost.

The information which causes the major trouble in the imagination is not so much the knowledge of the loss as the knowledge that the loss occurred as the result of an injustice. This is the knowledge that the ghost introduces. Its intelligence is calculated to incite anger as well as to provide an object of hatred against which that anger can be directed. Anger is both the root from which the desire for revenge will grow and the product of that desire, for as long as this emotion is met with obstacles and cannot expend itself against the hated object it will continue to increase in intensity. As an irascible passion, it differs from the concupiscible passion of grief. Grief is identified with the motion of withdrawal. Anger has a force and aggressiveness specifically designed to deal with obstructions. But combined with grief, anger evolves into that implacable desire for revenge.

IV A further observation about the role of the imagination in the revenger's madness can now be made. The imagination had two powers which were dangerous if allowed to exist unchecked—the power to call up objects from the memory and keep them before the mind's eye and the power to combine images perceived at different times to create totally new and more emotionally charged images. Both of these abilities assisted in the process of magnification that made the natural passion into a mad obsession. Should the revenger settle his imagination upon the offense, he could do himself no end of harm. "A man that studieth revenge keeps his own wounds green, which otherwise would heal and do well," says Francis Bacon in "Of Revenge."[18] To forestall this healing effect, the ghost of King Hamlet chose "remember me" as his call to arms. Once under the spell of this call, stage revengers do their utmost to keep their wounds green.

The dramatists rely heavily upon the first of these characteristics of the imagination in depicting the psychology of their heroes. In most plays the revenger takes deliberate steps to ensure that the memory continually feeds images of the offense to the imagination. Kyd, Chettle, and Tourneur use visible props to dramatize this point. Kyd's Hieronimo pulls his son's handkerchief from the corpse and dabs it in the dead boy's blood, then swears that "it shall not from me till I take revenge." More macabrely, he preserves Horatio's body, unburied, setting a precedent later stage revengers will follow:

> Seest thou these wounds that yet are bleeding fresh?
> I'll not entomb them till I have reveng'd.
>
> [2.5.53–54]

The skeleton Hieronimo displays at the end of *The Spanish Tragedy* turns up at the beginning of Chettle's *Hoffman*, whose avenger had followed Hieronimo's precedent, for the same purpose. Tourneur's Vindice also assures himself that time will not dull his memory of the offense by making Gloriana's skull a constant reminder of the injury. For nine years the skull has been "his studies' ornament" and the object of his meditation. These tokens become visual representations of the thoughts festering in the revenger's mind.

In *Hamlet* and *Antonio's Revenge*, oaths are used instead of mementoes—a difference possibly explained by their common descent through the *Ur-Hamlet* line rather than directly from *The Spanish Tragedy*. Both Hamlet and Antonio vow to erase ex-

traneous knowledge from the mind so that all thoughts concentrate upon the offense. Hamlet, for example, determines
that when his imagination looks into his memory it shall see one
thing:

> Remember thee!
> Ay, thou poor ghost, whiles memory holds a seat
> In this distracted globe. Remember thee!
> Yea, from the table of my memory
> I'll wipe away all trivial fond records,
> All saws of books, all forms, all pressures past
> That youth and observation copied there,
> And thy commandement all alone shall live
> Within the book and volume of my brain,
> Unmix'd with baser matter.
>
> [1.5.95–104]

Antonio takes a similar oath:

> May I be cursed by my father's ghost
> And blasted with incensed breath of heaven,
> If my heart beat on ought but vengeance!
> May I be numb'd with horror and my veins
> Pucker with sing'ing torture, if my brain
> Digest a thought, but of dire vengeance;
> May I be fetter'd slave to coward chance,
> If blood, heart, brain, plot ought save vengeance.
>
> [3.1.85–92]

Goffe, eager to display his familiarity with the tradition by
making allusions, picks up both suggestions in *The Tragedy of
Orestes*. Orestes imitates Hieronimo, Hoffman, and Vindice in
preserving his father's skeleton (he carries the bones in his
pocket). But not to be outdone by Hamlet or Antonio, Orestes
also makes a vow to apply his whole mind to one subject:

> Thinke on me, and reuenge: yes, those two words
> Shall serue as burthen vnto all my acts,
> I will reuenge, and then I'll thinke on thee:
> I'll thinke on thee, and then againe reuenge,
> And stab, and wound, and still I'll thinke on thee.[19]

The playwrights all stress this single-mindedness. The
madness is in essence an obsession, a disturbance of the
imagination. Just as the lover delays his own recovery from his

lovesickness by keeping the image of the beloved in his imagination, so the revenger exacerbates his own sickness by nursing there the memory of the offense.

With that central image of the dread event the imagination combines others which make the offense increasingly grotesque. Vindice's imagination is the most industrious, having united with the image of the dead Gloriana all of the traditional associations that come with the skull as a symbol of life's vanities. So closely has his imagination linked the general to the particular that whenever he thinks of one he passes automatically to the other. When he envisions "the bright face of my betrothed lady" he associates it with its potential to draw the "uprightest man" into sin.[20] When doting on her lost beauty he is soon wondering why the silkworm expends its "yellow labors" to deck out flesh that is in essence no more than this skull. When considering how Gloriana was by "the old duke poison'd" his mind immediately expands the image to "old men lustful." Because of this inflating activity of the imagination, Vindice carries not only his single burden of grief but all mankind's. What has happened to Gloriana becomes by this process of inflation a symbol of human evil and the necessity for revenge appears to Vindice an unavoidable duty to humanity.

Having concentrated all of his faculties upon a single area of experience, the revenger will be affected in two ways. First, he will gain new and deeper insights into evil. His reason will be led to probe his own experience of evil and out of his meditations will come a more profound sympathy with or understanding of the darker forces of the universe. This process, so obvious in *The Revenger's Tragedy* where Vindice's warped vision of reality as a world of darkness at noon forms the very matrix of the play, is even better illustrated in *Hamlet,* where it is too well known to require explication and too all-pervasive to submit to it. The revenger's fascination with evil may also be seen in a less perfectly realized form in those satiric speeches which Marston gives to Antonio:

> O, you departed souls
> That lodge in coffin'd trunks which my feet press:
> If Pythagorean axioms be true,
> Of spirits' transmigration, fleet no more

> To human bodies; rather live in swine,
> Inhabit wolves' flesh, scorpions, dogs, and toads
> Rather than man. The curse of heaven reigns
> In plagues unlimited through all his days;
> His mature age grows only mature vice,
> And ripens only to corrupt and rot
> The budding hopes of infant modesty;
> Still striving to be more than man, he proves
> More than a devil.
>
> [3.1.108–20]

Like Vindice and Hamlet, Antonio has discovered enough evil in the world to make him question the very nature of man.

At the same time that the revenger gains an acquaintance with evil, he will along the way rid himself of all that is good in him, thus becoming more and more like those malevolent forces that he decries against. Each playwright dramatizes this effect of the madness differently.

In *The Spanish Tragedy* the problem is handled symbolically. The slow painful stripping away of virtue is evidenced by a more obvious stripping away of Hieronimo's occupation as knight marshal. Hieronimo originally holds a respected judicial position in the court, gradually declines in efficiency, and finally casts off his marshal's robes in a fit of madness, while simultaneously developing a close affinity with the denizens of Hell. Tourneur also employs symbolism. In the allegorical setting of *The Revenger's Tragedy* Vindice leaves the House of Grace and Chastity which is associated with his intended marriage to Gloriana, and journeys to the Court of the World, where Gloriana's beauty becomes to him only a snare to deceive men and his better qualities give way to a sardonic delight in intrigue.

Marston and Shakespeare treat the matter with greater realism, though symbolic overtones are never completely absent. The loss of goodness, not central in Marston because of certain quirks in his personal vision, is acknowledged in at least one isolated incident. The Julio episode shows us what the knowledge of Piero's guilt does to Antonio's humanity. Noticing Piero's son in the church, Antonio determines to rip the boy open, "vein by vein, and carve revenge / In bleeding rases" (3.1.166–67). When Julio protests his innocence, pity and compassion surface in Antonio; for a moment, love seems about to prevail over anger. Immediately, however, the Ghost—that spirit of revenge that has taken over Antonio's imagination—closes the gates of the phantasy to any such humanizing emotion. It enjoins Antonio to repudiate all tender feelings toward Julio that might work to temper his fury. Goodness must be rooted out.

In *Hamlet,* Shakespeare also develops the syndrome on the more realistic level, using the prince's relationship with Ophelia as the key. One of the "forms and pressures past" that Hamlet erases from the table of his memory after the Ghost's visitation is his love for Ophelia, the most nearly pure character in the play. Shakespeare has made Gertrude and Ophelia the central mirrors of the young prince's diseased imagination. Once awakened to the existence of evil, Hamlet perceives the nature of Gertrude's errors more clearly than she herself does, just as he interprets the corruption of the kingdom under Claudius quite accurately. Yet he is blind to the virtues of Ophelia and erroneously attributes to her the same inconstancy and lust which he has discovered in his mother. The more obsessed with evil Hamlet's imagination becomes, the further he pushes Ophelia away from him, so that his repudiation of her becomes the dramatic expression of the suppression of his own innate purity and kindness.

This steady domination of the revenger's good qualities by the more ruthless ones fostered by his obsession is another of the signs of his madness. The phantasy, having focused upon the offense, develops a propensity to search into the foul corners and alleyways of life and becomes lost in them. Wasted and slightly maddened by so dank an environment, it begins to believe there is no other, until eventually it reaches a point where in coming upon a sunny landscape it focuses entirely on the shadows. What the phantasy sees, in this state, is there, but the vision of it is highly distorted.

V   The madness, of course, drives toward an action—the torture or death or damnation of the murderer. Two changes must occur in the revenger's psyche before he can commit that action. His will must be separated from the reason and aligned with the passions. And his picture of reality must be so thoroughly distorted that the contemplated action appears to his reason as a just action, for so long as the mind sees murder as an evil, it will back off from the deed. In other words, the revenger not only must have made the decision to act but must believe that the action is good. At such a point the madness will be complete. The unlikelihood of these changes occurring schematically in life prevents the playwrights from displaying them schematically in the drama, but both developments are generally denoted in some form.

The final corruption of the will, because it involves conflict and choice, the basic materials of drama, is easily rendered on the stage. Hieronimo's *Vindicta mihi* soliloquy, for example, is specifically designed to mark the moment at which the will aligns itself with the passion of revenge. In this speech Hieronimo fully commits himself to action and whatever delays occur thereafter arise from the difficulties of obtaining access to the victim rather than from rational doubt or conscience.

Kyd's play is constructed to build toward the moment of reversal at which the just man consents to murder. Not all revenge tragedies follow this pattern. For Vindice in *The Revenger's Tragedy* the will has hardened itself to this point long before the play opens; Vindice enters with a psyche already prepared to act and only awaits his opportunity. In Hamlet, the proclivity toward reason is so strong that the passion never gets an unbreakable grip on the will—it has several momentary victories but, when it most threatens to overwhelm, chance intervenes and removes the prince from the infected environment. When he returns, his perspective upon the situation has cleared; the Ghost has lost its control over his imagination. This difference in the state of the will of the individual protagonists has important effects upon our moral judgment of each revenger's action: while all revengers who take action must pay with their lives, Hamlet, obviously, is far less culpable than Hieronimo, and Hieronimo less so than Vindice.

To dramatize the ability of the mind to locate the Good in violence and murder, the playwrights frequently allow the hero to "discern" that he is an agent of God:

> Heaven applies our drift,
> And all the saints do sit soliciting
> For vengeance on those cursed murderers.
> [*The Spanish Tragedy* 4.1.31–33]

> O, my lusty bloods,
> Heaven sits clapping of our enterprise.
> [*Antonio's Revenge* 5.2.29–30]

> Heaven hath pleas'd it so
> To punish me with this, and this with me,
> That I must be their scourge and minister.
> [*Hamlet* 3.4.173–75]

> No power is angry when the lustful die;
> When thunder claps, heaven likes the tragedy.
> [*The Revenger's Tragedy* 5.3.47–48]

Whether the protagonist erroneously interprets the ghost as a divine messenger and assumes authority from it (as with Antonio) or whether he grasps at some less awesome event as a sign (Hieronimo derives his "divine authority" from Belimperia), he nonetheless proceeds upon his self-appointed mission of violence in the belief that he has a special dispensation from Heaven. Make no mistake—he may indeed have supernatural sponsors among deities representing the forces of nature; he may even, insofar as his own passions and choices have stirred up enough evil within him to set him on a path of self-destruction, actually be functioning to bring about the will of Providence (this without any divine compulsion being set upon him to deny him freedom of choice). Both influences—the playwright so desiring—may be operative simultaneously. But first and foremost there is always this fact at the height of the madness: the revenger believes he acts as a divinely appointed agent of justice because his distorted imagination, wherein he sees himself as the one just man left in the universe, has convinced him that the act of revenge will bring about a good, and that God therefore desires him to *act*.

VI   With the change in the direction of the will and its drive to champion a false good which presents itself as divinely sanctioned justice, the revenger is ready to kill. There remains but one final aspect of the psychology of madness to be considered: by this time the imagination is so overwrought that the revenger is not living in the real world. The world he "sees" is no longer perceived through the senses and taken in to be judged and interpreted; his vision originates in the imagination and form is superimposed onto objects outside. Objective fact is altered to fit preconceived notions of it.

The task of re-creating this internal reality upon the stage is no easy one for the playwright. Subjectivity itself is difficult to portray. And when the distortions taking place in the revenger's imagination are given concrete form, problems of credibility invariably arise. Many unsuccessful experiments were made in the attempt to dramatize this aspect of the madness.

One method used by the playwrights was to depict the disturbed imagination deliberately manipulating facts that do not fit with its private view of the world. *Antonio's Revenge* contains an unmistakable illustration of this approach. As Antonio thrusts his dagger again and again into young Julio's body, his mind is busy amassing evidence that no wrong is being done. The "logic" of the passions first separates Julio into two entities, soul and body. It then equates the life of Julio with the soul, which cannot die. Antonio, in freeing that soul from the inhibiting body, is actually releasing it. Julio lives on, in bliss. The rationalization goes further. Since the soul which is the real Julio no longer inhabits the body, that body cannot be Julio. For Antonio, "there's nothing but Piero left; / He is all Piero, father all; this blood, / this breast, this heart, Piero all" (3.1.199–201). Stabbing Piero is a just act. Anyway, since Piero himself still lives, there has been no murder. Marston here (and elsewhere in his drama) is fascinated by these manipulations worked by the passions upon the reason. He very consciously strives to capture the process through which Antonio's mind deliberately imposes upon the real Julio a more acceptable image put together by his phantasy and his passion.

Shakespeare, in *Titus Andronicus,* brings his protagonist to a similar stage. Again the distraught imagination twists the information conveyed to it by the senses and comes up with an interpretation of the data that better meshes with his passion for revenge—witness Titus's reaction when he meets a simple peasant carrying a basket with two pigeons in it:

> Titus.   News, news from heaven! Marcus, the post is come. [*To the peasant*] Sirrah, what tidings? have you any letters? Shall I have justice? what says Jupiter?
>
> Clown.   Ho, the gibbet-maker! he says he hath taken them down again, for the man must not be hang'd till the next week.
>
> Titus.   But what says Jupiter, I ask thee?
>
> Clown.   Alas, sir, I know not Jubiter; I never drank with him in all my life.
>
> Titus.   Why, villain, art not thou the carrier?
>
> Clown.   Ay, of my pigeons, sir, nothing else.
>
> Titus.   Why, didst thou not come from heaven?
>
> [4.3.78–89]

Titus insists upon taking this simple peasant for a "post" from Heaven bringing an answer to his prayer for justice. The stylization here, the attempt to suggest lunacy, should not obscure the fact that the "mistake" is Shakespeare's means of rendering the disordered imagination which is under such great psychic pressure that it has begun to view the outside world in terms of its own images and emotions.

The same kind of projection occurs in *The Spanish Tragedy* when Hieronimo responds to simple individuals in the real world, to whom he should relate as judge to supplicant, by transforming them, in his imagination, first into specters of his dead son, walking the world to urge him to revenge, then into a Fury, "sent from the empty kingdom of black night," and finally into "the lively image of my grief" (3.13.133–69). On stage the action seems naïve, but the episode is part of a full and consistent study of the process whereby the inside becomes the outside.

Tourneur uses a different technique. In an extremely subtle study of the revenger's psyche, he makes the world of the play itself a projection of the maddened mind of Vindice. So successful has he been in presenting, through Vindice's eyes, a world bereft of all decency, all human feeling, a world full of a "loathing and disgust of humanity" as it would have existed in the obsessed imagination of the revenger, that commentators have taken Vindice's vision for Tourneur's and deemed Tourneur mad.[21]

The mind's ability to experience the world in all its vital complexity has been destroyed; hence, there is no objectivity to the world Vindice sees. Everything in the outer world that his senses light upon is degraded as it passes through his imagination. Suspicious and cynical in approaching goodness and unable to fight the compulsion to test and corrupt it, he looks out upon the world not with the intent of seeing what is there but with the aim of uncovering its inconsistencies and perversions. The more evil he detects, the more his own pride in being the last just man is sustained. It is fitting that as a character Vindice should be little more than a personification of the imagination obsessed by the passion for revenge and that the other characters in the play are allegorical figures whose unreality renders the landscape more that of nightmare than of nature. We never *see* the morally healthy Vindice, except as a memory of Vindice's own imagination. We meet him in the advanced stages of the revenge-madness, and we view "reality" only through the filter of his imagination, as his mind projects itself outward onto the world.

Most Renaissance psychologists locate the end of any madness of passion—be it lust, jealousy, hatred, or revenge—in some act of uncontrolled brutality, the reason being that most frustrated or excessive passions turn at some point into anger and the anger invariably surges into violence. The course which Tofte postulates for jealousy is typical:

> [Jealousy] sometimes bursteth out so farre, and exceedeth beyond her bounds so much, as it turneth it selfe into extream Hatred, and from thence falleth into a Frensie, and Madnesse, not alone against the partie it loueth, or his aduersary or Riuall, but as well against all such, who, as he thinkes, may be any way an obstacle or let, to hinder or crosse him in his dissigne and purpose, whereupon haue ensued most cruell reuengements, and most horrible and sauage murthers, beyond all common sense and reason. . . .[22]

Revenge, more than any other passion, is destined to end in this way. La Primaudaye, marking out the course of the passion through grief and rage much as it has been described above, sees the rage turning into cruelty and the cruelty to inhumanity:

> Nowe, when the heart is hardened with Reuenge, it is turned into Crueltie, which is a priuation of pitie and compassion. For when Offence [i.e., grief] and Anger are set on fire, they exclude all good

thoughtes out of the minde, and perswade to all kinde of Crueltie, of
which there are three degrees. . . . Heereof followeth inhumanitie,
which is as if wee shoulde lay aside all humane affection and bee
transformed into brute beasts. Therefore wee may well conclude, that
all priuate Reuenge proceeding of enuy, or of hatred, or of anger, is
vicious and forbidden by God.[23]

So it is in revenge tragedy. The brutal act committed by the
revenger is what distinguishes the act of revenge from the act of
justice and makes void all of the protagonist's claims to sanity.

That many of the playwrights borrow from Seneca the incident in which the revenger forces the villain to feast upon his
son's body is no accident. What better symbol than this Thyes-
tean banquet for the utter state of depravity to which the
revenger's madness has brought him? Shakespeare makes this
banquet a central symbol of the revenger's insanity in *Titus
Andronicus*. When Titus enters the highest stage of lunacy, his
mind retains both its ability to handle logic and its ability to
recognize evil. The ordering faculties still function, at least to a
degree. What signifies that Titus's madness has reached its apex
is his becoming finally capable of committing atrocities:

> Hark, wretches, how I mean to martyr you.
> This one hand yet is left to cut your throats,
> Whiles that Lavinia 'tween her stumps doth hold
> The basin that receives your guilty blood.
> You know your mother means to feast with me,
> And calls herself Revenge, and thinks me mad.
> Hark, villains, I will grind your bones to dust,
> And with your blood and it I'll make a paste,
> And of the paste a coffin I will rear,
> And make two pasties of your shameful heads,
> And bid that strumpet, your unhallowed dam,
> Like to the earth swallow her own increase.
> This is the feast that I have bid her to,
> And this the banket she shall surfeit on.
>
> [5.2.180–93]

The horror is not gratuitous; it is a fiction designed to render on
the stage the full madness of revenge. The perverted imagination reveals itself in all its grotesqueness.

In terms of the accepted commonplaces of Renaissance psychology, then, the madness has its origins and its end in the

imagination. It began with an image of the offense, which was magnified to the level of obsession by various passions, especially anger, until it became so all-absorbing that it burnt away everything else. The passion became the mind, and imposed a barrier between the reason and reality.

No doubt some blurring of the distinctions between revengers has resulted from this attempt to discern the broader patterns of the madness. The evils of too large a generalization will be remedied in later chapters which treat each work individually. In the meantime, the points made in this chapter, ideally, will provide a sounder basis for aesthetic judgments of the various mad scenes which occur in revenge tragedy and will lead to new insights into the dramatic functions of these scenes.

Chapter 4
The Other Motifs

And, princes, now behold Hieronimo,
Author and actor in this tragedy,
Bearing his latest fortune in his fist;
And will as resolute conclude his part
As any of the actors gone before.
And, gentles, thus I end my play;
Urge no more words—I have no more to say.
                    He runs to hang himself.
            Thomas Kyd, *The Spanish Tragedy*

THE VARIOUS STAGES of the revenger's madness as rendered in the drama divide into two categories—every play has its period of preparation and its period of accomplishment. The motif of delay is closely associated with the former, while the motifs of the play-within-the-play and the multiple murders are utilized in rendering the latter. These motifs are not only linked together by the madness; they assist in analyzing and defining it.

I No discussion of the madness motif is complete without consideration of the concurrent delay, whose mitigating force makes the madness tolerable for the audience. The delay is a function of another aspect of the psyche customarily included in Renaissance formulations—the conscience—from whence, theorists wrote, man receives the intuitions that allow him to distinguish right from wrong. Not all of the wisdom stored in the understanding was derived from the reason through the external School of Experience; some of it had inner origins that testified to the existence of channels running between the human mind and the divine. When reason is overthrown, conscience still remains the last hurdle to be leapt by the man racing toward his own damnation.

Successful artistic effects often fit so harmoniously into their surroundings that the burdens they carry are taken for granted. Only when they are removed from their customary places and the great gap left by their absence becomes apparent is their importance realized and appreciated. Such is the case with the delay in revenge tragedy. All of us are on familiar terms with the trusty delay. We expect to see it report for duty some time during the second act, work hard straight through the rising action to the end of the fourth, and silently retire before the climactic moment in the fifth, when its job is done. Confident of its presence, we fall to grumbling about its faults—either it is too simple or too involved, too long or too short, too forward or too reticent. Then, tired of hearing it talked of, we complain about the tediousness of the subject. But let it fail to appear and we should sorely miss it.

Chettle in *Hoffman* dispensed with the delay. And with it went the complexity, the vitality, and the tragedy of the hero's plight. Clois Hoffman is placed in the same situation as Antonio and Hamlet: he has lost a father. Like them, he feels that wrongs have been done and like them he is possessed by the desire to avenge these wrongs. But Chettle gives his hero no doubts about his right to punish those who executed his father. Hoffman is ready to commit murder at the time we meet him and tortures his first victim to death early in act 1. The bulk of the play is taken up with Hoffman's attempts to eradicate the entire line of the family he feels has offended him.[1]

Chettle deliberately set out to make Hoffman a villain. He intuitively removed certain motifs from the configuration when creating his plot. Chief among the motifs to go was the doubt and subsequent delay. The effect of this omission is to transform the hero-revenger from a good man overwhelmed by passion to a monstrously inhuman one whose actions are barbaric and revolting. It becomes impossible for the audience to develop that double response of pity for the sufferings of the revenger and fear of the reprisals he will bring upon himself that is so important in the true Kydian form.

If the configuration is to hold together, the playwright working with it must find some means of suggesting through a conscience-derived hesitation that his hero is a moral being not easily brought to the act of murder. In previous chapters this view of the delay was asserted, perhaps too glibly. We shall here acknowledge that the delay motif involves many complexities and ambiguities and examine these more carefully.

Delay has a peculiar relationship to the configuration because its function in the plot differs from that of the other motifs; they all supply incident, it supplies time. Without the delay, there would be no plot at all. Were the revenger to kill his victim immediately, the major dramatic question of the revenge form would be answered and the play's dramatic focus distorted by the resulting need to find a new center of interest for the remaining acts. Where the murder does occur early, as in *Hoffman* and *The Revenger's Tragedy,* dramatists have been forced to supply other victims to keep the action going. Equally peculiar, where most of the other motifs occur in succession, the connections between them being chronological, the delay occupies essentially the same space of time that is dedicated to the madness. The delay and the madness develop simultaneously.

One way of looking at the relationship between delay and madness is that the delay deals with the external circumstances of revenge, while the madness tells of internal developments. Delay thus becomes linked with plotting; it is developed in terms of dramaturgical complication and ends at the climax. Madness is handled more through character delineation. It peaks at the climax and spills over beyond it. There is an inevitable element of arbitrariness in such a distinction, yet it does generally hold true that the playwrights use the delay to cover the temporal gap between the advent of the desire to revenge and the violent act precipitated by it, while filling out the spiritual distance that lies between these two extremes of the hero's psyche by intensifying the madness.

Let us express this point in another way. Both the novelist and the playwright have frequent occasion to portray internal spiritual conflict. The unlimited resources of the written word are available to the novelist for the purpose; he can halt the action to dedicate a paragraph or a chapter—even the entire book if he is Proust or Beckett—to a detailed description of the thoughts passing through a character's mind. He can expand the doubts of a second into a hundred pages or compress the vacillations of a year into three lines. Not so the dramatist. His duty to dramatize compels him to use the soliloquy sparingly. He can make other characters discuss the thoughts of a third, but such reports must allow for the speaker's biases and may in the end produce as little insight as do Polonius's descents into Hamlet's mind. A more trustworthy method of portraying complex and incompatible thoughts on stage is to extend the period of time between one action and the other. The period of time does not justify the action. But it does introduce the notion of internal struggle. The prolonged delay in revenge tragedy, while it serves a dramaturgical function, suggestively implies indecision, perplexity, procrastination, even as the revenger is actively working toward his goal. It is a dramatic symbol of the doubt within a mind that has to work itself to a point where it can accept its role.

From the various revenge plots, three common dramaturgical motives for delay can be isolated. None of these excuses for procrastination supports an assertion that the delay stems from qualms of conscience; rather, each seems realistic enough in terms of action to need no symbolic explanation.

In the beginning the delay occurs because the revenger does not know that murder has been committed; the death for which he mourns has been passed off as a natural death. While the hero remains uninformed about the murder, as in *Hamlet* and *Antonio's Revenge,* he is neither consciously or conscientiously delaying. He has no reason to reproach himself for inaction.

There is more cause to speak of conscience if one examines the variant upon this stage of not-knowing found in *The Spanish Tragedy* and Goffe's *Tragedy of Orestes,* where the revenger is aware that the loved one was murdered but lacks knowledge about the identity of the villain. Here again conscience does not loom large as a factor, for the revenger generally announces his readiness to commit the murder—provided he could only find out whom to kill.

Toward the middle of the play the delay becomes a conscious one; the revenger has identified his target but is prevented from acting for some valid and compelling reason. Either he wants sounder proof of his enemy's guilt or he lacks access to his intended victim. Generally, he is taking whatever steps he can to overcome the troublesome obstacle—Hamlet actively organizes his play, Hieronimo takes his evidence to the king, Antonio puts on the disguise of a fool. The delay appears to come from outside. And in truth this is no accident; the playwright means to say that the world is withholding justice from the revenger.

Further on, delay occurs when the revenger refuses to kill his enemy because the presented opportunity will not bring sufficient suffering to the victim. Hamlet's refusal to "drink hot blood" when he comes across a Claudius vulnerably at prayer hardly looks like a drawing back by the conscience. The stated reason for hesitation seems clear enough: so evil a man deserves a more fiendishly excruciating torture than quick death. The delay points, on the surface, more toward an imbalance in the revenger's psyche than to deeply rooted moral scruples.

The evidence offers little support for a claim that the delay calls attention to the promptings of conscience. In the first two instances, the delay appears to stem directly from the external situation, not the revenger's psyche, while in the third, where it does arise from within, the excuse for it scarcely suggests a devout Christian's recognition that vengeance belongs to God. But an understanding of the psychological complexities of the experience resolves the difficulties.

It has become a truism of the twentieth century to point out that human reactions to life, especially when the emotions are involved, are often paradoxical. That insight is fundamental to an understanding of revenge tragedy. The mind responds to the delays imposed by the outside world on two levels, one conscious and one subconscious. At the conscious level, the hero fights against the delay with all of his strength. He abhors it. Once the anger of the revenge passion is activated, it creates a psychological need for immediate retaliation. As a result any postponement of action seems intolerable to the revenger. Both Kyd and Shakespeare recognized that the revenger will experience a time-span that is relatively brief as interminable, chiefly because his desire to see justice effected is so intense. The revenger reacts to the delay with a sense of impatience, a feeling that the speediest of actions is but slothful tardiness. Yet the delay continues.

The foregoing facts support our earlier contention that the period of delay provides time for the madness to develop credibly. The frustrations incurred because release cannot be obtained through action are definitely understood by all of the dramatists to intensify the passion, making it increasingly probable that the event will end in some violent explosion. From this vantage point alone, the delay is an essential part of the configuration.

Meanwhile, a reaction is taking place in the subconscious. Without his being fully aware of it, the revenger welcomes the delay, because he really does not want to act. He would rather someone else took the responsibility. The evidence for this assertion lies in the very number of excuses the revengers find for avoiding action. Something within the psyche—call it conscience—is obviously working to postpone the moment when the terrible action must be committed. So long as the possibility of murdering is but a dream and its actuality far off, Hamlet or Hieronimo will indulge himself in the belief that he would commit the murder if he had the villain before him. But give him the name of the villain, and he immediately asks for more proof. Give him the proof, he must wait for an opportunity. Give him the opportunity, he perforce cannot use it: a better time will come. Yet the time never seems to be quite right. Individually, each one of the excuses is incontestable, but taken together they form a pattern of unexplained procrastination. The revenger appears to be morally unwilling or unable to commit the deed. Rationalization is one of the signs that the revenger has a conscience—difficult to prove through ordinary critical methods, but crucial in the Kydian configuration.[2] Without it, the delay would disappear, and Hamlet, Hieronimo, Antonio, Vindice—all would fill us with loathing, the same loathing we lavish upon Chettle's Hoffman.

II Once the madness reaches its height, the revenger moves out of the realm of delay toward action. The mad act takes place in the play-within-the-play.

In Renaissance drama one finds many types of theatrical performance within the larger play. Kyd employs several of these in *The Spanish Tragedy*.[3] He uses a framing action carried out through prologue, choral interludes, and epilogue to make the five-act tragedy seem like a play within itself, lets Revenge present a dumb show which serves the customary role of foreshadowing and predicting events, has Hieronimo supply an allegorical pageant at court to soothe and flatter the visiting Portuguese ambassador. Yet when *the* play-within-the-play is spoken of, any person familiar with revenge tragedy will forget all of these and automatically fasten on the final play within Kyd's play, Hieronimo's *Soliman and Perseda*—the play in which Lorenzo is murdered. It is this play that all of the playwrights who wrote in the Kydian tradition chose to copy.

There are several important points to be noted about the play in which the revenger commits his murder. First and foremost, it is the revenger's play; he writes, directs, stages, or otherwise controls it—this because the play must be a reflection of *his* mental state. In agreeing (however subconsciously) that the playlet must be a creation of the revenger himself, the playwrights set themselves a difficult task. They must provide a play written by the revenger without allowing for the protracted time that would be required for its composition. The plot cannot permit the revenger to sit down and write out a whole play, nor is he, as a character, psychologically in any condition to do so. In trying to explain how the play got written, the dramatists involve themselves in various technical awkwardnesses. Probably the best solution is Marston's, where the revengers leave the stage at the end of one act saying "let's think a plot" and return later in costume ready to perform. The audience accepts the fact that the planning has taken place in the interval and no further allusion to it need be made. In struggling with this problem, Kyd asks us to accept the *donnée* that Hieronimo had retrieved an old manuscript from the attic which just happens to suit the occasion perfectly. Shakespeare, more plausibly, allows the script to preexist in the players' repertory and makes the play specifically Hamlet's by having the prince compose crucial additions which shape it to fit his immediate needs. The result is greater credibility, without the sacrifice of the key factor in the play motif—that the play produced by the revenger must mirror his mind.

This brings us to the second point about the play-within-the-play: it sets up a world distinct from that of the real world. The separation is represented visually by the creation of a sealed-off space within which the play can be staged. In *The Spanish Tragedy* the Duke of Castile visits Hieronimo while he is readying the performance area, hanging curtains and arranging for a "throne." Hieronimo while he is readying the performance area, hanging curtains and arranging for a "throne." Hieronimo makes a special request of the Duke:

> Let me entreat your grace
> That, when the train are pass'd into the gallery,
> You would vouchsafe to throw me down the key.
>
> [4.3.11–13]

This natural precaution on the part of the revenger establishes a convention that is followed by subsequent dramatists—the play-within-the-play takes place in a closed room. The room is controlled by the revenger, who traps the victim within it, and all other parties are excluded from it. In *Antonio's Revenge,* Piero is cunningly persuaded to clear the banqueting hall:

> *Piero.* The maskers pray you to forbear the room
> Till they have banqueted. Let it be so;
> No man presume to visit them, on death.
>
> *Exeunt Courtiers*
> [5.3.57–59]

Piero himself is then invited to remain behind to feast with the maskers. Vindice, in *The Revenger's Tragedy,* arranges the meeting between the Duke and Gloriana in the "unsunned lodge, / Wherein 'tis night at noon," another sealed-off space, and the Duke assists Vindice in maintaining the convention of the closed room by sending his retainers off to make excuses at court for his absence (3.5.122–28). Goffe, interestingly, places greater stress upon the closed room than on the revenger's play. In *Orestes* the hero arranges to meet his victims, Aegystheus and Clytemnestra, in the "priuat'st room" in the palace, and the sense of circumscribed space over which Orestes has total control is strong throughout the scene in which he exacts his revenge. Only Shakespeare in *Hamlet* makes the playlet a public affair. The other dramatists literally wall off the world of the revenger to distinguish it from the world outside.[4]

The contents of this sealed-off world of the mind will naturally reveal a high degree of subjectivity. There will inevitably be an obsessive concern with the offense; invariably its action will involve a creation of the event for which revenge is desired, with the effect that the offense is moved out of the past and into the present. There will also be complete freedom to retaliate for the offense. No restraining forces that might block the revenger's will are invited to enter it. And justice will be done. Where, in the real world, the crime had gone unpunished, in the play world guilt receives its due.

The third characteristic of the play-within-the-play is that the revenge action occurs within it. The avenger pulls his victim into the play and murders him there.[5]

When the play dissolves, the revenger is returned to the real world and subjected to the judgment of its authorities. These authorities represent the order of earthly justice. The order that is reestablished after the play-within-the-play concludes is never perfect; Astraea and the Golden Age do not return. Tourneur, for one, makes this explicit: Vindice succeeds in banishing the Iron Age; however, the Silver Age that Duke Antonio will preside over will only be less corrupt, not Edenic. In *Hamlet*, the heroic perfection of earlier days does not return with Fortinbras, and in *Antonio's Revenge*, the noblest people in the Venetian world retire from the active life, leaving the state to the commonplace senators. There is an equilibrium but never a transcendence established.

Of all the motifs, the play motif is handled with the greatest fluidity. The varying degrees with which the element of unreality in the madness is suggested by different playwrights makes it impossible to formulate rigid rules for the play motif, and any argument in which the playlets are discussed outside of the context of the action leading up to them will not be convincing. This is especially true in *Hamlet* (though the extensive changes in the dramatic handling of the motif do not essentially alter its underlying meaning). We have chosen, therefore, to leave the particular analysis of each revenger's play to the chapter given over to that play. This generalization can be made in isolation, however: in every case the play—with its suggestion that the revenger is withdrawing from reality—is prepared for by the fact that the revenger goes into disguise.

The disguise could actually be taken as a motif in its own right, for it occurs in each of the plays. Hieronimo, though he does not don a costume, assumes the role of a hypocrite. Having determined to kill Lorenzo, he decides to cloak his ill will under a guise of friendliness:

> I will revenge his death.
> But how? Not as the vulgar wits of men,
> With open, but inevitable ills,
> As by a secret, yet a certain mean,
> Which under kindship will be cloaked best.
>
> [3.13.20–24]

He considers it wise to

> rest me in unrest,
> Dissembling quiet in unquietness,
> Not seeming that I know their villainies,
> That my simplicity may make them think
> That ignorantly I will let all slip.
>
> [3.13.29–33]

Ironically, his "disguise" enjoins him to the very behavior that the decision *not* to revenge would have involved—the controlling of emotions and the exercising of patience. It requires him to bend

> thy tongue
> To milder speeches than thy spirit affords,
> Thy heart to patience, and thy hands to rest,
> Thy cap to courtesy, and thy knee to bow.
>
> [3.13.40–43]

The distraught Hieronimo, at the height of his madness, suddenly becomes "mild as the lamb."

Kyd dedicates a full scene to a depiction of the canniness of Hieronimo in wearing the disguise effectively—that in which Hieronimo is reconciled to Lorenzo through the auspices of Castile. The scene takes place at court. Castile has heard rumors that Lorenzo has been "busy to keep back / [Hieronimo] and his supplications from the king" (3.14.77–78). Admitting the incident but making plausible excuses for his action, Lorenzo suggests a reconciliation, whereupon Castile sends for Hieronimo. Hieronimo gives a magnificent performance in this sequence. He grows incredulous at the idea that Lorenzo could be accused of any evil. He draws his sword in mock anger, threatening to carve up any man who would insult "the hope of Spain" and "mine honorable friend." He deplores "scandalous reports," laments that "the world is suspicious," and is "ashamed" that such base statements could be made. All of this is capped by an amazing line that highlights the new dishonesty of Hieronimo: "Should I suspect Lorenzo would prevent / Or cross my suit, that loved my son so well?" The sequence ends with a tableau of the revenger, Hieronimo, embracing his son's murderer. Hieronimo is so successful in feigning Christian meekness that Castile is fooled, Lorenzo is thrown off his guard, and poor Andrea flies into a rage at his seeming betrayal of the cause.

This disguise device is picked up by Kyd's successors. Marston makes Antonio choose the disguise of a fool as one which will give him the freedom he requires, whereas Shakespeare lets Hamlet don the famous "antic disposition." So, too, Vindice becomes Piato. As many commentators have pointed out, in *The Revenger's Tragedy* the personality which the hero develops under the pressures of the villainous disguise as malcontent becomes so integral a part of him that when he turns up at court again, this time impersonating himself, he and the disguise have been fused.

How does the disguise function? It is invaluable to the playwright from the point of view of the narrative. The disguise provides the revenger with protection in an environment in which evil forces seek to take his life, and it gives him access to the important personage whose life he himself would end. In the game of cat-and-mouse the hero plays with his adversary, the disguise is a necessary step toward the successful accomplishment of the revenge.

Philosophically, the disguise motif raises questions about personal freedom. When the revenger abandons his own role in society and assumes another, he gains the same kind of anonymity that modern man seeks from the urban environment: the necessity of accounting to his neighbors for his actions is removed. The disguise allows him to do things that he might not ordinarily do. This freedom has its pluses and minuses. As in the cases of Antonio and Hamlet, it differentiates the protagonist from his world and permits him to make observations upon his society that would not normally be tolerated. His insights reveal his philosophical superiority to the world around him. Antonio's attitude, in particular, shows us how consciously the motif was used for this purpose.[6] But, the playwrights indicate, the dislocation of the disguise also leads to a breakdown in the hero's character. Hamlet becomes abusive (note his cruelties to Ophelia, to Polonius, and to Gertrude). Hieronimo becomes an oily hypocrite. Vindice, playing Piato, is sent to corrupt his mother and sister. This tendency of the disguise to conceal—and even condone—moral deterioration gives us a foretaste of the play-within-the-play where the danger of the disguise emerges at its worst: the revenger, under the protection of his mask, commits murder.

This Machiavellian device, like the others in revenge tragedy, has a characteristic ambiguity. The revenger assumes the role in order to do a virtuous deed but ends up doing an opprobrious one. He prides himself on his wisdom but in using his reason for the purposes of revenge he is ultimately perverting wisdom. Forced by a corrupt society to seek justice through the only means possible in that environment—deceit—he is pulled into the vortex of corruption and takes on himself some of the stain of his antagonist. These characteristics of the disguise assist the playwright to effect the transformation between the madness and the play-within-the-play. It is a preparatory stage for the moment when the *individual* mask is enlarged as the revenger imposes a disguise upon the *world*, forcing it to participate in a "play" of his design.

III The functions of violence in revenge tragedy are beginning to be recognized.[7] The multiple murders, like the other motifs, have their basis in experience. They reveal that the revenger, once he allows the revenge passion to take possession of him, no longer has full control of himself or of the events that his actions will trigger. The multiple murders thus differentiate the

workings of this primitive justice from divine justice, the former
avenging like a tornado by wiping a swath across the affected area
and the latter generally directing its aim more specifically at the
guilty.

We touched upon the notion of excess that accompanies the
desire for revenge earlier, when we discussed the convention of
the ghost—the demands of that figure being extravagant and
insatiable:

> Invent some strategem of vengeance
> Which, but to think on, may like lightning glide
> With horror through thy breast. Remember this:
> *Scelera non ulcisceris, nisi vincis.*
> [Injuries are not revenged except where they are exceeded.]
> [*Antonio's Revenge* 3.1.48–51]

The ghost calls for actions that are horrible, inhuman, almost
unthinkable. The murders committed by the revenger *must* be
gory. They must spring from the insanity that temporarily possesses the hero through his contact with the ghost. Marston, who
best captures this element of violence, perhaps pushes beyond the
bounds of what a modern audience can tolerate, but there is no
gainsaying that he has fully captured the essence of the experience. A man feeling the kind of passion that revenge arouses is
not apt to be delicate.

The playwrights consider it important that at least one of the
many deaths be that of an innocent. This, like the blood and gore,
is an aspect of the excess. Julio must suffer at the hands of
Antonio. The whole Polonius family is destroyed before Hamlet
gets at Claudius. The good Duke of Castile is cut down by
Hieronimo. And three unnamed gentlemen and a lord go to their
deaths when Vindice attempts to revenge himself upon Lussurioso. In depicting this sacrifice of innocent lives the dramatists
establish a sense of the terrifying ferocity of the justice of nature.
The multiple murders help us to recognize and lament the waste.

That the guilty also perish in the bloodbath brought about by
the madness adds a positive note to the motif. The audience is
led by the multiple murders to a feeling that the revenger has
accomplished his goals. We may deplore the methods used to
dispose of the play's villains, but we acquiesce to the necessity of
their deaths; thus, our sympathies are never entirely divorced
from the avenger. Insofar as he does destroy the source of

pollution, he remains a hero to us. His act, punishing the guilty, has a beneficial and requisite effect.

An integral relationship exists between the motifs of the multiple deaths, the play-within-the-play, and the madness, both experientially and aesthetically. These deaths occur within the playlet for a reason derived directly from the dramatists' understanding of the revenge experience. The murders represent acts of madness, acts undertaken by an individual whose view of the world is highly distorted. The playlet captures and isolates the distortion, differentiates its unreality by radically shifting the dramatic mode from the naturalistic level to the symbolic. It suggests that the freedom provided by the disguise, the hysteria, the sense of being chosen to ferret out and eradicate injustice, has in it a high degree of illusion. Aesthetic considerations are also involved in the combination of these motifs. The play setting provides an essential control upon the effect of the madness and the murders on the viewer. The playlet distances the murders from reality just enough so that we do not lose sympathy for the revenger as he executes the ghost's command, whereas the violence perpetrated within the play forces us to recognize that he has gone beyond the bounds of humanity. Through the interaction of the play and the madness with the multiple murders motif, a subtle degree of tension is established which is essential to bring the audience to the proper emotional pitch for the tragic conclusion.

The test of any work of art is always to ask whether it would be equally successful if any part were to be removed. The effectiveness of the much-criticized multiple-murders motif is perhaps best understood by considering the emotional effect that its omission would produce. Were the violence to be removed from the configuration, we would find the madness tame. But far worse, we would no longer be prepared to accept the revenger's death. His demise would seem simply one more injustice and the sense that man was a victim of wanton gods would be so overwhelming as to be unbearable.

IV If the villain were to survive the revenger, our sense of justice would be highly offended. But the converse is also true: were the revenger to survive after murdering the villain, we would be equally shocked. No one—reader, critic, or audience—feels easy with Marston's ending to *Antonio's Revenge.* Moral law requires that the man who is guilty of murder must render up his own life in atonement, and aesthetic feeling demands, especially where so violent an act as the act of revenge is involved, that this law be adhered to without hedging. The configuration of motifs, if it is adequately to reflect experience, must conclude with the death of the avenger.

One response to the revenger's death seems inappropriate, though commonly voiced—the notion that a wrathful God has cruelly betrayed his "scourge and minister" after appointing him to do His work. Observation of the revenge configuration discloses that Heaven has forbidden impassioned actions all along. When the Christian God exacts punishment, He exacts punishment for sin, not for loyalty.

So long as this qualification is borne in mind, it is probably safe to suppose most playwrights take Providence, not Revenge, as the force of justice that requires the revenger's death. But no absolute statement can be made. In the death-of-the-avenger motif, too, ambiguities leave the matter mysterious. Had the playwrights resorted to the *deus ex machina* to bring about the death, the divine role would be clear. But they do not. Everything works out naturally: the revenger either commits suicide or is maliciously poisoned or is sentenced to be executed. Any sense of contrivance that exists is mainly a result of dramatic awkwardness: by and large the *aim* is to make the death appear as a natural consequence and an inevitable outgrowth of the madness. Still, despite the cause-and-effect relationship between events, there is a tragic dimension that gives a loftiness to the concluding action. In accomplishing his end, in defying the earthly order and remaining faithful to his conception of justice, the revenger achieves greatness. Part of that greatness is surely that it may have been bought at the cost of the soul. Inherent in the action is the suggestion that though God has not *caused* the hero's actions (they were freely willed), neither will He *overlook* them.

Another aspect of the final mystery is that Providence cannot be entirely separated from other orders of justice (at least not by human reason), for *all* are operating within its purview. The order of nature, in bringing the revenger to the state where he finds life no longer worth living, may be the cause of his suicide or, in hurtling him toward excess, may bring about the accident in which he is slain. In at least one play, *Hamlet,* the revenger's death occurs directly through the processes that exist within that order for the punishment of murder: Hamlet's excess initiates a retaliatory cycle and Laertes, the new revenger, exacts retribution from him. But in terms of the single revenge cycle Vindicta does not *require* the revenger's death: the Ghost of King Hamlet never demands the death of his own agent. On the other hand, while the order of the community does call the avenger to atonement, it rarely has the chance to exact punishment. With both Hieronimo and Hamlet, other forces have already taken care of this by the time the court becomes aware of the legal necessity. So with Vindice—for although Duke Antonio indicts him for the murder and his death is worked out through the forms of communal justice, some other force—perhaps Providence itself—first makes Vindice expose himself to condemnation. Both the natural and the communal forces are operative but, since neither by itself can explain the revenger's death, the effect left by the play is that something beyond the community and beyond the desires of Revenge is at work.

This feeling that Providence brings about the death of the avenger is reinforced by the attitude of the revenger himself as he nears death. We know, for example, that he is not going to come back as a ghost to demand retribution; the revenge cycle is terminated. He is satisfied. Hamlet's "the readiness is all" indicates an acceptance of divine will and a resignation to whatever judgment is passed upon him. Vindice, too, acquiesces to his fate, sees its rightness; he is content that his mission has been completed. We the audience sense from the revenger's resignation that somehow "that eternal eye that sees through flesh and all" has not been entirely detached from the events that have transpired.

The mystery remains insoluble. Yet there is no mistaking the sense of quietude and completion brought about at the end of the play by the revenger's death. We may not feel, as we do at the conclusion of the *Oresteia,* that an *ultimate* order has been instituted. In the *Oresteia,* there is a kind of perfection evolved through Athena's guidance that suggests a transcendent order. Not only is the community raised up; so also are the Furies. The three orders are integrated. In the Elizabethan plays, the three forces remain unreconciled. A permanent imperfection persists even in the new order established by the revenger. Nonetheless, the various acts of injustice have all been paid for. One has the feeling that each of the three orders has been placated; each has achieved its end. Were the concluding motif of the revenge tragedy configuration to be removed, this balance would be upset and the aesthetic equilibrium of the form destroyed.

Just as the ghost, the delay, and the madness motifs interact in such a way as to make them inseparable, so also the madness motif flows into the play-within-the-play, and the latter is closely related to the motifs of the multiple murders and the death of the avenger. These motifs may be put together in various ways, but each carries a burden of significance in relation to the archetypal experience of revenge that gives it an integrity which cannot be violated. Any alteration in a single motif requires corresponding alterations in the other motifs that will leave the configuration in tandem with the experience which underlies it. To alter the configuration without reference to the experience of revenge is to destroy its power to produce the superb insights into this fascinating passion that are found in the plays.

Chapter 5
The Revenge Experience as Tragedy

> And know ye all (though far from all your aims,
> Yet worth them all, and all men's endless studies)
> That in this one thing, all the discipline
> Of manners and of manhood is contain'd;
> A man to join himself with th'Universe
> In his main sway, and make (in all things fit)
> One with that All, and go on, round as it.
> Not plucking from the whole his wretched part,
> And into straits, or into nought revert,
> Wishing the complete Universe might be
> Subject to such a rag of it as he. . . .
>> George Chapman, *The Revenge of Bussy D'Ambois*

I IF THE ACTIONS of the revenge hero could be adequately explained solely in terms of Elizabethan psychology, an investigation of the works of men like Pierre de la Primaudaye and Thomas Wright could possibly be sufficient to unravel their mysteries. But when we experience the plays, we are instantly struck by the complex nature of our response to the hero. To be sure, one aspect of this response does tie in directly with statements on madness found in the contemporary psychological texts: the revenger does seem a man possessed and overruled by his passions. Yet we immediately recoil from the glaring inadequacy of such a characterization of Hamlet, Hieronimo, or Vindice. The revenger is a tragic hero, not a madman. His problem is not that he cannot get a grip on himself but that he is in the grip of a force beyond himself. Acknowledging in our-

101

selves this tension between approval and rejection of the revenger, we must ask the next question. Is this response appropriate to the plays? There is no evidence to make one suspect a different response was expected from the original audience. These contradictory feelings the plays arouse in us, which stand in marked contrast to the disapproving attitude toward revenge and revengers found in tracts of the period, should warn us that a reconstruction of the contemporary climate of opinion regarding the revenger's madness is not an adequate explanation of the experience rendered by revenge tragedy.

Knowledge of the official Elizabethan attitude toward revenge, because it alerts us to the fact that the playwrights not only use but go beyond it, helps us to understand just how original the insights of the revenge tragedies are. In juxtaposing the plays with the textbooks we get the feeling that the authors of revenge tragedies were saying to the accepted wisdom of the age, "Yes, but . . . ." "Yes, what you say is true, but you don't say everything. In fact, what you leave unsaid is vastly more important." Hamlet and Vindice continue to intrigue people because of what lies beyond the madness and touches mystery.

The fact that the revenge hero is angered by the murder of his father or son or the defilement of his beloved is not the root of the problem. Anger is the fitting response to such a grotesque act of malignancy. Murder and rape threaten the order of society. Only if someone is moved sufficiently to oppose them can order be maintained in the face of the towering human passions that drive men to such deeds. Within any established order, the emotions experienced by Hamlet, Vindice, or Hieronimo have a beneficial function. In the first place, anger must always be channeled directly against injustice; it supplies the force that resists injustice and works for the restoration of order. But beyond that, the mere presence in a society of a store of righteous indignation, with the potential force for justice that it represents, acts as an effective deterrent, discouraging violations of the order. But this anger and indignation must itself be restrained by the order if it is to function as a stabilizing influence. To this end, all societies have developed within their symbolism, customs that are designed to regulate the course of the emotion, customs aimed at making certain that when passion is elevated to the level of action that action will in fact redress an injustice and restore balance, not fly off into excess. In revenge tragedy the weakness ultimately rests not in the anger but in the defective symbolism.

Regulating the passions and therefore the actions of men is the primary function of society, and this can only be achieved through a healthy symbolism. Conversely, when the symbolism of a society fails to regulate the actions of men, particularly those of the good, capable, and well-intentioned men, then that society has entered a time of crisis. That this regulation is missing from the societies and consequently from the lives of the revenge heroes is crucial to an understanding of the action of the plays. The authors are all surprisingly clear and in agreement on this point, even when they are either cryptic or in disagreement on others. Each play is structured to reveal that the disorder is social and not individual. Further, the source of the disorder is internal to the society, not caused by external pressures. It is always the king or duke—that person who should represent authority and order in the society—who has transgressed and violated the order that he should both symbolize and maintain.

In *Hamlet* Shakespeare goes out of his way to establish the fact that "something is rotten in the state of Denmark." For an entire act he leads the audience to believe that Denmark's problems have some external cause. When the Ghost appears, he does so in that "warlike form / In which the majesty of buried Denmark / Did sometimes march".[1] The whole kingdom is drawn together in defensive preparations while King Claudius negotiates peace:

> . . . Now, sir, young Fortinbras,
> Of unimproved mettle hot and full,
> Hath in the skirts of Norway here and there
> Shark'd up a list of lawless resolutes
> For food and diet to some enterprise
> That hath a stomach in't, which is no other,
> As it doth well appear unto our state,
> But to recover of us, by strong hand
> And terms compulsatory, those foresaid lands
> So by his father lost; and this, I take it,
> Is the main motive of our preparations,
> The source of this our watch, and the chief head
> Of this post-haste and romage in the land.
> [1.1.95–107]

No doubt in retrospect, in the study, one may pick apart Claudius's initial speeches (1.2.1–128) to expose the oily hypocrisy there. However, anyone innocent of the play, hearing it for the first time in the theater (as it was meant to be experienced, and as we always must experience it regardless of how familiar we are with the text) would be impressed by his seemingly even-handed control of all aspects of statecraft. Only when the Ghost reveals that Claudius is the murderer is our attention swung around from looking to Norway for the source of corruption to finding it in the seat of judgment itself.

By focusing our attention on the possibility that a foreign power threatens Denmark before alerting us to the true source of the upheaval, Shakespeare has deliberately divided the world into external and internal and by eliminating one emphatically condemns the other. The problem is not an invading force, not Norway, nor Fortinbras, not the external world, but our own state, our king, our uncle, our mother, and, ultimately, ourselves.

As in *Hamlet,* so in all the revenge tragedies: we are confronted with a society at war with itself. The rift is internal and the source of the disturbance is in each case the organ that should be the fountainhead of order and stability, the one person in the state who stands for more than himself. The king, whose only justification for his authority to rule is that he is God's steward on earth, makes a mockery of the symbol of kingship by using the sacred office to legitimize tyranny, and thus undermines the whole symbolic structure of the civilization. Is it any wonder that men are without the guidance necessary to curb their passions and channel their emotions into fruitful conduct?

This rift in the social order is merely a manifestation of the more fundamental breakdown of the very symbolism developed by the society to interpret the universe. Thus, the disturbance among men reaches beyond the human sphere into the divine. It is not only the passion of the citizens within the society that lacks regulation when the ordering symbolism loses its power to transform the chaos of experience into a meaningful structure. For a people whose social order disintegrates, the entire order of existence is threatened. The natural forces that were formerly placated within that order break lose and demand propitiation directly.

The power that breaks out in the revenge tragedy, surging forth from the underworld to intervene directly in the lives of men, is the same power represented in Greek constructs of the universe as the Furies. But that power did not have access to the consciousness of the Elizabethans, whose minds were strangely taken up by man. In a sense the playwrights are recognizing this fact when they employ an intermediary—Andrea, Andrugio, Albanact—to go between these powers and mankind. The human ghost has a shape that would be understood by a people who lacked the direct consciousness of the gods evidenced in the primitive Greeks. Through it, the "Furies" can press their claims.

The ghost brings a gift of knowledge to the hero. In the sense that this knowledge is not common among men, it is a gift. In the sense that the knowledge wells up out of the region external to man that is the corollary to his passions, it is more of a curse. The knowledge the ghost grants irrevocably separates the hero from his fellow men, because it makes him the subject of his passions. But supernatural knowledge is heady stuff and the gods, particularly the Furies, do not give it without a purpose. Nor are they at all interested in the well-being of the individual they grace. The course of action they prompt the hero to through their gift of knowledge involves extraordinary self-indulgence. Even the hero recognizes this and would avoid it, except that in his passion he convinces himself he is God's avenging angel.

At the same time, the vision that isolates the hero and drives him mad does raise him above the world he lives in. As something outside the human order, the hero's madness places him directly in the realm of mystery. He has been removed from the order that binds men together. The message from beyond the grave gives the hero a wedge into the follies of man. Yet he is not lifted into a new order. Rather, he is placed in a void where vision and insight alternate with passion and illusion in an undifferentiated kaleidoscope. Ultimately, of course, he acts out of the blind passion that is symbolized by the excess at the end of the play. We feel he must die because he has fallen into sin. Nevertheless, his action has purged the state of the corrupting force it had harbored. But there is no epiphany. It is as though the disease is so deep-rooted in the society that the mere killing

of a Claudius or a Piero is insuffient. The problem was not that a
corrupt individual cast his shadow over a healthy society. If that
had been the case, then, as with the death of Macbeth, an epiphany of order would have ensued. But the pall that blankets the
society in the revenge tragedy is of a more universal sort.

The course of action of the revenge tragedy is not from disorder to order. Rather, it is from ignorance to knowledge. The
disorder is still there. The hero has been unable to dispel it
because his actions, the result of unregulated passions, were
themselves symptomatic of the disorder. Yet if the problem is
not solved, it has at least been identified. The problem lies in the
civilization.

II To fully comprehend where the revenge hero derives
his tragic stature from, we must know the state of the
civilization in Elizabethan England, not the state of the climate of
opinion. The revenger symbolizes certain things that were true
then and continue to be true today. The symbols used to render
that meaning have significance for us, but we cannot understand
the symbols unless we understand the civilizational epoch out of
which they come.

It is axiomatic that comedy can be written at just about any
point in history, whereas tragedy requires very special civilizational conditions for its creation. Ironically, though tragedy is
one of the supreme achievements of the imagination, it is not the
product of a civilization that is itself at its high point. Tragedy is
produced only in societies that have reached a point of crisis. We
are aware that to speak of a civilization in crisis is to make several
assumptions, assumptions about civilization and assumptions
about civilizational validity. In fairness to the reader, we shall set
these assumptions out fully before attempting to discuss tragedy
in terms of them. One is that at certain moments in history—
pre-Aeschylean Athens or the high Middle Ages—civilization
was achieved. Another is that something was present in these
eras and not in other eras which gave coherence to the popula-
tion. A third is that sociological or economical definitions of
civilization do not really recognize, let alone explain, this
achievement.

The characteristic that distinguishes a culture as a culture and at the same time distinguishes it from all other cultures, marking it as uniquely itself, is its symbolism. All cultures develop symbolism. Each one is different, but the purpose of every one of them is fundamentally the same: to render experienceable the interrelationships of the levels of being. The process of developing such a symbolism is the life work of a culture. So all-pervasive an activity is it that ironically much of it is carried out below the level of consciousness. The very language itself, as spoken universally throughout the culture, becomes heavily laden with the culture's symbolism of order. The metaphors arising from that language in the poetry, philosophy, and theology of any given epoch will be especially revealing about how that culture at that time perceived the order of the universe.

Nor should this process be surprising to any student of literature who is continuously discovering how garbled an understanding one age has of the values of another. What may seem surprising, however, is our insistence (developed below) that there is a causal relationship between the decay of a civilization and its failure to comprehend its own symbolism. Nevertheless, it is the symbolism that defines the culture. And this symbolism must lead the culture to civilization.

Furthermore, as the culture itself has a history of growth and decay, so has its symbolism. The growth and decay of the culture is more dependent upon the health of its symbols than upon either its army or its economy. To make a distinction in this process of growth and decline, it is useful to define a "civilization" as that period when a culture develops a symbolism which imparts a sense of coherence to the lives of its citizens by relating their everyday actions directly to the transcendental ground of being. At such a time the sacred and the profane, which otherwise would literally be worlds apart, merge into one cohesive, extended universe. To achieve this the symbolism must, metaphorically, place the culture directly over the center of being. When this alignment of being, the culture, and the individual is accomplished, they have a common axis. At such moments in history the individual is spared the anxieties of existing as a dislocated alien in his world.

These moments do not simply come about in the normal course of things. They are accomplishments perennially sought after but only occasionally achieved in the history of man. The very idea of a history of mankind presupposes that human nature is constant. And precisely because it is constant, the problem of order is the same for all men at all times. "Human existence in society has history," says Eric Voegelin, "because it has a dimension of spirit and freedom beyond mere animal existence, because social order is an attunement of man with the order of being, and because this order can be understood by man and realized in society with increasing approximations to its truth." Insights into the nature of the order of being are the accomplishments of individual men living at specific times and in particular societies. The Christian West is the heir to two unique insights that are of such magnitude and penetration that they can only be characterized as leaps in being. One is the "Hellenic experience of God as the unseen measure of man," and the other is the Israelite experience of the God who reveals himself to his people.[2] But no matter how monumental these leaps in being were, not the Hellenic nor the Israelite nor the Christian established the ultimate order of mankind. What was achieved in each case was that the struggle for the truth of order continued on a new historical level.

That is to say, the struggle to comprehend the order of being is the permanent subject of the history of man. The struggle is characterized as much by failure of insight as achievement and subsequent development of insight. The symbols which have illuminated the order of being for one generation are not necessarily superseded by the subsequent generation: they may as easily be misunderstood, corrupted, or forgotten. Much as the proponents of the myth of progress would have us believe that the history of man has been a story of continuous growth, the fact is that understanding achieved by previous generations is frequently garbled and lost. When this happens, though the wise may regret the loss, there will always be large numbers committed to the form of provincialism that proclaims that what is, is good. Thus a civilization may easily be in a state of crisis without the fact being generally acknowledged.

The times of Elizabeth and James were times of crisis not only for England but for all of Europe. The crisis, however, was not specifically the result of those movements we associate with the names of Copernicus, Machiavelli, Luther, and Montaigne.

These disruptions in the spheres of science, politics, religion, and moral philosophy were both causes and symptoms of the crisis. But the crisis itself was the breakdown of the medieval symbolism which had achieved an unparalleled integration of the individual with the ground of being.

Since the symbolism of the civilization we call the Middle Ages had located the society spiritually over an archetype by developing its structure out of the mythic unconscious of its citizens, the resulting cultural myth opened toward the ground of being by symbolically enacting the ground of being. Within such a context the citizen could rely on the value structure that surrounded him to solve his day-to-day problems as well as his metaphysical problems.

To keep all the activities of life wound together, the Middle Ages had developed an intricate symbolism that stitched the sacred and the profane together so that everyone lived simultaneously in both worlds. Each day was two inseparable days, where the rhythms of the workaday world were counterpointed by such ecclesiastical services as Matins, Lauds, and Prime; likewise, the natural rhythms of life—birth, marriage, and death— were supported by appropriate sacraments. The individual life in a civilization is woven into the structures and relations created by the symbolism of that civilization.

The hero performs a vital function for his civilization. His willingness to put his life on the line in defense of the civilizational values gives proof of their validity in a way no philosophical argument could hope to do. Although no national state has ever come near to achieving perfection, insofar as the order of the nation validly reflects the order of the universe, the defense of the nation is the defense of the order of the universe. The crown that Richard II failed was not the crown of the risen Jerusalem. Still, the crown did represent something quite real. It stood, anagogically, for the order in the universe. This was as near as imperfect man could get to that order. Using the crown as a symbol, he could see beyond it to the true order. The nation that no longer respects its heroes or, worse, no longer produces heroes is a nation that has lost its meaning. Then the Falstaffs become heroes.

Since the values of a high civilization transcend reason, neither nature nor science are exalted as sources of truth. Hope

and faith give it its structure and the warrior, saint, and phi-
losopher are its heroes. As there was no question in the Middle
Ages that the Crusaders were heroes acting in righteousness, so
there was no question that men like Saint Anthony and Saint
Francis were God's chosen. The symbols of the civilization inter-
connected the different orders of being. The result was that
though the saint, like the tragic hero, had to descend into himself to find his being, the journey was not made unaided. The
saint's descent is as real as the tragic hero's, but the path he
travels is well marked by the mythology of Christianity—this
gives a symbolic structure to the journey. Because this symbolism
is not a purely human invention but derives its validity from the
fact that it incorporates within it a perception of reality at its
highest order, the saint is never cut off for long from hope. Even
the dark night of the soul is no exception. Though it may be
agonizing, the saint knows where he is. Even when life becomes
frightening and hallucinatory (as in the temptation of Saint
Anthony), there is a symbolic formulation of experience that
explains what is happening to him. For the saint as for the
Christian hero, there is always present the very real possibility
that he may break under stress; nevertheless, his journey is
charted.

Unfortunately, the high civilization has its own destruction
built in. Although the ground of being is fixed and immutable,
man and his symbols are constantly changing. On the positive
side, this flexibility makes it possible for man to develop his
perceptions and his symbolism to the point where they put him
in touch with the ground of being. But this process of change
cannot be switched off when it reaches the point of equilibrium.
The conditions of life change and what was formerly an adequate symbol, largely because it related the experiences of a
particular time to the eternal, no longer illuminates. Furthermore, like all metaphors, symbols lose their freshness and must
be renewed.

And this is what happened in the Middle Ages. No sooner had
all of life been fitted into a pattern and that pattern and the
resulting sureness reached its highest state of refinement than
the language of that refinement developed the same symptoms
as the Greek of the age of Plato and Aristotle. In its sophistica-

tion, it begins to examine consciousness more closely. The language (in its metaphoric aspects) develops the capacity and desire for a more intricate exploration of experience. Man becomes more introspective, and he expends more of this metaphoric ingenuity peering into the self and less looking out into the world. But as the symbols turn inward they develop an opacity in the direction of being. The symbolic alignment of the culture with the ground of being begins to fail because not adequately attended to. Soon the symbols themselves block the view of that which they were to illuminate.

These developments mark the first step toward civilizational crisis. Things become more arbitrary as values that were formerly self-evident become less apparently so. And though polemicists willing to prove the validity of the old values are frequently abundant, the very fact that the self-evident needs champions to assert its claims is a measure of the decline. Increasingly, it becomes more difficult for the individual to align his actions with the right, because the metaphors necessary to penetrate through to the ground of being are no longer available to him in his language and just exactly what is right in a given circumstance becomes problematic.

While the myth crumbles, individualism flourishes. The individual has lost the ability to live his life in terms of the covering myth of his civilization. The more myth loses its essential quality as the cohesive force cementing the variety and multiplicity of society, the more the language of the culture turns inward exploring consciousness. The myth fragmentizes and the old symbolism is regarded as restrictive and limiting. To break out of the limitations of the symbolism which has failed him, the individual turns to more radical forms of metaphor. He seeks to create a personal language in an effort to open a line to the ground of being. Language now is no longer a civilizational property jointly held by all but becomes the property of each individual in his struggle to find validity for his actions. Language now becomes the property of the poets who can manipulate it to express their personal visions, while the rest of the culture, which has lost direct contact with the vibrant quality of words, is left with a degraded language, the control of which falls into the hands of sophists and hucksters who manipulate words to manipulate people. Ironically, in spite of this new power of the poet, he too is unconsciously aware that he cannot find meaning or purpose for or in his actions. This new language, charged with metaphoric intensity, is like a cluster of bombs hurled at the narrowing passage leading to the ground of being in an individual effort to blast one's way through. Paradoxically, it is the creation of this language itself that finally isolates the individual both from the ground of being and his community. Shorn of its myths, the civilization no longer performs its primary function of safely carrying the individual on his personal journey. It has broken apart into a treacherous ice floe that cuts people off from one another rather than uniting them.

The fact is, however, few people possess either the temperamental or the intellectual capacity to create their own symbolism from within themselves. As a result, the simple people are excluded from the world of poetry. At first they cling to their faith, which no longer has a symbolism adequate to engage the minds of the more sophisticated. Eventually the symbolism of the old faith atrophies because every poet is now developing his own private symbolism. Still, the belief of the common people holds fast at an almost silly level to a symbolism now hopelessly garbled and mistaken for literal truth.

Some have speculated that a civilizational decline is traceable directly to political corruption, while others have said that it is the moral fiber of a people that gives way first. Still others have tried to find in economics or demography the central cause of the collapse of a civilization. Obviously we have not the space here for an elaborate proof but we have tried to show that most of the problems a culture has in any of those areas can be dealt with, so long as the symbolism of the culture is healthy. Of course it goes without saying that the symbolism of a culture can be placed under stress by disasters in the economic, military, or political spheres. But so long as the language of the community remains vibrant and the mythology growing out of the linguistic symbols possesses sufficient vitality to keep the culture aligned with the ground of being, the vicissitudes of the material world will not overwhelm the citizens but be understood as part of the encompassing order. It was never part of the Christian mythology that there would be no suffering in the world. What that mythology did was supply a context within which suffering was made meaningful. Once that context was lost, suffering could no longer be understood and the world seemed absurd.

Tragedy is the creation neither of a civilization at its height nor of one which has utterly collapsed. Tragedy arises in a period of shifting civilizational values. The civilization is no longer compact and at one with its theological values, nor has it swung to the other extreme—the agnostic or atheistic society. Tragedy is produced in a civilization at a point where the consciousness of the individual is enlarged. At this stage, meaningful action is still possible, though many, including the heroes of revenge tragedy themselves, have strong reservations on the point.

But what is implied by the statement that action is meaningful? In the twentieth century, we have become too sophisticated to regard the world as "a proving ground for souls." Rather, we insist upon viewing the pains and pleasures of life as ends in themselves. There is, nevertheless, adequate evidence to indicate that the Elizabethan and Jacobean writers of tragedy stood on the other side of this issue, and if we are to understand what they were doing we had better acknowledge this fundamental divergence in world outlook.

A basic assumption they all shared was that though none of us made the world we live in and none have total control over choosing the situations we must act in, we are all nevertheless fully responsible for our actions. Consequently, one of the most important questions in life is, how does one conduct oneself in a world that was shaped and framed without regard to one's own desires? Basically, that is the situation the revenge hero finds himself in. He is a man who awakes to find himself a citizen in a civilization in crisis. As a conscientious man, he hungers for an ordering principle for his life and will not accept the illusions of order he sees those around him gravitating to. Yet no action available to him seems to have the potential of leading to truth. Still, so long as he continues to hunger after truth or justice and delays his actions, he only feels the pain of his desire but is no nearer his goal. On a purely logical level, his paralysis seems justified. Although he hungers for justice and truth, his society offers no taste of it, so he is at a loss as to what direction his search should take. Why should he take any road when all roads seem to lead to error?

It is at this point that tragedy makes its fundamental assertion as regards the nature of human existence. Tragedy insists on the redemptive function of action itself. Voegelin stresses this point in his study of Greek civilization:

> The truth of the tragedy is action itself, that is, action on the new, differentiated level of a movement in the soul that culminates in the decision of a mature, responsible man. . . . Tragedy as a form is the study of the human soul in the process of making decisions, while the single tragedies construct conditions and experimental situations, in which a fully developed, self-conscious soul is forced into action.[3]

The process of action has miraculously within it the potential of its own reformation. And revenge tragedy, more particularly, is asserting the paradoxical nature of this transformation inherent in action by saying that even action fraught with damnation may end in an epiphany.

III Although the Christian myth was still the official belief of England under Elizabeth, the one hundred years of Tudor rule, particularly the religious turmoil under Henry VIII, "Bloody" Mary, and Elizabeth herself, had effectively ended the self-evident quality the Christian symbols formerly possessed for Englishmen. As the sixteenth century drew to a close, England was obviously in a state of civilizational crisis. In hindsight it seems an ideal time for the writing of tragedy. And certainly the plays of Middleton, Shakespeare, Webster, and Tourneur contribute to the genre. But the Elizabethans should not have been able to write tragedy, for the destruction of the symbolism had gone too far. By the time of Marlowe, it was impossible to create a believable tragic hero who could achieve a genuine epiphany of knowledge as Oedipus had.

Marlowe is an excellent example of the Elizabethan plight. Here is a great dramatist whose innovations were to become the foundations for the later flourishing of the Elizabethan-Jacobean drama, yet one whose plays never achieve tragic stature. Marlowe was trying to do the impossible. He was centering his plays on the character of his heroes and their ability to reach within themselves and find a personal ordering principle. He created a series of *Übermenschen* who were also outsiders—a tyrant, a Jew, a homosexual, and a genius. One after another they are lacerated by life and, in true Promethean fashion, defy the limitations that shackle ordinary mortals. They cannot be denied their superhuman stature. But to make such Prometheans tragic is impossible: they lack the believability necessary to the tragic hero. Macbeth may grow into a bloody monster by the end of the play; nevertheless, he is still a recognizable human being. Tamburlaine never quite seems like a mortal man; he always remains somewhat fabulous.

Marlowe can be called the Michelangelo of the Elizabethan drama. Long before Michelangelo, Giotto had created a new realism both of figure and setting. He had, in painting, foreshadowed the nineteenth-century box set in the theater, and he used it for the same purpose as the dramatists would. His figures were made part of a distinct environment. Now though the gestures remained slightly generalized, the figures were rendered specific and recognizably human by the surrounding context. For two hundred years the basic premise of the box remained unchallenged. Then Michelangelo pulled man so far forward in the box that he destroyed the relation of the figure to the box. Two hundred years of artistic experiment ended in man's gigantism. Of course Michelangelo's figures are believable for what they are, but they are no longer human figures. The figures on the Sistine Chapel ceiling are neither us nor our heroes. They are super heroes. We can experience awe and wonder in their presence because they are, in every sense, far above us. When we look at them we are seeing the age of the giants. Not so the Christ and Saint Paul in Masaccio's *Tribute Money;* these figures are believable because, though transfigured, they could be us or our neighbors.

Marlowe is hardly terminating a long tradition in English drama. But he is doing the same thing with his dramatic heroes as Michelangelo did in his paintings. He pushed his heroes so far forward on the stage that the other characters fail to establish a limiting context within which the hero must realize his potential. He transcends the human dimension.

For Michelangelo, this gigantism should not be regarded as a failure of vision. He may be contrasting the Golden Age of his paintings with the fallen world of those who view them; hence,

the very chasm that separates us from them renders them believable. With Marlowe, the case is different. His titans do represent a failure of vision. But not just Marlowe's. Marlowe's
problem was representative of an age. One reason Marlowe
could not make a believable tragic hero is that the Elizabethan
Age could not believe in a tragic hero—one who, through a
descent into himself, could reach that epiphany of knowledge
that links the sacred and the profane.

The fact that tragedy is only written when a civilization
reaches a certain phase in its development implies that a necessary relation exists between the values of the community and
those expressed within the drama. Tragedy is, therefore, a
communal art form. Its success depends upon an overlapping of
public taste with the inherent demands of the tragic form. Most
importantly, the community's image of heroism must include
within its diversity the actions of a man who possesses a capacity
for gaining self-knowledge through suffering. They must believe in the possibility of descending into oneself and discovering
there the mythic connections that exist between the individual
and the deity. In short, the community must believe in the existence of tragic actions. That is, they must believe that action can
lead to epiphany. If they do not, there is no way in which they
could understand the symbolism of the action. Beyond being
believable, the hero who achieves the epiphany must be acceptable to the community as an archetype. His actions must express
symbolically one of the central experiences of their lives.

There can be no doubt as to whether the Elizabethans had a
concept of the hero. In the English-speaking world the notion of
the Renaissance man is derived from the heroic scale of the
Elizabethan Age. But this idea of the heroic was more akin to the
Marlovian *Übermensch* than to the tragic hero. They saw themselves as bigger than life. As the anagogic relation broke down,
the concept of the hero as one whose life enacted the civilizational
myth gave way to the fantasy of the rebel as hero. The hero was
one who stood against the existing order. Prometheus became
their hero. And the *hubris* of the Renaissance man was the attempt
to become the *Übermensch*.

Rather than the concept of the hero and the heroic acting as a
corrective to the excesses of their personal lives, the Elizabethans

had transformed those very excesses into an ideal. Man had become his own hero. As the Tudor monarchs led the nation further out of the Middle Ages, the people were faced with a confusing (not to mention highly dangerous) situation for many. Here was a ruling dynasty, whose right to the throne was itself questionable, propagandizing the nation with a reoriented symbolism in which the king would assume the roles formerly shared by king and pope. Again the secular and individual were being magnified at the expense of the sacred.

Where a civilization lacks the concept of the hero, it means essentially that it lacks the symbolism by which it can interconnect the orders of the sacred and the profane. Elizabethan England had not gone that far. But just as they had redefined the relation between the earthly and spiritual orders, so they had redefined the hero. For them the hero had to have the virtues they valued most in themselves—grandeur and defiance. Typical of a symbolism growing out of a time of crisis, the Elizabethan myth of the Herculean man tended to isolate its adherents from the ground of being. While isolating them, it increased their sense of self-importance. So grandiose had they grown in their own estimation that they were encouraged to challenge the order imposed by the ground of being with one of their own construction. Where the artist formerly thought of himself as a maker, he began to regard himself as a creator.

The Elizabethan era would not appear a propitious time for the writing of tragedy. Although it was a period of civilizational crisis, the values had shifted so far that it was already too late to construct a tragic action around a hero like Oedipus, who in the end fully comprehends the implications of his actions. Even so, if Marlowe's Herculean heroes were not tragic, they were Elizabethan. That was the kind of hero the people could believe in. The problem was how to make characters cut from the Marlovian mold into tragic heroes.

The Elizabethan dramatists were stymied. How to write tragedies that resolved within themselves the conflicting demands of a society which only accepted as heroes men cut from the Promethean mold, and the inner necessities of the tragic form itself, which requires that the tragic hero be a man who, though perhaps deficient to a degree, has at his core sufficient humility to acknowledge his *hubris?* Obviously the answer did not lie in creating more gargantuan protagonists. Nor was it tragic to see a villain such as Richard III brought low. The fact is, the beliefs of Elizabethan society and the tragic hero were irreconcilable. But if the Elizabethan absolutely insisted on a hero who was constitutionally incapable of tragic wisdom, perhaps the tragic form could be induced to be more yielding. No getting around the fact that without tragic knowledge there could be no tragedy. But would it be possible for the tragic knowledge to be present without the tragic hero participating in it?

Ironically, it was not Marlowe, but Thomas Kyd, a lesser dramatist, who intuited the solution to the dilemma. What is radical about *The Spanish Tragedy* is not the idea of a revenger as a protagonist; John Pikeryng had long since written his *Horestes,* in which this hero sought vengeance for the death of Agamemnon and in which the figure of Revenge appeared as a vice, and Marlowe was shortly to create the most intransigent of revengers, Barabas. Kyd's innovation is the creation of the revenge configuration itself. With it, Kyd introduced a dramatic form which was also a symbolic form. This was the solution the dramatists had been seeking. The revenge configuration presented them with a tragic situation involving a recognizably Elizabethan *hero* conducting the business of his life at a level believable to the theatergoing audience of the day. At the same time, the *play,* through the structure of the revenge configuration, transcended the limitations imposed by the community values and achieved tragic stature. Kyd's symbolic form made it possible for the play itself to actually "learn" more in the course of the action than the hero does.

Kyd taught the Elizabethan playwrights how to put together a dramatic action that operated on two levels at once. On the realistic level, it was simply the narrative of Hieronimo's search for justice, a search that leads him to madness and revenge. On the symbolic level, *The Spanish Tragedy* is a myth of the civilization. In this case the myth is not, as myths usually are, a symbolic narrative of the civilizational origins, but a symbolic rendering of where the civilization is now. Nor did Kyd's new myth provide the grounds for the troubled individual to comprehend his role in the world. That understanding could only come from a knowledge of the relation of the finite to the infinite, and this myth had as its burden the theme that that knowledge was to be denied to the hero, as it was denied to the Elizabethan citizen. On the symbolic level, then, the revenge tragedy would be a myth of the civilizational crisis of the Elizabethan Age. That is what the other playwrights who wrote revenge tragedies learned from Kyd, and what some, like Shakespeare, were able to learn from the revenge tragedy and apply to other tragic situations. It is that and not the "poor girl run mad" or the ghost screaming "Vindicta, revenge!" or the stage drenched in blood that captured the imagination of the Elizabethans.

IV Some critics have maintained that to stress the revenge aspect of the revenge tragedies is to distort the plays. Any passion would have done as well; revenge just happens to lend itself to heightened theatrical situations. So long as the plays are approached from this direction, the significance of the revenge configuration will continue to elude scholar and critic alike. They will go on searching for explanations for the incredible popularity of these plays. We miss the whole point if we regard revenge as just another passion. No other passion could have been elevated to a search for justice. That search is symbolic of the individual's quest for order.

Kyd saw in the revenger the possibility of creating an archetype of the Elizabethan man, an archetype the Elizabethans could themselves recognize. But not just any man overruled by the passion for revenge would do. Equally important as the kind of revenger is the kind of revenge. The revenge sought in the revenge tragedy is a very special kind. It must be distinguished from the Poe-like revenge, where an offense (real or imaginary) festers in the mind until, crazed by passion, the revenger strikes out. Villain-revengers like Barabas and the brothers in *The Duchess of Malfi* could be placed in this category, but not Hieronimo or Hamlet. Revenge tragedy probes beyond the anger and rage within each of us to investigate the whole question of justice and order in a society that is experiencing a civilizational crisis.

In each of the revenge tragedies the revenger is introduced as a man noted for his uprightness. Furthermore, the offense the revenger is called upon to avenge is always real—the revenger's passions toward his victim never arise from a morbid hatred or jealousy of some innocent person. It is exactly because the hero is a good man and the offense is real and cries out for punishment that the situation can become tragic. Were he not a man determined to do what is right himself and at the same time a man whose sense of righteousness is so strong that he cannot tolerate seeing justice withheld, he would not be caught in the peculiar situation we find him in. Like the heroes of many plays, the revenger must make a decision. Not, however, the decision Faustus must make between good and evil but between two conflicting goods. Nor is the revenge hero's situation analogous to that of the heroes of French neoclassical tragedy, men of the noblest of intentions who find themselves in situations where their virtues are at odds with one another. The heroes of French tragedy would do what is right but they are caught between conflicting obligations. To do anything is to injure someone who has a clear call on their loyalty. In Corneille, for example, the dilemma frequently grows out of the fact that within the structure of values in any society, it is possible for events to so fall out that two areas of a person's life simultaneously make incompatible demands of him.

This was not the kind of situation the revenge hero found himself in. He was not prey to demands put upon him by conflicting virtues defined within the same system of values. Rather, his will was the battleground for competing systems of value. In this regard, Hieronimo, Hamlet, and Antonio are symbolically undergoing the same spiritual stresses that men in the audience were subjected to. As the Christian symbols lost their grasp on the mind, men turned elsewhere for guidance and order. First there was the pull of pagan antiquity, which was followed by the rise of rationalism with its morality based on natural reason. So, like the revenge hero whom he watched agonizing on stage, the Elizabethan was himself bewildered by the array of conflicting systems of value he was to choose between. While the Christian symbols of the Middle Ages continued to be the symbols he generally thought in, these failed to inform and cover the actions of his life the way they had his father's.

The revenge hero finds himself in just such a situation. He has a father or a son murdered, a sister or a mother defiled. How should he revenge himself? Christian dogma tells him quite clearly that he should not revenge himself, that revenge is evil. He must practice the Christian virtue of patience. The injunction is unequivocal. Nor is his particular situation an exception: the rule applies directly to him. And he is a good man, neither rebellious nor headstrong. Yet somehow he cannot align his will with the sanctions of his culture. The symbols have lost the stature of unquestioned authority and have become one of several possible courses of action.

The ghost is the key to understanding the symbolic reverberations that link the plays to the Elizabethan world. Christianity had, by several devices, been largely successful in placating the natural order. But that could only remain true so long as the people found the symbols adequate for the events in their lives. The Elizabethans did not. One of the first things that occurs when a universal system fails in its universality is it loses its power as the voice of justice and order. This was the situation in Elizabethan England, symbolized in the revenge tragedy by the emergence of the ghost. The Furies have ceased to be placated.

In each of the plays a horrendous crime is committed but the agencies of justice are paralyzed. With injustice mounting on injustice, nature itself, that incomprehensible and seemingly capricious force which nonetheless takes cognizance of men, becomes offended and cries out for redress. The irrational which had been held in check breaks forth to intervene directly in the affairs of man.

This is one way that the plots of the revenge tragedy reveal a society in which civilization has broken down. There is another. It has become a commonplace of the criticism of Elizabethan-Jacobean drama to point out that the typical plot moves from order into disorder with a new order achieved at the end. One can find this movement in any number of Shakespeare's tragedies. It is a pattern that is apparently present in all the revenge tragedies. There is, however, a significant difference between the order in Scotland under Duncan and that in the Denmark of Claudius or the Spain of *The Spanish Tragedy*. As we pointed out earlier, in *Hamlet* Shakespeare is at great pains to establish what appears to be a well-run kingdom in which all rejoice except

Hamlet. But we quickly learn that this apparent order is just that—an illusion. So it is with each of the revenge tragedies. Now we are in a position to see that the order at the opening of the play was like the order in Elizabethan society itself. It appeared wholesome but was incapable of rendering justice and therefore was no order at all.

As is so often the case, *The Spanish Tragedy* is the most schematic. Once Hieronimo learns of his son's murder, he turns for justice to the authorities whose job it is to maintain the order of society. A large portion of the play then deals with his growing sense of betrayal as justice is denied him. In contrast, we meet Hamlet and Vindice when their sense of betrayal has already reached full bloom. The important thing is that they all find themselves in societies others believe to be functioning but which, they learn, are characterized by a seeming order that reveals itself as a communal fantasy.

If the hero of the revenge tragedy does not completely comprehend the nature of the decision he was forced to make, there is good reason to believe that his author was in much the same state. The revenge tragedies present an instance where the authors are discovering their theme in the writing of their plays. They had no theoretical structure available to them that gave cognitive expression to what they were intuiting to be the nature of a particular kind of revenge and what the existence of that kind of revenge said about the nature of the world. Their insight, in part as old as tragedy itself, had not found articulation in either the philosophy or the theology of their day. Like their heroes, the authors of revenge tragedy were on their own, forging through the symbolic action of their drama the articulation of their insight.

It is this quality of being isolated and confused that marks the revenge hero as an archetype for the Elizabethans. The highly ordered, systematic world picture with its degrees and correspondences had become an illusion covering a growing spiritual chaos, much as the perfumes and high fashion of the court masked the foul breath and inadequate hygiene. But just as physical corruption can be masked to an extent, so can spiritual chaos be covered up in daily life. The revenge hero, however, is not living at the level of daily life. He is not allowed the luxury of self-deception. The revenge hero had to face what the intelligent Elizabethan knew but was too busy erecting defenses against to face. For the individual living in a civilization which has entered the stage of crisis, the problem of aligning one's will with the reality of the civilization (as would be natural were the civilization healthy) has lost its meaning. The hero is enjoined to act, yet everything he turns to for guidance in action proves insubstantial. His only recourse is to construct a meaning to life from the order he finds within himself.

There is no place for the revenger to turn but inward; he must begin his descent into himself in his search for justice. What is meant by the "descent into himself"? Voegelin describes it in careful detail in his analysis of the inquiry undertaken in Plato's *Republic*:

> The depth of experience is not unrelieved night; a light shines in the darkness. For the depth can be sensed as misery, danger, and evil only because there is also present, however stifled and obscured, the sense of an alternative. The illuminating inquiry . . . is not carried from the outside to the initial experience, as if it were a dead subject matter, but the element of seeking is present in the experience and blossoms out into the inquiry. The light that falls on the way does not come from an external source, but is the growing and expanding luminosity of the depth. On the one hand, therefore, the concepts of the inquiry do not refer to an external object, but are symbols evolved by the soul when it engages in the exegesis of its depth. The exegesis has no object that precedes the inquiry as a datum, but only levels of consciousness, rising higher as the Logos of the experience becomes victorious over its darkness. The inquiry continues, on rising levels of logical penetration, the substantive struggle between good and evil that rages in the depth. On the other hand, therefore, the concepts and propositions do not primarily tender information about an object, but are the very building blocks of the substantive stature into which the soul grows through its inquiry.[4]

In being forced to fall back on his inner resources—to look within himself for the ordering principles he cannot find in the external world—the revenge hero is like the Greek tragic heroes before him. But unlike Orestes and Oedipus at least, he cannot find within himself that epiphany of knowledge that would warrant our saying that, though he suffered greatly, the knowledge he won by it more than justified the pain. Hieronimo learns nothing. Antonio is self-deluded and Hamlet's insight that "readiness is all" is small comfort for the carnage it cost. Revenge tragedy, then, does not conform to what is commonly regarded as the basic format of the tragic vision, which can be stated briefly in the triad *do-suffer-know*. The revenge hero never achieves tragic knowledge. What he does is all that can be expected of a hero in a society incapable of producing either saints or heroes with tragic insight. The revenge hero enacts the tragic journey into the self. That it is an aborted journey does not diminish the heroism of the effort.

But that is true of Elizabethan and Jacobean tragedy in general. Certainly none of Shakespeare's tragic heroes gains an epiphany of knowledge through his suffering. Though they are both quite believable, neither Othello nor Macbeth learn much through their suffering. When Othello dies he has learned considerably less than Hamlet. As grand a creation as Macbeth is, his final nihilistic view is in sharp contrast to the hopeful tone of the end of the play itself. Macbeth does raise himself to a height of grim stoical courage when facing death that lends him a perverse dignity. One cannot but admire this man. Yet his suffering has not gained him wisdom. There is something of the Marlovian man about him, except that where Faustus and Tamburlaine are exotic, Macbeth is quite believable. He shares with them the same defiance of the gods merely because they are gods. They all seem to be saying "Even if we are wrong and our error brings us to grief, we will not go down in penitance but in defiance." The Shakespearean hero who comes nearest to tragic wisdom is, of course, Lear. Significantly, the meaning Lear finds within himself brings him to the verge where tragic hero merges with Christian saint. This was an ever-present problem for the dramatists. It was all but impossible for them to create a believable hero capable of learning enough by the end of the play to generate a tragic epiphany without being confronted in the final moments of the drama by the spectacle of their hero transforming himself before their eyes from a tragic protagonist into a saint. In Lear's scene with Cordelia he approaches sanctity but then moves away from it. For all his insight, he remains a violent old man ("I kill'd the slave that was a-hanging thee") and dies happily deceived. The necessity to have a believable figure as hero transcends the genre of revenge tragedy and is characteristic of all tragedy of the period.

This question of the believability of both the hero and the action was one of the paramount considerations that guided the dramatists to their unique success in the field of tragedy. It was their dogged determination to be true to the nature of the experience they were writing about that confronted them with what looked like the insurmountable problem of bringing the action to a truly tragic conclusion. It should be noted that we have deliberately not used the term "realism" here, because the question of verisimilitude is not at stake. It is not the quality of being able to capture surface nuances that we are referring to. By the believability of the play we are referring to that quality that grows directly out of the dramatists' commitment to the concept of the redemptive dimension present in action. Not that they set out to prove it; rather, they firmly believed it. This ruled out dramas centered around outlandish action pursued by fantastic creatures who could only live in poets' imaginations. Nor should the hero be a man consciously seeking redemption. The point is that out of the actions of life itself—the morally ambiguous and compromising acts that characterize all of our lives—redemption can grow if only we have fortitude enough to live the action through. They understood that the only way action could be shown to lead beyond itself was to be absolutely faithful to the nature of the action itself. If they violated the natural course of the action, the audience would say, "but that's not true: people in that situation don't act that way." Far from implying the realism for which T. S. Eliot condemned the Elizabethans for introducing into the drama, this is the believability that one finds in Sophocles. As a member of the audience, one is carried with Oedipus every step of the way on his dreadful journey because one says, "Yes, I know he is wrong, yet I must admit I would have done the same thing."

That is where the psychology of revenge comes into the revenge tragedy. As we watch the plays, we are not witnessing a pastiche of theatrical conventions. We are watching a fictional character work his way through a real action. Although the character is unreal, we know the action all too well. It is revenge. And we have all felt its grip. Because the dramatists had studied how real human beings act in revenge situations, they were able to distill from the psychology of revenge those key elements that could at the same time present a thoroughly recognizable revenger while they were raising the action from the level of case history to that of symbol. So, as a member of the audience, one says, "I know exactly how he feels; I have tasted the hunger for revenge myself, and while I don't know whether he is right in what he is doing, I do know passionately the emotions he is feeling."

Scholars, with their dedication to research, have tended to ignore this aspect of Elizabethan drama in favor of ferreting out the literary sources of the plays. But they forget that the only reason we are even dimly interested in the influences operating on the imagination of the Elizabethan (in a way that we are not at all interested in the eighteenth-century dramatist) is that the experiences they rendered in their drama are intensely true. One of the primary fascinations about the revenge tragedies is the accuracy with which they render experience. But the accurate portrayal of a passion is not in itself tragic. An indication of the depth of their dedication to the believable is that even where their loyalty to this principle might have caused their dramas to fall short of the tragic, they did not sacrifice it in an effort to heighten the significance of the play by suddenly granting the hero insights that could never have grown out of the play's action. Where it was not possible for the hero to gain tragic knowledge, they did not violate the experience.

In a demonstration of incredible artistic integrity the dramatists time and again remained true to both the experience of revenge and the tragic journey into oneself despite the fact that it meant that they must leave their hero's tragedies aborted. Yet the dramas themselves are not aborted. Tragic knowledge is imparted to the audience nonetheless. Throughout each of the plays it has been implied that while the tragic protagonist is the pivotal figure and prime mover of the action, he is never to be seen as the sole focal point. Contrary to what many hold to be the way to read drama, in the revenge tragedies we are never invited to identify or empathize with the protagonist. The tragic structure of the revenge motifs grants us adequate distance so that we in the audience are able to perceive the working out of an order that the hero lacks either the ability or opportunity to find.

To say that the revenge hero, or for that matter the hero of Elizabethan-Jacobean tragedy, is not granted an epiphany is not to say that the dramas lack tragic epiphanies. What Thomas Kyd taught the Elizabethans was how to write tragedies in which the play itself as a symbolic form learned more than the hero. At the end of any Elizabethan-Jacobean tragedy, the audience is in a position to know a great deal more than the hero ever did. The drama as a whole has a meaning greater than the actions of the hero. This can only be true where the action has been constructed in such a way as to become a symbol itself. Kyd's symbolic constellation of revenge motifs achieves this purpose. Through them, the tragic journey of the hero took on greater significance. It was not just Hieronimo or Hamlet, but Hieronimo and Hamlet as representative men seeking order in a time of civilizational crisis. If the plots of the revenge plays located the action in Spain, Denmark, or Italy, the symbolic structure placed them like templets directly over contemporary England.

Part II
The Motifs and the Artist's Personal Vision

Chapter 6
The Spanish Tragedy

Yet still tormented is my tortured soul
With broken sighs and restless passions,
That, winged, mount and, hovering in the air,
Beat at the windows of the brightest heavens,
Soliciting for justice and revenge:
But they are plac'd in those empyreal heights,
Where, countermur'd with walls of diamond,
I find the place impregnable; and they
Resist my woes, and give my words no way.
                    Thomas Kyd, *The Spanish Tragedy*

I ANY DISCUSSION of revenge will inevitably become a discussion of justice, for the passion of revenge is inextricably tied up with Justitia; it is born of a violation of justice, nourished by a fanatical desire to obtain justice, and laid to rest by the exacting of a "wild" kind of justice upon the offender. In *The Spanish Tragedy* Kyd set about to examine the relationship between justice and revenge. His efforts are tentative and experimental, and the results, as the many spoofs of Hieronimo reveal, easy prey to parody. Despite its title, the play remains more a melodrama than tragedy, for plot and situation are pushed so strongly that these qualities dominate the characters, few of which are developed as credible human beings. Not that Kyd's interest in plot derives from attempts at sensationalism; on the contrary, plot here is at the service of the theme. Close examination of Kyd's personal vision reveals an unflagging concern with the theme of justice.[1]

131

Much of the play seems designed to explore the complex forces which lead to a loss of faith in the system of earthly justice. For this purpose Kyd found the trial scene useful: his play is filled with judicial sessions in which mundane authorities attempt to sort out right from wrong. An official inquiry is needed to determine whether Horatio or Lorenzo deserves credit for capturing Balthazar. A judgment is required when Villuppo accuses Alexandro of murder. A verdict must be reached as to the extent of Pedringano's guilt in the slaying of Serberine. A hearing is requested to probe into Horatio's death and Lorenzo's part in it. Each of these trial scenes isolates some condition of existence that tends to prevent the magistrate from making a faultless decision. This questioning of the effectiveness of earthly courts puts God himself on trial, for, as Hieronimo reminds us, if He allows crimes to go unpunished on earth, He cannot be deemed a just God. The play itself, however, never doubts the existence of a divine order. Rather, it portrays a society in which man displays an increasing reluctance to wait for divine justice to work, even, at times, an inability to recognize the divine presence. Trials and judgments, then, give form to this play whose primary focus is upon justice.

Hieronimo is one of the many judges in this play of trials, but th symbolism of his role is usually misread. Critics are aware that behind the action lies the ordering structure of Christianity—specifically the doctrine so succinctly explained by La Primaudaye, that earthly magistrates hold their power through the will of Heaven and are responsible for carrying out that will among men:

> Therefore wee may well conclude, that all priuate Reuenge proceeding of enuy, or of hatred, or of anger, is vicious and forbidden by God, who commaundeth vs to render good for euill, and not euill for euill. For hee hath ordained the meanes, whereby hee will haue vengeance executed among men. Therefore hee hath appointed Magistrates to execute it according to his Lawe, and following his ordinaunce, not with any euill affection, but with iust indignation proceeding from loue, and from true zeale of iustice.[2]

Realizing that Kyd accepts this premise, commentators frequently argue that Hieronimo, as knight marshal, is to be understood as just such a magistrate, that he has specific authority, through his office, to act in God's place.[3] Throughout *The Spanish Tragedy*, however, the King of Spain makes the important magisterial decisions. Kyd identifies him, not the marshal, as God's deputy. That one of Hieronimo's major goals is to bring evidence of Lorenzo's guilt *to the King* is a good indication that Hieronimo's own powers are limited. The old man recognizes in his sovereign an authority he himself does not possess, and so should we. This distinction between the two defenders of God's justice in *The Spanish Tragedy* is significant.

Hieronimo himself cuts a poor figure as a judge. His occupation makes little sense if we try to view it realistically. For a man of his position, he seems incredibly naïve. His actions as knight marshal during the course of the play definitely do not suggest long years of experience in dealing with evil. On the contrary, whenever we watch him witnessing courtroom scenes, we find him reacting with surprise; Hieronimo seems to be completely innocent of all previous knowledge of evil. Nor does his role as marshal give him power—he is confronted with evil of great magnitude but has no jurisdiction in the case. We are meant to view the knight marshal as a subordinate, who can only function so long as the order represented by the King remains sound.

More important than Hieronimo's role as judge is his role as an everyman who thinks the world should be just and who tries to be so himself. Hieronimo has a solid reputation for honesty. And Kyd presents him as a man seeking justice:

> There is not any advocate in Spain
> That can prevail, or will take half the pain
> That he will, in pursuit of equity.[4]

Hieronimo's profession, then, is metaphorical as well as realistic; it reinforces our view of Hieronimo as a person who expects justice to be prompt and fair in its workings.

If Hieronimo's abilities in the judicial chair are played down, the King's are not. The King is unquestionably the representative of divine order on earth, both for the playwright and for Hieronimo. The first act of the play depicts the sovereign in the role of Solomon, the archetypal judge. The Spanish King is rational and wise. He is introduced at the center of an orderly court, celebrating the end of a war whose cause was just, and because just, victorious. As he is quick to reward those subordinates who have served him well, so he is ready to forgive his enemies, Portugal's Prince Balthazar (an enemy and a prisoner) being granted both the freedom of the court and the companionship of the Spanish prince, Lorenzo. But above all, Spain's King is conscientious in seeking to determine the right, hearing evidence calmly, weighing it objectively, passing judgment equitably. The closing lines of act 1, scene 2, toward which the entire scene has been building, do much to establish the King as an admirable magistrate. Here both Horatio and Lorenzo claim to have captured Balthazar, and since both desire the resulting rewards and honors, the King must arbitrate the matter:

King.	Will both abide the censure of my doom?
Lorenzo.	I crave no better than your grace awards.
Horatio.	Nor I, although I sit beside my right.
King.	Then, by my judgment, thus your strife shall end:
	You both deserve, and both shall have reward.—
	Nephew, thou took'st his weapon and his horse;
	His weapons and his horse are thy reward.—
	Horatio, thou didst force him first to yield;
	His ransom therefore is thy valor's fee:
	Appoint the sum, as you shall both agree.—
	But nephew, thou shalt have the prince in guard,
	For thine estate best fitteth such a guest;
	Horatio's house were small for all his train.
	Yet, in regard thy substance passeth his,
	And that just guerdon may befall desert,
	To him we yield the armor of the prince.

                                                              [1.2.175–90]

The situation is delicate, for there are conflicting claims, and the prize cannot be split down the middle and divided equally. Kyd does all he can to suggest that the King administers justice conscientiously.

In this opening sequence, a definite order is assumed. Christian values are still operative. The Spanish King grounds his decisions in a belief that the ultimate justice flows from "heaven and the guider of the heavens" (1.2.10–11) in the hope of recreating that justice within his kingdom.

Far from presenting a utopia though, Kyd acknowledges that the complexities of life make the administration of justice a perplexing affair and require the exercising of the keenest discrimination and judgment on the part of the magistrate. He is also realist enough to know that these qualities are not always present, and, moving his scene to Portugal, he shows the human aspects within the magistrate that make earthly justice fallible. The Viceroy of Portugal has personal faults that make him a poor magistrate. His mind is preoccupied so entirely with himself that he is blind to the natures of those around him. After Alexandro is falsely accused by Villuppo of murdering Balthazar on the battlefield, it becomes necessary to exercise judgment. The Viceroy accepts "an envious forged tale" as fact, refuses to allow the defendant to answer his accuser, weighs all the evidence upon the scale of his own emotions, and condemns a loyal counselor to death. Villuppo's action tells us that evil is always present in the world, while the Viceroy, with his extreme self-centeredness, makes himself the emblem of the unjust magistrate by failing to ferret out that evil for correction.

This being the case, the individual must have some other recourse, or the world must be deemed absurd. Therefore, in the companion scene which concludes Alexandro's trial, Kyd supplies a confirmation that divine providence is operative in the world. Alexandro, condemned to death for a crime that was never committed, places hope of his vindication in the divine powers (" 'Tis heaven is my hope" [3.1.35]). Such hope seems futile as his persecutors prepare to burn his body in "flames / That shall prefigure those unquenched fires / Of Phlegethon" (3.1.48–50). Before the fire can be lit, however, an ambassador enters bringing proof of Alexandro's innocence and instant reprieve. Providence appears to intervene in earthly affairs: the innocent and the guilty are identified, as heavenly justice proceeds to right an earthly wrong. These two opening scenes, portraying as they do first the wise magistrate and then the wise subject, establish for the audience what we might call the old order, which still views the universe in Christian terms.

After witnessing the trial of Alexandro in its entirety, we can discern the real purpose of the Portuguese episodes. Alexandro is Kyd's touchstone. His action—the action of unshaken faith—is the action that would be taken in the face of gross injustice by a man who accepts his society's symbols.

With the appearance of the younger generation, a new order is suggested, one that runs along beneath the surface and no

longer operates on the same premises. The new morality of the
youthful aristocrats is a disruptive element which serves to
undermine the present rulers and, in its manipulation of them,
to render them impotent. As Balthazar and Lorenzo take over
the stage from the King, destroying the atmosphere of reconciliation by murdering Horatio, justice ceases to function. The
effect is that the King appears to have lost his power to control
evil.

The "policy" of Lorenzo characterizes this new element, more
pervasively evil, and the kind of justice it fosters is illustrated in
the trial of Pedringano. The degree of injustice here involves
more than the personal error and bad judgment that Kyd
recognized in depicting the Viceroy. The flaws in the
Portuguese court look almost innocent when set beside the
Machiavellian philosophy of Lorenzo, who makes a mockery of
the whole judicial system by using it to serve his own corrupt
ends. Pedringano's trial is the only trial at which the sane
Hieronimo is portrayed in his official capacity. Yet for all his
determination to "see that others have their right," Hieronimo is
completely blocked by Lorenzo from uncovering the truth.

Everyone is familiar with this comically ironic scene in which
Pedringano struts about with impudent self-confidence until the
executioner puts an end to his bravado. Kyd displays here his
usual sure grasp of the complexities of life; this trial, like the
previous ones, is filled with perceptive observations about the
difficulties involved in the process of judging.

The truth is that Lorenzo had ordered Pedringano to kill
Serberine and has promised to pardon him for the deed. Lorenzo, the only person with all the facts, does not appear in court.
Nevertheless, he controls the proceedings. Pedringano refuses
to tell the truth to Hieronimo because he expects Lorenzo's page
to deliver the pardon. The page encourages these hopes by arriving with a box, but withholds from Pedringano the information that the box has no pardon in it. Hence, factors that throw a
different light on the nature of the prisoner's guilt are never
discovered during the trial. The judge, ignorant of the circumstances, has no way of counteracting this kind of injustice. Yet
Hieronimo believes he has a clear-cut case; he orders Pedringano's death.

What we have in this scene is a shrewd dramatization of the insight that any single human action can be interpreted in several different ways, the degree to which such interpretation approaches the truth relating directly, in these instances, to the amount of information available to or withheld from the perceiver. Each individual knows a part of the truth, but no one individual possesses the whole. The court and its presiding judge are always at the mercy of this fact of life, as well as of another, that out of various degrees of self-interest the individuals involved may choose to withhold the information they do have. So keen are Kyd's perceptions that the critic may get bogged down in the detail and miss the larger point made by this scene. What the audience must understand from the trial of Pedringano is that the values Lorenzo has introduced into the system have undermined and perverted it. What remains is only an illusion of order. The alignment between divine and human justice has been thrown out of whack.

At the end of this trial scene, when the executioner finds a letter to Lorenzo on Pedringano's corpse revealing the truth, Hieronimo is made aware of the discrepancies between appearance and reality. Although the revelation comes too late to save the defendant, it does raise Hieronimo to the ultimate level of awareness by exposing Lorenzo's guilt. This makes Hieronimo the first member of the old order to perceive the misalignment that so clearly speaks of a civilization in crisis.

The split between the old order and the new is dramatized in still another way. Kyd has subtly given the community a motivation that directs its actions throughout the play. The King is working from the beginning to the end to establish peace between Spain and Portugal, a peace to be effectuated by the marriage of Balthazar and Bel-imperia. But the success of that peace is subject to the degree to which the King can persuade Bel-imperia to subordinate her personal desires and find fulfillment as part of the resulting larger order. Although Lorenzo and Balthazar, for more selfish reasons, also work to effect the marriage, their method of winning Bel-imperia's consent—murdering Horatio—turn her permanently against Balthazar. Bel-imperia is confirmed in her irrational hatred of the husband proposed for her by the King. This element of irrationality, a

decided threat to communal efforts toward justice, is a counter-
force which, throughout the play, is completely out of harmony
with and even incomprehensible to those forces striving to establish the order of reason and a new Golden Age. The King's
failure to detect this factor and to placate it in some fashion is
another clue that his control is slipping.

Those scenes of the play which show men at work doling out
justice inform us that while the old order still exists, the real
control in this society no longer rests with it. It has lost its power,
and the elements that are moving in to fill the vacuum work to
make a mockery of earthly justice. Under these circumstances,
the individual begins to doubt the concepts on which social order
is based.

Hieronimo, finding society's justice unsatisfying, has two
other kinds of justice available to him in *The Spanish Tragedy*.
There is, first of all, the justice of nature, championed by Bel-
imperia, which has its visual manifestation in the pagan deities of
Hades. Directly opposed to it is the justice of Heaven. Since
scholars commonly lump both together,[5] the distinction must be
strongly emphasized. If the justice of Heaven and the justice of
Hades are equated, the insights of Kyd's personal vision are
easily obscured. The two realms have distinct functions in the
play as alternative forces operating on Hieronimo's psyche, the
former appealing to his faith and the latter to his instinct. The
old order has taught Hieronimo that "time is the author both of
truth and right, / And time will bring this treachery to light"
(2.5.58–59), that the Lord will exact vengeance on the guilty, and
that his duty is to exercise patience. At the same time, he is also
cognizant of a certain parental duty to his son, of the gross
unfairness of the world's failure to punish Lorenzo, and of an
inner urging which tells him his belief that Lorenzo should die
for the offense is right. In one mood Hieronimo will "beat at the
windows of the brightest heavens, / Soliciting for justice"
(3.7.13–14); in another, he will "go marshal up the fiends in hell,
/ to be avenged" (3.12.77–78). Hieronimo himself never equates
the two realms; he vacillates between them.

As we have seen, the existence in the universe Kyd has constructed of a source of justice beyond the mundane world is first
testified to by the King in act 1—

> Then bless'd be heaven and guider of the heavens,
> From whose fair influence such justice flows.
>
> [1.2.10–11]

—and later by the miraculous vindication of Alexandro. Hieronimo repeatedly displays not only an awareness of this higher order but an awareness of what his behavior should be in relation to it:

> Ay, Heaven will be revenged of every ill;
> Nor will they suffer murder unrepaid.
> Then stay, Hieronimo, attend their will;
> For mortal men may not appoint their time.
>
> [3.13.2–5]

But the actions of Lorenzo have shaken Hieronimo's faith.

As Kyd realized. one of the natural reflexes of man is to question the existence of anything that cannot be immediately confirmed through his senses. The doubt of an invisible Eternal Good is never more intense than at moments of undeserved suffering. When evil manifests itself in the world and is not met immediately with a thunderbolt that will blast it out of existence, man characteristically begins to complain. Hieronimo, too, is quick to despair:

> Oh sacred heavens! if this unhallowed deed,
> If this inhuman, barbarous attempt,
> If this incomparable murder thus
> Of mine, but now no more my son,
> Shall unreveal'd and unrevenged pass,
> How should we term your dealing to be just,
> If you unjustly deal with those that in your justice trust?
>
> [3.2.5–11]

This impatient view is, of course, set in perspective. The scene in which the calumnies of Villuppo are exposed in a mysterious way that reveals Providence at work immediately precedes Hieronimo's exhibition of doubt and weakening faith. But unfortunately, Hieronimo, back in Spain, can profit little from this distant miracle. Only the audience, which is given a more elevated level of knowledge throughout the play, can benefit from it. Hieronimo's experience tells him that Heaven no longer hears the prayers of man. Its walls have become impenetrable; they "give my words no way" (3.7.18).

The justice of nature functions quite differently throughout
the play. Its judges are Pluto, Proserpine, Minos, Aeacus, and
Rhadamanthus, with the Furies lurking not far off. These
judges appear in the prologue in response to the needs of the
Ghost of Andrea, who has been wandering homelessly about the
underworld, a spirit unable to rest. They seem at first a rather
harmless group (Pluto and Proserpine, for example, do not involve themselves in long deliberations over Andrea's case but
merely amuse themselves with it for the brief moment that it
commands their attention). Yet as the play proceeds references
to these infernal deities become more ominous. Though never
physically brought on stage after the prologue, Pluto and
Proserpine and their minions remain vividly present in the language of the characters. Not only do Andrea and Revenge
constantly speak of them. Hell becomes the landscape of
Hieronimo's mind:

> I'll go marshal up the fiends of hell,
> To be avenged on you all for this.
>
> [3.12.77–78]

> I'll down to hell, and in this passion
> Knock at the dismal gates of Pluto's court,
> Getting by force, as once Alcides did,
> A troop of Furies and tormenting hags
> To torture Don Lorenzo and the rest.
>
> [3.13.109–13]

> Then sound the burden of thy sore heart's grief,
> Till we do gain that Proserpine may grant
> Revenge on them that murdered my son.
>
> [3.13.119–21]

It is clearly the realm of the irrational that Kyd depicts in these
ravings of Hieronimo's troubled imagination, and in a sense its
ways are as mysterious as those of Heaven. The fiends and Furies under Proserpine's command are not only embodiments of
the fierce passions rising in the revenger but also infernal forces
justifying and giving authority to those passions. Although our
acquaintance with Proserpine begins with whim, it ends on a far
more tragic note. During the course of the play, Hell, because it
sanctions the act of revenge which Heaven forbids and thus
seems to promise justice, ironically becomes the final symbol of

hope for Hieronimo and Isabella, a hope born of despair of obtaining justice in any less violent way.

We must, therefore, acknowledge that in his concern with justice Kyd spans the whole range of possible human responses—he examines justice as manifested at the levels of Heaven (the order of Providence), earth (the order of the community), and Hades (the order of nature). It is in the context of this very comprehensive vision of justice that his revenge tale is told—*The Spanish Tragedy* is the story of one man's attempt to understand justice within a civilization that is at a point of crisis and of his tragic failure to do so.

II Since Kyd chose the figure of Revenge as the presenter of his play, he apparently attached importance to this primitive form of justice. In reacting against the exclusive emphasis critics have placed on Kyd's revenge themes, we should bear this in mind. The passion of revenge seems to have fired his imagination. His "The Murder of John Brewen" explores it from another angle, and speculations are high that Kyd himself wrote a *Hamlet*. Kyd's own contemporaries found what he had to say about revenge significant. An examination of the experiential basis for the revenge motifs reveals a depth of perception in his work that justifies the same detailed attention on our part.

Few revenge tragedies have only one revenge action, though most are so constructed that there appears to be only one. Kyd initiates this pattern in *The Spanish Tragedy*. In the main action, Horatio is the victim, Lorenzo the offender, and Hieronimo the revenger. In a parallel framing action, Andrea, Balthazar, and Bel-imperia, respectively, take these roles. But the framing action is not a subplot. The relationship is one of identity. The death of Horatio functions as a reenactment of the death of Andrea, and thereafter the two actions become joined. Kyd's Ghost lives entirely in the afterworld of the framing action.

Bowers is sometimes criticized for his statement that the Ghost of Andrea is "superfluous, and, indeed, need never have been introduced," but his remark reflects a feeling most readers have.[6] The opening sequences *are* cumbersome. To get his ac-

tion going and point it toward excess, Kyd needs a multiplicity of
characters—Andrea, Revenge, Bel-imperia, and Horatio. Later
dramatists need only one—the ghost itself. Admitting from the
start that the ghost motif is awkwardly handled, we must try to
understand why Kyd found it essential.

The ghost motif seems designed to illuminate several aspects
of the experience of revenge. For one thing Kyd embodies in
Andrea the desire for vengeance. The Ghost's "hopes" are simple—he wants to injure those who have harmed him. Primarily
he wants Balthazar slain, yet it suits him that Revenge should
promise to turn his enemies' "joys to pain, their bliss to misery"
(1.5.9). The desire is simple but not static. It is worth noting that
the Ghost's passion is much like that of the revenger; it
intensifies as the frustrations to its fulfillment increase. Initially,
Andrea's desire is almost unstated. Once Revenge comes to his
aid, he grows more and more insistent upon having his will, until
at last he is imploring all the inhabitants of Hades to come and
enforce his right:

> Awake, Erichtho! Cerberus, awake!
> Solicit Pluto, gentle Proserpine!
> To combat, Acheron and Erebus!
> For ne'er, by Styx and Phlegethon in hell,
> O'er-ferried Charon to the fiery lakes
> Such fearful sights as poor Andrea sees.
> Revenge, awake!
>
> [3.15.1–7]

And though at first he viewed the methods of Revenge with
dismay, at the end we find him delighting in the carnage. Certainly Andrea is identified with the revenger's desire to see his
foes suffer.

Andrea's desire is given a definite "objectivity." His other-
worldliness raises it to the level of a force of nature. In this
picture of the dead man's ghost roaming the underworld in
search of justice and finally hovering about the earth with the
guarantee that his death will be revenged, we have echoes of a
tradition that goes back beyond Seneca, its immediate source for
Kyd, to the ancient Greeks, who sought in their literature and in
their mythology to find symbols for the implacable natural
forces that are premoral.[7] Sponsored by the deities of the nether

world, given "authority" by its highest powers, Andrea becomes an Anglicized surrogate for the Furies.

While linking the Ghost to Hell, Kyd has been careful not to associate him with Lucifer. Within the framework of the Christian mythology there are only two external powers that can operate on the individual, one for good and one for evil, God and Satan. Throughout the medieval period, passion, when it breaks away from the reason to overwhelm the psyche, is characteristically "located" in Hell. Kyd seems a bit uncomfortable with this situation. By depicting Hell in pagan rather than satanic terms he manages to neutralize the symbols somewhat and thus to soften the judgment made upon the order of nature, while still allowing it supernatural authority.

Because this mysterious force represented by Andrea is in essence irrational, part of its reality is a tendency to run to excess. Andrea is therefore presented with Revenge at his side. His allegorical companion symbolizes the inevitable destruction which this particular passion will produce. The certainty of Revenge that events can work out in only one way stems from the fact that the passion he personifies has a predictable course. Revenge, by his very presence, throws over the play the suggestion that fate or destiny is at work.

Though the passion has a predictable course, it cannot develop in the abstract; to grow it must take root in the human psyche. Having chosen to keep the force separate from the beings it acts upon, Kyd was confronted with a dramaturgical problem—how are the Ghost's demands to be communicated from Hades to earth? Remembrance is the spark that bridges the gap. Revenge himself reminds us of this when he describes himself as a "mood" that "solicits the souls" of the living. Since psychologically the connection occurs through the memory, there must be someone on earth, a dear one, whose memories of Andrea breed in his imagination the same desires that the Ghost itself harbors. Kyd solves the problem of communication between the two worlds by inventing Bel-imperia. This willful young woman becomes the spokesman for Andrea and Revenge in the human world.

Too frequently Bel-imperia is interpreted as an intermediary between God and Hieronimo, assisting him to carry out the di-

vine will. Because her letters, timed to arrive after Hieronimo's
various complaints about the lack of divine intervention, seem to
be providentially supplied and because, at her urging,
Hieronimo takes it for granted that saints and angels support his
cause, commentators view Bel-imperia as a touchstone whose
approval of his actions should win ours.[8]

This is hardly the case. Although Bel-imperia is indeed an
intermediary, she is brokering between Andrea and Hieronimo
and consequently is the agent through whom Revenge can make
good his promise to the angry Ghost. Kyd supplies visual proof
of the connection by allowing her scarf to pass from Andrea's
corpse to Horatio (1.4.42–49) and thereafter to become the
bloody handkerchief that serves Hieronimo as a token of his
desire for revenge (2.5.51, 4.4.122–29). Bel-imperia's role
parallels Hieronimo's; she, too, is a revenger. But she is more.
She is a compulsion. Behind her lies the power of Proserpine. It
is Bel-imperia who first introduces thoughts of chaos into the
world which the King of Spain has just restored to order:

> But how can love find harbor in my breast
> Till I revenge the death of my beloved?
> Yes, second love shall further my revenge:
> I'll love Horatio, my Andrea's friend,
> The more to spite the prince, that wrought his end.
>
> [1.4.64–68]

Her passion for revenge, aroused against Balthazar by the loss of
Andrea and doubled when Balthazar kills her second love, is
eventually communicated to Hieronimo. Bel-imperia's function
during the remainder of the tragedy will be to bring Hieronimo
to the point of murdering her enemies.

Kyd wisely sensed that it was not enough to locate the origins
of the revenge passion in external forces, for there was very
definitely also a psychological aspect to the problem. To suggest
the subjective side of the revenge, Kyd employs a second ghost,
that of Horatio, which "speaks" to Hieronimo as Andrea had
"spoken" to Bel-imperia. This ghost has no objective reality
whatsoever. Hieronimo imagines Horatio's ghost to have come
"from the depth, / To ask for justice in this upper earth"
(3.13.133–34), but this ghost is a hallucination. Hieronimo's own
psyche imposes an image of Horatio upon a character who is, in

reality, Don Bazulto. This imaginary ghost testifies to the extent
to which the old man's imagination has fixed itself on the idea of
revenge. Symbolically, however, the ghost of Andrea and the
ghost of Horatio, taken together, suggest the twin sources of the
passion for revenge—one the universal force, the other the subjective passion.

Obviously dramatic economy is not a virtue of *The Spanish
Tragedy* where the ghost motif is concerned. In trying to put the
irrational forces behind the passion for revenge on stage, Kyd
surrounds his revenger with a real ghost, an illusory ghost, an
allegorical figure, and a vindictive young lady. Yet concepts
basic to the revenge experience are embodied in these figures.
Kyd is struggling to find appropriate symbols for the experience.

III Much of the conflict of the main revenge action arises
from Hieronimo's refusal to accept a world that is imperfect. This seemingly irrational world—"no world, but mass of
public wrongs"—nearly comes to replace Lorenzo as his major
antagonist. Hieronimo's passion for revenge is in a very real
sense a passion for justice and what drives him mad is his inability to accept the fact that the world is essentially unjust.

Kyd has understood that the individual's deep resentment of
an undeserved injury and his angry urge to punish the offender
is the emotional basis for society's more sophisticated forms of
justice—the laws and the courts which have replaced primitive
codes of revenge in maintaining social order. As such, the desire
has a positive value. Only here it wells up through the
fragmenting social scheme of justice which was built over it to
permanently intervene between man and the natural order.
This thematic framework provided by Kyd's personal vision
must be kept in mind as we trace Kyd's use of the madness
motif.[9]

At the beginning of the play, Hieronimo's frame of mind
could not be further from that of lunacy. Introduced in scenes
which imply that order has prevailed over anarchy and justice is
being meted out with equity, Hieronimo is not only sane but

even at the peak of happiness. Seeing Horatio honored fills his heart "withover cloying joys." The banquet scene for which he prepares a play-within-a-play in act 1 is in marked contrast to the parallel banquet scene in act 4. Now, Hieronimo is in no way isolated from the community by madness, as he will be when he presents his second play. He is at peace with himself, and his masque-message contributes to the growing harmony between countries. Hieronimo's sanity is the sanity of the good man—this is the first hallmark of the Kydian revenger.

But in Hieronimo's happiness, his "sanity," there is an element of naïveté and innocence. Knight marshal though he may be, this virtuous man has been living at the level of appearances. He believes that the world is just, that the rewards and punishments it metes out have something to do with desert. He is little prepared to comprehend injustice on a mammoth scale. Yet this is exactly what Kyd forces Hieronimo to face. He must learn that the order he has been content with is at least ineffectual if not absolutely corrupt, a fact that had escaped his vigilance because he had never before personally experienced the injustice growing in his community.

When Horatio is murdered, the painful process of adjustment is initiated. The event seems to Hieronimo beyond comprehension:

> Who hath slain my son?
> What savage monster, not of human kind,
> Hath here been glutted with thy harmless blood,
> And left thy bloody corpse dishonored here,
> For me, amidst this dark and deathful shades?
> [2.5.18–22]

Hieronimo is stunned by the magnitude of the injustice, and this causes him to question not only the world which did not foresee and prevent the evil deed by eliminating its perpetrator but also the heavens whose natural rhythms "assisted" the evildoers:

> Oh, heavens, why made you night to cover sin?
> By day this deed of darkness had not been.
> Oh earth, why didst thou not in time devour
> The vile profaner of this sacred bower?
> Oh poor Horatio, what hadst thou misdone,
> To leese thy life, ere life was new begun?

> Oh wicked butcher, whatsoe'er thou wert,
> How could thou strangle virtue and desert?
>
> [2.5.24–31]

The effect of this confrontation with evil is to shatter Hieronimo's faith in everything he had previously believed in. His whole world has fallen apart:

> O world! no world, but mass of public wrongs,
> Confus'd and fill'd with murder and misdeeds.
>
> [3.2.3–4]

Under the impact, Hieronimo begins to question the symbolic patterns developed by his society to structure reality. The Christian symbols no longer seem adequate. A God who treats His subjects so unjustly is no "just" God. Slowly, Hieronimo turns away from received wisdom and struggles to redefine justice for himself on the basis of his own experience. Thus forced to make the search into self that brings enlightenment, he will gain a heightened awareness of the nature of existence but, because he is filled with an anger that will block out large areas of reality from his new perspective, his knowledge will never progress to the stage of transcendent clarity.

If we remember that the madness Kyd depicts has both a real and a symbolic level and approach it first at the realistic level as a madness of inordinate passion, we can best appreciate how Kyd solved the difficulties of dramatizing it. Psychologically, the development of the madness involves two distinct kinds of movement—undulating and linear. Both reflect a basic characteristic of the human mind (that the mind rarely proceeds uninterruptedly through life at a single level of knowledge but shifts from one level to another). Both had to be reflected in the action if the dramatic presentation was to be accurate and convincing.

The first kind of movement is recognized but not always understood.[10] It allows for the minute-to-minute alterations which take place in the psyche. Throughout acts 3 and 4, Hieronimo moves into and out of madness as his passion wars with his reason. These undulating movements of the madness create the dramatic tension which allows us to see the conflict between conscience and instinct, the two natural tendencies of the mind controlling human notions of justice. In terms of the revenge tragedy symbols, the undulating movement is the vacillation between moods of delay and moods of madness.

Let us illustrate. Hieronimo is never more fully committed to revenge than he is in act 2, when he first discovers his son's body. In the intense concentration of passion as he vows revenge, there is a definite flick of madness:

> Seest thou this handkercher besmear'd with blood?
> It shall not from me till I take revenge.
> Seest thou those wounds that yet are bleeding fresh?
> I'll not entomb them till I have reveng'd.
> Then will I joy amidst my discontent.
>
> [2.5.51–55]

But his determination does not remain at this level. Each time we meet him, he enters leaning toward one course of action and moves round to the opposite persuasion before the episode is concluded. In this constant wavering between madness and delay, during which Hieronimo is continually making choices, we are made aware that the human mind is constantly in flux and that when one defines the state of being of any particular individual, one is merely speaking of that state of mind which dominates more often than the others competing with it.

This inclusion of the undulating movement gives the dramatic rendering of the madness a complexity that saves it from seeming overly schematic. But it would confuse matters if the order were totally obscured. Kyd therefore uses the linear movement to accent the major moments of decision and to reveal the basic direction in which the mind is moving. The over-all pattern is a descending one, progressing from sanity to insanity; Hieronimo's psyche is steadily moving toward the irrational.[11]

This descending movement into madness is underscored by Kyd in several ways. The most obvious is the progress from sanity to insanity at the level of plot. At first, Hieronimo, finding his untried faith in the justice of heaven wavering, seeks desperately to fend off madness by commanding God to display His might. Losing this round, he makes a highly irrational attempt to force justice from the earthly powers. Finally, as the madness overwhelms him, he embraces the justice of nature, because that is the only form of justice condoning the violent action circumstances have made him see as the necessary action. This linear movement ends in a very literal lunacy that reflects symbolically on the moral state of the psyche.

Other less obvious techniques are employed by Kyd to suggest the over-all direction of the psychological descent from rational to irrational modes of behavior. All are techniques of intensification. There is, first, the increasingly erratic behavior at the official level: Hieronimo becomes ever more ineffectual as knight marshal, temperamentally "resigns" the office, and acts in the end, at Bel-imperia's advice, in the private capacity of impassioned father. There is, second, Hieronimo's growing tendency to identify himself and his cause with the forces of Hades. Whereas the old man initially associates Hell with Lorenzo, he comes more and more to see its denizens as his allies. There is, finally, the steady deterioration from objectivity to subjectivity in Hieronimo's perception of reality. This last form of intensification involves a unique method of characterization worked out by Kyd to reflect a psychological truth and deserves further comment.

One of Kyd's major insights into the madness of passion was that the imagination obsessed with revenge would eventually begin to project itself onto the exterior world. Hieronimo's passion for justice causes him to misinterpret events to which he is a witness as well as to impose upon them meanings derived from his own psyche. For example, there are several trial scenes in the play wherein Hieronimo, officially presiding, is forced to witness various kinds of injustice. In each of these scenes, a judgment is going to be made. In each, Hieronimo is, in a sense, struggling to exert his power over the world to make it behave justly. And in each, he fails. The more evidence he acquires of the injustices of the world the more his rage grows, and the more his rage grows the narrower his vision becomes. His mind seems to be constantly striving to reconstruct a world of its own in which events work out as Hieronimo would like them to.

At the trial of Pedringano, the displacement is small; Hieronimo, still knight marshal and sitting in judgment at the session determined to dispense true justice, is fairly objective. He is enraged by Pedringano's insolence, the more so because this murderer puts him in mind of his son's, but his anger causes little distortion in his view of the world. The major misconceptions on his part are those resulting from a lack of adequate information or the deliberate presentation of false evidence. Such misconceptions are characteristic of the world, in which no human being is omniscient and even the most equitable judge cannot be sure he has all the facts. In the light of the information he has access to, Hieronimo interprets the events of this trial correctly.

The madness shortly begins to work on his psyche and in future scenes Hieronimo no longer sees with full objectivity. The tendency of his passion to color what his reason sees is suggested in the next trial scene in which Hieronimo participates, that in which he petitions the King for the prosecution of Lorenzo. Here Kyd makes a distinct contrast between reality and Hieronimo's illusion. In a state of despair as the scene opens but determined to try one last means of obtaining satisfaction, Hieronimo approaches the King with his new evidence. Unfortunately, Hieronimo has timed his arrival poorly, for the King is engaged with the Viceroy about important matters of state. His preoccupation makes it easy for Lorenzo to step in between Hieronimo and the King, and once again justice is withheld, as the King rebuffs the suppliant. In no condition to remain patient and state his case clearly, Hieronimo flies into a rage and the "trial" is aborted.

Two kinds of illusion are operative here; Hieronimo is alerted to one but blind to the other. What Hieronimo sees is that the order of the community is a fantasy. The King is a representative of justice—his chief role in the state is that of lawgiver, administrator of justice—and he is not fulfilling his duty. As important as the peace to be effected by the marriage of Balthazar and Bel-imperia may seem, all of the preparations are based on illusion, for Bel-imperia's attitude toward Balthazar is far from that of a loving bride, and in advancing Balthazar in the state the King is in reality thwarting, not advancing, justice. Because he remains uninformed about the true nature of the relationship between Balthazar, Lorenzo, and Bel-imperia, the King is unwittingly neglecting his central function as God's magistrate, and worse, creating a chasm between the order of the community and the order of Heaven which ordinarily finds expression through it.

This kind of illusion is widely recognized by modern critics, particularly Anne Righter.[12] The other kind, Hieronimo's illusion, is not. The insight that Hieronimo gains from his madness, that the order of the community has become a farce, has also thrown Hieronimo so deep into himself that instead of stoically grasping the general truth that the ground of being remains firm even though the world may drift off center, Hieronimo assumes that life has no meaning. He takes the rebuff as the result of personal malice and, in a self-inflicted rage, tosses away the marshalship that has associated him with justice. His distorted vision of the episode contains a degree of illusion even greater than the King's. The old man envisions himself surrounded by enemies, against whom he may defend himself only by gathering together an army of fiends from Hell.

Kyd takes pains to make Hieronimo's blindness to reality more obvious by following the marshal's exit with a view of the King that is in direct conflict with the one Hieronimo projected. Here is the King as he really is, full of paternal concern and noble generosity:

King.	Gentle brother, go give to him this gold,
	The prince's ransom; let him have his due,
	For what he hath, Horatio shall not want;
	Haply Hieronimo hath need hereof.
Lorenzo.	But if he be helplessly distract,
	'Tis requisite his office be resign'd,
	And given to one of more discretion.
King.	We shall increase his melancholy so.
	'Tis best that we see further in it first,
	Till when, ourself will exempt the place.

[3.12.92–101]

This gesture of good will is not sufficient to dull our feeling that justice has been withheld. Still, we are meant to see that Hieronimo's imagination has begun to breed spectacular fantasies.

The process by which the maddened Hieronimo projects his psyche onto the exterior world becomes even more overt in the next trial scene Hieronimo participates in, where the old peasant Don Bazulto appeals to him for justice for a murdered son. Hieronimo's imagination has become so absorbed with his desire for revenge that he now sees very little of reality. No longer is he the equitable judge who would go to all lengths to insure justice; Hieronimo views Don Bazulto's case only as a reflection of his own. His response to Bazulto's plea for justice for *his* son is "No, sir; it was *my* murder'd son!" (3.13.80), and he proceeds to reflect upon the case only insofar as it seems to him a chastisement for his own delay. His mind breaks down further under the stimulus of this episode, and the result is another series of projections of his subjective world upon the real one. Having been reflecting upon the similarities between Bazulto's case and his own, Hieronimo takes the next step of actually transforming Bazulto into Horatio:

> Sweet boy, how art thou chang'd in death's black shade!
> Had Proserpine no pity on thy youth,
> But suffered thy fair crimson-color'd spring
> With withered winter to be blasted thus?
> Horatio, thou art older than thy father:
> Ah, ruthless fate, that favor thus transforms!
>   [3.13.146–51]

No matter how frequently Bazulto insists that he is, in truth, "a grieved man . . . that came for justice for my murdered son," Hieronimo persists in imposing an identity of his own making upon the suppliant. If Bazulto is not a ghost, then he must be "a Fury . . . sent from the empty kingdom of black night" and if not a Fury, then "the lively image of my grief." The only reality in Hieronimo's world now is the reality of the offense.

These three trial scenes, each marking a different stage in the linear development of the madness, have an inner coherence that scholars often overlook. Each is designed to reveal that the revenger's passion becomes a kind of fixed idea in which the mind concentrates all its awareness upon the injury and the resulting loss, thereby blocking out any other knowledge from the imagination.

In all of these manifestations of madness one obsession remains paramount; Hieronimo's single-mindedness takes the form of an obsessive desire to make the world behave justly. When viewed in these terms, the desire is immediately recog-

nizable as an irrational one. But because Hieronimo approaches
it only as the wish to see the murderers of his son duly punished,
the desire presents itself as perfectly reasonable. Kyd has made
Hieronimo the embodiment of human reason as it seeks to find a
direct relationship in the world between actions and rewards.
The playwright understood that at the level of appearances, the
world does work in ways that come tantalizingly close to being
comprehensible to human reason and that when the world is
irrational and baffles the understanding, it often appears only to
have slipped a cog. From the point of view of human reason, the
immediate response is that human action—action such as a man
like Hieronimo might contemplate—can put the world back in
gear. When one is as completely convinced of the reasonable
nature of the world as Hieronimo is, one becomes increasingly
frustrated and angry at its reluctance to be reasonable in one's
own case, seemingly in this case alone. One becomes incensed
and demands "what is only reasonable" as one's right. Under
these conditions, the desire for reason becomes so intense that it
is transformed into an irrational passion. The pressures placed
upon the mind by that passion prevent the reason from functioning and bring to a halt the mind's journey toward enlightenment. Hieronimo's experience demonstrates that the very
human commitment to a belief in the power of reason, if put to
the test, paradoxically will be shown to be irrational, because the
world ultimately is not reducible to human terms.

The problem, of course, is that the insight which the revenger
gains from his confrontation with injustice—the insight that the
world is unjust—though valid, is only a partial insight. The injustice must be seen in a larger context, for it is only in the light
of the whole that one can discover the implications of injustice,
either for the individual or for the world. To fully differentiate
the insight, the revenger would have to accept the fact that in the
final analysis, the world is not rational but rather is radically
mysterious. Hieronimo, ironically enough, was in touch with a
symbolic construction of reality from which this deeper insight
could have come:

> Ay, Heaven will be revenged of every ill;
> Nor will they suffer murder unrepaid.

> Then stay, Hieronimo, attend their will;
> For mortal men may not appoint their time.
>
> [3.13.2–5]

But his was an age of doubt, not an age of faith, and his belief in this symbolism could not survive the ultimate test. Hieronimo's passion prevents him from accepting the insight that the Christian symbolism provided. His psyche is so busy constructing its own reality that it can see no other. The suffering that the madness of revenge inflicts upon Hieronimo thus, unfortunately, never raises him to a point of transcendence.

IV The compulsion set up by the underworld figures and the madness induced by Hieronimo's irrational desire to make the world behave reasonably eventually culminate in the play-within-the-play, within which the act of revenge is finally committed.

The immediate stimulus to Hieronimo's plan of action is Bel-imperia. Her role in pushing Hieronimo into action should not be interpreted as depriving Hieronimo of free will: Kyd has already made much of Hieronimo's moment of choice in the *Vindicta mihi* speech, where the hero elects the course of revenge. Rather, Bel-imperia's presence at the beginning of act 4 is a reminder that the order of nature (not Heaven) lies behind the madness. The irony of the scene is that Hieronimo completely misunderstands the origins of Bel-imperia's authority.

As usual, Kyd sets up a direct contrast between the reality and the illusion. Throughout the play, Bel-imperia has been a primary advocate of the justice of nature:

> But how can love find harbor in my breast
> Till I revenge the death of my beloved?
> Yes, second love shall further my revenge.
>
> [1.4.64–66]

> Revenge thyself on Balthazar and him:
> For these were they that murdered thy son.
> Hieronimo, revenge Horatio's death.
>
> [3.2.28–30]

> Hieronimo, why writ I of thy wrongs,
> Or why art thou so slack in thy revenge?
> Andrea, oh Andrea! that thou sawest
> Me for thy friend Horatio handled thus . . .
>
> [3.9.7–10]

When the last act opens, Bel-imperia is sent out on stage to bombard Hieronimo with the arguments that later playwrights will put directly into the mouths of stage ghosts. Her plea is the plea of natural instinct:

> Hieronimo, are these thy passions,
> Thy protestations and thy deep laments,
> That thou wert wont to weary men withal?
> Oh unkind father! Oh deceitful world!
> With what excuses canst thou show thyself
> From this dishonor and the hate of men,
> Thus to neglect the loss and life of him
> Whom both my letters and thine own belief
> Assures thee to be causeless slaughtered?
> Hieronimo, for shame, Hieronimo,
> Be not a history to aftertimes
> Of such ingratitude unto thy son:
> Unhappy mothers of such children then,
> But monstrous fathers to forget so soon
> The death of those whom they with care and cost
> Have tender'd so, thus careless should be lost!
> Myself, a stranger in respect of thee,
> So loved his life, as still I wish their deaths.
> Nor shall his death be unreveng'd by me.
>
> [4.1.4–22]

Her argument for the justice of nature is forceful; indeed, we all half wish Hieronimo will heed it. It reminds us that there is a compulsion acting upon Hieronimo which he cannot ignore: he would be an unnatural father who abandoned the attempt to bring his son's murderers to justice.

But since Hieronimo distrusted this woman's urgings in his rational stages, we must wonder when he reasons that her approval can bestow Heaven's blessing upon his cause:

> But may it be that Bel-imperia
> Vows such revenge as she hath deign'd to say?

> Why, then I see that heaven applies our drift,
> And all the saints do sit soliciting
> For vengeance on those cursed murderers.
>
> [4.1.29–33]

Again Hieronimo views events in terms of his desire: what could be more arbitrary than the connection Hieronimo makes between Bel-imperia's vow of revenge and Heaven's patronage? The revenger's madness has reached a stage where his vision of the world is so distorted that it no longer bears any relation to reality. Normal prohibitions against murder have been converted into a divine authorization to kill. This final bit of self-deception brings Hieronimo to a point where he can act.

In depicting Hieronimo at the height of his madness, Kyd wished to distinguish between the real world, where plans for Bel-imperia's wedding to Balthazar are going forward, and the revenger's world, where a limited subjective reality has been substituted for the whole. What better symbol for this purpose than a play, which is itself an imaginary world? It represents a "creation" of Hieronimo's mind as credibly as his vision of Bazulto does. In it the original offense can be transformed from an event of the past to a "reality" of the present, indeed, the sole reality of life itself, just as it is the sole concern of the maddened mind. Hieronimo can step into this imaginary world with all the authority of an avenging angel and arrange events exactly as he pleases.

Significantly, though Balthazar calls for a play to celebrate his marriage to Bel-imperia, Kyd insists upon putting Hieronimo—the revenger—in control of the performance. Hieronimo is the author of the play:

> When in Toledo there I studied,
> It was my chance to write a tragedy—
> See here, my lords—   *He shows them a book.*
> Which, long forgot, I found this other day.
>
> [4.1.75–78]

He is also its director—he will assign the parts and manage the production, Whatever the results, they will be entirely of *his* invention.

Kyd not only put the revenger in control of the play, he also made him choose a play in which the original offense is dupli-

cated. In it, Soliman and the Bashaw, finding Erasto an obstacle
to Soliman's lust for Perseda, kill this lady's innocent lover. The
actions of Soliman and the Bashaw are the actions of Balthazar
and Lorenzo; Erasto's fate is Horatio's, and Perseda's loss is
Bel-imperia's. Through this restaging of the original crime, the
revenger's refusal to allow it to become an event of the past is
given visual presentation on the stage. In addition, we are able to
watch Hieronimo arranging the world in such a way that perfect
justice can be effected. This time, when "Horatio" is stabbed
Hieronimo kills the murderer on the spot.

In his final speech, Hieronimo will argue that the only true
reality is that of his play-within-the-play:

> Haply you think—but bootless are your thoughts—
> That this is fabulously counterfeit,
> And that we do as all tragedians do:
> To die today (for fashioning our scene)
> The death of Ajax or some Roman peer,
> And in a minute, starting up again,
> Revive to please tomorrow's audience.
> No, princes—
>
> [4.4.76–83]

The "show" was real, says the revenger, and those slain in it will
never rise again. But in the play Hieronimo is no longer the
impartial advocate he claims to be. In order to carry out the
action demanded by the Ghost and Revenge, he has had to cast
himself in the role that Lorenzo should have played, that of
Soliman's corrupt Bashaw, while Lorenzo took the place that was
Horatio's. Hieronimo, that is, unwittingly reveals himself to be
the villain of his piece at the very moment that he has assumed
the role of God's agent; he has transformed himself into the
image of Lorenzo. As he ironically remarks, "I'll play the murderer, I warrant you" (4.1.131).

The symmetry through which Hieronimo murders Lorenzo
and Bel-imperia dispatches Balthazar should not obscure the fact
that the justice of nature, though it, too, restores order, cannot do
so without excess. This is testified to by the several other deaths
which occur in or as a result of the performance—the so-called
multiple murders. Events in Hieronimo's play do not work out
exactly as Hieronimo had intended. The two planned deaths
explode by a chain reaction into five. Bel-imperia stabs herself;

this Hieronimo did not foresee. Hieronimo puts a knife into the Duke of Castile, an innocent bystander, an act of excess by which he literally forfeits the title of a just man which he has metaphorically thrown off with his robes of office. And he himself is driven to suicide. Hieronimo's desire for justice, though commendable and necessary in the situation, results in a blood bath more horrible than the one he witnessed in the bower.

This culmination of the plot in multiple murders is not simply a matter of "cramming as much horror and complication as possible into a denouement."[13] These deaths reflect the nature of the experience, in which cruelty and excess is the rule. Much critical ink has been spilled in seeking reasons for Hieronimo's murder of Castile, when the point is precisely that there is *no* reason for it—it is a mad act, an act of cruelty and of waste, and one dramatically calculated to differentiate the justice of nature from earthly or heavenly justice. The frame story in which the ghost of Andrea and his allegorical companion claim credit for this "fated" ending and exult in it informs us that such waste is the inevitable result when the spirit of revenge is unleashed in the world. Like the ghost, the madness, and the play-within-the-play, the multiple murders express an integral aspect of the archetypal experience of revenge.

A word should be said in closing about the final motif of the revenge plot, the death of the avenger. Of all the conventions, this one is best understood. The point is obvious: however lofty his aims, however beneficial his actions, the revenger, having committed murder, must atone for his crime. His dedication to justice ironically involved him in actions that violate the very standards he means to uphold, thus rendering him subject to the same penalties he would exact from his foes. Once the revenger has acted, his death is inevitable; the only freedom of choice remaining to the playwright (if he is faithful to the moral and aesthetic requirements of the experience) lies in the choice of method by which to effect the death.

Because of his focus upon the revenger's psychology, Kyd elects to emphasize the relationship between revenge and despair: he makes Hieronimo take a course which Shakespeare, interestingly, allows Hamlet only to consider and reject—that of suicide.[14] The solution is an ideal one. Hieronimo has maintained throughout the play that he died when Horatio died:

But hope, heart, treasure, joy, and bliss,
All fled, fail'd, died, yea, all decay'd, with this.
From forth these wounds came breath that gave me life;
They murder'd me that made these fatal marks.

[4.4.94–97]

Life has been a living death to him, and he has considered suicide frequently, remaining alive only to see the murderers into
their graves. With the mission accomplished, he can say, "My
heart is satisfied," and go to his rest. Hieronimo's own peace of
mind allows us to accept his death with greater ease. Moreover,
his willingness to die attaches to his actions as a revenger the
aura of sacrifice, so that the death takes on larger significance.
Hieronimo becomes an emblem of a man who has given his life
"in pursuit of equity." Kyd had to strain a bit to get a knife into
Hieronimo's hands, but the decision to end the revenger's life in
suicide renders the final motif of the configuration satisfying
both dramatically and experientially.

V It was suggested in chapter 5 that revenge tragedies are
   tragedies in which the viewer learns more from the action than the hero does. How is this true of *The Spanish Tragedy?*

As the action of the play unfolds, the audience always knows
more than the characters. It has viewed the action from a higher
perspective, perceiving hidden causes for events that baffle
those on stage, and thus is schooled to recognize, by the end of
the play, that the universe is mysterious in its workings and that
its mysteries must simply be accepted.

Through its revenge action, the play suggests that concepts of
justice, though advanced by society, also have an emotional basis
closely linked with feelings of kinship and familial loyalties. But
by displaying the destructive power of this instinctual passion
when let loose, it also illustrates the necessity for the order of the
community, which placates such forces of nature by providing
formal methods of punishing offenses against justice.

Although Hieronimo's play-world contained a high degree of
illusion, it has the effect of exposing the communal fantasy and
bringing the community (at least temporarily) into closer align-

ment with the ideal. The revenger, in his passion to do justice, exceeds the mark by such an extent that the act of retribution, in its grotesqueness more than in its justice, serves as the impetus to reawaken the community to a new sense of the urgency for order. Aware at last of the corruption in Lorenzo and Balthazar, the court can perhaps correct the misalignment that has developed between itself and Providence.

But the workings of the divine order, within which the other two are encompassed, remains mysterious. We cannot understand *why* all this should happen to Hieronimo. Although as events turn out he has given his life in the cause of justice, he receives neither reward nor recognition for his services. Ironically, the community, because it cannot tolerate actions called for by an order alien to it, cannot approve of his gift but must punish him. Nor can Hieronimo himself enjoy the fruits of his success, for to put himself in touch with the order of nature has cost him his sanity. Even Heaven cannot recognize Hieronimo's gift; his actions involve both a deliberate rejection of the divine command that "thou shalt not kill" and the greater sin of despair.

In the epilogue, we are once again reminded that the destiny to which Hieronimo's passion subjected him had its roots in the order of nature. The chaos which had appalled the earthly court delights Andrea, who finally comprehends how Revenge operates and proceeds to plan further torments for Balthazar and Lorenzo, while forgiving Hieronimo. Andrea is no more an agent of God than Hieronimo, however, and his judgments must not be taken for those of Heaven. If by some mysterious order in the universe the promptings of the Ghost brought Hieronimo to a point where his errors served a higher purpose that might be spoken of as providential, it is not because Providence *chose* Hieronimo and made him a victim. The *choices* were Hieronimo's—freely willed. That they culminated, paradoxically, in a destruction that implied victory and a victory that induced destruction is simply another inexplicable mystery in a world that is, to human reason, essentially and ineradicably incomprehensible.

Chapter 7

Antonio's Revenge

What satisfaction outward pomp can yield,
Or chiefest fortunes of the Venice state,
Claim freely. You are well-season'd props
And will not warp or lean to either part:
"Calamity gives man a steady heart."
  John Marston, *Antonio's Revenge*

I IN PLANNING THE FINAL MOMENTS OF *Antonio's Revenge,*
Marston tried to capture the sense of release that follows
an act of vengeance. The intense emotional pressure which had
driven the revengers for much of the play is crowned by a period of elation, in which Piero's murderers exult in the success of
their plot to kill him. But then, suddenly, desire is gone. In the
end exuberance gives way to a quiet exhaustion that hints at
world-weariness. Psychologically speaking (and Marston is "psychologically speaking" for much of the play), the insight is a valid
one. The dramatist has erred, however, in attempting to connect
this release from passion with the release from sin. He does this
by equating the misery Piero has inflicted upon Antonio and Pandulpho with the tragic suffering that elevates the
soul, thus endowing the calm with a spiritual significance that
dominates the psychological one. The play tells us that as the
deed has purged the psyche of passion, so the suffering which
necessitated that deed has purified the "elate spirits" who perpetrated it; for Marston, the revengers' great woe has been the
agency of their spiritual rebirth.[1]

161

We can readily believe in the "do" of this tragedy, but never in the "suffer" or the "know." The conclusion Marston has written for *Antonio's Revenge,* wherein the avengers, after brutally murdering their victim, are "religiously held sacred," violates not only dramatic convention, which calls for the death of the avenger, but our whole sense of reality. Marston's attempt to end his play on a note of calm has, for this reason, been met by a thunderous clamor from outraged critics:

> It becomes preposterous lenience in the dramatist when he [Antonio] is allowed to end his days "In holy verge of some religious order."[2]

> There is something shocking in the complacency with which the final butchery of *Antonio* is accepted.[3]

> The naïve cathartic assumptions of these [last] lines betray an ethic of revenge as involuntarily sanctimonious as it is collusively brutal.[4]

Various explanations have been offered for Marston's callousness. Bowers sees the root cause in "the obvious influence which the morality of Seneca exercised in the play," whereas Samuel Schoenbaum accuses the playwright of "identifying himself with the forces of violence, enjoying vicariously the piling up of horrors." At the other extreme is R. A. Foakes's argument that *Antonio's Revenge* was written as a parody and its ending should not be taken seriously.[5] Although this new theory has attracted much attention, it has not found general acceptance, and we are still left with the old fact—that in failing to condemn his revengers, Marston unwittingly condemned his play.

This ill wind which blows against Marston's judgment might be turned to some good. We might see in this widespread and instinctive feeling that *Antonio's Revenge* should have closed with the revenger's execution a confirmation that the motifs of revenge tragedy have an integrity that must be respected. Kyd's motifs establish a configuration designed to conform to the experience of revenge. When properly used they remain vehicles which assist the playwright in his explorations of the passion by concretizing the abstract concepts involved in the experience. Marston, in employing the revenge plot developed by Kyd, has unfortunately attempted to wrench certain individual motifs out of their place in that configuration in order to make them serve new purposes and, in doing so, has provided interesting evidence that the original relationship between the motifs is permanent and meaningful.

The task of analyzing Marston's use of the revenge play is made both more difficult and much easier by the playwright's imposition of the villain-hero or retribution form upon his revenge plot.[6] Throughout *Antonio's Revenge*, two actions are being carried forward simultaneously. One, modeled after *The Spanish Tragedy* or an early *Hamlet,* dramatizes the ever-increasing madness of the hero, Antonio, as he falls under the influence of the revenge passion. The other, reminiscent of *Richard III,* traces the decline and fall of the villainous tyrant, Piero, who wreaks havoc in the state for four acts and is brought down by Nemesis in the fifth. At first glance it may seem that these two forms could be joined without peril, for there are many similarities between them. The tyrant-king of the retribution plot, who exercises his Machiavellian schemes at the expense of the suffering populace, has much in common with the Machiavellian villain of the revenge play, whose act of murder causes equal suffering to a specific individual. Both villains are emblems of injustice; both are somehow above the law and thus immune to punishment, and both must be removed from their positions of authority by extraordinary means. In both cases, they are brought down by a worthy man who takes it upon himself to execute the divine will. Yet, despite these similarities, the differences between the forms are significant enough to work against a successful merger.

The difficulties in analyzing *Antonio's Revenge* arise because the two modes, when chained together, ultimately prove contradictory, so that readers are never sure which point of view the playwright is taking at various moments in the play. The contradictions, at least as Marston handled them, are irreconcilable. For example, the perspective of the audience is different in each of the plot forms. In *Richard III,* the villain is at the center of the action; the emphasis is upon the proliferation of evil deeds and the monstrous nature of the man who commits them. Richmond, the individual elected to destroy the villain, enters only in the last scene, surrounded as it were by angels and trumpets, and his sole act is to slay the tyrannous monster. Because the hero's entrance is delayed, the question of his moral state is never raised. The audience, knowing little more about him than that his cause is just, can easily accept him as the divine agent through whom order is to be restored. In Kyd's plot, on the other hand, the action is deliberately focused upon the revenger. He is on stage from the beginning, for the revenge form explores the moral and psychological state of this individual as he responds to the monster. This hero's public role is mixed inextricably with a private one, and there is always a question whether he is being motivated by Apollo or simply by the Furies. The feeling of the viewer is that he is watching a tragedy of self-destruction that will presumably end with the hero's death. Marston, in joining the two forms, has given Antonio the roles of both Richmond and Hieronimo, thus driving to exasperation the audience which tries to make sense of the play's ending. Antonio must commit atrocities during a fit of madness and yet be "religiously held sacred" for these very deeds. From the essential incompatibility of these parts spring the difficulties of coping with the whole.

Yet once this fundamental fact about the structure of *Antonio's Revenge* is grasped, the author's objectives are a bit easier to see. It is obvious from Marston's handling of the play, especially in act 5, that he put the two forms together consciously. It is also obvious that his imagination was captured by the revenge rather than the retribution plot. Piero is depicted rather mechanically—Marston gives him a set of barely credible motives to account psychologically for his hatred of Andrugio and Antonio and, to pump him up to the level of monster, thrusts him into the stereotyped role of the Machiavellian. With a few more strokes to suggest the old Vice, the portrait is completed. Marston devotes far more attention to the characterization of Antonio. Clearly the psychology of the revenger intrigued Marston, and his greatest insights may be found in his depiction of the emotional states into which the passion for vengeance casts the individual. Moreover, insofar as Marston connects those states with tragic suffering (what Antonio calls "woe"), the response he demands from his audience is pity (Prologue 21–27, 5.3.163–86).[7] It seems safe to suppose that one reason for the introduction of the retribution plot was its capacity to justify the deed of revenge. What better way to gain sympathy for a revenger whose suffering is to be seen to raise him above the world than by identifying the revenger with the saintly hero of the retribution play?

Whatever Marston's reasons for combining the two forms, the facts that most concern us here are (1) that both are undeniably present throughout the play, (2) that because of a basic incompatibility they cannot exist together without alteration, and (3) that Marston, sensing this, has made definite attempts to square the revenge tragedy motifs with the demands of the retribution plot. Since the combination of forms affects Marston's handling of the madness, the ghost, the play-within-the-play and, above all, the death of the revenger, *Antonio's Revenge* becomes an excellent source for the study of revenge tragedy motifs. In it one may perceive both the degree to which Kydian motifs can be shaped to fit a playwright's own personal vision and the degree to which they will resist alteration.

II Most commentators would agree that Marston is deeply involved in his writing in the murder scenes. They might question the aesthetic merits of these sensational scenes, but they would certainly admit that nowhere else in Jacobean drama is the brutal inhumanity of the passion of revenge documented with such actuality. Since any search for scenes which reveal the essence of the revenger's madness must culminate in *Antonio's Revenge,* our examination of Marston's use of the revenge tragedy motifs can profitably focus upon this one. Where Kyd in depicting the madness came at it obliquely by imposing a symbolic lunacy upon Hieronimo and where Shakespeare tastefully distanced us from the madness of Hamlet by imposing between us and it an "antic disposition," Marston goes right to the core of things—here is the madness of revenge in its full heat.

Antonio, like Hieronimo, is sane when we meet him. Sane and virtuous: here, too, the madness grows out of the shock administered to a good man by some sudden confrontation with evil. Things begin to fall apart for Antonio when the malevolent actions of Piero impinge upon his comfortable world. Piero prevents the wedding between Mellida (his daughter) and Antonio, on the pretense that Mellida has been caught in bed with Pandulpho's son Feliche. He has Feliche killed and Mellida impris-

oned. Having blocked the marriage, Piero then maliciously
poisons Antonio's father Andrugio. These schemes, which
function in the retribution plot as demonstrations of the cruelty
of the tyrant, serve in the revenge plot as the offense which
introduces the good man to the experience of injustice. Thus,
though Antonio enters the play at "the solsticy / And highest
point of sunshine happiness" (1.2.178–79), with all the expectations of a fortunate bridegroom, Piero exerts an influence which
moves him from the height of joy to the depths of gloom.

The effect of this shock, in *Antonio's Revenge,* is to break down
the cooperative relationship that normally exists between reason
and passion. The opposing responses of Pandulpho and Antonio illustrate this psychic division. Marston seems to have hit
on a technique now familiarly discussed in terms of the "double"; he has embodied in Antonio the impetus toward revenge
(in other words, the preparation) and in Pandulpho the drawing
back from it (that is, the procrastination). By splitting the revenger in half, with Pandulpho embodying his reason and
Antonio his senses, the playwright can look more intensely at the
workings of each area of the psyche under the impact of the
injustice.

The intensity that we observe in Antonio, generally assumed
to stem from the playwright's attempts to appeal to the jaded
tastes of his audience or from his own "precariously balanced"
mentality, results more from the fact that Antonio is an embodiment of raw passion. Marston has firmly identified him with
the sensing areas of the psyche. In keeping with the psychological theories of the period, which saw grief as the seedbed for
the revenger's anger, Antonio is first associated with "boundless
woe." Not only is he smitten with all the physical symptoms of
excessive sorrow—his moist entrails crumpled up with parching
grief, his heart beating in punching anguish, and, as an outward
sign of this inward turmoil, his arms wreathed in abject melancholy; in addition his grief is magnified, here and throughout
the play, by means of Senecan hyperbole and inflating imagery:

> Cracks not the joints of earth to bear my woes?
>
> [1.2.268]

> Pigmy cares
> Can shelter under patience' shield, but giant griefs

> Will burst all covert.
>
> [2.2.4–6]

> Let none out-woe me; mine's Herculean woe.
>
> [2.2.134]

As a result, Antonio seems plunged so far into sorrow that ordinary means of assuaging it no longer apply. There is an aura of madness in this inordinate grief which defines the transformation that has taken place in Antonio under the influence of the shock administered by Piero. Bereft of reason by his "unbounded woe," he is a solid knot of passion.

In contrast, Marston depicts Pandulpho, the second revenger in the play, as the voice of unadulterated reason; his presence in *Antonio's Revenge* serves to indicate that there is another response to injustice than passionate fury, that of rational endurance. Pandulpho would not "cry, run raving up and down / For my son's loss . . . turn rank mad, / Or wring my face with mimic action" (1.2.312–14). He instead erects a barrier between his mind and ill fortune by wrenching evil into the form of good. He forces the world to conform to reason by personally removing evil from the environment.

A mistake often made by commentators dealing with *Antonio's Revenge* is to see Pandulpho as a touchstone. While at moments the old man seems to fulfill this function, as in the set debate with Piero in act 2, scene 1, at other times his behavior is far from ideal. Like Antonio, Pandulpho goes to extremes; his insistence upon reason is excessive. We can see this in two ways—through Pandulpho's emotional and through his philosophical responses—but for the time being we need note only the first of these. Marston's point here is not that Pandulpho lacks the emotions that Antonio displays so freely but, rather, that Pandulpho is deliberately attempting to cover up his emotions. That Pandulpho, in order to hold himself in check upon learning of his son's death, has to make such a grotesque overcorrection as to burst into laughter signifies immediately that all is not well. Commenting upon Feliche's mutilated body, which has been hung up in ignominy on the palace wall, he says to Antonio:

> Look, sweet youth,
> How provident our quick Venetians are

> Lest hooves of jades should trample on my boy;
> Look how they lift him up to eminence,
> Heave him 'bove reach of flesh. Ha, ha, ha.
>
> [1.2.306–10]

Pandulpho is properly reprimanded by Alberto for this lack of decorum. Pandulpho's reactions are highly strained. He is under a degree of stress of such magnitude that to maintain rational control he has to distort his whole personality. He goes beyond keeping his emotions in check and tries not to feel; to do this is to be inhuman.

This contrast between Pandulpho and Antonio is often recognized as a contrast but rarely seen as a contrast between two extremes. Through it Marston intimates that the shock which Piero's cruelty has inflicted upon the psyche works to split the sensing faculties and the rational faculties apart, so that neither can function correctly. The actions of the characters are more symbolic than realistic, and the structure of this first act, centering as it does upon the effects of evil upon the psyche, should warn us that we are not dealing with a conventional cause-and-effect plot.

Marston's plot technique is to focus upon intense moments in the experience of revenge and to render, in semisymbolic terms, the impact of the experience upon the mind of the revenger. Two of the most illuminating episodes in this regard are those which occur in act 3—the appearance of the Ghost and the resulting murder of Julio.

The central scene of *Antonio's Revenge* describes Antonio's visit to the tomb of Andrugio, his dead father, in Saint Mark's Church. As noted in chapter 1, Marston has economically united in this ghost functions that Kyd incorporated only through a chain reaction from Andrea to Revenge to Bel-imperia and Hieronimo. Marston's ghost speaks directly to the revenger. It informs Antonio of hidden facts—

> I was empoison'd by Piero's hand;
> Revenge my blood! Take spirit, gentle boy.
> Revenge my blood! Thy Mellida is chaste;
> Only to frustrate thy pursuit in love
> Is blaz'd unchaste. Thy mother yields consent
> To be his wife and give his blood a son,

> That made her husbandless and doth complot
> To make her sonless.
>
> [3.1.35–42]

and urges him to action:

> Thou vigor of my youth, juice of my love,
> Seize on revenge, grasp the stern-bended front
> Of frowning vengeance with impeised clutch.
> Alarum Nemesis, rouse up thy blood,
> Invent some strategem of vengeance
> Which, but to think on, may like lightning glide
> With horror through thy breast.
>
> [3.1.44–50]

Here in act 3, the Ghost is associated only with the revenge plot. Significantly, Marston presents it as an elemental force. It has an external reality, a supernatural existence, which makes it a personification of the universal sense of outrage against murder. Andrugio seems to be an embodiment of that law of nature which time has dignified with the title of *lex talionis*.

The passage in which it calls for vengeance presupposes that its authority is derived from a Vindicta or a Nemesis (not Heaven). The Ghost's justice bears little resemblance to the luminous justice of Astraea. Its justice is the black justice of "stark dead night," of clammy graves and moldy sepulchers, of "numb'd horror," "sing'ing torture," and spurting blood. Andrugio preaches the justice of nature, and, fittingly, requires Antonio to do obeisance at the altar of Vengeance (3.1.206). Nowhere does the Ghost, at this stage of the play, claim kinship with Providence; in fact, he ascends from and returns to a place no more ethereal than his coffin (3.1.34, 3.2.96).

Yet even about the coffin, one is reluctant to be too flip. There is something prodigious about Marston's use of Andrugio's monument as an altar, something primitive but powerful in the hint that Antonio's grief reaches into the grave, into the earth, and perhaps even deeper, into Hades to attract this wandering spirit which is seeking revenge. By making the tomb into an altar, Marston removes Antonio's revenge from the sphere of personal vindictiveness within which Piero operates. Andrugio's tomb becomes the center of that order of being that is represented by the Ghost and attaches to him the weight of religion.

At the same time, Marston recognizes that the forces of
vengeance which the Ghost speaks for work through human
psychology. In this sense, this spirit of revenge "enters" the revenger, intensifying the madness that had until now taken the
form of excessive grief. Antonio's grief is quickly elevated into
rage; this rage is soon pulsing through his entire being. A new
stage in the madness of revenge has been reached.

The immediate psychological effect of this intensification of
passion is to narrow the vision of the revenger even further:

> May I be cursed by my father's ghost
> And blasted with incensed breath of heaven,
> If my heart beat on ought but vengeance!
> May I be numb'd with horror and my veins
> Pucker with sing'ing torture, if my brain
> Digest a thought, but of dire vengeance;
> May I be fetter'd slave to coward chance,
> If blood, heart, brain, plot ought save vengeance!
>
> [3.1.85–92]

Preoccupied with his rage, Antonio tends to blot out all other
areas of experience from the psyche. This extreme single-
mindedness, characteristic also of Hieronimo, Titus, and Hamlet, and most especially of Vindice, is a primary symptom of the
revenge-madness, one essential to the build toward the concentrated personal world of the play-within-the-play and thus
one Marston is right in utilizing.

Not only does Marston's ghost kindle anger, it prompts Antonio to one of the worst excesses in revenge literature—the
murder of Julio. This scene has never been much appreciated;
Bowers, in fact, calls it "a purely gratuitous piece of business
brought in merely to make the audience shudder."[8] Indeed, as
one of those discrete scenes so characteristic of *Antonio's Revenge,*
it does pull loose from its surroundings. Quite obviously, it occurs too early in the play. The two-act gap between the death of
the boy Julio and the impact of that death upon Piero looms
large as a flaw in the play's construction. Moreover, with this
murder coming where it does, the audience is led to feel that if
Antonio is psychologically prepared to kill, he might just as well
have killed Piero as Julio, so that, as Bowers remarks, the "delay"
here seems calculated mainly to stretch the play out for another

two acts.[9] However, if we heed Hunter's warning, that it is the "separate attitudes," the "extreme states of mind," and not "the process by which these were arrived at" that interest Marston,[10] and if we concentrate on the attitude of excess which Marston is exploring, we can better accept the fact that Julio replaces Piero as Antonio's victim.

The Julio scene contains at least two insights into the madness of revenge which should be noted. First, Marston has attempted to reflect what the revenger would be feeling in Antonio's situation—intense anger coupled with a sense of frustration arising from the inability to hurt enough. Not reason but anger makes Antonio hesitate to kill Piero. Second, the dramatist has understood how the mind, under the pressure of a raging passion, can find an outlet for its pent-up emotions by striking out at surrogate targets. Once having hit upon the idea of injuring the Duke through Julio, Antonio transfers all of his rage to the boy and performs the murder with the same irrational fury he will muster in killing Piero in act 5. His mind transforms the boy into Piero.

Marston's insight into the psychology of revenge goes still deeper. He realizes that however extreme the degree of irrationality, there is a portion of the subconscious that rebels against the inhumanity involved in deeds of revenge. Consequently he portrays Antonio deliberately manufacturing in his mind a way of seeing Julio which makes the deed no murder. To Antonio's warped mind, the real Julio resides in the "dislodg'd soul" and since that soul lives on—unharmed—to be "twined with the soft'st embrace / Of clear eternity," no guilt is incurred.[11]

In constructing this scene Marston shows himself aware of how the madness motif can disclose that passion has affected the revenger's ability to view reality clearly. Antonio's mental state at this point is complex; on the one hand, he chooses to kill Julio because of his awareness that "injuries are not revenged except where they are exceeded," and on the other he must minimize to himself the horror of his deed, shaping it, in his mind, in a form that disguises its essential cruelty. Antonio's failure to recognize the fallacies in the argument that the body can be treated apart from the soul impresses upon us the extent to which his powers of perception are distorted. Insofar as it reveals how passion manipulates the mind in the revenger's plunge into excess, the Julio scene is not gratuitous.

So far we have been looking entirely at the "sensual" faculties of the revenger and neglecting the role of the reason. But Antonio is not the only one shattered by the cruelties of the tyrant; Pandulpho suffers as well. It was suggested earlier that Pandulpho's "rational" attempts to stifle the emotions aroused by the death of his son Feliche were futile and, in fact, opened him up to a charge frequently made by Renaissance psychologists against the Stoics, that they were "blocks" or "stones." It was also mentioned that Pandulpho attempted to push the reason too far in another way—through his philosophical responses. In act 4 Marston demonstrates this second inadequacy in the attitudes embodied in Pandulpho.

In the fourth act, Pandulpho breaks down. The implication here is that the Stoical philosophy does not adequately come to terms with injustice.[12] While Marston, like Kyd, hints that human reason cannot comprehend the mysterious quality of the world, in which such arbitrary evils as those wrought by Piero are abundantly in evidence, his personal vision leads him to take a slightly different approach to the problem than that found in *The Spanish Tragedy*. Whereas Hieronimo had to learn that the world was unjust, Pandulpho has known this fact all along; the instability of the world is one of the basic tenets of his philosophy as a Stoic (1.2.329–37). Pandulpho does not look for reason in the world but in man. His error lies in believing that man can cope with a world in which all coherence is gone, solely through his use of reason. Eventually he discovers that human reason cannot hold up under stresses of the kind which Piero imposes, at which point *his* world falls apart:

> Man will break out, despite philosophy.
> . . . I spake more than a god,
> Yet am less than a man.
> I am the miserablest soul that breathes.
>
> [4.2.69–76]

Pandulpho's excessive dedication to reason ultimately leads him back to the place where Antonio began: both feel themselves the "most miserable, most unmatch'd in woe" (4.2.80).

III As we have seen, Antonio and Pandulpho embody different aspects of the psyche, and up to this point they
have had contrasting attitudes about how to deal with Piero.
Reason has been reluctant to use violence and has responded
with a withdrawal from the oppressor and an attempt to transform evil into good by a deliberate act of the mind. Passion, on
the other hand, has gone to the direst extremes of cruelty,
striking out obliquely with an uncontrollable urge to retaliate but
achieving nothing in the way of abating the oppression. In the
interaction between the two revengers, there has only been the
inevitable cycle of preparation and procrastination, madness
and delay, with Antonio, for the most part, willing to move
ahead with full steam and Pandulpho applying the brakes. Neither really has been able to solve the problem of freeing the
psyche from the pressures exerted upon it.

In the meantime, Piero has proved himself unfit to rule. The
allegiance to virtue that governed the decisions of Kyd's King
and Duke have disappeared from Marston's state, where the
Machiavellianism of Lorenzo has taken over. The Duke of
Venice defends the politics of power and self-interest against
moral absolutes and finds honest men like Pandulpho an embarrassment. Act 1, scene 1; act 2, scenes 1 and 2; and act 4, scene 1,
dedicate themselves to displaying the tyrannical nature of this
villain. We watch Piero attempt to corrupt first Strotzo, then
Pandulpho, then Ballurdo. We see him banish those who do not
succumb to his wiles and exterminate those who do. We hear
him talk of the necessity of the ruler to "converse and cling to
routs of fools / That cannot search the leaks of his defects"
(4.1.112–13). Piero's allegiance to Machiavellian precepts, his
ruthless ambition, his careless disregard for his subjects (whom
he expects not only to endure but to praise his cruel acts), and,
finally, his intention to "conquer Rome, / Pop out the light of
bright religion (4.1.266–67)—all make him the epitome of the
corrupt ruler, as well as an emblem of new and destructive
trends in the political sphere.

How does one cope with such injustice? Marston's notion
seems to be that individual action is the only possible answer. For
him, the evil in question is so extraordinary that it is insupportable and under such conditions the natural and just approach is

to rebel against it. The action he envisions is the kind of heroic fortitude that combines the physical strength of a Hercules with the righteous anger of Saint Michael. Like the Herculean hero described by Eugene Waith, Marston's hero must exhibit "the power of the active man, called upon to shape the world in which he lives."[13]

By bringing Antonio and Pandulpho back together at the end of act 4, Marston signals that this stage in the cycle of oppression has been reached. Once reason, in the person of Pandulpho, has determined that evil of this magnitude is beyond the power of man to excuse or endure, the delay will end. Pandulpho's conversion arouses Antonio to action. It gives him direction just as he gives Pandulpho energy and drive. Thus, we have the image of passion and reason joining together, and in their unity "standing triumphant over Belzebub."

Significantly, it is right at this point—the moment the union is effected—that the playwright places renewed emphasis upon Piero's role as a tyrant and upon the call from the community for his removal. The evils of Piero, like those of Shakespeare's Richard III or his Macbeth, are said to be so great that to slay him is to "rid huge pollution from our state." Where the revenger usually acts alone, and with secrecy, Marston gives Antonio and Pandulpho the support of the whole society that customarily belongs to the hero of the retribution form. The rebels' plans are bolstered by the local citizens who are enraged by Piero's "ill-used power" and "deep villainy," by the individual states of Venice who are "swoll'n in hate" against the tyrant, and by Galeatzo, "the Florence Prince, / Drawn by firm notice of the Duke's black deeds" (5.1.14–15) to back the uprising. Heaven, too, according to Pandulpho, "sits clapping of our enterprise" (5.2.30). This unanimous encouragement continues even after the deed is committed. Antonio and Pandulpho, as the heroic individuals through whom harmony is restored to the kingdom, are offered in reward for their services everything that "outward pomp can yield, / Or chiefest fortunes of the Venice state" (5.3.140–41). All of this belongs entirely to the retribution plot. In Kyd's play the progress is from order to the utter chaos of madness and Hieronimo's bloody tragedy. But Marston, in the cause of "justice," deliberately counteracts this trend by giving his heroes the authority of a Richmond.

Further evidence that Marston intended the union to be seen as
a positive force leading to perfect justice can be gathered from the
care he has taken to pattern the murder to reflect the original
crimes exactly. In the final act of the play, the positions of Piero
and Antonio are reversed. Piero is now the bridegroom that
Antonio was in the first act and Antonio and Pandulpho the
oppressors. In this conclusion nothing is done to Piero that is
not specifically related to his own crimes. As he had killed
Pandulpho's son, so Antonio has killed Julio. As he had murdered
Antonio's father, so he, a father, will be murdered. As he had
prevented the marriage of Antonio and Mellida, so his own marriage will be disrupted. And most important of all, as Piero had
had neither pity nor remorse for his victims, so none must be
shown to him. Marston's concept of perfect justice has no room in
it for mercy. T. F. Wharton is quite right in emphasizing "the
precision with which punishment is fitted to crime."[14]

Unfortunately the emotional effect of this concluding action
upon the audience is not what Marston sought. He apparently
wished us to believe that order will be restored with the reunion
of Antonio and Pandulpho. But what we seem to have witnessed
in Pandulpho's decision to join with Antonio is the surrender of
reason to passion. The effect of Pandulpho's transformation appears rather to confirm Antonio in his madness than to raise him
out of it: Antonio responds with renewed fury and the action he
plans is no more "just" in the real sense than was his inhuman
assault upon poor Julio. The truth is that the kind of justice a
revenger effects is a "mad" justice and one cannot write truly of
the experience, as Marston does, and not come up with a scene
that erupts into insanity.

IV Despite all of Marston's efforts, the retribution plot fails
to convince us that its heroes are worthy of the admiration it requires us to give them. One reason for this is that it
cannot override the essential integrity of the revenge motifs;
they insist upon making their own statements. Another reason is
that Marston's profound insights into the passion of revenge,
which he never attempts to disguise, completely undermine his
conscious efforts to justify the passion. These are, of course,

really two aspects of one fundamental problem—Marston's ability to understand the *experience* of revenge but not its *implications*. What Marston grasps in this play is the psychology of the revenger. His empathy with the revenger is so great that there is almost no separation between character and author: he can follow Antonio into the very depths of the madness. Consequently he informs certain of Kyd's motifs—those dealing particularly with the passion, such as the ghost, the madness, and the play-within-the-play—with more immediacy than Kyd himself had given them. But his strength, unfortunately, does not extend to the metaphysics of revenge; here he lags well behind Kyd. Marston's point of view remains that of the revenger. It proceeds toward the personal emotional release that Antonio and Pandulpho feel after the ordeal is over, not toward any comprehensive statement about the complex and fascinating interrelationships between natural justice, earthly justice, and heavenly justice. The metaphysical statement that Marston makes at the end of the play (if one can claim at all that the play makes any consistent metaphysical statement) is reminiscent of Euripides: the irrational is so much an integral part of reality that ultimate reality is actually irrational; thus, passion is a truer guide to the truth than reason is. To act in accordance with the natural order, as Antonio and Pandulpho do, is to accept the will of the gods and to be lifted up, as a result, into a priestly class which it is beyond the powers of the rational community to comprehend. Now the revenge tragedy form, with its obligatory madness of the revenger, presupposes that a commitment to the irrational *limits* the amount of truth which the psyche can attain to through the descent into the self, for the very reason that the irrational keeps one preoccupied with the self. Thus, because Marston is not in tune with the metaphysical functions of the form, he fails to make those corrections in the motifs that must be made if the configuration is to serve his vision.

Let us look first at what happens to the motifs in act 5. First, Marston adapts the convention of the ghost to suit his own purpose without realizing that the motif has an integrity of its own which makes it totally unsuited for this use. When bringing the retribution plot together with the revenge action in preparation for Piero's overthrow, Marston foists upon the Ghost the duty of bestowing Heaven's blessing upon the saviors of the state. This is achieved in the soliloquy of Andrugio which opens act 5. The Ghost enters, still hovering about as the "clutch'd fist" of vengeance with which he was identified in act 3 but now ready to fall and "crush life's sap from out Piero's veins" (5.1.3–6). Then, through subtle movements of rhetoric, "vindicta" becomes "fate," fate is transformed into "Providence," and suddenly Providence and the Ghost become one. Both sit on high and peer down "t'attend the last act of my son's revenge" (5.1.11). The Ghost is now asking us to believe that the performance we are about to witness is sponsored by a just Heaven.

Insofar as Antonio and Pandulpho are conceived in roles which parallel those of Richmond or Malcolm, they must have the endorsement of Heaven, and the Ghost, with its supernatural origins, seems the likely candidate for the honor of bestowing it. But by now the Ghost is too closely associated with the excessses of revenge to serve this dual function. It operates quite well as the embodiment of the vindictive temperament and as such it can naturally applaud the outrages which occur within the masque, but it becomes silly when, while doing so, it purports to represent a Being who has always counseled turning the other cheek. This attempt to fuse the two forms through the agency of the ghost leads only to confusion: we cannot accept the old ghost in its new role.

So it is with the motif of the play-within-the-play; it, too, works only so long as Marston is using it for its original purpose and breaks down when he attempts to make it work against itself. Marston employs a masque for the climactic scene in which Piero is finally murdered. Of course, the purpose of this particular motif in the revenge tragedy form *is* to dramatize murder— indeed, often mass murder. And it does more. In *The Spanish Tragedy*, the play-within-the-play is designed to reveal the world of the revenger; it provides a way of getting into his mind at a moment when his madness is at its height. The play is not only Hieronimo's creation but also his attempt to order the world as he wants it to be. He shapes a world which he can step into and act in with complete freedom from the restraints which hold sway in the objective world; only within this fantasy world can he bring himself to the act of murder. The play-within-the-play, with its frenzied author and its babel of foreign languages, suggests for Kyd a mad world, a world grotesquely distorted in its perception of reality.

The masque-within-the-play in *Antonio's Revenge,* created jointly by Antonio and Pandulpho, functions in a similar way as a sealed-off world into which the revengers can step to take action. It goes even further in projecting onto the stage an image of the mind which is possessed by the passion of revenge than Hieronimo's play did. In this fantasy world the revengers allow themselves the freedom to indulge their every vengeful whim. Marston is expert in reproducing these violent fantasies. He places the obsession with the original offense at the forefront of the psyche (5.3.81–91). Growing out of the obsession he sees the desire to inflict every kind of suffering that can be imagined, and the imaginations of Marston's revengers are fertile. Pain alone is not enough—the torture of being forced to look upon the scorched remains of his son's limbs is only a prologue to a greater affliction planned for Piero, that of death. But death brings an end to suffering; before Piero can be granted that release, the revengers will have him "die and die, and still be dying. / And yet not die till he hath died and died / Ten thousand deaths in agony of heart" (5.3.105–7). They are driven to demand still more; they must have Piero damned so that his agony will continue even into the next life. Every emotional release from name-calling to brute violence upon the person of the offender is given expression, and coloring all (rendered by Marston in the joy with which Antonio throws himself into the dance, the glee of the spectator-ghost, and the state of exultation in which the parties afterwards vie for the credit of the deed) is the sense of exhilaration and pleasure the revengers obtain from the final consummation of their desire. Theatrical sensationalism, yes. But sensation which captures in all its savagery the ultimate essence of the madness of revenge.

Obviously a play-within-the-play which symbolizes the culmination of the revenger's madness is hardly a suitable climax to the retribution plot. If Antonio is to be accepted by the audience as a divine agent, the play-within-the-play must be dropped, or at least significantly toned down. The tyrant's crimes, however horrible, should not be made an excuse for another's inhumanity. For this very reason, Shakespeare, when using the retribution plot, originally made a battle the agency of the overthrow, usually one led by the lawful heir to the throne. In a battle the blame does not fall on any individual but is dispersed among many; even better, the tyrant may be killed in a fair fight. For the hero to remain blameless, he must dispose of the usurper officially and without personal passion. But Marston's intuitions into the mad world of the revenger go deep. He seems to have been unable to resist the temptation to include in his play a full study of the triumph which the revenger feels when his desire is finally fulfilled. Consequently, his play-within-the-play sits rather awkwardly on the retribution plot. It, too, fails to provide a convincing image of perfect justice.

There is another aspect of the play-within-the-play (as it takes its place in the configuration of motifs which make up the revenge tragedy form) that Marston has ignored. The effectiveness of the play as a setting for the long-postponed murder results from the contrast it allows the author to make between two ways of viewing reality—the subjective reality of the revenger revealed to us in the play can be set against objective reality as seen through the onlooker's reaction to the performance. As the play-within-the-play closes, the focus changes, and we see the revenger's deed from a wider perspective. In the world outside of *Soliman and Perseda*, Hieronimo will be held responsible for the mad act his subjection to passion has led him to commit. The feeling we are left with, once we draw back and look with the King's eyes upon the effects of Hieronimo's excess, is that the act of Hieronimo, though it in some strange and incomprehensible way may fulfill a higher purpose, is horrid and barbaric. Through Antonio in *The Revenger's Tragedy*, a similar perspective is provided upon Vindice's masqued actions. This double level of awareness is denied by Marston. The senators here, spokesmen for the larger community, view the "gory spectacle" of Piero's mangled remains from the vantage point of the revengers. Upon making the boast that "I pierc'd the monster's heart / With an undaunted hand" (5.3.122–23), Antonio is judged by the civil powers as a man to be "religiously held sacred, even for ever and ever" (5.3.128). The feeling we are left with in this case is again one of contrivance.

The death-of-the-avenger motif is similarly violated. Strangely enough, Marston shows himself fully aware that this

last motif is grounded in reality. He consciously acknowledges
that the demise of the revenger is required not by theatrical
convention but because the revenger, having exceeded the limitations of human prerogative, must pay for his presumption. We
glimpse this recognition through several statements on Antonio's part to the effect that when his work is done he means to
commit suicide (3.1.13–16, 4.2.18–22), as well as through the
admission by Pandulpho that self-destruction would be the natural sequel to their deed (5.3.147–48). The decision of the revengers to seclude themselves in a monastery is further evidence
of Marston's awareness that there was guilt attached to the revenge action; he was sensitive enough to realize that he could not
crown Antonio the new Duke of Venice and apparently made
some effort to satisfy the demands of the revenge tragedy form.
But he never endows Pandulpho or Antonio with the spirit of
humility and repentance which would have made their retire-
ment an acceptable alternative to suicide. On the contrary, he
thrusts upon the form his own personal feeling that the revengers had more than paid their reckoning in enduring the
suffering imposed on them by Piero and had been somehow
purified by the experience. They go off cleansed and purged. As
Peter declares, this strikes us as "preposterous lenience." Experience leads us to demand that Marston adhere to the convention.

Certainly it has not startled the readers of this essay to hear
again that the last act of *Antonio's Revenge* does not work. But
this, of course, is not the point being argued. The point is that
the motifs we have been speaking about have a relationship, one
to another, that is firmly grounded in the experience of revenge.
As a consequence, though their order can be altered, their number increased or decreased, and their specific meaning sometimes even changed (as is the ghost's in *The Atheist's Tragedy*), the
adaptations made in the motifs cannot be arbitrary but must take
into consideration the concepts behind the motifs. While
Marston was aided by the motifs to render his insights into the
passion of revenge with great impact and actuality, he was unable to use them in the way that others have done, to suggest on
stage the complex interworkings of the various levels of justice
that the faculties of man must try to comprehend. In not condemning his revenger, Marston ironically condemned his play.

Chapter 8

Hamlet

'Tis now the very witching time of night,
When churchyards yawn and hell itself breathes out
Contagion to this world. Now could I drink hot blood,
And do such bitter business as the day
Would quake to look on.

Shakespeare, Hamlet

To DISCUSS *Hamlet* solely in terms of revenge is somewhat like attending to the trellis rather than the rosebush it supports. Shakespeare's *Hamlet* transcends the revenge theme, and any criticism of it from this point of view alone can hardly be exhaustive. Yet the revenge theme in *Hamlet* cannot be ignored, for it is the basis of the play's structure: an interpretation that neglected it would be inadequate in the opposite direction. Nor could any study of the revenge tragedy motifs themselves be complete without considering *Hamlet,* the keystone of the genre.

Up to this point we have been dealing with flawed plays. *The Spanish Tragedy* was mocked even in its own time for its exaggerated rhetoric, and Hieronimo, because of his constant attitudinizing, has become to us more a comic figure than a tragic one; we will sooner smile at his hysteria than weep over the poignancy of his situation. The value of Kyd's experiment, as drama, lies primarily in the impulse it gave to subsequent writers to venture into new channels. *Antonio's Revenge,* too, has a mechanical quality that puts us off. Since its characters lack both credibility and scope, they do not win our admiration, and the episodes, occasionally interesting in themselves, never really convey to us a sense that each scene follows inevitably from its predecessor. *Antonio's Revenge* remains of interest for scholars mainly as a result of plot similarities between it and *Hamlet,* which have led to speculations of their common origin in a Hamlet play by Kyd. Because of the aesthetic inferiority of these early works, the revenge play has gained, both in its own time and ours, the reputation for vulgarity.

In *Hamlet,* we find everything transmuted. A finer imagination is at work and its effects upon the material are evident at every level of the play, from dramaturgical invention to intellectual scope. The revenge experience is now linked to another, a wider experience, the experience of knowing. Shakespeare's protagonist, thrust into the dilemma of the revenger, focuses on his own mind's reactions to the experience as much as on the experience itself. Of necessity he must also probe the mind of Claudius, and in the process he inspects as well the minds of Gertrude, Polonius, and Ophelia. All of the other major characters desire to unlock and enter Hamlet's mind. The very structure of the scenes reflects this basic human drive to know. In one scene after another Shakespeare utilizes the "observation sequence," wherein a concealed character spies on another in the attempt to creep unawares upon his thoughts and capture them. So strong is this idea that the play itself seems to ask, how much can one man see of another man's mind? How completely can he comprehend his own? And how far can he penetrate into that unseen realm beyond, the "undiscover'd country" to which the human mind is the only gate?[1] Again and again the revenge motifs are adapted to illuminate these, the central questions of human existence. It is a testimony to the basic rightness of Kyd's impulses that in expressing this personal vision through the revenge tragedy form, Shakespeare not only uses all of the motifs found in the prototype but respects their essential integrity as a configuration grounded in experience.

I   Our initial experience in *Hamlet* is of the ghost. And this is as good a place as any to begin an examination of the refinements Shakespeare made in the form. Earlier scholars, in writing about the evolution of the revenge-tragedy ghost, uni-

versally express a sense of relief when King Hamlet takes over
from Andrea and Andrugio. J. A. Symonds's response is typical:

> Shakspere, who omitted nothing in the tragic apparatus of his pre-
> decessors, but with inbreathed sense and swift imagination woke
> those dead things to inorganic life, employed the Ghost, all know
> with what effect, in "Hamlet" and "Macbeth" and "Julius Caesar." It
> is not here the place to comment upon Shakspere's alchemy—the
> touch of nature by which he turned the coldest mechanisms of the
> stage to spiritual use. Enough to notice that, in his hands, the Ghost
> was no longer a phantom roaming in the cold, evoked from Erebus to
> hover round the actors in a tragedy, but a spirit of like intellectual
> substance with these actors, a parcel of the universe in which all live
> and move and have their being.[2]

Symonds's enthusiasm is matched by many in the generations
that followed him. But often, as here, the improvements in the
motifs are discussed almost exclusively in terms of dramaturgy.
The skill with which the motifs are radically altered to fit
Shakespeare's personal vision, and yet altered so carefully that
they retain their integral relationships with the experience of revenge, is still rarely appreciated, even in *Hamlet*. In analyzing the
ghost motif, therefore, we shall attempt to distinguish between
those refinements stemming from Shakespeare's superior
dramaturgical instincts and those occurring because of his
deeper insights into life.

One of the dramaturgical functions of Kyd's ghost was to provide exposition; Andrea acts as a prologue. Not so in Marston, who preferred to emphasize the effects of the ghost upon
the revenger. Marston let Piero acquaint the audience with his
own villainy and delayed the ghost's entrance until the time
came for Antonio to learn what Piero had already told the
viewers. Shakespeare, by beginning his revenge action in the
middle, creates a situation in which the ghost both apprises us of
past events and informs Hamlet of Claudius's guilt. This magnificent bit of restructuring permits Shakespeare to come immediately to the crucial point in the revenge action, without
spending two acts (as Marston does) on the static lamentations of
grief. It also provides him with a compelling and suspenseful
introduction to his play. This early introduction of the ghost
focuses the drama squarely upon the question "what will Hamlet
do with the information given him by the Ghost?" Shakespeare's

use of the ghost as an expository device goes far beyond anything that his predecessors had done for dramaturgical bril-
liance. It makes the ghost an integral part of the action.

   The skillful positioning of the ghost's revelation is not all that
differentiates this ghost from earlier ones. Shakespeare's ghost,
as many have noted, has been given a character. Earlier playwrights were satisfied if their ghosts communicated an aura of
terror. It was enough that there was on stage "a voice mouthing
vengeance."[3] The point was made. Shakespeare's ghost is hu-
manized. It appears in a "fair and warlike form," the customary
"foul sheet" of the earlier ghost abandoned for martial armor.
No ghost before King Hamlet had been particularized so vividly:

> So frown'd he once when in an angry parle
> He smote the sledded Polacks on the ice.
>
> > [1.1.62–63]

> It was about to speak, when the cock crew.
> And then it started, like a guilty thing
> Upon a fearful summons.
>
> > [1.1.147–49]

> > Look with what courteous action
> It waves you to a more removed ground.
>
> > [1.4.60–61]

These details are quite aside from those that describe King
Hamlet while he was alive; the details here vitalize the Ghost *as
ghost*. On the bulwarks we see him move "with martial stalk," we
watch him appear and disappear at will, and we find him "as the
air, invulnerable" to the sword thrusts of the baffled soldiers.
Later we learn that the Ghost has a keen interest in the world he
has been separated from and would influence its events; he desires to be revenged upon Claudius but—a humanizing detail
much appreciated by critics—would protect Gertrude. We also
discover something about the way the Ghost spends his time in
the afterworld—Old Hamlet, having been "sent to my account /
With all my imperfections on my head," apparently has sins
upon his soul which he must expiate and is therefore "doom'd
for a certain term to walk the night, / And for the day confin'd to
fast in fires." The suffering which he undergoes in his "prison
house," he informs us, is as horrible to imagine as the crime

which put him there. These details have a definite dramatic
purpose; they endow the ghost of Denmark's former king with a
vivid and memorable character. Where Marston's Ghost is
plainly and simply an embodiment of the passion he symbolizes,
Shakespeare's is that and a particular human soul as well.[4]

Yet Shakespeare has not sacrificed those supernatural qualities which give the ghost its significance in terms of the revenge
tragedy form. He clearly links his ghost with the world beyond.
Much theological discussion has been occasioned by the references to purgatory made by the Ghost, but Robert West is correct in warning that it is unnecessary to search for—is indeed
impossible to pin down—the religious denomination of this
wandering spirit. The same references to the afterworld which
serve to humanize the Ghost also emphasize, as West asserts, "its
tenuity, its frightfulness, its special knowledge, and the dubiety
of its nature and purposes," in other words, its mystery.[5] The
fear and awe with which its sudden appearances and unearthly
manner inspire those who first detect it work in the same way. As
the onlookers—Marcellus, Bernardo, and Horatio—are "har-
rowed with fear and wonder," as they "tremble and look pale,"
as they connect the appearance of the apparition with "some
strange eruption to our state" and set it in the context of the
times when "graves stood tenantless and the sheeted dead / Did
squeak and gibber in the Roman streets," we, too, experience
their terror. No ghost is more humanly real than the Ghost in
Hamlet, yet at the same time no ghost is less of this world.

Few people would challenge the supernatural reality of the
Ghost, but not all understand clearly the reason for Shakespeare's insistence that the Ghost is not a figment of Hamlet's
imagination.[6] Many, for example, believe that the Ghost is issu-
ing a command that has a divine origin—Hamlet is, for them, a
hand-chosen agent of God, even though the Ghost's demands
contradict the orthodox teachings of Holy Writ.[7] Because
Shakespeare has the Ghost call attention to the difference between its brand of justice, which is to be applied to Claudius, and
a higher justice, that to which Gertrude is subject, one is probably correct in assuming that the playwright did not wish to
identify the Ghost's justice with Heaven's. Moreover, the dramatic origins of the Ghost in an amalgamation of Kyd's Andrea
and his allegorical companion Revenge, the presentation of this

figure as something that loses its power under the influence of
the Savior, and the Ghost's own emphasis upon Hamlet's being
bound by a natural rather than a religious duty, all suggest that
Shakespeare, like his predecessors, viewed the Ghost as an embodiment of the spirit of revenge. Yet like them he sees this
spirit as something more than human instinct. It does exist
within the individual—Hamlet's "O my prophetic soul" testifies
to this—but, as a "force" of nature which all men recognize, it
has at the same time an ontological reality, a universality, that is
as mysterious and as difficult to comprehend as is the Ghost
itself. Shakespeare has used every device in his power to assert
both the reality and the compelling authority of this irrational
external force which the Ghost embodies.

That authority, of course, and the nature of the offense which
draws the specter back to earth to make his demands, distinguishes this revenge from those (like Ferdinand's in *The
Duchess of Malfi*) involving perverse and diabolical fury far out of
proportion to the cause. If the Ghost tells us anything, it tells us
that the crimes of Claudius are so insupportable that Nature
itself has broken form, thrusting itself "unnaturally" into the
human order to insure that the crimes will not go unpunished.
Shakespeare, it should be noted, presents the authority as having a binding effect upon the avenger; the action of *Hamlet* is far
less concerned with the revenger's movement toward a decision
to abandon the divine and embrace the natural (as in *The Spanish
Tragedy*) than with his attempt to comprehend the relationship
between the two conflicting imperatives. Shakespeare's Ghost
has a near-absolute authority that makes it a forceful antagonist
to the Everlasting whose canons Hamlet would also adhere to
and thus places the prince in the classic tragic situation: either
way that he moves will be right—and thus wrong.

While Shakespeare's Ghost retains the symbolic role it had
held in *The Spanish Tragedy* and *Antonio's Revenge*, stirring Hamlet into a rage against Claudius and thus initiating the fatal impulse toward excess, it is also made the carrier for a new theme.
This Ghost embodies, simultaneously, its creator's vision of
human perfection. We are told that in his lifetime the elder
Hamlet was a judicious king, a valiant warrior, a devoted husband, and a beloved father. But he is even more than this.
Hamlet could envision man to be "noble in reason," "infinite in

faculties," in action "like an angel," in apprehension "like a god," because he had such a model before him in the person of his father:

> See what a grace was seated on this brow:
> Hyperion's curls, the front of Jove himself,
> An eye like Mars, to threaten and command,
> A station like the herald Mercury
> New lighted on a heaven-kissing hill,
> A combination and a form indeed,
> Where every god did seem to set his seal
> To give the world assurance of a man.
>
> [3.4.55–62]

The elder Hamlet shows us man raised to his highest potential. Still the former king is more. Constant comparisons are made between him and Claudius that indicate what Denmark has had to settle for in his place—one brother with an eye like Mars, the other but a mildewed ear; the former a fair mountain, the latter a barren moor; the first Hyperion, the second a foul satyr. Through the juxtaposition of the two characters and their respective reigns, Shakespeare associates the dead king with the noble past, the usurper with a "poisoned" present, so that King Hamlet emerges as a symbol of an irrecoverable Golden Age.

Many commentators speak as though Shakespeare's modifications of the ghost motif can be explained simply on the principle of good taste. Not so. The new symbolism assigned to the Ghost arises from the necessities of Shakespeare's own personal vision. In taking up the revenge form, Shakespeare uses it to explore in depth a concept that has been only latent in the earlier tragedies we have examined—the attempt of the revenger to come to terms with evil. Both Hieronimo and Antonio puzzle over the problem but in neither play is the theme so integrally related to both character and plot as in *Hamlet*.

Evil impinges itself upon Hamlet initially through his widowed mother's hasty acceptance of Claudius. Her callousness adds to his realization that a great man such as his father can die, the painful knowledge that greatness can be forgotten "within a month." Already he begins to question the value of life. His later disovery, that Claudius had murdered his father, shatters him completely, and where before he only longed for death now he actively contemplates suicide. If this is what the world is like, concludes Hamlet, then no action is worthwhile. At the same time, the father whose very loss has led him to this conclusion enjoins Hamlet to undertake the ultimate act of murder on his behalf. This is the basis of Hamlet's dilemma and the conflict from which plot, character, and theme will develop. It becomes essential, therefore, because of the nature of Shakespeare's vision, not only that the Ghost embody the spirit of revenge but also that it epitomize human dignity, majesty, and worth.

It is a testimony to the genius of Shakespeare that these seemingly incompatible demands of the form and the vision have been reconciled. A labor of Hercules is required to yoke together a ghost conceived after Kyd as that vengeful unrelenting force which is released into the world to restore order when an imbalance is created and the ghost as Shakespeare's personal vision required it; that is, to superimpose upon the prototype that majestic demigod we see through the reminiscences of Hamlet and Horatio. The adaptation is as radical as the one made by Marston when he attempted to present the ghost as the agent of Heaven, and we have just noted how badly Marston failed in tampering with the motif. Yet Shakespeare has *not* failed.

Why do we not reject Shakespeare's Ghost? One reason is that to facilitate the merger Shakespeare has played down the Ghost's connection with excess, leaving this aspect to develop from the action of the play rather than from the will of the Ghost and instead associating the Ghost subtly, through its solicitude for Gertrude, with compassion. The events which convey the sense of excess, Polonius's death, for example, or Ophelia's madness, remain direct by-products of Hamlet's pursuit of vengeance, but they seem to occur accidentally. Neither Hamlet nor the Ghost is made responsible in the brutal way that their counterparts in *Antonio's Revenge* are responsible for the death of Julio and the subsequent cannibalistic defiling of that boy's body. Given Hamlet's character (and the playwrights invariably seem to make their ghosts reflect the characters of their revengers), it is more fitting that the excess, though inevitable, should arise as an accidental rather than a deliberate result of the revenge passion. This dramaturgical structuring which slightly divorces the excess from the original demands of the ghost helps us to accept the exalted role which the ghost now plays.

There is another technique used to render the adaptation in the ghost motif acceptable. The perfection associated with Old Hamlet has to do with his former life and, being a picture of the past, is somewhat detached from his present activities as a vindictive ghost; indeed, the fact that so magnificent a personage was less than immortal, and the human condition such that he could be reduced to the level at which we find him on the battlements, serves more to sharpen our sense of loss than to make us question Shakespeare's artistry. Thus, the very nobility of the Ghost's past tends to convince us that what it asks of Hamlet is far more reasonable than what Andrugio had asked of Antonio, even though in essence the request of both ghosts is the same. Shakespeare has so controlled our responses that the image of the old king as a paragon of men is never tainted by his demand for vengeance but, on the contrary, his demand seems the more justified, on the grounds that the corruption which set in upon his death must be reversed. An adaptation that in lesser hands might have come across as a gross contradiction appears in Shakespeare's no discrepancy.

It will do us no good to appreciate Shakespeare's artistry if we are not clear about exactly what this ghost does ask for, as the demand made upon the prince dictates the action of the entire play. Exactly what does this spirit of revenge demand? And is that demand just? The Ghost asks Hamlet to punish Claudius for a heinous deed, a deed for which the punishment of death is well deserved. It demands that Hamlet respond in terms of the law of nature—blood for blood—not in terms of courts and trials (a course which in any event is impossible because of Claudius's position as the highest authority in the realm). Hamlet must kill his uncle, mercilessly, in cold blood. There is a justice to the Ghost's demand for the king's death, and certainly this deed of Hamlet's will have beneficial results for the state, which Claudius is polluting. In fact, Shakespeare sets up the situation in such a way that Hamlet cannot refuse to comply, for Claudius *must* be punished and, the plot tells us, *only* Hamlet can do it. Yet though the end is good, the means to that justice involve irrational actions which will in their turn need to be punished. To do what the Ghost asks is to risk damnation, to avoid it seems like cowardice, and to escape the whole problem through suicide is only to arrive back at square one—daring damnation. Hamlet has two choices—dishonor or self-destruction—and recognizes early the ironic injustice in his own plight. A further danger in the situation, one Hamlet does *not* foresee, is that where the order of nature is involved what begins as a desire for justice can run amuck and end in inconceivable waste. Here again there is the potential for injustice. The Ghost's demand, while having a strong element of justice and even necessity about it, has also, in itself and its effects, a tendency to initiate further injustice. The situation is unavoidably tragic.

II Let us now turn to the knotty problem of Hamlet's madness. It is hoped that the revenger's madness has been presented in this book in terms that will allow the reader to accept the word *madness* as a suitable name for the mental state which surfaces in young Hamlet after he meets with the Ghost. Nevertheless, Hamlet is the least maddened of all revengers. As we have defined it, the revenger's madness is a state of mind originating in a temporary fit of excessive passion but later magnified into an obsession by the subsequent refusal to expel the root cause of that passion from the mind. In avengers like Titus or Hieronimo, the fits increase in intensity and duration and occur with greater and greater frequency, while the periods of lucidity diminish concurrently. But all revengers are not equally distraught. The personal vision of the playwright, combined with the character traits he has given his hero, determine the extent to which the revenger lapses into insanity. In this play we find a revenger who has a surprisingly high degree of control. Thus, in insisting upon the madness of Hamlet, we are asserting only (1) that Shakespeare has drawn a mind in which the passion of revenge has gained a definite foothold and (2) that passion's effect upon the psyche is a primary subject of the drama. Hamlet never goes the full route into lunacy.

Definite refinements have been made upon the madness motif in *Hamlet.* An important step in appreciating what Shakespeare had done with this motif is to recognize that two separate conventions are involved. There is the "antic disposition," which, technically, must be understood in terms of the disguise convention and compared to Hieronimo's third-act impersonation of the patient man, Antonio's transformation into a fool, and Vindice's appearance as Piato. Then there is Hamlet's "sore distraction," which involves the actual state of his psyche as it attempts to deal with the injunction placed upon him by the Ghost. Strictly speaking, the madness motif pertains only to the sore distraction. Yet the disguise and the madness motifs in revenge tragedy are closely related, for, as we have seen, the disguise underscores the dislocations of identity taking place in the hero. It is thus in Hamlet: the disguise, that is, the antic disposition, indicates that "nor th' exterior nor the inward man / Resembles that it was." Because of this, and also because the particular disguise Hamlet chooses is that of lunacy, the antic disposition must be considered in any discussion of the madness itself. "Antic disposition" and "sore distraction" then, or disguise and madness—to these two conventions Shakespeare has given intense life.

Exactly how do the two motifs of disguise and madness interact in *Hamlet*? What Shakespeare has done with them exceeds what he has done with the ghost. It is obvious from *Titus Andronicus* that Shakespeare realized the purpose of madness in the revenge story—that a good man will commit the act of murder only in high passion. His problem was to make the madness credible without making it stagy or sensational. Given his personal vision of Hamlet as the courtier, soldier, scholar, it would not do to send him out to fire arrows at Jupiter. Some more subtle dramatic device was needed to convey to the audience the sense that Hamlet is "mad."

Fortunately the source story already contained the perfect solution; in it, the revenger feigns madness. Shakespeare uses the madness of craft with double effectiveness. First, though the antic disposition does not replace the madness, it emphasizes Hamlet's distraction by making his mental state a matter of central concern to others (and thus to the audience) from the moment Hamlet returns from his interview with the Ghost uttering "wild and whirling words." Second, while making the question of the madness more central, the antic disposition simultaneously distances us from Hamlet's real madness and consequently renders that madness more mysterious.

Let's take the last point first. Because Hamlet drops into his chosen role and out of it as occasion demands, the disguise creates an ambiguity that is reflected in the endless critical debate over Hamlet's madness—is he mad or is he not? And if he is mad, *when* is he mad? Certainly in many instances we are perfectly aware that Hamlet has switched into his antic disposition, and at such moments we are far more conscious of the operation of intelligence and a quick wit than of a warped imagination:

Polonius.	What do you read, my lord?
Hamlet.	Words, words, words.
Polonius.	What is the matter, my lord?
Hamlet.	Between who?
Polonius.	I mean, the matter that you read, my lord.
Hamlet.	Slanders, sir; for the satirical rogue says here that old men have grey beards . . .

[2.2.191–97]

As Polonius says, there is method in such madness, and we delight in it, as Hamlet himself does. In this sense Hamlet's "playing" serves to unveil the hypocrisy in others. But there are moments when the distinction between reality and role is not so clear, moments when it seems that Hamlet *has* to grasp at the role to disguise emotions that are about to overwhelm him. Such is the case in the "nunnery scene" with Ophelia. Here the antic disposition blends with something that lies very deep in Hamlet's troubled consciousness. The scene is so written that it will never really give up its essential mystery and reveal to us where Hamlet's acting ends and his own agony begins. There are also moments when we are not sure whether Hamlet is feigning at all. The ambiguities constantly being generated by the antic disposition make it impossible to distinguish where sanity ends and madness begins. The uncertainty is deliberate. Through it, Shakespeare shows us that the revenge passion has thrown Hamlet off balance. He also makes us feel the limitations one man labors under when he would know another man's mind.

This brings us back to our initial point about the antic disposition. If Hamlet's own behavior as he endeavors to seem mad tends to make us wonder about his real state, so also does the constant reiteration by everyone else of the statement that Hamlet is mad. Hamlet's ruse gives the opposing forces at the court their primary motivation in the early acts of the play—their desire to discover the reason for his alteration. As a direct result of this disguise, Shakespeare is able to fill the play with

references to Hamlet's madness. These come primarily from
Claudius and Gertrude:

Claudius.   Something have you heard
                          Of Hamlet's transformation; so call it,
                          Sith nor th' exterior nor the inward man
                          Resembles that it was.

                                                          [2.2.4–7]

Claudius.   An' can you by no drift of conference
                          Get from him why he puts on this confusion,
                          Grating so harshly all his days of quiet
                          With turbulent and dangerous lunacy?

                                                          [3.1.1–4]

Gertrude.   And for your part, Ophelia, I do wish
                          That your good beauties be the happy cause
                          Of Hamlet's wildness.

                                                          [3.1.37–39]

Claudius.   I like him not, nor stands it safe with us
                          To let his madness range.

                                                          [3.3.1–2]

Gertrude.   O gentle son,
                          Upon the heat and flame of thy distemper
                          Sprinkle cool patience.

                                                          [3.4.122–24]

Claudius.   How does Hamlet?
Gertrude.   Mad as the sea and wind when both contend
                          Which is the mightier.

                                                          [4.1.6–8]

The king and the queen, who are continually discussing
Hamlet's "lawless fit," are echoed by enough members of the
court to make us feel that everyone in the play is convinced of
the truth of the charge:

Horatio.   He waxes desperate with imagination.

                                                          [1.4.87]

Polonius.   I have found
                          The very cause of Hamlet's lunacy.

                                                          [2.2.48–49]

Rosencrantz. Good my lord, what is your cause of distemper?

                                                          [3.2.337]

Against this kind of subliminal persuasion that Hamlet is mad,
we have the prince's own protestations ("I know a hawk from a
hand-saw" and so on); however, these are undercut by his occasional admissions to the contrary. In actual fact, Ophelia's comment leaves the most lasting impression on us; it seems to express so much of what we feel:

> O, what a noble mind is here o'erthrown!
> The courtier's, soldier's, scholar's, eye, tongue, sword,
> Th' expectation and rose of the fair state,
> The glass of fashion and the mould of form,
> Th' observ'd of all observers, quite, quite down!
> And I, of ladies most deject and wretched,
> That suck'd the honey of his music vows,
> Now see that noble and most sovereign reason
> Like sweet bells jangled out of time, and harsh;
> That unmatch'd form and feature of blown youth
> Blasted with ecstasy. O, woe is me
> T' have seen what I have seen, see what I see!
>
> [3.1.150–61]

Ophelia has been misled in this scene by Hamlet's disguise. But
such is the poetry of her speech, such her love of Hamlet (resembling ours), that her lament seems to catch the essence of
Hamlet's character and situation.

In short, though we know intellectually that Hamlet feigns
madness, we submit emotionally to the repeated suggestion that
Hamlet is no longer himself. Thus, through this double use of
the antic disposition to create ambiguity and to provide a bar-
rage of witnesses who doubt Hamlet's sanity, Shakespeare gets
the effect of a madness without debasing Hamlet. Nowhere else
in revenge tragedy is the disguise used so inventively or so pro-
foundly.[8]

By itself the dramaturgical manipulation of the audience described above is not sufficient to render fully the experience of
madness which is so essential a part of the tragedy of revenge.
Shakespeare is neither dishonest nor unwilling to confront the
task of representing the madness on the stage as it really is. But
here again, Shakespeare goes far beyond the commonplace.

Undoubtedly Shakespeare means us to see that the burden the
Ghost has imposed upon Hamlet has altered the prince and that
the alteration takes the form of a "distraction." Hamlet himself

chooses this term to express the effect of the Ghost's revelation
upon his psyche:

> Remember thee!
> Ay, thou poor ghost, whiles memory holds a seat
> In this *distracted* globe.
>
> [1.5.95–97]

Significantly he uses the term again in his apology to Laertes at
the end of the play:

> This presence knows,
> And you must needs have heard, how I am punish'd
> With *a sore distraction*. What I have done
> That might your nature, honor, and exception
> Roughly awake, I here proclaim was madness.
> Was't Hamlet wrong'd Laertes? Never Hamlet!
> If Hamlet from himself be ta'en away,
> And when he's not himself does wrong Laertes,
> Then Hamlet does it not, Hamlet denies it.
> Who does it then? His madness. If 't be so,
> Hamlet is of the faction that is wronged,
> His madness is poor Hamlet's enemy.
>
> [5.2.228–39]

This speech has puzzled critics. Prosser, as we have noted, finds
it incomprehensible: "Samuel Johnson and others have wished,
and with good warrant," she says, "that Hamlet had not offered
his nonexistent madness as a defense. The curious wording of
the speech may, of course, be simply a lapse on Shakespeare's
part."[9] Prosser rightly sees that for Hamlet to lie at this point
would be an act of grotesque cowardliness and senses that, on
the contrary, he means to be supremely honest. In truth, his
admission to Laertes is both a polite acknowledgment that in his
distraction he had indeed wronged his friend and a sincere request for forgiveness. It also records the deeper insight into
himself which Hamlet has gained during the period of that distraction.

There could be no better example of the difficulties arising
from the alteration in the meaning of the word *madness* over the
centuries. Hamlet will always be misunderstood by those who do
not associate inordinate passion with madness and who thus fail
to realize that he is hardly claiming a clinical lunacy. The con-

ceits of the speech are grounded in the Elizabethan concept that
to act in passion is to be divided from reason and thus from
oneself. Shakespeare has chosen a moment when it is impossible
for the prince to play false to allow Hamlet to reveal an awareness that he has indeed been sorely distracted. Having this authority from Hamlet himself, let us look into the nature of the
distraction.

Exactly what does the real alteration in Hamlet's character
involve? How does this alteration differ from those which stem
from his disguise? First, there is the change that gives Hamlet
the dimensions of the tragic hero. Under the impact of the confrontation with evil, Hamlet is thrust off the level of appearances, turned away from the shadows of the cave, so to speak,
toward the light. One aspect of his madness involves a descent
into the self which is both painful and elevating. There is a
potential for illumination in this suffering and, though Hamlet
(unfortunately) dies before attaining full knowledge, his desperate attempts to comprehend the nature of the universe which
could harbor so much evil raise him, even in his madness, far
above the less sensitive creatures who surround him.

Nevertheless, the passion takes the usual toll. His initial efforts
to come to terms with his situation are hampered by the disorientation of his psyche. For example, there is a marked narrowing of the vision in the altered Hamlet. Shakespeare follows
his predecessors in pointing out this tendency of the disturbed
imagination to limit its focus:

> Remember thee!
> Yea, from the table of my memory
> I'll wipe away all trivial fond records,
> All saws of books, all forms, all pressures past
> That youth and observation copied there,
> And thy commandement all alone shall live
> Within the book and volume of my brain,
> Unmix'd with baser matter.

[1.5.97–104]

This narrowing of the vision originates, of course, with Hamlet's
grief. The shock of his father's death and the subsequent insen-
sitivity of his mother to the loss changes Hamlet's attitude toward the world, which he begins to look upon in disillusion. The

ghost, with its revelation that the old king's death was not a natural one but a murder "most foul, strange and unnatural," gives his son further justification for disgust. Moreover, the betrayal of friendship which Hamlet detects soon afterward in Rosencrantz and Guildenstern and the seeming betrayal of love which occurs when Polonius makes Ophelia desert Hamlet push him still further into the belief—very real to him but actually only a partial truth—that evil has pervaded every aspect of existence. Hamlet discovers that the values he and the others have lived by constitute nothing more than a communal fantasy and that if he is to find justice he must seek for it within himself.

Being so narrowly focused upon evil, Hamlet's vision of it becomes supersensitive. Not only has he grasped the exact nature of Claudius's guilt. Better than anyone Hamlet analyzes as well the general frailties of mankind—recoiling from the ugliness of particular vices:

> Nay, but to live
> In the rank sweat of an enseamed bed,
> Stew'd in corruption, honeying and making love
> Over the nasty sty!
>
> [3.4.91–94]

recoiling also from the innate sinfulness of the species:

> Why wouldst thou be a breeder of sinners? I am myself indifferent honest, but yet I could accuse me of such things that it were better my mother had not borne me. I am very proud, revengeful, ambitious, with more offenses at my beck than I have thoughts to put them in, imagination to give them shape, or time to act them in. What should such fellows as I do crawling between earth and heaven? We are arrant knaves . . . .
>
> [3.1.120–28]

But, alas, generalizing from his own experiences, Hamlet unfortunately sees evil even where it is not, making Gertrude's frailty the failing of all women and condemning the honest Ophelia along with the rest. His new outlook makes him reject *all* that is good in himself and in the world. As a result, Hamlet takes up a position at the opposite pole from the one he held in his days of innocence. His grand vision of the universe and man's exalted place in it is replaced by a feeling that he is surrounded by a "foul and pestilent congregation of vapors." Man is reduced to a "quintessence of dust." Hamlet sees all of the world in terms of his own problem and is blinded to other areas of life. Remarkable though his insights may be, they generate an excess which is unhealthy. His limited view of existence is a misleading and dangerous one.

Another result of this concentration upon evil is that Hamlet becomes excessively self-righteous. Just as he is extreme in his searching out and labeling evil, so also he is excessive in his demands for perfection. He tends to set himself up as a god (a very *stern* god), passing judgments not only on Claudius, Gertrude, Ophelia, Polonius, Rosencrantz, and Guildenstern but on human frailty in general. Yet he fails to deal equally sternly with his own shortcomings, except to note them in passing. He does recognize that he has faults; he throws that bone to us. But once he has stated them, they are to be dismissed. There is no deep remorse, only the conviction that he himself, as heaven's scourge and minister, must singlehandedly chastise, punish, and reform errant humanity. There is a real heroism in Hamlet in his attempt to carry out the mission which the Ghost has assigned him, yet, ironically, his good qualities and his valid insights into the grubbiness of the world backlash on him into a form of pride, a callousness toward human life that is a further indication of his alteration.

Shakespeare, like Kyd, presents the distraction not as a given state but as a state that one passes into and out of. The critic is most nearly correct if he writes that Hamlet has *moments* of madness. Of those moments, two stand out as distinctly belonging to the distraction rather than the antic disposition. During and just after the interview with the Ghost Hamlet may definitely be described as mad, and he enters this distracted state again at the end of the play-within-the-play. In this latter moment his madness reaches its greatest intensity. But the degree of madness even at this point falls far short of that found in any other revenger.

Were Hamlet less intelligent than he is, the perception that the time is out of joint, combined with the overwhelming desire to set it right which is a distinguishing characteristic of the Kydian revenger, would drive Hamlet into a lunacy rivaling that of Hieronimo or Titus. Certainly Hamlet never questions the necessity of the act of revenge. When he hesitates to kill

Claudius, he does so either because he is not sure that the Ghost's word regarding Claudius's guilt can be trusted or because he believes Claudius's soul stands on better terms with Heaven than he would have it. The question he does ask, however, is "Is it worth it?" Granted that there is a need to act, the very fact that the world is so sordid that the action is required raises the question for Hamlet of whether that action is worthwhile. Rather than rushing headlong into passion, Hamlet is constantly intellectualizing the problem, with the consequence that the madness is greatly attenuated.

A primary point about Hamlet's madness is that Hamlet continually brings it under control. Shakespeare has envisioned a revenger whose comprehension of his situation is far greater than that of his predecessors and who therefore cannot help subjecting his own situation to the scrutiny of reason. Consequently, though in Hamlet there is the usual war for supremacy between the reasonable soul and the sensitive soul, here the scales tilt on the side of reason, with the result that the intensity of the madness is much reduced. This creates a problem for Hamlet, for as long as he insists upon handling on an intellectual level a matter which is best dealt with in a high rage, he is unable to accomplish his end. This is the uniqueness of Shakespeare's revenger: Hamlet's mind is one which is compelled to reason things out, and though he tries hard to work himself into a passion, the very act of thinking so precisely on the event turns his mind back to the intellectual aspects of his situation. Where Hieronimo, Titus, and Antonio push themselves further and further into madness, Hamlet, though his desire is the same as theirs, paradoxically keeps pulling himself *out* of it.

This tendency to nail down his passion with the hammer of logic is best illustrated by the soliloquy at the end of act 2. Meditating upon the ability of the player to muster up passion "all for nothing, / For Hecuba!" Hamlet condemns himself as a "dull and muddy-mettled rascal" and, deploring his "delay," works himself up into the passion he has envied. However, when anger overtakes him and he begins to rage at Claudius ("Bloody, bawdy villain! / Remorseless, treacherous, lecherous, kindless villain!"), Hamlet immediately draws himself up—the conduct that necessarily accompanies the revenge action he rejects as unbecoming. To be in the passion is to behave "like a very drab, a scullion." The result is a return to logic. The mental processes of the soliloquy are halted and their direction reversed with "About, my brains!" and for the remainder of the speech Hamlet proceeds not through passion but through logic. (Guilty creatures sitting at a play have proclaimed their malefactions. The guilty Claudius will see a play; he will confess his guilt.) The irascible anger of the revenge passion is brought under control.

Still, the attempt to proceed logically toward his end is constantly being frustrated because the end itself is an irrational one. The immediate purpose of the play-within-the-play—to determine whether Claudius is guilty or innocent—seems sane enough, but its ultimate aim is that implied by Hamlet's "If 'a do blench, I know my course." No matter how salutary it may be in its public effects, as it relates to Hamlet personally this intention involves the prince in an act of murder. Because the mission which the Ghost has thrust upon him commits him to an end directly counter to reason, his efforts to think his way out of this dilemma remain unsuccessful. The commitment itself (as it affects him psychologically) betrays the predilection toward madness.

Certainly Shakespeare's treatment of the madness motif is far more complex than any we have seen so far. The various strands that go into its design are so intricately woven together that it becomes impossible to isolate and meticulously label any one. The antic disposition, technically belonging to the disguise convention, contributes skillfully to the madness motif and therefore creates more than one paradox. It conceals Hamlet's intentions from Claudius but also warns the latter that Hamlet must be watched. It allays our suspicions that the lunacy is anything but feigned, yet subtly arouses in us the feeling that Hamlet is indeed distracted. The sore distraction is also mysterious. Hamlet's flights into passion and his steady commitment to pursue revenge to its inevitable end inform us that Hamlet has embarked upon a course linked with madness in all of the orthodox treatises of the period. Yet his remarkable intelligence, his unquestionable virtue, and his supersensitive insights into the nature of his predicament make us hesitate to doubt his inherent sanity. The result is that while the madness is there, it never intrudes hysterically upon us, diverting our attention from the truly dramatic to the merely theatrical. Shakespeare has seen the essential relationship of the motif to the archetypal experience and has utilized it as it was designed to be used, but his personal vision has deepened and extended its original significance. In the process the "madness" itself is transformed. Ironically, the "mad" Hamlet becomes, in the words of C. S. Lewis, an image of "man—haunted man—with his mind on the frontier of two worlds, man unable either quite to reject or quite to admit the supernatural, man struggling to get something done as man has struggled from the beginning, yet incapable of achievement because of his inability to understand either himself or his fellows or the real quality of the universe which has produced him."[10]

III Just as Shakespeare's Ghost, depicted as the spirit of a great and noble man, seems at first divorced from its vengeful forebearers and as Hamlet's madness, projecting as an antic disposition, is only gradually perceived to cloak the traditional distraction, so the play-within-the-play in *Hamlet* appears to have little in common with the conventional fifth-act massacre in which the protagonist takes revenge upon the offender.

In a majority of the revenge tragedies, the play-within-the-play occurs in the concluding moments of the action. Shakespeare has moved the play-within-the-play forward from act 5 to act 3; it no longer belongs to the denouement but becomes, as Righter points out,

> the strategic center of the plot, the turning-point of the action [as well as] the centre of the tragedy in a more symbolic sense, the focal point from which a preoccupation with appearance and reality, truth and falsehood, expressed in theatrical terms, radiates both backward and forward in time.[11]

In other revenge tragedies, the play-within-the-play becomes a trap, designed to isolate the murderer physically in a locked room, thus rendering him vulnerable to attack. Although Hamlet calls his play "The Mousetrap," his primary intention in planning it is not so much to trap Claudius in body as to trap him in mind. Claudius's conscience is what Hamlet wishes to prick; he means only to make the king reveal his guilt. Hamlet's play-within-the-play seems more a test of the Ghost's honesty than an attempt to maneuver Claudius into a sealed-off world where his power no longer protects him.

In other revenge plays, the protagonist kills his enemies within the mock play—one murder, if not several, gives evidence of the horrors to which the madness of revenge can lead. Hamlet commits no murder in the Gonzago play. Significantly, where Hieronimo, Titus, Antonio, and Vindice made themselves the heroes of their own productions and played the roles of murderers, Hamlet remains outside of his play, as in fact, does his victim.[12] This arrangement clearly distinguishes Hamlet from the other revengers. He sits in judgment of the play; he does not participate in it. He is trying to understand the real world, not to create a subjective one. The play-within-the-play motif, too, has been civilized by Shakespeare's pen.

All of these changes are dictated by the requirements of Shakespeare's personal vision as regards the character of his revenger. The revenger is an unusual kind of tragic hero, and Hamlet is unique even among these. In tragedies such as *Macbeth* or *King Lear* or *Oedipus Rex,* the protagonist is a person who sets up a counterground to the ground of being at the very outset of the play. These heroes try immediately to establish a world defined in terms that they find compatible with their own desires, one which denies or ignores reality. The action of the drama concerns their attempt to assert the validity of this counterground and their consequent failure to do so. In revenge tragedy the situation is slightly different. The protagonist starts out in touch with the ground of being and is later called upon to commit an action which requires him to establish that counterground. This is accomplished only at the end of the drama in the play-within-the-play, at which point we see the illusory world established by the hero and find it a world describable in terms of madness. Once the playwright postulates a revenger who exercises a high degree of control over his madness, as Shakespeare does in *Hamlet,* he is bound to give the play-within-the-play a link with reason that previous revenge plays, with their insistence upon the hero's subjection to the passion, could not have had. Hamlet is unique among revengers in that while he does try to manipulate events in his world, he is at the same time constantly trying to discover how his own thoughts and actions fit into the universe established in the symbolic constructions of his society. Any world that he creates, therefore, must exhibit that innate rationality which is as much a part of him as is the irrational goal that rationality must serve.

The greater objectivity of the world Hamlet creates in *The Murder of Gonzago* is best appreciated when set against the subjective world put together by Hieronimo in *Soliman and Perseda*. The contrast makes the specific functions of each playlet clearer. Righter (and subsequent critics) stress that in *Soliman and Perseda* "everything that seems illusory is in fact real," meaning that the greater truth is to be found in Hieronimo's version of events.[13] The judgment of the event made by his audience, however— that Hieronimo has acted against reason and human law—reflects another valid level of truth. Hieronimo himself, far from being an exponent of reality, is guilty of several kinds of deception. He undertakes actions in the play which violate the very nature of art by usurping its illusion as a cloak for reality: he deliberately deceives the spectators. The actors are also cheated; they are asked to take on roles and find that other actors, who were to murder them in play, are playing in earnest. Moreover, the revenger is deceived about the role he himself is playing. Hieronimo casts himself as God's agent of justice but is in reality a murderer. The illusory nature of Hieronimo's world is further emphasized by the chaos resulting from the old man's decision to instruct each of his players to speak in a different foreign language. Under these conditions the action could only come across to the theater audience as babble, and the resulting confusion serves to underscore the chaos in Hieronimo's mind. This is all set in perspective when the illusion ends and Hieronimo is forced to step back into reality, where his actions are looked upon as heinous. In *Soliman and Perseda,* art is used to deceive; the revenger has reached that stage of madness which tries to make illusion into reality.

This is not the case in *Hamlet.* In turning to art for assistance, Hamlet shows himself to be a learned and judicious critic. He clearly understands "the purpose of playing, whose end," he says, "is, to hold as 'twere the mirror up to nature: to show virtue her feature, scorn her own image, and the very age and body of the time his form and pressure" (3.2.20–24). It is significant that Hamlet does not *enter* the play himself; for him there is no illusory world in which the normal laws of society are inapplicable.

He has not set up an antiworld where his own will reigns supreme. In preparing *The Murder of Gonzago* for its courtly audience, Hamlet creates an objective world, one which reproduces fairly accurately a reality that those outside of it— Claudius, in particular—can recognize and respond to meaningfully. So accurately does this play-world copy nature that Claudius, discerning his own deeds in the vile actions of Luciano, is nearly brought to repentance. Thus, there is a great difference in the degree of objectivity between the world created by Hamlet and that created by Hieronimo. In watching *The Murder of Gonzago* one never has the feeling that the play was created by a madman. Hamlet's drama seems to do exactly what Hamlet says drama should do—hold a mirror up to nature.[14]

Obviously the play motif has been adapted to fit the dramatist's personal vision. Still, the changes are all instituted in ways that retain the relationship of the motif to the experience which underlies it. If the script was drawn from the player's repertory, it is nonetheless viewed as a creation of the revenger. Hamlet, like his predecessors, still plans the production, selects the script, and authors key lines in it. In addition, though the world Hamlet creates has a greater degree of objectivity, it remains limited in scope, centering strictly upon the poisoning of a king. It gives us evidence that Hamlet's vision of life has been noticeably narrowed. Again, the play-within-the-play may come earlier in the text, but only because Shakespeare has compressed the whole of the Kydian form into three acts. As rational as Hamlet's stated purpose of catching the conscience of the king may be, the prince is taking this honorable course only because he ultimately has a more sinister goal to which the first is a necessary bridge. Hamlet has told us that if the king "do blench, I know my course." The irrational purpose which lies latent in Hamlet's heart and comes to the surface after Claudius interrupts the play will bring Hamlet to the point of murder before the third act ends.

The actions characteristic of the revenger's madness which are omitted from the play-within-the-play, instead of being contained within it, follow immediately after. Ultimately we find that the experience previously connected with the play motif is not violated at all, for under the spell of the play Hamlet does meet his victim in a closed room—Gertrude's closet—and he does kill. The connection between Hamlet's play and the murder has gone unnoticed because Polonius dies in the place of the king. This innovation—allowing the hero to stab the wrong man—artistically disguises the strictness with which the configuration is adhered to; nevertheless, the death of Polonius is far more significant in the structure of the play than has generally been noticed.

Most scholars will agree that on his own Hamlet was unable to push his psyche into a madness sufficiently violent to allow him to bring the revenge to its obvious conclusion. The play-within-the-play, however, works Hamlet up into a state of excitement having every symptom of the required madness. Hamlet watches the play, sees the offense reenacted, and obtains certain proof of Claudius's guilt. The spirit of revenge, awakened in him by the experience, kindles an exhilarated anger in Hamlet's psyche. Though he wills to be only "cruel, not unnatural," yet in truth he loses control. During the remainder of the act his passion increases as his mind becomes more and more absorbed in the emotions aroused by the performance.

Hamlet's motive for presenting the play was logical, but his reaction to it is not. In the scenes growing out of "The Mousetrap," Shakespeare engages Hamlet in three actions which display his madness. All three take place within the framework of a journey to his mother's chamber, where he has been summoned to answer for the offense given by his play. Shakespeare sets the tone of this section by bringing in thoughts and images that explain at once why the eternal abode of Revenge was figured by poets of his era as adjacent to Hell. Hamlet goes into the scene feeling the same kinship with the irrational elements of the universe that Antonio and Hieronimo had voiced:

> 'Tis now the very witching time of night,
> When churchyards yawn and hell itself breathes out
> Contagion to this world. Now could I drink hot blood,
> And do such bitter business as the day
> Would quake to look on.
>
> [3.2.388–92]

This speech of Hamlet's, better than any other, suggests the state of mind the play-within-the-play has left him in.[15]

In the first of the three actions displaying the passion of re-

venge at work within Hamlet's psyche, Shakespeare gives his
protagonist the opportunity to complete his revenge: Hamlet
comes upon Claudius praying. As the paths of these two antagonists cross, we no longer see any objectivity about Hamlet's attitude toward Claudius. The prince is ready to murder his uncle:

> Now might I do it pat, now 'a is a-praying;
> And now I'll do 't.

[3.3.73–74]

Here again, the old logic which is so characteristic of Hamlet
pulls the young man back from his outburst of passion, but this
time it is a diseased logic—macabre, sinister, unhealthy. It is the
logic of the committed revenger:

> That would be scann'd:
> A villain kills my father, and for that
> I, his sole son, do this same villain send
> To heaven.
> Why, this is hire and salary, not revenge.
> 'A took my father grossly, full of bread,
> With all his crimes broad blown, as flush as May,
> And how his audit stands who knows save heaven?
> But in our circumstance and course of thought
> 'Tis heavy with him. And am I then revenged,
> To take him in the purging of his soul,
> When he is fit and season'd for his passage?
> No!
> Up, sword, and know thou a more horrid hent:
> When he is drunk asleep, or in his rage,
> Or in th' incestious pleasure of his bed,
> At game a-swearing, or about some act
> That has no relish of salvation in't—
> Then trip him, that his heels may kick at heaven,
> And that his soul may be as damn'd and black
> As hell, whereto it goes.

[3.3.75–95]

Hamlet, finally, does not kill the king. But his hesitation has no
root in pity, piety, or remorse. It is a perverse delay, stemming
directly from an excessive passion—a madness—that can never
be adequately explained in terms of his "antic disposition." And
that madness was aroused by the play-within-the-play.

In this first episode Hamlet's own thoughts give testimony to the disturbed state of his psyche. In the second, the same extremity in Hamlet's behavior is conveyed to us through Gertrude's fear. So distraught is Hamlet as he rushes in upon his mother hurling charges of guilt that Gertrude is concerned for her life ("What wilt thou do? Thou wilt not murther me? Help ho!" [3.4.21–22]). The actor playing Hamlet must take his cue from the queen's response; he must behave with a ferocity that will inspire terror. Once more we see that Hamlet is at last possessed by that passion which the Ghost had wished to stir in him and which he had chided himself for lacking.

The second episode leads into the third. While in this passion, Hamlet lunges with his sword at a voice behind the arras, suspecting that the king is hidden there, and kills old Polonius. His impulsiveness here and the callousness which follows the deed strike us as strange and unnatural. This, too, is something Hamlet would not have done in a saner moment. It, too, testifies to the strong effect the play-within-the-play has had upon him.

These three episodes culminate in the climactic confrontation between Hamlet and the queen. About this scene Hamlet might well lament, "How all occasions do inform against me." Chance would have it that when Hamlet finally does reach an emotional state that leaves him ready to "drink hot blood," he happens to be summoned by his mother rather than his uncle and, thus involved, expends all his energies against her. With the time so ripe, Hamlet occupies himself with a matter that is only secondary, much to the chagrin of the Ghost, who reappears to remind him of the more important goal:

> Do not forget! This visitation
> Is but to whet thy almost blunted purpose.
>
> [3.4.110–11]

By the time Hamlet finishes with the queen, his passion is exhausted; the opportunity for action has again slipped away.

Throughout this dialogue with Gertrude, Hamlet remains highly overwrought, and, intriguingly, the action growing out of the play-within-the-play ends with a discussion of whether or not Hamlet is mad:

Hamlet.   Look where he goes, even now, out at the portal.
                                                          Exit Ghost

Queen.   This is the very coinage of your brain,
               This bodiless creation ecstasy
               Is very cunning in.
Hamlet.   Ecstasy?
               My pulse as yours doth temperately keep time,
               And makes as healthful music. It is not madness
               That I have utt'red. Bring me to the test,
               And I the matter will reword, which madness
               Would gambol from. Mother, for love of grace,
               Lay not that flattering unction to your soul,
               That not your trespass but my madness speaks.
                                                  [3.4.136–46]

The treatment of insanity in this concluding scene puts before us
once again those mysterious questions always being raised in
Hamlet: How far can one human mind be entered by another?
What can Hamlet know of Gertrude's soul? What can she know
of his, or of her own? Which of them is really right about the
Ghost? These mysteries are pondered when Gertrude, amazed
by the responses of Hamlet to the sudden appearance of the
Ghost (which she herself cannot see), calls her son mad. The
queen is wrong, first because the Ghost is quite real and second,
as Hamlet points out, because she would rather clutch at the
notion that Hamlet is demented than admit the accuracy of the
pictures he has drawn of her. But her errors do not make her
statement untrue. Gertrude is right enough about the emotional
turmoil going on in Hamlet's mind. Hamlet, on the other hand,
claims perfect sanity. "It is not madness / That I have utt'red,"
says he. "My pulse as yours doth temperately keep time, / And
makes as healthful music." Hamlet, too, is wrong, though more
nearly correct than Gertrude. He is correct in that no "ecstasy"
of his brain had produced the Ghost, as his mother supposes. He
is also correct in asserting that his accusations concerning Gertrude's behavior contain much truth. If his mind can still make
these logical connections, he is no lunatic. Still, Hamlet is mistaken when he claims absolute sanity. This is a play in which the
audience usually knows more than the characters do, more even,
than the tragic hero himself knows. The audience, having heard
Hamlet's satanic logic in the scene with Claudius, having viewed
demeanor so wild upon his entrance into Gertrude's chamber
that the queen was moved to scream for help, and having had

the dead body of Polonius on the stage before them through the remainder of the scene to testify to the extent to which Hamlet was overwrought and distracted—this audience would hardly acquiesce to the statement that Hamlet was "temperate" or that no hint of madness was evident. The three episodes following Hamlet's "Mousetrap" are deliberately designed to depict the kind of excessive passion that the Elizabethans would have classified as a madness.

The elements that we expect to find associated with the play-within-the-play—a madness and a murder—are present, if not in the play, then directly following it. Hamlet's play, like the other motifs in this tragedy, reflects a harmonious merger of the old form and the new vision. In at once affirming Hamlet's sanity and giving rise to his most extended bout with madness, the play-within displays the complexities of the human mind, which can pursue the most irrational of ends in a seemingly sane and reasonable manner and can appear the most serene when the volcanic passions lurking in its depths are closest to erupting.

IV Emrys Jones has argued that Shakespeare's plays should be seen in terms of a two-part structure, and this certainly appears to be true of *Hamlet*.[16] The play breaks down into two parts—that leading up to an outbreak of madness during which Polonius is killed and that falling away from it. In the first half, Hamlet is attempting to manipulate events (and, as he laments, finds that nothing he does works out as he intends it to). He wants to organize the world in terms of revenge. In the second half, Hamlet lets the world take its own course, confident that "there's a divinity that shapes our ends, / Rough-hew them how we will" (5.2.10–11). Significantly, though Shakespeare makes no fuss about it, once Hamlet resigns himself to the will of Providence, the Ghost, so potent an influence on Hamlet when he was teetering on the brink of madness, is not heard from again.

Although Hamlet has come in slow stages to see more about the ground of being itself, he never has time to reach a full awareness. Unfortunately, the forces he had already set in motion by entering into commerce with the Ghost cannot be laid to rest. What we find in the denouement of the play is a study of the way the destructive forces initiated by the Ghost work to restore the balance in nature only through tremendous waste and ruined potential. The motifs through which this final aspect of the experience is worked out include the excess (or multiple murders) and the death of the revenger.

Earlier in this chapter we stated that the excess was embodied in the action of the play rather than in the behavior of the Ghost. Let's now examine Shakespeare's adaptation of this excess motif in more detail. Directors often think of the Polonius / Ophelia / Laertes episodes as extraneous to the main action, as one of several subplots included only to provide contrast to the major plot, and thus feel free to cut such scenes drastically. But this accusation of structural superfluity is invalid. Many scenes that may appear tacked on are logically inevitable to the action itself.

The murder of Polonius is the most important act of excess growing out of the catalytic play-within-the-play. Surely this *is* excess. The follies of Polonius were hardly mammoth enough to merit so terrible a fate. Nor did Hamlet wish to harm him. Yet his death is directly attributable to the revenge desire. In the attempt to restore justice, the revenger inadvertently commits a gross injustice: here is excess.

This event, the climax of Hamlet's sore distraction, is pivotal in the structure of Shakespeare's drama.[17] It, in a sense, completes the action in which Hamlet is the revenger, just as it initiates the revenge action of Laertes. Hamlet has committed the deed, ironically missing his target but nevertheless setting in motion the same inevitable consequences as surely as if he had killed the real villain. Shakespeare creates an interesting variation on a theme (but a variation perfectly in line with experience because it even more clearly defines the nature of excess) by having most of the waste in the story of Hamlet's revenge follow from a murder that Hamlet never intended to commit.

Polonius's death has consequences almost immediately in the madness and death of Ophelia, another example of the chaos wrought when passion is let loose. She, too, falls prey to excess. Hamlet speaks of the way the base nature, coming between the "fell incensed points / Of mighty opposites," is cut down. The innocent nature suffers a similar fate. Ophelia's death corresponds in significance to the deaths of Marston's Julio and Kyd's

Duke of Castile, but the dramaturgy is far superior. In keeping with his general tendency to avoid hysteria, Shakespeare stresses the victim's innocence instead of the revenger's fury and arranges matters so that her death occurs through natural causes rather than intolerable violence. With the motif so manipulated, the audience is able to feel the loss more directly, while being conscious at the same time that the characteristic excess which flows out of the passion of revenge brings that loss about.

Another wasteful death, that of Laertes, also follows from Hamlet's stabbing of Polonius. Much has been made of the contrasts between Laertes and Hamlet, which are well enough known to need no repeating here, but the experiential relationship of the episode to the motif of excess is often ignored. The plot structure suggests a theme that is strangely Aeschylean: one revenge action inevitably begets another. Once Hamlet has killed Polonius, Laertes, his son, is bound to seek the life of Hamlet. It is a remarkable twist (and a precedent Tourneur will follow) that Shakespeare actually concludes Hamlet's revenge action and begins a new one in the middle of the play. Yet the "new" revenge action is a natural—indeed, an inevitable—development from Hamlet's own flubbed attempt to kill the king. It exposes still another aspect of excess.

In Laertes' revenge action, all of the relationships are changed. Hamlet is now the villain. Claudius, stepping out of that role, plays a very dishonest "ghost" to Laertes' avenger, spurring this young man to excesses far less fortuitous than Hamlet's are and revealing in that role why poison is so frequently associated with him. Assisted by Claudius, Laertes traps Hamlet in a kind of play-within-the-play with rapiers, and the excess stemming from Laertes' attempt against Hamlet's life leads to the unplanned deaths of Claudius and Gertrude, as well as to the death of the avenger, Laertes himself. The whole sequence of revenge is played over again in little, and the effect is to reinforce the lessons offered earlier about the uncontrollable nature of revenge.

Through this step-by-step destruction of the Polonius family, excess is embodied in the action of the play. Accidental though this waste may be, Hamlet wreaks as much havoc merely by harboring the desire to kill Claudius as other revengers do in actually committing the deed. Once again we find that Shakespeare, in pressing into service a revenge tragedy convention, disguises it skillfully, refines it aesthetically, and nonetheless uses it perceptively to illuminate the archetypal experience which gave it birth.

V It is always a mistake to assume, especially with Shakespeare, that a playwright is doing only one thing at a a time. This is particularly true in *Hamlet* and nowhere more so than in the fourth and fifth acts of the play. On one hand, we can speak of Polonius's death as the murder we normally associate with the end of the play-within-the-play, of its giving rise to the multiple deaths so characteristic of the revenge action, and of its being the direct cause of Hamlet's demise. On the other hand, we can still speak in act 4 of Hamlet's delay, for Claudius is still alive, Hamlet's motive is still to slay him, and the major dramatic action of the plot is still building to that moment when Hamlet will force the poisoned wine down the villain's throat. And we should speak of it, for the primary conflict, the most interesting conflict, is the cat-and-mouse game between Hamlet and his villainous uncle. For the first time, the protagonist and antagonist of the revenge tragedy form no longer merely coexist in lines of action that run parallel, as in *Antonio's Revenge*, but are mighty opposites, men of indominable energies and piercing minds truly pitted one against the other.

Hamlet is the first revenge play in which the delay lingers on as a theme after the curtain has fallen on the play-within-a-play. It is also the one play in which the full value of the delay motif is realized. On the simplest level, the delay is caused by the need to test the validity of the ghost's message and to determine Claudius's guilt. But the delay continues on beyond that point, and the very causes that extend it had existed even before the test was conceived. There is unquestionably something deep in Hamlet, something on which he himself, for all his self-analysis, cannot put his finger, that is responsible for his procrastination.

Some authorities have argued that there is no delay. Those who take this stand have Hamlet's constant musings to refute them:

> Yet I
> A dull and muddy-mettled rascal, peak
> Like John-a-dreams, unpregnant of my cause,
> And can say nothing . . . it cannot be
> But I am pigeon-liver'd, and lack gall
> To make oppression bitter, or ere this
> I should 'a' fatted all the region kites
> With this slave's offal.
>
> [2.2.566–80]

> Now whether it be
> Bestial oblivion, or some craven scruple
> Of thinking too precisely on th' event . . .
>
> [4.4.39–41]

> Do you not come your tardy son to chide,
> That, laps'd in time and passion, lets go by
> Th' important acting of your dread command?
>
> [3.4.106–8]

Since Hamlet can thus chide himself for procrastination, it becomes folly to ignore the motif of delay. One may feel, with Robert Nelson, that "Hamlet upbraids himself too much" or that "these are the reproaches of an impatient man" rather than a slothful one, yet one must admit that Hamlet *does* make an issue of the delay.[18] And well that he does.

In these speeches the prince speaks of a condition in which there is a will to action and a simultaneous inability to act. Many critics therefore locate a flaw in Hamlet. Hamlet himself has spoken of persons whose characters are marred by "some vicious mole of nature," and such critics assume that Shakespeare means us to apply this circumstance to Hamlet himself. Since Hamlet attributes his procrastination to his "thinking too precisely on th' event," his intellectualization of the revenge problem is linked to the tragic-flaw theory and taken to be the flaw.

The drawback is that *Hamlet* is not a tragedy of character in the same sense as is *Macbeth* or *Othello* or *King Lear:* in those plays there would be no tragedy if the protagonist were not ambitious or jealous or rash. Macbeth, Othello, and Lear are each faced with a right choice and a wrong choice and were they constitutionally able to make the right choice the problem which caused their suffering would have solved itself. The tragedy in *Hamlet* is a tragedy of situation, as in *Oedipus Rex* or *Antigone,* one in which the protagonist must make a choice between two right actions, so that either choice will be wrong. Hamlet *must* kill Claudius; no one but Hamlet can bring him to justice. Yet killing is an unnatural act, repulsive to the human mind. Moreover, in doing the deed Hamlet will doom himself; he no more than Claudius can commit murder and live. The tragedy lies in the situation and Hamlet's awareness of it; therefore, the tragic flaw theory is unnecessary.

What, then, are we to make of Hamlet's excuse for procrastination—of such remarks as Hamlet's "thinking too precisely on th' event," "conscience does make cowards of us all," and so on? What is the "craven scruple" that Hamlet suspects exists within him? We submit that in the delay Shakespeare has embodied an instinct which is as deeply seated in the human psyche as the instinct for justice—the innate awareness that it is wrong to kill. Hamlet tries with all his will to suppress it but it keeps coming back to him, not in the form of such moral platitudes as might flow from a George Barnwell but in the form of an irrepressible fear of damnation. The point is nicely made by C. S. Lewis, who would trace Hamlet's hesitation "not to a physical fear of dying, but to a fear of being dead" because, he supposed, "any serious attention to the state of being dead, unless it is limited by some definite religious or anti-religious doctrine, must paralyze the will by introducing infinite uncertainties and rendering all motives inadequate."[19]

There is much truth in Lewis's speculation. Because of the mysterious nature of the Ghost and the magnitude of the demand it makes, Hamlet can never be completely confident that his act against Claudius will be a justifiable one. He finds it difficult to align himself wholeheartedly with the forces that the Ghost represents; he goes beyond the Ghost and questions the authority itself. One of his major purposes in introducing *The Murder of Gonzago,* it will be remembered, is to determine whether the Ghost is an evil spirit sent to play upon his hatred for Claudius and to encourage him to damn himself. The well-being of his soul after death is a question of primary concern to Hamlet throughout the play. Even in act 5 when he asserts the rightness of the deed he has undertaken Hamlet puts the matter in such a way that he could as well be expressing doubt as certainty:

> Is't not perfect conscience
> To quit him with this arm? And is't not to be damn'd,
> To let this canker of our nature come
> In further evil?

[5.2.67–70]

Because he chooses the interrogative rather than the imperative form in addressing Horatio, Hamlet appears almost to be asking for reassurance. Is it a damnable act? Is it not? Horatio gives no answer. Nor can Hamlet. The only thing of which he seems to be certain is that he will have to pay with his own life for killing Claudius ("A man's life's no more than to say 'one' "; "since no man of aught he leaves knows, what is't to leave betimes?"). Thus, it is likely that the fear of the undiscovered country which first made him hesitate over suicide and later holds him back from taking revenge stems from his own sense that the act, necessary as it might be, is a damnable one. No man can take the life of another with impunity.

For most of the play, Hamlet tries to crush his own awareness of this fact. In a way it shames him. He sees the recognition of any authority beyond that of the ghost as cowardice. To be truly brave, to live in accordance with the dictates of honor, is to dare damnation, as Laertes does, to throw conscience and grace to the profoundest pit of hell, and to be willing to cut one's enemy's throat in church. Hamlet is not so reckless. But he views his scruples again and again as "craven."

Shakespeare's profound treatment of the delay, adapted to serve his personal vision by giving us still another glimpse of the mysteries of the human condition, illuminates the revenge experience in two ways. First, more clearly than any other dramatist, Shakespeare uses the delay to render the full significance of the act of revenge to the revenger. It is a damnable act, and for the first time we are shown how this knowledge affects the psyche of the hero. Just as Hamlet is the only revenger to question the authority of the ghost and to dedicate a good portion of his energies to testing its honesty, so he is the only one to be fully conscious of the possible effects of the deed of revenge upon his eternal life and to specifically articulate his fears. In other revengers—Hieronimo, Titus, Antonio, and Vindice—the intellectual process is so thoroughly anesthetized by the madness that they fail to perceive their continually devolving spiritual state and end blinded by illusion. Hamlet, at least, perceives all the ironies and complexities, the paradoxes and the tragedies of the situation. Second, Shakespeare's handling of the delay throws a fuller light upon the importance of the madness convention as symbolic of a state of mind which is essential to the revenge act. What Shakespeare is saying about the relationship between the delay and the madness confirms what we have been attempting to stress throughout this book—that given Elizabethan patterns of thought, the revenger must go mad in order to commit the deed, for what man in full possession of his reason would willingly choose damnation? Revenge is, in the end, a crime of passion. The "craven scruple," whether one part wisdom and three parts cowardice or one part cowardice and three parts wisdom, is only overcome by a rage so close to insanity that it has no perception of reality. How Hamlet yearns in his will to be so steeped in passion! Yet because his intellect resists the madness he must remain, in his own eyes at least, a procrastinator.

What is the solution to Hamlet's dilemma? There comes a point in the play when Hamlet overcomes his fear. At this point he undergoes a second transformation, this marked by a change in the direction of his will. Where formerly he had seen himself as a scourge and minister, acting on behalf of Heaven, had in his pride and his impatience with evil developed a stern intolerance of the failings of others, and ironically had found chance and accident consistently frustrating the ends he had willed, he comes, after his journey abroad, to view events in a wider frame of reference. His vision remains limited; it is still a relatively pessimistic one, still very much more aware of the world's evils than of its goods. Yet the self is less at the center of Hamlet's thoughts. His attitude toward death in the graveyard scenes has dimensions that were completely lacking in his first soliloquy, where Hamlet feels death in an immediate and personal way. His perspective seems to have been expanded, and part of that new perspective includes a change in attitude toward the human will. Hamlet moves toward a solution to his dilemma by resigning his own will to that of Providence. He still feels compelled to kill the king, but he has progressed to a point where he can abandon active plotting.

Having discovered through his experiences a higher authority than the Ghost, Hamlet will be guided by that authority. Here again we find Shakespeare altering the conventional motif. This transformation in the hero entails a new cause for delay—Hamlet must wait for Heaven to provide the proper moment for Claudius's death. Other revengers have "waited" for Heaven to act, of course, but they waited complainingly, with impatience and rage and doubt. There is none of this now in Hamlet. In this second part of the play delay has been transformed into "readiness." Where the delay in attaining the necessary state of madness in the first half of the play had been a reproach which required the Ghost to reappear to "whet thy almost blunted purpose," the delay, under Providence, brings a sense of quietude and acceptance of the world as it is, in place of the earlier desire to organize and manipulate the world.

This handling of the delay, too, is a reflection of Shakespeare's personal vision. Hamlet's dilemma is the dilemma of man, and the only solution, as Shakespeare poses it, is to accept it as part of the inevitable condition of being human, to admit the fact that man is caught in a situation which allows for heroism and allows for illumination but exacts its return for these glories in suffering. To live life at the level of full awareness is to discover that the human condition is necessarily a tragic one. This alteration does not distort the motif; rather, it relates the delay more solidly and meaningfully to those motifs which surround it—the madness, over which for the first time the delay has won out, and the death of the avenger, which Hamlet is now spiritually prepared to accept with dignity.

VI There is nothing really unexpected about Shakespeare's use of the death-of-the-avenger motif. That Hamlet die is every bit as morally and aesthetically essential to the play as that Claudius be disposed of. Were Claudius to live, we would have to believe that the world is absurd, as Rosencrantz and Guildenstern do when they venture onto Tom Stoppard's stage. Were Hamlet to live, the world would seem immoral. As it is, the play tells us that the universe, though incomprehensible, is nonetheless ultimately just. This is the burden that the final motif must carry, and Shakespeare brings it off magnificently.

One of the remarkable things about Shakespeare's handling of the death of Hamlet is the careful way the playwright controls the emotional responses of the audience so that the ending of the play conveys the desired tragic effect. What Marston had failed to do, Shakespeare succeeds at: he retains our sympathies for the hero and makes us believe in his suffering.

As in *Antonio's Revenge,* there is the suggestion in the last act that events are being watched by an eternal eye. Not that Heaven applauds the revenger's excess—far from it. Shakespeare simply has Hamlet introduce the notion that Providence has been acting in his life all along:

> Our indiscretion sometime serves us well
> When our deep plots do pall, and that should learn us
> There's a divinity that shapes our ends,
> Rough-hew them how we will—

[5.2.8–11]

And he indicates, in Hamlet's meditations on death, that things are continuing thus:

> There is special providence in the fall of a sparrow.
> If it be now, 'tis not to come; if it be not to come,
> it will be now; if it be not now, yet it will come—
> the readiness is all. . . .

[5.2.219–22]

More important, Hamlet (as we have seen) has put himself in divine hands. The action in the final scenes—that is, the competition between Hamlet and Laertes—is to be taken as the expression of the will he has chosen to obey. With very skillful dramatic planning, Shakespeare obtains a delicate balance that allows us to see that Providence is at work while at the same time maintaining that the ways of Providence are mysterious. If the effect of this introduction of Providence upon Hamlet is to free him from the pressures that worked upon his psyche under the influence of the Ghost, the effect upon us is to direct our attention to a center of responsibility other than the order of nature, so that we no longer hold Hamlet totally culpable for the ensuing carnage, though, in actual fact, it stems from his earlier commitment to revenge.

To further enable us to sympathize with Hamlet, Shakespeare shifts a great deal of the responsibility for the deaths that follow to Claudius. In the earlier acts Claudius had maintained appearances. He had looked reasonable; in rejecting him Hamlet seemed peevish and ungrateful. So long as Hamlet remained in control of the plot, Claudius was distanced from us. Hamlet's abdication of control put Claudius in command of the action. This dramaturgical strategy has the happy result of letting the king's own intrigues become the means through which he is brought down. But at the same time it draws the usurper-king closer to the footlights, displays his infinite resourcefulness in exploiting others, and at last exposes his wickedness. With Claudius emerging as the villain and Hamlet taking on more and more the aspect of victim, our emotions fall in line with the planned ending. So appalled are we by the actions of Claudius, as he makes both young men his dupes, that we give our sympathies entirely to Hamlet.

The machinery involved in Hamlet's death is skillfully disguised in the rush of events at the close of the drama. It is Laertes who gives Hamlet his death wound, thus providing Hamlet with the distinction of being the first revenger to suffer from this retribution before he has actually taken revenge—the villain, Claudius, is still very much alive. This inverted order of events is rendered feasible by the filial relationship of Laertes to Polonius. Despite the injustice of Laertes' methods, the wound which he gives Hamlet is deserved, for Hamlet must answer for the murder of Laertes' father. With his time on earth now at a premium, Hamlet hastes to finish off Claudius, not in cold blood but in a burst of passion which comes naturally from him when Laertes informs him of the king's vile role in the duel. The wounded Hamlet lives to die *after* Claudius, and thus also appears to die as a result of *killing* Claudius, and the demands of the convention are thus at once preserved and refreshed.

In handling the death-of-the-avenger motif Shakespeare avoids the trap that Marston fell into of being too explicit about the relationship between the various orders of justice, of reducing them to coherence and thus making the mysterious into the ridiculous. What Shakespeare does not tell us is whether Hamlet's final passionate stabbing of Claudius is a reversion to the self that was under the control of the Ghost—for it *is* an act of passion—or whether at this moment Hamlet is being guided by Providence. If the former is true, presumably the act is a damnable one. *Is* Hamlet damned? No answer is provided. Often as the question has been raised during the course of the play, we are not invited to ask it now. Horatio, in saying may "flights of angels sing thee to thy rest," hints at salvation, but he is no seer, has no authority to predict, and so must be understood to mean only that Hamlet is at peace; his words are best taken as a tribute to the greatness that is gone.

A question that can be asked, however, is, what has Hamlet learned? The death of the avenger motif, here, does not include within it tragic knowledge, not in the sense that Oedipus or even Lear attain that knowledge.

The tone of the play, established by the complex blending of the form, the action, and the language, tells us that we are witnessing a tragedy. And tragedy implies a knowledge achieved through suffering. The play raises this expectation of tragic awareness only to dash it. By continually pointing to unrealized potential, particularly through metaphor, the play suggests the level that could be achieved, making the audience painfully aware that there is no transcendance in the killing of Claudius. As the reunion between Lear and Cordelia suggests the possibility of universal reconciliation, a reconciliation never realized, so Hamlet's dazzling flashes of insight suggest a higher order of justice than is ever attained.

The tragedy in the Elizabethan-Jacobean plays is experienced through the tragic form of the play itself and is not identical with the knowledge gained by the hero. *Hamlet* is an excellent example of a play that knows more than the hero does. Prince Hamlet has unique potential. He could have become an ideal king. He is honorable, sensitive to the needs of others, mindful of his duties, a keen observer of other men. Nor is his intelligence merely witty; there is wisdom in the wit. This depth of intellect, absent in the Marlovian heroes, who were supreme in power but not wise, makes Hamlet seem a fine prospect for gaining the tragic insight that they were denied. Indeed, he has insights that flick at a higher order of justice: witness his "use every man after his own desert, and who shall scape whipping?" At these moments he is at a level which could have led to a tragic insight, had it been sustained. But though Hamlet knows more at the end of the play than he did at the beginning, he is also more deceived both about the world and about himself.

His failure to achieve insight into the universal order is echoed in the order that is finally reasserted. Here, as within Hamlet, there is a gap between the potential level of order and the order actually established. This is not that magnificent order that grows out of the reconciliation of the opposing deities, as in *The Oresteia*. It is an order much like the order achieved at the end of Shakespeare's other major tragedies. We witness dull, decent, blunt, earnest men initiate a new order. It will be an order superior to the one it must replace in that it will partake of justice. However, as these men never achieved the level of insight implied in Hamlet's "use every man after his own desert, and who shall scape whipping?" it will not be an order that opens to the ground of being. Thus, though the play ends with order reasserted, another higher order is suggested to the audience, with no one on the stage being conscious of it, and the character most likely to have attained knowledge of it having died before acquiring it.

Once again, then, the revenge tragedy motifs fit into the configuration—they are closely interlocked, one with another, dramaturgically inseparable, their positions dictated by the experience of revenge and their meanings enhanced by Shakespeare's personal vision of the human condition. The Ghost initiates the revenge action by demanding that the imbalance created by his death be righted. The demand upon Hamlet works through the passions and therefore pushes the psyche toward madness, a state which is resisted by the rational and intellectual powers of the mind, causing hesitation and delay, and one which requires a disguise for the revenger to continue to operate in the world. Once the passions are engaged, they are not easily subdued; thus, the combined impetus of the ghost and the madness now manifest themselves as excess, that wasteful process through which nature attempts to right the balance and return itself to harmony. Pushed to the extreme, the revenger will slay the villain, committing a deed which restores the balance but creates a new upset, the latter being quieted only by his own death. Individual motifs are radically altered in *Hamlet*, but their integrity is always maintained.

Chapter 9

The Revenger's Tragedy

The best and brightest, having tainted their luster in the pursuit of honor, having picked up some of the foulness of their environment, must go under. But they are no more to be lumped with their victims than Hamlet is to be lumped with Claudius because in the process of combating Claudius's wrongs he too dips his hands in blood. There are taints and taints; there is corruption and corruption. *The Revenger's Tragedy,* even before it is a tale of the good contaminated, is a tale of good versus evil.

Jonas Barish

I TOURNEUR, it seems, has treated the revenge tragedy motifs like juggling balls; he has tossed them up in the air, flung them over and around one another, dropped a few, and caught the rest as they landed. The long delay is relegated to a one-sentence statement that the offense against Gloriana occurred several years in the past. Gone, too, is the ghost. Vindice knows who killed Gloriana, so no wandering spirit from Hades or Purgatory need shock him with the news. Even the madness seems suppressed. The hero rails often about other people's madnesses but never laments, as Antonio does, that he has "thus run mad, / As one confounded in a maze of mischief," or admits, with Hamlet, that "I am punish'd / with a sore distraction."[1] On the other hand, the play-within-the-play seems to have been duplicated endlessly. There are two masques in act 5, and, if we accept the argument of one critic, Vindice not only produces an additional play in act 3 but, in fact, the whole of *The Revenger's Tragedy* can be taken as his play-within-a-play.[2] And so it goes. Is

Tourneur idiosyncratic in producing these variations, unaware or unconcerned with the uses to which his predecessors had put the motifs? Or are these alterations made necessary by his personal vision, and do the motifs still comment meaningfully on the experience of revenge?

To answer these questions, one must have some sense of the play's structure. Larry Champion voices a puzzlement that many scholars probably feel when he writes that

> strangely, Act I concludes, not with Vindice's establishing his scheme for either immediate or eventual dispatch of the Duke, but with Hippolito's binding certain lords with oaths before heaven to revenge the ravishment and death of Antonio's virtuous wife. And Act II confuses the issue even further . . . [it] scatters the plot, setting in motion several additional layers of Vindice's intrigues but failing even to mention what the spectators in the first act saw as the dominant motif of the tragedy. . . . [And] by the middle of Act III the basic intrigue of the drama is settled and the antagonist dead.[3]

The play does make sense, despite this seeming chaos, for Tourneur has so arranged the details of the plot around Vindice, its motivating force, that the ultimate impression is one of unity. He strives to make it appear that there is only one action; however, the tragedy is better understood if its principle plots are distinguished. Basically the play has three—possibly even four—parallel plots. Vindice's attempt to obtain revenge upon the Duke, though it begins in the middle of an action and ends quite early in the play, is certainly the main plot, for the events pertaining to Gloriana are central to both the author's and the protagonist's purposes. The more extended action in which Vindice seeks revenge against Lussurioso, generally assumed to be part of the Gloriana action, is best approached as a second plot. It clearly has its own beginning, middle, and end. Distinct from both of these is the relatively undeveloped plot in which Antonio seeks justice for an injury committed against him by the Duchess's Youngest Son. The other minor episodes may be seen either as brief independent plots or as episodes in the longer plots—the Duchess's desire to be revenged upon the Duke, which arises out of the action involving the Youngest Son but seems to move thereafter under its own steam, is the primary example.[4]

Each of the three major actions involves an offense that cries out for justice. But the offense is no longer the murder of a father or a son; Tourneur makes it an offense against the beloved. The parallelism between the three offenses is striking. In the first, the aged Duke has sought to seduce Vindice's fiancée, Gloriana; in the second, his son and heir, a man in the prime of maturity, attempts to seduce Vindice's sister Castiza; in the third, his adolescent stepson rapes Antonio's wife. Tourneur sets one seduction in the past, one in the future, and one in the present, and distributes the ages of the debauchers to indicate the ongoing nature of the problem. All three of the ladies are presented as paragons of virtue. Their seducers are personifications of lust—the corruption of the court, the lechery of the present line of princes, has "poisoned" or violently dishonored beauty and chastity as it is poisoning the realm itself.

That each of the touchstones is seen in relation to sexuality is not coincidental. The starting point of Tourneur's personal vision is that love has been perverted. Honorable love is presented in the play as a stabilizing force. Those characters who lack stability are characterized by lust, the perversion of love, and their instability chafes against the order that love strains to uphold. One of the major ironies is that virtue has a beauty that attracts the lecherous eye and arouses a desire for possession, but in attempting to possess that beauty lust destroys it. Paradoxically, the very fidelity and stability of the chaste women, their desire to live by the values taught by love, subjects them to abuse and suffering.

Tourneur is often criticized for the immaturity of his vision. But is his vision really immature? In making lust rather than murder the root cause of injustice in his state, he warns against an attitude that, in our own century, has been widely accepted as valid—the belief that sexuality alone can give meaning to life. In an age of decline, the one virtue that appears to maintain its validity is sexuality. When love, in its best sense, and the more intangible virtues such as honor or chastity lose their hold on the imagination, sexuality can be confirmed on the sense endings. At the same time it appears to possess metaphysical potential. Basically sexuality is a biological drive, yet operative within it is a subtle interplay between the biological and the symbolic. How-

ever, once the symbolism is shifted so that sexuality no longer
functions as a component within a love relationship but becomes
an end in itself, sex becomes a god. As G. K. Chesterton points
out:

> The effect of treating sex as only one innocent natural thing was that
> every other innocent natural thing became soaked and sodden with
> sex. For sex cannot be admitted to a mere equality among elementary
> emotions or experiences like eating and sleeping. The moment sex
> ceases to be a servant it becomes a tyrant. There is something
> dangerous and disproportionate in its place in human nature, for
> whatever reason; and it does really need a special purification and
> dedication.[5]

Cut loose from the only context that can give it a meaning
beyond itself, sex becomes demonic. It seeks to become the only
value. But though a paradise in itself as long as the sex act lasts, it
has no meaning beyond the moment. True, one can reconfirm
one's existence moment by moment in sex. However, there is
never the feeling of contact with Being at a higher level. Nor can
an imaginative or intellectual probing of sexuality for meaning
reveal anything that will render the other activities of life
meaningful—not that sexuality is meaningless but that, independent of love, it is incapable either of informing the rest of life
with meaning or of sustaining its own meaning for human life.
In its diabolical urgency, it becomes both capricious and destructive of human relationships.

To the members of the Duke's family in *The Revenger's
Tragedy*, sex has become god. It is the sole end of life. But lust
does not produce stability of character; those ruled by it are
committed to "opportunity," to "occasion," to "fortune." When
they are thwarted, whether in their desires for lustful pleasures
or in other areas where they must face the pressures of life, they
cannot accept the rebuff. Instead of reacting, as Castiza, Gloriana, and Antonio's wife do, with fortitude and patience, they are
immediately turned to another vice—the vice of anger, which
accelerates rapidly into the desire for revenge. In most instances
the "justice" they seek is nothing more than the psychological
gratification of hurting someone who had thwarted their desires.

The actions of the Duchess make it clear that Tourneur was

consciously depicting the process through which the thwarting
of the will produces a longing for revenge. Although her
youngest son is being tried for rape, has confessed his guilt, and
will not repent, she nonetheless pleads with the Duke for his
release. Eventually the Duke overrules the judges, who would
hang the offender; however, he is slow in doing so and merely
defers judgment, while the doting mother would have the boy
pardoned unconditionally. Her will thus frustrated, the Duchess
determines to seek revenge for the presumed injury. There is no
real justice in her plan to get even by committing adultery;
moreover, the lustful act that is to be the act of vengeance is one
the Duchess was already looking for an excuse to commit. Her
desire for revenge is merely the peevish response of an unstable
character already ruled by lust to her failure to get her own way.

So it is with Spurio. He, too, has no stability of character. Born
a bastard he feels the world has heaped abuse on him. Consequently, Spurio, too, is angry. He also seeks revenge for the
wrongs which he lacks the patience to endure:

> Duke, thou didst do me wrong, and by thy act
> Adultery is my nature . . . .
> The sin of feasts, drunken adultery:
> I feel it swell me; my revenge is just,
> I was begot in impudent wine and lust.[6]

There is, of course, an ironic truth to Spurio's statement that
"my revenge is just." But his decision to cuckold his father is no
more a sign of the return of Astraea to the world than is his
stepmother's plan to commit adultery. It merely reveals his own
malevolence.

Spurio describes another way that lust breeds revenge. The
process begins in the "whisp'ring and withdrawing hour," where
gluttony is transformed into lust. The offspring of the illicit
union, deprived of the love that permeates the natural family
relationship, becomes resentful and perverse and harbors an
undying hatred for the parents who so cheated him. Spurio is
walking proof of this truth: the lust of the parents spawns a
desire for revenge in the children.

These cases depict the metamorphosis of lust into revenge in
basically evil characters. In contrast, an act of lust by an evil man
may twist love into a desire for revenge in a good man. The

Duke's conduct toward Gloriana, in rewarding her fidelity and
chastity with death, transforms the love of Vindice into a desire
to retaliate that debases an originally pure love and destroys the
lover. In this case, not only a real *love* but a real *injustice* underlies
the desire for vengeance. Vindice's personal drive to punish the
Duke, thus associated with a desire to cleanse the state of its
consuming vice, consequently bears within it certain admirable
qualities. As a good man driven to revenge by evil, Vindice
moves in a different sphere from that inhabited by Spurio and
the Duchess; he is not seeking mere self-gratification. Insofar as
justice is pursued through passion rather than law, however, his
desire cannot earn our wholehearted approval. It, too, bespeaks
of chaos and instability.

By making the act of lust the offense which sets revenge raging in the world, Tourneur fuses the two passions at the most
fundamental point in the structure of his play. In his world the
perversion of love (the most basic disorder in the individual)
becomes the pervading cause of the perversion of justice (the
root source of disorder in the state).

Having noted the general context in which Tourneur placed
the revenge motifs, we are in a better position to study the
adaptations he made in fitting them to his personal vision. A
word of caution is necessary before turning to the conventions
themselves. The revenger in Tourneur's play is more highly
stylized than any of his predecessors. Vindice, like the other
figures in *The Revenger's Tragedy,* is the embodiment of a passion,
only slightly more fleshed out than Lust, Ambition, or Envy.
Obviously there is far more to Vindice than there was to Revenge in *The Spanish Tragedy,* but the two share a common ancestry. Both belong to the world of allegory. Of all the Kydian
revengers, Vindice is the least developed. In judging him, one
must not look for the complexity of character one grew accustomed to in keeping company with Hieronimo or Hamlet.

II "Tourneur dropped the ghost," said Muriel Bradbrook.[7] But did he? Ghosts and skeletons are not so far
apart, after all, one being the spiritual and one the material
remains of the deceased. Either might serve as a reminder of the

lost loved one. Provided the playwright does not need a means of informing his revenger about the details of the offense, the skull can serve much the same purpose as did the earlier ghost. And so it does in *The Revenger's Tragedy.*

Tourneur probably made the switch initially because the connotations which came ready-packaged with the skeleton, closely associated with the grave as it was, better suited his personal vision than those of the supernatural which surround the ghost. By substituting the skull he could exploit its traditional function as a *memento mori*, making ironic contrasts between its two "unsightly rings" and the "heaven-pointed diamonds" once set within them or between the "ragged bone" and the three-piled velvet that vainly bedecked it. Nevertheless, though the skull is central to the personal vision, it also serves Tourneur in many of the same functions that were served by the ghost.

The skull of Gloriana, the source and constant reminder of Vindice's anger, was obviously the catalyst in transforming the protagonist from what he was to what he is. His opening soliloquy is a meditation. The skull, both his "studies' ornament" and the subject of his study, does not merely teach him about the frailness of human life. It fans his desire for revenge. Viewing it, he first recalls the loveliness of the lady. His mind passes from the living Gloriana to the dead one, and he meditates upon the outrage which the Duke committed against her. This meditation is a quasi-religious one; it leads Vindice to thoughts of the deity he worships and issues in a prayer to that deity:

> Vengeance, thou murder's quit-rent, and whereby
> Thou show'st thyself tenant to Tragedy,
> O keep thy day, hour, minute, I beseech,
> For those thou hast determin'd.
>
> [1.1.39–42]

His thoughts cannot rise up to heaven. He descends into himself and fixes his mind on Vengeance. This brooding upon the skull keeps Vindice's emotions at high pitch. We are obviously to assume that Vindice finds frequent occasions for such brooding.

Besides keeping the offense fresh in Vindice's mind, the skull gives him authority to revenge that offense. The ghost in *The Spanish Tragedy, Antonio's Revenge,* and *Hamlet* stood for the spirit of revenge in the universal sense in which revenge is a primitive

urge for justice sensed by each individual—it represented
something outside the psyche as well as something inside it.
Thus it was always seen by several people so that its reality might
be attested to. Since it came from a world beyond, it gave the
revenger authority to do the deed. To be sure, its "authority,"
the law of nature, was lower than that of the law of man or the
law of Providence, but it was sufficient to motivate the revenger.
The skull serves a similar function for Vindice. But Tourneur
apparently wished to suggest that the spirit of revenge origi-
nated in the individual psyche alone. Given this source of authority, the skeleton was a better symbol than the ghost. The
skull has no supernatural origins. It is a "dumb" god, and since
its commands are only the commands one's emotions draw from
interaction with it, it can be made to "authorize" whatever one
wishes it to authorize. In the ultimate sense, Vindice's authority
for the deed comes only from his own will.

The skull, then, can be viewed as a substitution for the ghost.
As such, it retains the original functions of providing the revenger with a source of authority and of winding up his passions
to their full height by keeping the memory of the offense vivid in
his mind. But the authority is now seen to be subjective.[8]

III In denouncing the tendency of the human being to live
for the "bewitching minute" rather than for eternity,
Vindice describes those whose lives are governed by the passion
of lust as "mad people." The truly mad creatures are not those in
Bedlam, but we who have our reason and abuse it. Ironically,
Vindice is describing not only the Duke, Lussurioso, the
Youngest Son, and those like them in the world outside of the
play, but also himself. As revenger, he has taken on a role that
makes him "near kin to this present minute." Vindice can see the
crimes of others, but he is morally blind to his own failings.
Having given himself up to a passion even more irrational than
lust, for it leads to the greater sin, Vindice is also "mad."

The substitution of the skull for the ghost is useful to
Tourneur in this regard—it enables him to establish Vindice's
madness quickly. By associating his hero with a skull in the
opening scene he achieves an effect he could not have created

with a ghost. Revenge ghosts inspired awe. Each in some way manifested power—Andrea, assisted by Revenge and championed by Proserpine, wielded the power of destiny, Andrugio of violence, King Hamlet of regality. All were mysterious. When we see Hamlet confronting the Ghost, we have a sense of fear. We admire his courage in meeting it. When we see Vindice with his skull, our impression is different. There is no power, no mystery, no awe about a skull, only morbidity, even perversity. Tourneur exploits these connotations of the grave in his opening scene. The viewer, confronted immediately with the visual image of man and skull, senses some disorientation in Vindice's mind. His behavior seems abnormal.

Although Tourneur uses the conventional madness, he alters the usual relationship between the madness and the delay. Tourneur is the first to begin his revenge tragedy at the end. Kyd, Marston, and Goffe start at the beginning. They show us the revenger at an especially happy moment. Hieronimo basks in the reflected glory earned by his distinguished son. Antonio enters on his wedding morning, filled with joy. Orestes happily welcomes his father back to Argos after ten years' absence. Shakespeare introduces his revenger a bit later, after the offense against him has been committed. But he provides us through Ophelia with a glimpse of the carefree Hamlet of the Wittenberg days, and he lets us meet Hamlet before the prince becomes aware of the full magnitude of the offense. Moreover, all four authors attempt to convey the shock which their respective protagonists experience, and they then trace the long, painful process which involves procrastination as much as it does preparation. Tourneur omits all of this. He introduces Vindice only after Vindice is emotionally ready to commit the deed.

In *The Revenger's Tragedy,* the conventional "delay" is condensed into one sentence which tells us that the offense against Gloriana had taken place some nine years in the past. All we know of Vindice's actions during the period between the Duke's commission of the deed and Vindice's appearance at the court is that Vindice has been brooding the whole time upon the injury. This we learn from the fact that the skull has been "my studies' ornament" (1.1.15). What battles he had with himself over the pleasures and agonies of killing the Duke we can only guess at. All we can be sure of is that, since he has finally come to court

ready to act, such waverings are now behind him. Vindice is well
into the madness when we meet him.

Because the revenger's delay is one of the traits which earns
him the audience's sympathy, its absence leads many
commentators to align Vindice with the villain-revenger.[9] Vindice's dramatic ancestry, however, is not in the line descending
from Chettle's Hoffman, Marlowe's Barabas, or Marston's Piero,
who personify evils of one sort or another, nor is he related,
even distantly, to Shakespeare's Aaron the Moor, whose malignancy is motiveless. Vindice becomes a villain, as do all revengers who allow their passion for justice to drive them beyond
the limits of human prerogative, but this very passion for justice
marks him as the true kin of Hieronimo, Antonio, and Hamlet.
Although Vindice's virtue has already been tainted by the madness as the play opens, we are to assume that, at the time of his
betrothal to Gloriana and before her death at the hands of the
Duke, Vindice was a good man.

Tourneur suggests his protagonist's earlier virtue in two
ways—through his loathing of the Duke and through his respect
for Gratiana and Castiza. Since we first meet Vindice presenting
the vices of the Duke and his sons to us as despicable and sub-
human, we associate him immediately with the forces of good,
and since we also see him as a member of the one family in the
play which stands for virtue, we link him as much with Gratiana
and Castiza as with the vice-ridden family which rules the
court.[10] Thus from the beginning we have the ambiguity typical
of revenge tragedy: Vindice means to be good, believes he *is*
good, and ultimately does bring about good (goals never associated with the villain-revenger), but he has become so intensely
involved in his crusade against evil that his actions become more
and more perverse.

Tourneur is less eager than Kyd or Shakespeare to acknowledge the mysterious nature of justice or to stress its ultimate
incomprehensibility to the mere mortal. The evils in the world of
this play are not so much inherent in the universe as they are
signs of the corrupt will of man. As Lussurioso says, "it is our
blood to err, though hell gap'd loud" (1.3.73). All of the characters are caught in their moment of error; we know no more
about them than their particular sin, the sin by which they have
chosen to define their lives. Tourneur's is the vision of satire

rather than of tragedy. Fittingly, therefore, he allows Vindice's madness to find expression in the unbalanced railing of the satirist.

One of the chief characteristics of the conventional madness is the exaggerated obsession with evil, manifested in the narrowed but perceptive vision of the revenger. So it is with the satirist, as Alvin Kernan's analysis of the similarities between the two roles so clearly indicates: both satirist and blood revenger

> find themselves in a world where virtue has been dispossessed by vice and in a once healthy society now become morally sick. Both are unable to hold their tongues but discover in themselves an agonized compulsion to reveal the truth by speaking out, and to unmask the world's pretenses to virtue by clever arrangement of events and scene. Both find it necessary, though for somewhat different reasons, to probe to the very source of infection in the state and cut it out of the body politic.[11]

How natural, then, that Tourneur should make Vindice the satirical presenter of the allegorical pageant. The device allows Vindice to maintain a semblance of rational control impossible in the lunatic while indicating how the passion for revenge has affected his vision and warped his mind. His attitude toward lust becomes the image of his madness.

It is important that we recognize Vindice's obsession as an obligatory aspect of the revenger's madness, for many who do not tend to assume that the bitterness spills out of Tourneur himself. Hieronimo, Antonio, and Hamlet all began their careers as revengers by pledging to shut from their minds all thoughts but thoughts of revenge. Each, by carrying out this pledge, is driven to madness. Tourneur relies upon our awareness of this tradition. We see in Vindice the same preoccupation with evil, the same depth of insight into its nature, the same inability to relate to goodness in the normal ways. His attitude toward Gloriana becomes twisted and vulgar; he sees her beauty only as something which aroused lust. He cannot accept the virtue of his mother and sister on faith but feels a compulsion to "test" them. Vindice has developed the macabre sensibility that we find in Hamlet when he converses with the gravedigger (but he lacks Hamlet's composure). The narrowness of the world of *The Revenger's Tragedy* itself is in a sense the result of the fact that Vindice is its presenter. We see only what he shows us, and what he shows us is a reflection of a mind which has deliberately narrowed its focus because of its irrational preoccupation with evil.

There is, of course, that element of inspiration in the madness which both Mack and Kernan recognize in defining Jacobean uses of the aberration in literature.[12] Vindice, in his altered state, pierces through the layers of corruption to the realities beneath. Having kept company with the mask of death for nine years, he is vividly conscious that all vanity ends in the grave, where "three-pil'd flesh" becomes "worm's meat"; he alone perceives that every mortal must one day answer to "that eternal eye / That sees through flesh and all" (1.3.66–67). Clearly and sharply Vindice isolates the definitive vice of each person at court. The realities perceived in his mind become the landscape of the play, and in this sense the landscape projected onto the stage resembles that of Dante's *Inferno,* where each sinner is trapped for eternity in the posture that reflects his most characteristic desire. The emblematic scene in which the Duke kisses the poisoned skull of Gloriana is not far removed, either in its conception or in its revelation of truth, from those in which Paolo and Francesca whirl about forever caught in the incessant winds of passion or Farinata rises cursing from his tomb to arrogantly affirm his wrath. Narrowly focused though it may be, Vindice's vision is deep and penetrating, stripping away appearances and exposing grotesque realities.

Yet, and here again Tourneur has shaped Vindice's madness in accordance with the experience that underlies the convention, the very obsession which makes a prophet of Vindice also causes him to usurp an authority that society cannot tolerate in the private individual. Comprehending injustice does not give one the right to enforce it. Like Marston's Antonio, Vindice feels that Heaven applauds his deeds:

> No power is angry when the lustful die;
> When thunder claps, heaven likes the tragedy.
>
> [5.3.47–48]

But he is wrong.

IV Both of the elements we have been discussing, the skull and the madness, come together in act 3, scene 5, and are joined with the play-within-the-play. Vindice's use of the skull here is sure testimony to the distortions which his passion for revenge has created in his mind, while the play he organizes provides us with an illustration of his attempt to reshape the world in terms of his own desires.

Because Vindice functions as the presenter of *The Revenger's Tragedy* and is both its prologue and chorus, there is a sense in which the whole drama may be seen as Vindice's play-within-the-play, for the nightmare world of the play reflects his way of seeing, and even actions which he does not witness (the Ambitioso / Supervacuo episodes, for example) are so constructed that they *seem* to be part of his vision. Vindice enters the world of the court as Hieronimo enters his *Soliman and Perseda* and through his various "roles" exerts a similar kind of control over the characters.

Nevertheless, Tourneur follows the lead of Kyd, Marston, and Shakespeare in his actual handling of the play-within-the-play convention. In his main plot, following Shakespeare in *Hamlet,* he has crowded all of the revenge tragedy form into the first three acts, with the last two given over to the matter of excess. Thus, in the climactic death scene of the Duke, we find deliberate echoes of the Kydian "play-within," where the revenger's play gives us a glimpse into the psyche which has created it. The effect, one more often used in the novel or film than in drama, is that of the close-up: we have had a panoramic view of Vindice's mind and now we will be given a close-up that provides heightened intensity. In the playlet concluding the secondary plot, on the other hand, Tourneur imitates Marston; he not only picks up the masque from *Antonio's Revenge,* but doubles it, and in his ending permits his own Antonio to pass judgment on Marston's by restoring the conventional conclusion wherein the revenger goes to his death along with his victims.

Let us look first at the Kydian pattern. Many scholars have commented upon Tourneur's use of two masques at the end of *The Revenger's Tragedy,* and the first of these is invariably assumed to fulfill the play-within-the-play requirement of the revenge tragedy form. Few have noticed, however, that Vindice views his earlier plot to lure the Duke to the unsunned lodge in theatrical terms. To him, it is "my tragic business" (3.5.98), and he choses the setting deliberately for its appropriateness to the action he plans to present. Vindice himself arrives in costume, his role being that of Piato the pander. Gloriana, too, "shall bear a part" in the play (3.5.100). Vindice attires his dead mistress in a velvet gown and provides her with a mask, not, he assures us, "only for show / And useless property" (3.5.99–100) but because she is to be his leading lady. The Duke too will take part in the play; he will, in fact, along with Vindice and Hippolito, be both actor and audience. The role he plays in the improvised drama will open his eyes to the meaning of his actions in real life. The action of the main revenge plot, that involving Vindice's attempt to obtain revenge upon the Duke for his murder of Gloriana, thus ends with a play-within-the-play.

But Vindice is constructing more than a play; he is also constructing that private world symbolized by the "sealed-off room" of revenge tragedy, in which there is no reality but the reality of his own passion for revenge. In this world the Duke's crime against Gloriana is ever present, as it is ever present in his obsessed mind. The presence of the skull and the reenactment of the original offense staged by Vindice serve to dramatize in visual terms the actual process going on in his psyche, where his continual brooding upon the past keeps the offense fresh and prevents the healing effects of time from allaying his grief. In this world there are no restrictions, legal or moral, to keep the passions in check, and Vindice's imagination is free to indulge itself in every cruel fantasy, in the attempt to retaliate for the injury done him. Above all, in this world Vindice's own will is supreme: the Duke is rendered powerless the moment he enters it, and Vindice is no longer subject to his authority. Not only is Vindice freed from subservience to the Duke. He is, in this world created out of his own madness, an instrument of Heaven and therefore has divine authority for anything he might do. All the conditions in this closed-off world allow the revenger to act. With Vindice ordering events, justice is immediate and final—the Duke is poisoned in the very act of defiling Gloriana.

Naturally any close-up of Vindice's mind must take into consideration his profound insights into the nature of lust, that particular evil his mind has fastened on. The play that Vindice stages becomes what Kernan has described as a scene of truth.[13] The gorgeous trappings that in the Duke's world conceal or ameliorate the degradations involved in the act of lust—the

lecherous passion of the seducer and his misuse of power, the
defiling of virtue, even the corruption of the pander—are
stripped away, and the act is revealed to be an act that poisons
not only the body but the soul of all who participate in it. The
"scene" created by Vindice's psyche projects before us an accurate image of lust, but of course it also reveals a mind obsessed
by the subject. As with Hamlet's attitudes toward Ophelia, those
of Vindice are no longer balanced by an appreciation of chaste
love that would serve to counter the repulsion toward its misuse.

The world which Vindice creates in his "play" is no less a true
image of revenge; this passion, too, is seen for what it is as the
psyche of the revenger is flashed before us in close-up upon the
stage. Two points might be made: first, that the revenger believes he is doling out perfect justice, and, second, that Vindice's
justice dissolves into that deliberate and excessive cruelty which
is so integral a part of the advanced stages of the revenger's
madness.

As Vindice conceives it, the revenge is not complete unless the
Duke, as he dies, is brought face to face with the meaning of his
actions. Justice requires him to experience the horror of his own
sins; his "eyes" must "see" what he has wrought:

> Brother,
> Place the torch here, that his affrighted eyeballs
> May start into these hollows. Duke, dost know
> Yon dreadful vizard? View it well; 'tis the skull
> Of Gloriana, whom thou poisoned'st last.
> [3.5.144–48]

Having poisoned Gloriana, the Duke must in justice die by poison. Death for death, however, is not enough. There is more:

> Pooh! 'tis but early yet; now I'll begin
> To stick thy soul with ulcers. I will make
> Thy spirit grievous sore: it shall not rest,
> But like some pestilent man toss in thy breast.
> [3.5.171–74]

The justice of revenge also requires torture. As Vindice was
forced to endure the loss of his betrothed, so the Duke must
experience the loss of his wife to Spurio. His "eyes shall see the
incest of their lips" (3.5.181), and "if he but wink, not brooking
the foul object," Vindice and Hippolito are ready to "tear up his

lids / And make his eyes like comets shine through blood"
(3.5.196–98). The two brothers make a reality of their vengeful
fantasies that again graphically demonstrates the obsessed state
of the imagination under the influence of the revenge passion.

Following a precedent set in *Hamlet* where the play and the
murder are moved forward into act 3, Tourneur has used up the
action called for by the revenge tragedy form in only three acts.
But to further illuminate the experience of revenge, he has included a subplot which involves Vindice in a revenge action
against another member of the ruling family, Lussurioso. This
action, too, will culminate in a play-within-the-play.

The subplot relates to the major plot in two ways. Because
Lussurioso attempts to commit the same crime his father had
committed (he would seduce another of Vindice's loved ones),
the secondary plot provides the audience with a visual substitute
for the crime against Gloriana. Seeing this attack upon the chastity of Castiza, we can sense the outrage Vindice felt nine years
ago; the Duke's guilt becomes more concrete against this background and Vindice's desire for revenge upon him is more
readily acceptable.[14] Additionally, the subplot provides Tourneur with another means of showing how the passion of revenge
leads to excess, in that we see Vindice becoming habituated to
crime. Having killed the Duke, he finds it easier to plot against
Lussurioso, and the second time round he kills four people instead of only one.

Vindice's progressive deterioration is marked out in three
stages, each distinguished by the disguise he is wearing. In the
first instance, Vindice, an honest man, wishing to gain entrance
to the court world where only malcontents and flatterers receive
advancement, has presented himself to Lussurioso as Piato, a
"man o' th' time," that is, a pander. The disguise is obviously an
unnatural one. It requires a transformation in Vindice: he must
"quickly turn into another" (1.1.134). As Hippolito affirms,
Vindice is far enough from himself that it seems "as if another
man had been sent whole / Into the world" (1.3.2–3). The disguise also forces him to act in ways contrary to his nature, for in
his first interview with Lussurioso he finds himself sworn to be-
tray his own sister.

Transferred from the House of Gratiana to the world of the
court, Vindice progresses a step further into the madness: he

reaches a point where he can actually take pleasure in the hunting and trapping of his enemy. His initial irritation soon becomes overlain with a grotesque glee as he goes beyond justice and engages in violence for its own sake. Leslie Sanders puts it well: "Vindice's journey is a journey into madness in the sense that he creates an alter-ego and loses all grasp on himself."[15] Eventually there is no longer a real Vindice; he has entered so far into deceit that he *is* the man he pretends to be. To put on the role of Vindice again is to put on a new disguise.

In this second stage of his stay at court, Vindice has less ado to fit in with the times. The work that he formerly had to "put on that knave" to do, he can now do in his own person. Again Hippolito stresses the point—"Y'are yourself" (4.2.1); "Now thou art thyself" (4.2.4)—and Vindice repeats the lesson "I'll turn myself" (4.2.32). "Disguised" as Vindice, he is no longer engaged in the relatively menial assignments of the pander; he has been promoted to the calling of murderer. It is both comic and ironic that he is assigned to murder himself, for in pursuing revenge he is destroying what is best in him.

The masque supplies Vindice with his third disguise, and at this point Tourneur begins to juxtapose Ambitioso and Supervacuo more noticeably to Hippolito and Vindice. In parallel scenes, he shows the concern of each pair of brothers with the conduct of their mother. Since the intervention of Supervacuo and Ambitioso into the Duchess's affair with Spurio comes to naught, the episode's only function is to link these brothers with Hippolito and Vindice, who in the next scene display a parallel interest in Gratiana's moral state. There is an important distinction, of course. Supervacuo and Ambitioso are interested only insofar as their mother's behavior throws shame upon themselves, whereas Vindice and Hippolito are truly concerned for their parent's virtue; they would purge her of evil and take sincere satisfaction in her tears of repentance. Even as Vindice finds it easier and easier to eradicate those sinners he has singled out for death, he never fails to honor the virtue whose cause he believes he is defending. Vindice's *methods,* nevertheless, are identical to those of his victims; therefore, he and Hippolito finally become as culpable as Supervacuo and Ambitioso. In the masque-within-the-play in act 5, these revengers not only come in disguised in the costumes designed for the Duchess's sons,

having copied the patterns "e'en to an undistinguish'd hair almost," but also commit the very deed—the murder of Lussurioso—that Supervacuo and Ambitioso had planned to per-
petrate. The point seems incontrovertible: the revengers, in
pushing their desire for justice into the realm of excess, have
reduced themselves to the level of the villains.

Needless to say, in the multiple murders we have still another
example of the way the desire for revenge runs out of control
and involves the innocent. Vindice sets out to bring the Duke to
justice but is soon bent also upon thrusting a sword into Lussurioso. We might excuse him for this, for Lussurioso, too,
abuses his power. But when Vindice finally annihilates the
prince, he takes the lives of several lords simply because they
happen to be there on the dais with Lussurioso. The indictment
and subsequent execution of the Fourth Lord for deeds perpetrated by Vindice also illustrates how things go out of control.
With the stage strewn with corpses and our memory fresh with
Vindice's growing pleasure in the "quaintness" and "wittiness" of
his vengeful devices, we are left with no doubts that revenge, in
its irresistible charge toward justice, is as destructive as it is
beneficial.

V   Throughout *The Revenger's Tragedy* the author has indi-
cated that there are detectable laws in the universe
through which justice will eventually triumph. One of them is an
idea made theatrically current by those comedies of Jonson and
Middleton written around the same time as *The Revenger's Tragedy,* that evil will finish off evil. Ambitioso kills Supervacuo to
gain the ducal title, and Spurio, for the same reason, puts a
sword through Ambitioso. The instability of the evil nature,
combined with its propensity toward wickedness, makes it inevitable that such fatal quarrels will break out. Vindice, in his
Hamlet-like efforts to manipulate and control, merely frustrates
the natural operation of this tendency. In act 1 Spurio lies in wait
for Lussurioso outside of Castiza's house, meaning to kill him.
By diverting Lussurioso from the tryst, Vindice ironically saves
Lussurioso from a just punishment. In act 5 Vindice performs
the very murders that would have been effected in the masque
minutes later by Ambitioso and Supervacuo. The author seems

to say that revenge is unnecessary. The Hieronimonian impatience, the Machiavellian plotting, and the Herculean fury of the revenger accomplish only what would have occurred in time through the warring passions of the victims.

More overt is Tourneur's insistence upon the law that Chaucer's Chanticleer proclaimed abroad—"Murder will out." Planted throughout the dialogue is the suggestion that the murderer will give himself away:

> Who e'er knew / Murder unpaid?
>
> [1.1.42–43]

> Murder will peep out of the closest husk.
>
> [4.2.202]

> No doubt but time
> Will make the murderer bring forth himself.
>
> [5.1.146–47]

> When murd'rers shut deeds close, this curse does seal 'em:
> If none disclose 'em, they themselves reveal 'em!
>
> [5.3.109–10]

Granted, says Tourneur, that the earthly courts have succumbed to human corruption (as in the case of the Duke's judgment of the Youngest Son) and even in better times will fall short of perfection because of human fallibility (as when Antonio condemns the Fourth Masquer for the wrong offense). Yet mysterious forces are in evidence that work to maintain order, and wrongs are ultimately exposed.

Thus it is that, in a characteristically Middletonian fashion, Vindice is moved to overreach himself.[16] Unable to resist boasting, he claims credit for the murder of the Duke and is promptly imprisoned by Antonio. The incident, though well prepared for, strains belief; however, its aesthetic rightness does much to overcome the dramatic awkwardness. Were Vindice to live, our objections would be stronger.

In the play's third plot there is another covert suggestion that justice might have been effected without the violence inherent in the vendetta. Antonio, the protagonist, had as much cause to seek revenge as had Vindice. Far from making attempts on the life of the youngest son, Antonio had instead brought the case into court and, failing there, remained patient. By the end of the

play the Youngest Son has been put to death through the workings of an ironical fate, while Antonio himself has been elevated
to the highest office in the state and charged with the task of
maintaining justice under the new order. Antonio's route has
been at least as effective as Vindice's.

As is to be expected of the revenge form, the play opens out
after the masque, as the earthly authorities pass judgment on the
events that occurred within it. One is probably safe in guessing,
if only from the allusion contained in Antonio's name, that
Tourneur was making a direct comment—in fact a
correction—of Marston's treatment of the death-of-the-avenger
motif in *Antonio's Revenge*. The boasting of Vindice parallels that
of Pandulpho, Alberto, and Antonio, who would not "lose the
glory of the deed" and who vied for recognition from the
senators of Venice. Tourneur's Antonio, the counterpart of
these Venetian elders, makes a contrary judgment: the revengers are not to be "religiously held sacred." What they have done
once, they may do (and indeed already have done) again. Whatever the benefits of their action to the state, and to Antonio
personally, they have committed a crime. For that they must be
punished. By having Vindice acquiesce to the judgment placed
upon him, Tourneur affirms its rightness—aligns himself, so to
speak, with Antonio. Certainly he makes it clear that Antonio
ushers in no Golden Age—even *he* is subject to human error. Yet
the revenger cannot be allowed to triumph. Having had his
"minute" and misused it, 'tis his "time" to die.

Much of the interest in Tourneur's use of the revenge tragedy
materials lies in the way they constantly make allusions to earlier
scenes and sequences. Tourneur comes at a point in the tradition when the motifs are so well known that he can simply sketch
in their outlines and depend on the audience to grasp the point,
and he is therefore free to range a bit from the stricter format.
His transformations are imaginative. Vindice, with Gloriana's
skull, rings changes on the convention of the ghost. The change
reverberates with echoes of the skeletons cherished by Hieronimo and Hoffman and skillfully develops a theme that was
latent in *Hamlet* when the prince picked up the skull of Yorick.
New meaning is given to the roles of minor characters like Pedringano, Strotzo, and Lorrique by Tourneur's inventive decision
to combine the tool villain's role with the conventional disguise.

The satire, so unsuccessfully worked into *Antonio's Revenge,* here becomes a thematic medium through which Vindice's madness is rendered believable. Variations are played both upon Kyd's play-within-the-play and Marston's, with the allusions to the latter preparing for a deliberate overturning of Marston's interpretation of the death-of-the-avenger motif. Yet the changes are all held within limits. The alterations are never so radical that the motifs become wrenched out of their places in the configuration or divorced from the experience they were designed to portray.

Chapter 10
The Derivative Play:
Goffe's The Tragedy of Orestes

> It seems clear that Goffe at least partially understood the psychology by which the sudden shock of the murder of a father, the consequent turning-inward of grief and the forced repression of the normal outlet of instant vengeance, would so work on the character of an erstwhile good man that, when the path was made clear, his pent-up emotions would burst out in terrible retribution. Goffe comprehended that such an action was made possible by the buckling of the revenger's moral nature under the burden of an unbearable wrong which he had been too long helpless to right.
>
> Fredson Bowers, *Elizabethan Revenge Tragedy*

THE ARTISTIC MEDIOCRITY of Thomas Goffe's *The Tragedy of Orestes* has relegated to near obscurity a Kydian revenge play dating from around 1623. This oversight is unfortunate, because Goffe's interpretation of the form has immense value for critical purposes. Insofar as the work was written by a student at Christ Church, Oxford (and there performed), *Orestes* offers a detailed description of what a young man living in the Jacobean era understood Kydian tragedy to be; it is the nearest thing we have to a contemporary dissertation on the genre. Because Goffe is a completely derivative artist, no personal vision intervenes to obscure the essential outlines of the form. All of the motifs occur in a pure state that simplifies analysis, while wholesale importation of key scenes and speeches from such plays as *Antonio's Revenge* and *Hamlet* tells us much about their thematic importance. The usefulness of this play as a critical tool suggests the need for a modern edition.[1]

244

Throughout this book we have claimed that revenge tragedy motifs were interpreted in their own time in a way that no modern critic has attempted to interpret them. A radical departure in method has been made here from the methods previously used in analyses of revenge tragedy. Yet thus far only internal evidence from those plays normally called revenge tragedies has been produced to support the contention that the public, as well as the playwrights, recognized the symbolic content of the motifs. In Goffe's play, however, a record has been preserved that indicates how the English playgoing public understood the revenge play. This young man, a near contemporary but a nonprofessional, someone apparently not personally acquainted with the dramatists writing for the London theaters, sat down to write a revenge play and produced a text that confirms the theories set forth in this book.

Goffe, in a university setting, wanted to create a drama based on Greek myth for his university audience. There is evidence that he had both Greek and Latin plays—Euripides and Seneca, for example—available to him. To accomplish his goals he might simply have translated the Greek texts, ending up with a play that alternated strophes with antistrophes, gave a major role to a chorus of elders, banished all its violent action from the stage, and so on. But he does not. The English tradition of revenge drama so dominates Goffe's imagination that his *Orestes* comes out looking more like another revenge play than it does like any previous adaptation of the Orestes myth.

Except for a very different kind of madness, none of the motifs are to be found in the classical sources. Thus, when Goffe chose to turn the Orestes story into a revenge play, his first task was to isolate the elements that made *The Spanish Tragedy, Antonio's Revenge, Hamlet,* or *The Revenger's Tragedy* revenge tragedies and the next was to find ways of incorporating these elements into his Greek story. With amazing acuity he selected the ghost, the delay, the madness, the disguise, the multiple murders, and the death of the avenger. Although his revenger writes no play-within-the-play, Goffe achieves the same effect by emphasizing the sealed-off room. These motifs he insists upon even where changes must be made that violate the original myth. In the Greek, Orestes' madness does not occur until after he has murdered Clytemnestra and Aegisthus: the Furies torment

Orestes because he has slain his mother.[2] Goffe moves the madness forward to the moments immediately following Agamemnon's death (it begins when Orestes experiences the shock of seeing his father brutally killed) and lets it increase in intensity as the action progresses. He also adds a few extra murders to provide for the excess. Finally, he sentences Orestes to death, even though in Greek versions Orestes is invariably cleared of all criminal intent. This reshaping of material that had already been cast in dramatic form into the motifs recognized today as comprising revenge tragedy indicates public awareness *in the era* of such motifs.

More significant than Goffe's use of the motifs are the relationships he develops between them. Since he is drawing upon four or five different plays in constructing his own (including some, like *Macbeth,* from outside the revenge tragedy tradition), any kind of jumble could have been made of the motifs, had Goffe's understanding of them been that of twentieth-century critics. Since the mad Cassandra wanders about his stage, he might have considered this a sufficient dose of madness and left Orestes completely sane, or he could have had the Ghost of Agamemnon appear to Aegystheus, as Banquo's ghost appears to Macbeth. No particular order or relationship need have been observed. But despite the diversity of his material, Goffe comprehends it well enough so that one can immediately see in *Orestes* a faithful reproduction of the configuration.

Though to Goffe and to us it seems appropriate to view Orestes' actions in terms of the revenge passion, very different interpretations had been put upon the myth in the English tradition. The existence of John Pikeryng's dramatization of it in 1567, called in its day an interlude but containing an odd blend of chronicle and morality, demonstrates how possible it had been for an Englishman to view the Orestes story quite differently. Pikeryng, who has less contact with the Greek, is paradoxically far more faithful to the Aeschylean spirit of the myth. The essential outlines of the story are not violated as in Goffe. Where Goffe's alterations directly pertain to the hero's psychology and character, so that the myth is changed at its very center, Pikeryng's additions come in the form of extra characters, external trappings, elements that are nailed onto the central structure like ornamentation on a facade.

I A tendency has developed among recent critics to push the origins of revenge tragedy back beyond Kyd to Pikeryng: what was a miracle of spontaneous generation is reduced to a case of plodding, mechanical, and inevitable evolution. These critics read into Pikeryng's *Horestes* a concern with the passion of revenge and attempt to identify revenge themes in every episode of the interlude.[3] But these are concerns of the critic, not of Pikeryng. When Pikeryng's play is set beside Goffe's, the differences are more striking than the similarities. Pikeryng, writing about twenty years before Hieronimo's spectacular entrance into theater history, is innocent of all knowledge of the so-called revenge tragedy motifs. Although insanity is an integral part of Orestes' story in Greek tellings, even the madness is missing from this early play. Pikeryng gives little real thought to the *experience* of the revenge passion; he is rather transmitting a historical story very much as he found it in John Gower and William Caxton, adding to it, as Gower had done, the moral that murderers like Clytemnestra will e'er long be brought to justice.[4] As David Bevington points out, "the hero's spiritual struggle is not integral to the action."[5]

If we glance at Pikeryng's construction first, we will better appreciate how important a witness the Goffe play is to the significance of revenge tragedy motifs. The Tudor play contains thirteen brief scenes.[6] The majority of these recount the events leading up to Orestes' killing of Clytemnestra, with the main action being grouped into three stages. In the first section (scenes 2, 4, and 5), Pikeryng establishes the rightness of Horestes' mission. When Horestes enters, he is puzzling over the dilemma he finds himself in. Contemplated from the point of view of law, Clytemnestra's evils oblige him to punish her. Yet natural instinct (what he calls "paterne love") tells him that because Clytemnestra is his mother he should forgive and pity her. Horestes asks the gods to resolve the question:

> O godes therfor sith you be iust, unto whose poure and wyll
> All thing in heauen, and earth also obaye and sarue untyll
> Declare to me your gracious mind.
>
> [212–14]

A character presenting himself as Courage enters at this point, proclaiming that the gods, requiring Horestes to revenge the

wrong done to Agamemnon, have sent him as their messenger
and guide. To dispel any hesitancy in accepting this as adequate
authorization, Pikeryng buttresses it by having Horestes seek
sanction from King Idumeus, who with his advisor, Councell,
sides with "Courage" in approving the deed. Horestes is opposed in scene 4 by Dame Nature, who takes the side of Clytemnestra, but Pikeryng makes his hero firmly victorious in the
debate with Nature through Horestes' argument that the laws of
god and man both demand the murderer's death:

> If that the law doth her condemne, as worthy death to haue,
> Oh nature wouldst thou wil that I, her life should seem to saue:
> To saue her lyfe whom law doth slay, is not iustice to do,
> Therefore I saye I wyll not yeld, they hestes to com unto.
>
> [520–24]

This scene, not in Pikeryng's sources, has been interpreted as
his attempt to render the ambiguities of the revenge passion on
stage, but Horestes' tone here is authoritative, not willful. The
debate aims at reinforcing Horestes' insistence upon the superiority of justice over natural instinct. The position of "Courage"
is thus twice upheld. This section concludes with a tender part-
ing between Horestes and Idumeus after the latter has equipped
Horestes with troops for the war on Mycenae.

Although sketchily presented, the psychological conflict is
similar to that found in the seventeenth-century plays, but the
forces operating on Horestes are exactly reversed in their demands. In Kydian tragedy, natural urges press for the act of
revenge, law for patience and rational restraint. Here the opposite is true. Law is on the side of action, Nature against it.
Pikeryng recognizes that there is a large element of disorder in
the unnatural position Horestes must take toward his mother;
hence, he makes the Vice partly responsible for his hero's decision. Yet he takes pains to build up support for the necessity and
justice of drastic action in this case.

The loophole in conception which allows critics to turn Pikeryng's presentation topsy-turvy and read into this preparatory
section a "passion for revenge" that Horestes ought to subdue in
himself is that the character of Courage is actually the Vice,
Revenge, in disguise. The viewer's immediate response is to assume that if Revenge is the authorizing figure, the authorization

probably does not amount to much. Horestes is being deceived; the gods would send no such sign. Pikeryng even seems to encourage this attitude, for in the comic introduction to the play, Revenge masquerades as Patience in order to tempt two rustics into a quarrel, thus setting a precedent that would militate against our taking "Courage" at face value. The Vice is presented as a tempter. And he does try to stir Horestes up.

> Com on Horestes sith thou hast, obtayned thy desier.
> Tout tout man, seke to dystroye, as doth the flaming fier:
> Whose properte thou knoest doth gro, as long as any thing
> Is left wher by the same may seme, som suckcor for to bring.
>
> [331–34]

But Horestes is never really portrayed as tempted. He is given an autonomy and a dignity throughout the play that lifts him above the Mankind role. Pikeryng gives us the feeling that the Vice carries out Horestes' commands rather than Horestes his.

This Vice is far from a conventional Vice. He is vestigial, retaining few medieval traits beyond the characteristic one of troublemaker. He is definitely meant to be amusing—often, like his predecessors, a comic butt. As deceiver, he is not effective, for we are expected to believe that Horestes does indeed have the backing of the gods. Nor is the Vice vengeful, in the sense that the Elizabethan playwrights allegorize revenge. This Vice might better be called Discord. His primary desire is to foster enmity, and the virtue opposed to him is harmony. Yet even as Discord, his behavior is inconsistent. The simple fact is, Pikeryng is not entirely sure what to do with the Vice.[7] Therefore all that a critic can say of Revenge is that he is far too closely associated with the enforcement of earthly and divine law to be either the totally evil figure that a Vice is expected to be or the totally passionate incitement to excess that the Kydian ghost becomes.

Section two of the interlude treats of Horestes' attempts to carry out his mission. Delay is never a question in Pikeryng's conception. Certain that the gods approve of his intent, Horestes presses forward with his troops, conquering the lands lying in his path and arriving finally before the gates of his native city. With Egistus gone to raise an army in the provinces, Horestes does battle first with Clytemnestra's forces, which he easily defeats. His courage fails him, however, when his mother begs for

her life. Momentarily weakening, he has her imprisoned rather
than executed, while he attends to the threats now posed by the
army of Egistus. This opposition, too, is overcome. But Egistus
wins no clemency: Horestes orders that he be hanged immediately for his crimes (a feat which by some astonishing manage-
ment of stage effects is accomplished in full view of the audience). Clytemnestra is then brought out, sentenced to death by
Horestes, and herded off by Revenge who must carry out the
judgment.

Revenge delights in and the author deplores the ravages of
war which afflict the populace as Horestes pursues his mission.
Critics seize upon this and the fact that Revenge is made
Clytemnestra's executioner to insist that some guilt is attached to
Horestes for harboring this Vice within himself. This argument
has less force when one realizes that Pikeryng deliberately
omitted the cruel death meted out to Clytemnestra in his
sources, where the gods instructed Horestes

> That he hire Pappes scholde of tere
> Out of hire brest his oghne hondes,
> And for ensample of alle londes
> With hors sche scholde be todrawe,
> Til houndes hadde hire bones gnawe
> Withouten eny sepulture.[8]

What better sentence, had it been in the playwright's mind to
suggest the horrors instituted by the revenge passion. How
tame, beside this, is Revenge's speech to Clytemnestra, as he
leads her off to execution:

> Let me alone, com on a way, that thou weart out of sight,
> A pestelaunce on the [,] crabyd queane, I thinke thou do delyght,
> Him to molest, com on in hast, and troubell me no more,
> Com on com on, ites all in vaine, and get you on a fore.
> [998–1001]

The emphasis here is on humor. Pikeryng is obviously not
concerned with depicting excess. Only the guilty die, and
Horestes' hands are never stained by blood. He is given the role
of a divinely appointed judge doling out reasoned justice for
crimes that have too long gone unpunished.

In the final phase of the action, various leaders of state question Horestes' authority and, as in the Greek forms of the myth,

force him to stand trial at Athens for his actions. Pikeryng never suggests that Horestes is wrong, merely that his purposes are misunderstood. Menelaus organizes the trial, to which such famous kings as Nestor and Idumeus are summoned, and acts as attorney for the prosecution. Defending the dead Clytemnestra, Menelaus presents the act of matricide as an inhuman act and points out the destruction Horestes' wars have wrought. His arguments are not allowed to stand. Horestes speaks authoritatively on his own behalf:

> O ounckel that I neuer went, reuengment for to do,
> On fathers fose tyll by the godes, I was comaund there to
> Whose heastes no man dare once refuse, but wyllingly obaye
> That I haue slayne her wylfully, untruely you do saye.
> I dyd but that I could not chuse, ites hard for me to kycke,
> Syth gods commaund as one would say, in fayth against the prick.
> [1155–60]

Idumeus testifies to the truth of Horestes' claim that he was an instrument of the gods, and Nestor's overwhelming acceptance of the arguments for the defense leaves Menelaus no choice but to concede his error. Menelaus is persuaded to marry his daughter Hermione to Horestes, and the play ends with Horestes being triumphantly crowned by Truth and Dewtey. Revenge in Pikeryng's play is driven off by Amite.

Alternating with the scenes of high seriousness are comic interludes, many of them farcical variations on the fight. Usually in the dialogue of these scenes, one character or another uses the word *revenge,* and scholars have attempted to build this sparse evidence into the argument that the comic scenes thematically depict revenge. But again discord seems a better description. In one scene, two rustics come to blows over a dead pig. In another, two soldiers, Haultersycke and Hempstringe, quarrel over who is the better soldier. In a third, slightly more serious but still having elements of slapstick, a soldier is overcome and beaten by a woman he has attempted to imprison. Stage directions reveal a keen interest in the comic altercation: "Let the vice thwacke them both and run out" (181–85), "flout hym on the lipes" (447–48), "giue him a box on the eare" (473–75), "beate him" (760–61). These scenes of altercation among the lower orders underscore through contrast the nobility of Horestes' handling of his charge against Clytemnestra and

Egistus. But they are best understood in the light which Bevington places them. The author, Bevington notes, has invented
historical motivations for the vice figures of morality tradition
"in order to preserve their captivating brand of comedy."[9] The
scenes tell us nothing whatsoever about the emotion of revenge.

Despite the attempts of commentators to see in this play the
same conflicts that are present in Elizabethan revenge tragedy,
the conflicts acknowledged by Pikeryng are not those of Kyd or
Shakespeare, nor are psychological conflicts within the hero
thematically central. The play does acknowledge that its protagonist will have certain qualms about killing his own mother, both
before and after so doing, for such an act is highly unnatural. It
asserts that under normal conditions matricide is a horrendously
inhuman crime. But Pikeryng reminds his audience again and
again that Clytemnestra has forfeited her right to Horestes' respect by murdering Agamemnon, and characters in the play tell
us that Horestes is obliged to put down any natural feelings he
might have toward her. The emphasis is not placed, as in revenge tragedy, upon the conflict between two different modes of
justice making different demands upon the hero. The action
stresses, rather, that the mother's neglect of her duty to her
husband causes the son to neglect his duty to her. Crime leads to
a desire for vengeance, that to war, and the kingdom is poten-
tially destroyed. Only man's observance of his duty to the gods
can resolve the discord.

Gower had employed the myth to preach the lesson that one
should not choose to love in a place where love can only be
furthered by murder, for the gods will see that the murderers
are brought to justice. Pikeryng uses it to say that justice must be
upheld in the commonwealth. He subscribes to the age's belief
that people in high places must live virtuously, for what they do
is emulated by those below them:

> For lo the unyuersaull scoll, of all the world we knowe,
> Is once the pallace of a kinge, where vyces chefe do flow.
> And as to waters from on head, and fountayne oft do spring,
> So vyce and vertue oft do flo, from pallace of a kinge.
> Whereby the people seing that, the kinge adycte to be,
> To prosecute the lyke, they all do labor as we se.
>
> [631–36]

Once the people find that the prince can commit high crimes and escape punishment, they will be tempted to follow suit; consequently, evil deeds committed by rulers must not be tolerated. If their faults go unrevenged, "a thousand euylles would insu" (628).[10] Beyond this, Pikeryng's action teaches the proper relationship of soldiers to their king and of a king to his men, portrays rulers gaining wisdom by consulting with wise counselors, discusses the importance of amity to a kingdom—in short, suggests that each member of the state must fulfill his role if the commonwealth is to thrive. Pikeryng's moral is delivered at the close of the play by Dewtey:

> Where I Dewtey am neclected, of aney estate,
> Their stryfe and dyssention, my place do supplye:
> Cankred mallyse pryde, and debate,
> There for to rest, all meanes do trye.
> Then ruin comes after, of their state whereby,
> They are utterly extynguyshed, leuinge nought behynde,
> Whereof so much as their name we maye fynde.
> [1379–85]

Truth follows this up with the moral of Gower that murder will out:

> He that leadeth his lyfe, as his phansey doth lyke,
> Though for a whyle, the same he maye hyde:
> Yet Truth, the daughter of Tyme, wyll it seke,
> And so in a tyme, it wyll be discryde.
> Yet in such tyme as it can not, be denyed
> But receaue dew punnishment, as god shall se,
> For the faute commytted, most conuenient to be.
> [1386–93]

Pikeryng is writing his chronicle at the tale end of the morality tradition, and his presentation of Horestes' revenge has remnants of a form his audience would be familiar with. Many characteristics of the medieval style are recognizable. The bulk of the play is written in fourteeners, this being the meter used for the scenes of high seriousness. These are interspersed with song interludes, many in doggerel verse. Allegorical figures abound—Counsell, Dewtey, and Truth, Nature, Provision, Fame—even Nobelles and Commones make an appearance. These allegorical personages debate with or advise the hero and make pronouncements to the audience. Of course, Pikeryng introduces the Vice. But never, as in the plays to come, is the Vice of Revenge unmasked and revealed as the evil passion who has deceived and overthrown the Everyman he endeavors to guide. Horestes is never demeaned by insanity or excess, nor is he really "driven" by Revenge. Only in retrospect, and then with great strain, can one find in Pikeryng anything faintly resembling the concepts that first appear in Kyd and are subsequently used by Goffe in his *Orestes*.

II By the time Thomas Goffe turns to the Orestes myth (1623), revenge tragedy has taken on a life of its own. Totally different conventions exist, conventions so strong that even though Goffe had access to Greek plays as well as to the various transmissions of Dictys used by Pikeryng, his play resembles none of these. Goffe, like Pikeryng, shapes his material in the form dictated by his own age. His *Orestes* not only contains all of the revenge tragedy motifs but approaches these motifs as parts of a configuration; the motifs all relate to a central experience. Goffe displays a definite awareness that the revenge tragedy motifs deal with the effects of the passion of revenge upon the psyche.[11]

Goffe's handling of the passion differs markedly from that of his predecessors in an important respect. Goffe is a derivative poet. Rather than grappling with the raw experience, he goes to the work of others for his insights. As a result, his grasp of the revenge experience is less profound. The subtleties rendered through the motifs by Marston or Shakespeare, his chief models, are beyond Goffe's capacities as a dramatist to re-create, and some escape his notice altogether. His scenes, like the echoes they are, frequently ring hollow. In watching Orestes progress through the madness we find ourselves reminded more of other plays than of life.

The alterations Goffe has made in the configuration are thus controlled by two factors—first, his need to reshape the original Greek myth so that its story reflects the various stages of the passion and, second, his tendency to express that passion through already existing bits of language and structure.

In the original myth, Orestes is a small boy when Clytemnestra and Aegisthus murder Agamemnon. He is smuggled away immediately after the murder, usually by Electra, to be brought up elsewhere, in hopes that he will someday return to wreak vengeance upon the slayers of his father. The plays of Aeschylus, Sophocles, and Euripides all begin years later, with Orestes' return to his native land, his reunion with Electra, and their formulation of a plan to carry out the revenge.

Goffe alters this. He begins the play with Agamemnon's return to Troy, but makes Orestes already a young man of Hamlet's or Antonio's age. He sends Orestes onto the stage in a mood of joy, exultant over the happy prospects that reunion with his great father seems to promise:

> My empty soule is now fild to the top,
> Brimfull with gladnesse, and it must runne o'r.
>
> [1.3.2–3]

The pattern is the familiar one of revenge tragedy: Goffe sets the hero up for a devastating blow to his sensibilities. In the following scene, Clytemnestra and Aegystheus slay Agamemnon in his bed and withdraw, while Orestes, prompted by fearful dreams to investigate the commotion, comes smack upon the bleeding corpse. The young man is subjected to the same shock that revengers before him had experienced, a shock which transforms his joy into unappeasable grief.

In the Greek plays (and in Pikeryng) Orestes is never in doubt about who murdered Agamemnon, despite his long absence. In Goffe, the identity of the murderers now remains unknown, and the hero must learn who killed his father before he can take action. Enter the delay. The delay is, as usual, one means of keeping the plot flowing. The play extends itself for an act or two while this complication is being overcome. At the same time, the postponement of the revenge leaves the hero in danger and establishes a conflict between him and his antagonists that renders the action more dramatic. The Jacobean Orestes, sensing his vulnerability, flies the court until he can identify his enemies and sends back word that he is dead. His plan is to "put a new shape on, / And liue alone, to heare how things goe here" (2.3.65–66). Still, the delay, and the "new shape" Orestes faces it in, have significance beyond that of dramaturgical practicality. Goffe retains only one of the several symbolic overtones of the

delay, yet a principal one—the tendency of the delay to intensify
the desire for revenge. The delay induced by the lack of knowledge increases Orestes' passion, and there is a steady build toward madness.

In Aeschylus and Euripides, the madness devolves upon the
hero *after* the revenge is accomplished, when the Furies taunt
and whip his conscience. Goffe roots the madness in the shock
Orestes experiences upon discovering the murder. The playwright follows Kyd, Marston, and Shakespeare in rendering the
madness as a madness of inordinate passion and, in addition,
traces its development through stages of grief, anger, and barbaric inhumanity. When Pylades, Orestes' faithful friend, points
out how quickly sorrow can convert itself to irrational anger, we
know exactly where we are:

> *Orestes.*   I haue lost a father, a deare, deare father,
> A King, a braue old King, a noble souldier,
> And yet he was murdered: O my forgetfull soule;
> Why should not I now drawe my vengefull sword,
> And strait-way sheath it in the murderers heart?
> *Minos* should neuer haue vacation,
> Whilst any of our progeny remain'd.
> Well, I will goe and so massacre him,
> I'll teach him how to murder an old man,
> A King, my Father, and so dastardly
> To kill him in his bed.
>
> *Pylades.*   Alas, *Orestes!*
> Griefe doth distract thee: who ist thou wilt kill?
>   [3.2.16–27]

Such choric commentary on the madness is neither Greek nor
medieval but distinctly Jacobean:

> *Pylades.*   Alas, where be his wits?
> He stands declaming against senselesse worms,
> And turns more senslesse then the worms themselues.
>   [3.4.40–42]

The sore distraction Orestes suffers expresses itself in
speeches marked by the characteristic rant of inordinate passion,
derived not so much from a sympathy for the passion as from a
prolonged study of revenge tragedy. Orestes' wild "declamation
against senselesse worms" is a curious blend of Hamlet's

philosophical musings on Yorick's skull and Vindice's grim meditations on Gloriana's:

> *Enter Pylades & Orestes, with his arme full of a dead mans bones and a scull.*

  Orestes.   O giue leaue to descant on these bones:
                 This was my Fathers scull; but who can know
                 Whether it were some subiects scull, or no:
                 Where be these Princely eyes, commanding face,
                 The braue Maiesticke looke, the Kingly grace,
                 Wher's the imperious frowne, the Godlike smile,
                 The gracefull tongue, that spoke a souldiers stile?
                 Ha, ha, worms eate them: could no princely looke,
                 No line of eloquence writ in this booke,
                 Command, nor yet perswade the worms away!
                 Rebellious worms! could a King beare no sway?
                 Iniurious worms! what could no flesh serue,
                 But Kings for you? By heauen you all shall sterue:
                 Had I but known't; what must my father make
                 A feast for you? O ye deuouring creatures!
  Pylades.   Now some *Archilocus* to helpe him make
                 Vengefull Iambiques, that would make these worms
                 To burst themselues; Passion must please
                 It selfe by words, griefe told it selfe doth ease.
  Orestes.   You cowardly bones, would you be thus vncloth'd
                 By little crawling wormes! by *Ioue* I neuer thought
                 My Fathers bones could e'er haue beene such cowards:
                 O you vngratefull wormes how haue you vs'd him;
                 See their ingratitude: O ambitious creatures,
                 How they still domineere, or'e a Kings carcasse.
                                         [3.4.6–30]

Goffe carries the grotesque so far that it becomes ludicrous, yet the sequence is instructive. Goffe presents it as a display of his artistry in depicting a revenger's madness. He obviously knows a mad scene is required and strives to create one worthy of the subject and the form. One can see intelligence at work in this attempt at originality. It should also be said, to Goffe's credit, that he is not slavishly copying. He is using *imitatio* as it should be used—the borrowed material is adapted to a fresh and original purpose and the reader is given the double delight of recognizing the old and enjoying its new form. Unhappily, the "enjoyment" provided in this passage is not as great as Goffe might have wished. The scene has so little of the dignity of Shakespeare's graveyard scene that the comparison becomes an embarrassment. One has the feeling that even a madman would not express himself in this fashion. The vulgarity of the execution makes us appreciate the stroke of genius that led Shakespeare to employ the antic disposition to create the effect of madness in *Hamlet*. But it should not lead us to overlook Goffe's obvious awareness that the madness is to be suffered by the revenger, that it occurs as a result of pressures caused by the murder and the provoking delay in obtaining redress, and that it develops in the imagination as destructive excesses of grief and anger prevent the operation of reason.

Goffe makes the same effort to breathe new life into the ghost motif. He understands that knowledge of the murder should come to the revengers from the order of nature. But Orestes does not go the battlements of the castle, as Hamlet does, or to the tomb of his father, as does Antonio, to communicate with the darker powers. This revenger imitates Macbeth. He and Pylades make a pilgrimage to the cave of a sorceress called Canidia. The hope is that

> by her we may
> Haue leaue to looke in *Pluto's* register,
> And read the names of those most loathed Furies,
> Which rent thy Fathers soule from out his truncke.
> [3.2.100–3]

Or better still, Canidia may "prompt vs some Ghost" who will tell them "which kild the King of Greece, great *Agamemnon*" (3.5.7, 18). Goffe obviously knows that his audience will expect the sorceress to raise a ghost and plays with their expectations. Canidia, instead, summons Sagana, Veia, and Erictho, three witches, who together cast a charm that reaches down into Hades and draws forth "the shapes of those that kild the King":

> Infernall Musique.
> *Enter in a dumbe shew Aegystheus, and Clytem. with their bloody daggers, looke vpon the bed, goe to it, and stab, and then make a shew of gladnes and depart.*
> [3.6.26.1–4]

Here is a clever amalgamation of two unforgettable scenes—as Orestes and Pylades watch Clytemnestra and Aegystheus kill

Agamemnon, so Macbeth watched Banquo's heirs emerge from the dank mists, but so also did Hamlet watch Luciano pour poison into the sleeping Gonzago's ear.

This direct vision of the murder replaces the recounting of it by a ghost. Yet the meaning of the ghost motif is not radically altered. The forces advocating vengeance are still located in the Plutonic underworld. From them Orestes takes his authority to act. Equally important, the knowledge Orestes gains through the supernatural presentation leads him into excess. In response to the vision, Orestes reacts as Antonio or Hamlet had reacted to the ghost. He takes over Andrugio's Senecan motto, "Reuenge is lost, vnlesse we doe exceed" (3.6.93). For him the worst torment he can exact upon Clytemnestra and Aegystheus will be "too little":

> Hell and the furies shall stand all amaz'd,
> *Alecto* shall come there for to behold
> New kindes of murthers which she knew not yet:
> And nature learne to violate her selfe.
> [3.6.105–8]

In most versions of the story Orestes kills only Clytemnestra and Aegisthus. Not so here. The excess reveals itself through a series of murders. The first of these, appropriately, is reminiscent of the death of Polonius. A chief attendant and adviser to Aegystheus named Misander overhears Orestes and Pylades devising their plan to gain access to the palace and threatens to expose them. Misander becomes the first victim. Orestes then reaches a stage of inhumanity that has no parallel in *Hamlet;* for the second of the multiple murders, therefore, Goffe relies on Marston. In preparation for it, Goffe adds to his play a character that earlier versions of the story had no reason to develop, an unnamed son of Clytemnestra and Aegystheus. This child, born, christened, and reared in act 4, is murdered in act 5. Crowning all is Orestes' murder of Clytemnestra and her lover. And before the play is over, Strophius, Electra, Pylades, and Orestes also lose their lives.

The murder of the young child recalls Antonio's murder of Julio; Goffe offered his audience an unmistakable reworking of Marston's scene. Orestes first undertakes the task of persuading Electra, who has charge of the child, to surrender it: "Tush, I

must haue it, it shall haue no hurt, / Worse then my Father"
(4.5.205–6). From here on, the pattern is straight out of the
Antonio play. Orestes gains custody of the boy; then, as he goes to
kill the child, he is moved to compassion. Immediately, the
Ghost of Agamemnon steps in to suppress whatever tender
thoughts might impede the act of revenge:

> Orestes.   Would thou wert not my mothers, I could weepe,
>   But see, O see now my relenting heart,
>   Must now grow flinty, see my Father, see,
>   Now to shew pitty were Impiety.
>   *Enter Agamemnons ghost passing or'e the stage all wounded*
> Ghost.   Why flaggs reuenge? see thy now yeelding soule,
>   Made me burst ope my strong iawd sepulcher,
>   And rip the seare-cloth from my wounded breast,
>   O can a child smile blanke the memory,
>   Of all these horrid wounds, which make me grone,
>   In the darke cauerns of the vncoucht earth,
>   From whence I come for to infect thy soule
>   With ayre of vengeance, may make *Acheron,*
>   Yes, and our selues at the performance quake.
>   [4.7.17–29]

The phrases are Andrugio's. Borrowing still more of them, the
Ghost goes on to authorize the atrocities Orestes will commit:

> Fruite of our loynts, first vigor of our youth,
> Looke on these wounds, as on the *Gorgons* head,
> And turne thy heart to stone, houering reuenge
> Is falne into thy hands, O graspe her close
> By her snake knotted front, and make her doe
> Things may incite a horror to her selfe.
> Forget all, mother, in that disloyall witch,
> Whose damned heate raging in strumpets blood,
> So soone did condiscend to murder mee.
> By all the rites of Father, I coniure thee:
> By *Atreus, Atreus,* he whose reuengefull soule
> Is eccho'd through the world superlatiue;
> Doe thou make *Nemesis* as great a feast,
> And be enthroniz'd in her firie chaire,
> In her triumphant chariot euer ride,
> In which Beares hurry her from the wombe of hell,
> And beare this Title as thy deserued hire,

> The braue reuenger of thy murdred sire.
> Thinke on me, and reuenge.
>
> [4.7.30–48]

To this command, Orestes responds with the customary promise of single-mindedness,[12] and in this mood goes on to stage his revenge, inviting all the fiends of hell to "take a place, / As 'twere spectators at a first daies play" (4.7.82–83). Again the source of the emotions is the literature, not the experience—the language calls to mind the earlier play rather than the actuality of the revenge passion. Yet Goffe obviously knows that the multiple murders must suggest the presence of excess.

Although Goffe does not capture the psychological realities of the revenge emotion that Marston does in portraying the Julio episode, his dramaturgical judgment is sounder than Marston's. Since the revenger designed the incident to torture his enemy, Goffe places it within the confines of the final act, where the ultimate brutalities are committed, rather than locating it in the third act as in *Antonio's Revenge*. Thus repositioned, the torture of the child can now have its full effect upon the person it was intended to distress. Its impact is felt by Aegystheus, not (as in Marston) by the audience alone.

The staging of the climactic murders goes far beyond the strict necessity with which Aeschylus's Orestes or Pickeryng's carries out his duty before the gods. Goffe knew well that the revenge play must conclude with a display of the shocking inhumanity of the revenger's madness. Indeed, this Orestes is so thoroughly warped by his passion that he makes his predecessors seem like dilettantes. Having lured Clytemnestra and Aegystheus into the private chamber alloted for the meeting, he ties them to their chairs. This begins a long torture sequence. He stabs the child so that its blood spurts out at them, smearing their faces. He pulls "great Agamemnon's bones" from his pocket and displays them, thus rousing himself to a higher fury. He fills silver cups with the dead boy's blood and forces Clytemnestra and Aegystheus to drink from these, then stabs his two victims to "let out, / The blood you dranke before." Orestes takes care that their wounds are not immediately fatal, reasoning that "who strait threats death, knowes not to tyrannize." The victim must "feele hee dies," and he regrets that he was able to repay the offenders with only one death, who deserved a hundred. Undoubtedly Goffe understood—and capitalized upon—the relationship between madness and excess. He also reveals some faint understanding that the madness motif must culminate in a sealed-off space controlled by the revenger, for he makes Orestes insist that the meeting be held in the "secretst room" of the palace and has him exclude all but the concerned parties. In the appointed chamber, Orestes is free to enact his most revolting fantasies—and does.

Neither in Greek tragedy nor in *Horestes* does the protagonist die; in both he is ultimately justified, cleared of all stain. Goffe ignores all precedent—all precedent, that is, but the precedent of revenge tragedy tradition. His Orestes commits suicide.

In shaping the Orestes myth to fit the death-of-the-avenger motif, Goffe follows *Antonio's Revenge* to a certain point, then veers off on his own. Both playwrights make much of the exultation which the revenger feels after accomplishing his goals. Orestes, after the vengeful murders, feels triumphant and would blazon his glory to all the court:

> Now friend, I see my father liue againe,
> And in his royall state at *Argos* Court:
> This is the night in which hee first came home,
> O blessed powers of hell, diuine *Canidia*,
> Now am I satisfied, now hath reuenge perfection.
> ·   ·   ·   ·   ·   ·   · This night who would conceale?
> Now soule triumph, whilst that my deeds shall shine,
> I'th face o'th Court, and all the world know't mine.
>
> [4.8.133–43]

This exultation is inherent in the revenge experience, and Goffe retains it.

From the closed room where Orestes' maddened imagination had free play Goffe, like his predecessor, moves to the larger world. Here the playwrights diverge. In Marston, the hero was glorified almost to the point of sanctity. In Goffe, the senators condemn the revenger. Tyndareus, chief among them, is appalled by the bloody scene Orestes is so proud of. Orestes turns from him to various other lords of Argos for support, demanding the crown as Agamemnon's rightful heir. They, too, denounce him. Both Orestes and Pylades are banished from Argos. Goffe's solution brings his ending more in line with the experience than was Marston's.

Goffe punishes Orestes with a real lunacy: throughout act 5, which covers the exile, the hero is displayed as a bona fide madman. These final scenes combine allusions to the mythological source (where Orestes is hounded and maddened by the Erinyes after committing the murders) with echoes of mad scenes from *King Lear* and *The Spanish Tragedy*. As Poor Tom is to the crazed Lear, so Cassandra is to Orestes. The two mad characters, meeting, become one another's tormentors. Yet their relationship reminds us as much of that between Hieronimo and old Bazulto. Orestes, in his lunacy, projects images from his mind onto the outside world, mistaking Cassandra for his mother, seeing the dead bodies of Strophius and Electra as Clytemnestra and her lover, and filling the invisible air with demons from hell that lash and whip him. His mind indulges in a wholesale importation of underworld characters, all looming forth in the imagery of his speeches to suggest the hellish landscape of the guilty mind. This final lunacy thus has significance beyond classical allusion. The madness is also conceived as an assurance to the audience that "time / Hath brought true punishment on euery crime" (5.5.45–46). The imagination, by setting itself upon revenge, has converted the human mind into a hell.

The play ends on a more positive note. There is some movement among the senators to forgive Orestes, after he has duly suffered for his crimes, though it comes too late to be effected. In the final scene of the play, a renewed emphasis upon the friendship of Orestes and Pylades restores to the pair some of their early nobility in preparation for their joint suicide. But they are never excused. Tyndareus delivers the epilogue, in a speech that might describe the inevitable end of any good man who gives himself up entirely to the passion of revenge:

> Witnesse *Orestes* here,
> VVho was his owne tormentor, his owne feare.
> VVho flying all, yet could not fly himselfe,
> But needs must shipwrack vpon murders shelfe:
> And so his brest made hard with miserie,
> He grew himselfe to be his enemy.
>
> [5.8.30–35]

These sentiments demonstrate how little Goffe's play has in common with Pikeryng's *Horestes*. This revenge hero has no dispensation from gods who wish to see justice done and who excuse his deeds because extraordinary measures are called for to protect the commonwealth. Orestes is essentially self-motivated, or as Goffe expresses it, empowered by Hell. Having the authorization of the Furies, Orestes appropriates to himself a kind of superhuman stature. But his hatred grows so intense that he becomes inhuman rather than superhuman. Because "murder it selfe is past all expiation," is in fact "the greatest crime that Nature doth abhorre" (4.5.61–62), Orestes must die.

One would be wrong to study Goffe for deep psychological insights into the revenge passion. Goffe's imagination expresses itself in the lively combination of speeches and episodes from the plays of his masters. No personal vision informs these poetic alterations. He explores neither the inner depths of the psyche nor the structure of the universe. One looks in vain within his drama for any serious concern with the complexities of human existence. Traditional Christian morality is accepted, and Orestes' revenge is presented as a moral atrocity punishable in conventional ways. Goffe's main interest in the material is dramaturgical. His talents are applied to the task of giving a modern form to a classical story, the chief end being to create surprising and original effects by inventively blending and thus revitalizing familiar elements.

This superficiality caused Goffe to overlook some of the more subtle symbolic aspects of the revenge tragedy motifs. In using the conventions, he hardly probes the depths of the experience underlying them. His characters always remain puppets passing through other playwright's plots. Yet Goffe perceived the relationships between the motifs. Where he made adaptations in any motif, his substitutions do the work that that motif was designed to do. Though young, he was intelligent. He had absorbed the fundamentals of the madness so thoroughly that the psychological process which the configuration of motifs was designed to depict remains intact. The motifs still function within the context of a unified experience. Given the *Orestes,* we can safely conclude that nonprofessionals (as well as professionals) perceived the motifs to exist as a configuration and they understood, though with varying degrees of comprehension, that the motifs reflected the stages inherent in the violent course of the passion of revenge.

Chapter 11
Delimiting the Genre

"*The Malcontent,* by attention to themes of corrupt state-craft, and by use of Senecal stage conventions, is related to plays loosely ascribed to the 'revenge tradition' " (Bernard Harris, Introduction to *The Malcontent*). "One may now reconsider *The Duchess of Malfi* . . . in the light of the relation of the John Webster's use of the theme of revenge for honour in it and his use of the same theme in his two other major plays. . . . *The White Devil* has the dramatic form of a tragedy of blood revenge" (Elizabeth M. Brennan, "The Relationship between Brother and Sister in the Plays of John Webster"). "Middleton's greatest expression of the working of revenge on character and after-circumstance occurs in the *The Changeling*" (Fredson Bowers, *Elizabethan Revenge Tragedy*).

I SCHOLARLY ATTEMPTS to make John Pikeryng the progenitor of the revenge tragedy tradition raise a question that should be dealt with in this study.[1] Of the several plays that have found their way onto lists of revenge tragedies, which actually are revenge tragedies? And how can one tell?

If the term *revenge tragedy* means any play of the era sporting a revenger and one or more of the conventional motifs, then an inclusive attitude would be most appropriate. In this case the list might welcome such diverse works as *Horestes, Gorbuduc, The Jew of Malta, Locrine, The Malcontent, Julius Caesar, The White Devil, The Duchess of Malfi,* and *The Changeling.*

But what is to be gained by defining revenge tragedy so broadly that it cuts across well-established genre borders to herd

together a mass of plays having very little in common, as if the
term acquired more prestige as the genre acquires more members? This inclusive tendency leads to several problems. Primary
among them is the question, where, and on the basis of what
criteria, does one draw the line? Is *Julius Caesar* a revenge tragedy? If it is, what of *Macbeth*? And if either *Macbeth* or *Julius
Caesar* or both are revenge tragedies, then surely *The Jew of Malta*
is also. Does the term extended thus far serve any useful purpose?

Without more rigid criteria, a play's status will as likely be
determined by the personality and preoccupations of a particular critic as by anything in the play itself. Some critics are pre-
disposed by nature to be inclusive. Others assume an inclusive
attitude because their theories require it. For example, take a
critic touting the thesis that plays containing revengers, ghosts,
and multiple murders had proved themselves good box office
material. He would want to show that dramatists were under
pressure to provide more of the entertainment audiences had
developed a taste for. Such a critic would be obliged to find a
profusion of revenge tragedies, since the existence of many revenge tragedies is fundamental to the idea that revenge tragedies were produced in response to a popular demand.

So long as no objective standards were available to define a
revenge tragedy, such subjective inclusions and exclusions were
inevitable. With the discovery of the revenge configuration, all is
changed. The recognition of the configuration and an understanding of how it functions supplies us with a fairly objective
means of delimiting the genre. Not that this discovery will end
all controversy on the subject. Judging in any given play whether
the motifs are used to illuminate the psychology of revenge,
whether they serve some other thematic purpose, or whether
they are solely ornamental requires more of the scholar or critic
than an ability to spot a formula; keen insight and a mature
understanding of human nature will always be needed. The critic's task remains difficult. Even if the issue were approached on
all sides with a degree of good will and intellectual rigor un-
common in our profession these days, we could not hope for
unanimity. There is thus no point in examining the claims made
for every play ever designated as a revenge tragedy in an effort
to make a final determination in each case. Such an exhaustive

approach is neither desirable nor necessary. Demonstrating how such judgments can be made is more to the point.

We have tried to avoid the proprietary attitude scholars frequently develop toward the genre they are studying. When they come to organize their roster, they do so after the fashion of major league team-owners—striving through fair means or foul to get all the stars on their club. Naturally the *importance* of a genre is largely dependent on the quality and to some extent the number of works included in it, and the *prestige* of working on a particular genre is directly related to its importance. Such considerations should not be allowed to obscure the question. We have attempted to define the limits of the genre accurately without regard to the politics of the profession.

We have also borne in mind that the critic's ultimate responsibility goes beyond categorizing. Assigning a play to a certain genre tells us very little about its value as a work of art. Consequently, in this chapter, we have allowed ourselves the liberty of straying now and then from the problems of genre to avoid an emphasis upon classification that could overshadow the more important aspects of aesthetic and thematic value.

Four tragedies often linked with the genre have been selected for discussion: Chapman's *The Revenge of Bussy D'Ambois,* Tourneur's *The Atheist's Tragedy,* Webster's *The Duchess of Malfi,* and Middleton's *The Changeling.* These plays are important in their own right in the history of Renaissance drama. All of them have revengers. All utilize a significant number of the revenge tragedy motifs. The differences between them, however, are instructive.

II The case for including *The Revenge of Bussy D'Ambois* in the genre seems unambiguous, whether one likes the play or not. The most telling point in favor of its inclusion is that Chapman intended to write a revenge tragedy. Nor can there be any doubt of his intention. He tells us so. He calls his play *The Revenge of Bussy D'Ambois* and styles it "a tragedie" on the title page. Whether the play achieves tragic stature is not at issue here. For the moment, we are engaged only at the descriptive level, and Chapman describes his play as a revenge tragedy.

Of course by itself that answer is too pat. But it contains a large element of truth which, thus overstated, is brought to the fore—that the decision to write a revenge tragedy is as conscious an act as the decision to write a sonnet or a short story. Although it may be a matter of critical judgment whether one's play achieves the level of tragedy or whether one's sonnets deserve to be set alongside Shakespeare's and Donne's, it is a matter of intention—of what one sets out to do—whether one has written a revenge tragedy or a sonnet in the first place. The point is even more important when considering plays like *Macbeth* and *Julius Caesar*. These are obviously not revenge tragedies, and Shakespeare left not one shred of evidence that he intended them to be. It may indeed take centuries to determine the true worth of a poem, but it does not take four hundred years of criticism to make a poem an ode. When Chapman handed *The Revenge of Bussy D'Ambois* to the actors in 1611, he may very well have told them, without fear of contradiction, "Here is my revenge tragedy." For critics today to tell Shakespeare that perhaps he was unaware of it but in writing *Macbeth* he wrote a revenge tragedy seems presumptuous.

Beyond Chapman's intention, there is considerable internal evidence that *The Revenge of Bussy D'Ambois* is in fact a revenge tragedy. First there is the relation of the play to the source material. In *The Revenge,* Chapman returned once again to French history for his subject, this time to continue the story of Bussy D'Ambois which ended in an earlier *Bussy* play with the murder of Bussy by assassins hired by Montsurry. When writing *The Revenge,* Chapman departed from his sources, for there is nothing in them about either revenge or revengers, nor for that matter about Bussy's brother, Clermont. Although the play ostensibly deals with French history, the entire revenge plot, including the revenging protagonist, is a deliberate invention of Chapman. Then there are the motifs from the revenge configuration incorporated into the play. Chapman did not use all the motifs. He did, however, structure his play to utilize as many as were compatible with his theme. The play does indeed address the subject of the passion of revenge.

But why insist upon the obvious? Certainly *The Revenge of Bussy D'Ambois* belongs to the genre: one cannot deny it its place among revenge tragedies. Yet it is there almost on false pretenses. Chapman had not the least interest in the dramatic theme of revenge. In this play the author's own concerns no longer merge with but dominate—even disregard—the archetypal experience. His mind is unwaveringly focused on his own personal vision. In 1610–11 Chapman was consumed with the notion that Stoicism was the one rational response to the dilemma of the world. He wished to write a play about his new faith. As Clermont converts the Guise to Stoicism and the Guise tries to convert the court, so Chapman hopes to proselytize among the audience.

Chapman puts the Stoical man on stage to demonstrate how this ethical, reasonable man would conduct himself in the world. He wanted to depict a man who had so fully incorporated into his person the ethical tenets of Stoicism that his every response to the trials of the world is morally and intellectually correct. *The Revenge of Bussy D'Ambois* was to be the tragedy of a good man, the tragedy of a man who, unlike other tragic heroes, has nothing more to learn from experience. His experiences during the course of the play will simply confirm what his philosophy has taught him.

Clermont is like other tragic heroes in finding himself locked into a complex web of relationships that place him under obligations not always compatible with his philosophy. This revenger, too, exists in a world from which justice has fled, a world populated by Monsieurs who make pride and insolence the badges of high birth and greatness, Montsurrys who grace their titles by cowering in fear when challenged to fair fight, Balignys who declare that "treachery for Kings is truest loyalty" (2.1.32).[2] Here, if anywhere, barbarism has replaced civilization. Robert Lordi has aptly described the corrupt court world that Chapman's hero must function in:

> The play opens with Baligny, the chief Machiavellian intriguer, and Renel, lamenting the sad state of the "declining kingdom" where murder is "made parallel with law" (1.1.1–4). . . . Most of the subsequent dialogue emphasizes the decay of the present as opposed to the golden past. In former times, we learn, kings sought only the common good and permitted great scope to man's individual liberty with the beneficent result of a natural and wholesome relationship between king and subject (19–22). Now, that relationship has become perverted by modern statecraft, dominated by policy in the service of

absolutism, with the result that truth and justice are "gagg'd and tongue-tied" (13–18). Kings, full of pride, now rule by power, and ever more "fearful of the good / Than of the bad," have banished all virtue so that their subjects study only "self-love, fraud and vice" (23–29). Nobility too has suffered a decline and is now in a state of decay. In former days, a man's nobility was a natural consequence of his virtues and valorous deeds: a noble's chief ambition was directed toward scaling walls and over-topping turrets of his country's enemies. Fame was the reward he sought; there was neither honor without worth, nor wealth without desert. Through virtue he conquered all (48–53). Now, "idleness rusts" all: nobles expend their energy not "in public wars," but in "private brawls"; not "in daring enemies," but in "courting strumpets"; consume their "birthrights / In apishness and envy of attire" (38–42); and spend their time in practicing "what they most may do with ease, / Fashion, and favor; all their studies aiming / At getting money" (66–68).[3]

Clermont's inclination is to withdraw from such a world. He apprehends a truth that everyone around him has forgotten, that man's purpose in this world is to discern the nature and will of the universe, and its Creator, in order to align his own will with that Will to which he is subject:

> Good sir, believe that no particular torture
> Can force me from my glad obedience
> To anything the high and general Cause
> To match with his whole fabric hath ordain'd:
> And know ye all (though far from all your aims
> Yet worth them all, and all men's endless studies)
> That in this one thing, all the discipline
> Of manners and of manhood is contain'd:
> A man to join himself with th' Universe
> In his main sway, and make (in all things fit)
> One with that All, and go on round as it;
> Not plucking from the whole his wretched part,
> And into straits, or into nought revert,
> Wishing the complete Universe might be
> Subject to such a rag of it as he;
> But to consider great Necessity
> All things as well refract as voluntary
> Reduceth to the prime celestial cause;
> Which he that yields to with a man's applause,
> And cheek by cheek goes, crossing it no breath,
> But like God's image, follows to the death,

> That man is truly wise, and everything
> (Each cause, and every part distinguishing)
> In nature with enough art understands,
> And that full glory merits at all hands,
> That doth the whole world at all parts adorn,
> And appertains to one celestial born.
>
> [4.1.131–57]

To perceive the absolutes and to live in accordance with them is his goal. During the course of the play Clermont tries to do this. But as he would be an active man rather than a contemplative one, total withdrawal is not possible. The creatures of policy and intrigue will not allow Clermont to isolate himself, and even his own sense of honor keeps drawing him into the coils of the world.

Chapman sought a structure for his play that would give Clermont the maximum opportunity to demonstrate the strength of character one derives from a commitment to Stoicism. To accomplish this to the highest degree, he involves his hero in two plots, each bristling with moral ambiguities for the Stoical man. In one plot Clermont's role is principally that of a subject to the King of France. As such, he is not the initiator of actions but a person acted upon. The dramatic question of this plot could be expressed generally as, how can a good man be the loyal subject of a corrupt ruler?

In the second plot, the revenge plot, Clermont is cast as the active agent. He must be the revenger. Chapman saw in the revenge plot an action that could engage his hero in the kind of ambiguous and contradictory situation where his Stoicism could come to the fore and save him. An ordinary man might react with rage and hysteria. The Senecal man could fulfill his mission in complete control of his passion, refusing to enter into its madness and its violence. In choosing the latter course, Clermont displays his superiority to the general run of mankind.[4]

Chapman's concerns fostered a radical shift in approach in the handling of the revenge element. *The Revenge of Bussy D'Ambois* renders a judgment on the ethic of revenge. Earlier playwrights had been motivated by the desire to illuminate an experience. Meaning and significance arose almost as a by-product when the audience, witnessing the effects of the experience upon the soul which suffered through it, gained a fuller comprehension of the destructive nature of that experience. Possibly, having lived through that experience vicariously, a viewer might manage to avoid making a similar error in his own life. But the playwright structures his material in a dramatic rather than a homiletic fashion, always using experience as his touchstone. Chapman's starting point is vastly different, as his dedication to Sir Thomas Howard indicates. He conceived the end of tragedy to be "material instruction, elegant and sententious excitation to virtue, and deflection from her contrary, being the soul, limbs, and limits, of an aut[h]entical tragedy."[5] The difference between Kyd's or Marston's approach and Chapman's is the difference between showing how men act and showing how men ought to act.

This movement from the experiential to the didactic seriously weakens the ability of the revenge form to elevate its hero to tragic status. Having appropriated the revenge tragedy form, Chapman is not content to write yet another revenge tragedy. He has in the back of his mind the goal of illustrating where the previous revenge heroes had gone wrong. As he saw it, the error of earlier revenge heroes was to get caught in the madness of revenge. Clermont never does. He stands aloof while Charlotte and Tamyra both go mad for revenge. Therein lies the problem of the *Revenge* as a revenge tragedy, and for that matter as a drama. The play is chockablock full of sententious speeches by Clermont but never one that shows us his soul. That was the great thing about the revenge tragedy: it ripped the revenger apart so that we saw him exposed to the depths:

> O world! no world, but mass of public wrongs . . .

> Now could I drink hot blood.

> [I'll] cut his throat i' th' church.

There is no such passion in Clermont. Since we do not see the passion, we do not feel that the philosophical calm is earned. He is contrasted with characters who feel emotion, but we never witness him conquering his own. Clermont as Stoical man never feels anything. He is set forth by Chapman as an ideal man, and he strikes us as a paragon of prigs.

Ironically, we never get to know Clermont because he never stops talking. The talk never reveals the man behind the philosophic "position papers" he is endlessly delivering. His response to every situation is too high in the head. Not surprisingly, that is the problem with the play as a whole. It was written too high in the head. Chapman never trusted his subconscious to take over. The play remains an act of will, with the author's hand and mind ever present. Although one of the germs in the genesis of a revenge tragedy or a sonnet is the conscious desire to write one, the success of the effort hinges on how far the artist trusts his subconscious self to transform a concept into a living experience.

Tourneur's *The Atheist's Tragedy* belongs to the genre for the very same reasons that Chapman's does: Tourneur intended to write a revenge play, he engaged his hero in a revenge action, he utilized a significant number of the revenge tragedy motifs, and he worked with the motifs in terms of the configuration. *The Atheist's Tragedy* has been seen as a response to Chapman's play and might be thought of as initiating a dialogue between Chapman and Tourneur.[6] As his subtitle indicates, Tourneur, too, treated of the honest man's revenge. This play continues the approach to revenge on the didactic level, being, like Chapman's, a comment on the experience rather than a rendering of it. Tourneur focuses on a particular aspect of the breakdown of the world order occurring at that time—the tendency to see the self as the measure of all things and to make the individual will the sole arbiter of value. The atheist D'Amville denies both God and Providence, clinging to an amoral rationalism as the justification for his deeds. The Christian faith of Charlemont, set in contrast to this atheism, is continuously put in peril but eventually validated.[7]

In offering Christian patience in place of Chapman's Stoical calm, Tourneur restores a degree of warmth and emotion to the character of the hero. But, as revenge tragedy, *The Atheist's Tragedy* suffers from the same flaws as *The Revenge of Bussy D'Ambois*: its protagonist, similarly bled by his creator of every serious human weakness, is neither believable nor tragic.

Because both plays concern themselves with the rational attitude toward revenge, far-reaching alterations have been made in the motifs. So radical are these changes that the revenger's madness itself, the central and unifying motif, has all but disappeared, and with it the violence and the excess that gave the form its characteristic intensity. Yet both authors were unmis-

takably aware of the conventions, and there is good evidence in
both plays that each felt compelled to utilize the motifs.

Despite the similarity of intention in the two pieces, the truth
is that in Tourneur's alterations the basic integrity of the configuration is preserved whereas in Chapman's it is disregarded; the
motifs seem to have been retained in the *Bussy* play merely out of
a sense of obligation. In Chapman we have again the situation
found in Marston—the integrity of certain motifs is violated,
with the consequence that aesthetically the conventions work
against the play rather than with it.

Let's confine our inquiry to two motifs—the delay and the
death of the avenger.[8] Where the madness dominated earlier
Kydian plays, in both *The Atheist's Tragedy* and *The Revenge of
Bussy D'Ambois* the delay motif becomes paramount, for, given a
personal vision in which the revenger does not succumb to the
passion, there is no call for a symbolic madness. Obviously any
plot constructed around the delay will not have drama as its
major asset. Indeed, both plays are almost unbearably static. But
Tourneur, whose play is in many ways less grand than Chapman's, shows a greater awareness of the experiential basis of the
delay motif.

Chapman's handling of the delay provides interesting evidence that a playwright cannot invent external causes for the
delay at random and expect the revenge plot to hold together;
the external causes must impinge upon the revenger. The plot
of *The Revenge of Bussy D'Ambois* gets right to the point. Clermont
has already initiated the revenge action. He has written a challenge to Montsurry, which Baligny delivers in act 1. To stave off
the actual meeting of villain and revenger until the final act,
Chapman employs two devices. First, Montsurry refuses to accept the challenge and locks himself off from the world, barring
Clermont all access to him. Meanwhile, King Henry sets a trap
for Clermont, makes him a captive of the royal army, and (un-
intentionally) prevents him from pursuing Montsurry.

This solution creates several problems. One is that neither of
these delays touches the psyche of the revenger. He responds to
both with complete calm. Or, more truthfully, he does not respond. That Montsurry ignores the challenge hardly flusters
him. Chapman never uses the motif to open up the character of

Clermont; the refusal is enlisted only to shift the responsibility for the delay conveniently to Montsurry, whose fear and lack of nobility highlight the courage of Clermont and emphasize the justice of the cause. What strikes the audience, however, is that Clermont fails to follow through on his challenge. We wonder that the hero has so little feeling for his dead brother, and because the revenger himself seems in no hurry to fight the duel, we cannot muster up much interest in it either.

An equally serious problem lies in Chapman's decision to place the scene of Clermont's arrest at Cambrai, where Clermont has gone for no particular reason except to be deceived. The notion that a revenger would plan a casual vacation in the midst of his quest for justice borders upon absurdity. But this is exactly what Clermont does. At a moment when any other revenger would rather "be numb'd with horror and my veins / Pucker with sing'ing torture" than let "my brain / Digest a thought, but of dire vengeance," Clermont's mind is on "purpos'd recreation" (4.1.111). With the slightest attention to the art of plotting, Chapman could have corrected this fault. He might easily have arranged matters (for instance) so that Clermont was captured on his way to the house of Montsurry. The delay would then have seemed inevitable, the complication dramatic. But Chapman shows no dramatic instinct. The gratuitous excursion to Cambrai remains in the text as a further sign of the revenger's lack of interest in the task he has been singled out to perform.

Tourneur handles the delay differently. Charlemont, Montferrers's son and the revenger of *The Atheist's Tragedy,* is to represent Christian virtue and to establish a model of patience that the atheist-villain, D'Amville, will at first despise and later envy. The provocation will be as serious as any revenger has had to face. D'Amville gets Charlemont sent off to the wars; meanwhile, he murders Charlemont's father, spreads the news that Charlemont has been killed in battle, and marries Charlemont's fiancée Castabella to his own son. The hero, a paragon of men, with all the faith that Hieronimo lacked and far more self-control, must take no action to revenge himself. Tourneur recognizes that to make such a hero the driving force in a plot is impossible. He therefore adopts the villain-hero form used by Marston in *Antonio's Revenge,* letting D'Amville motivate the action and portraying Charlemont as a passive victim. The revenger is called upon only to respond to adversity with patience and faith. His delay, consequently, does not look like disinterest.

Moreover, in *The Atheist's Tragedy,* the revenger's emotions are involved. Though he is even more passive than Clermont, Charlemont experiences great difficulty in remaining so. It becomes as hard for him to obey the Ghost's command to stay sane as it was for Hamlet to work himself to the necessary peak of madness. Twice Charlemont struggles with pent-up passions— once when he flies at Castabella, denouncing her for marrying so swiftly after his reported death, and again when he accidentally scuffles with Sebastian, D'Amville's son. Caught in a moment of frustration and anger with this young man at his sword's end, Charlemont comes so near to killing him that the Ghost of Montferrers has to intercede:

Charlemont.	Th'art a villain and the son of a villain.
Sebastian.	You lie. *They fight.* SEBASTIAN *is down*
Charlemont.	Have at thee. *Enter the* GHOST OF MONTFERRERS
	Revenge, to thee I'll dedicate this work.
Montferrers.	Hold, Charlemont!
	Let him revenge my murder and thy wrongs
	To whom the justice of revenge belongs. *Exit*
Charlemont.	You torture me between the passion of
	My blood and the religion of my soul.[9]

Tourneur's decision not to eliminate passion entirely from a form that has as its organizing principle one of the most furious of human passions seems a far better solution than Chapman's.

Because the delay fails to incite frustration, the revenger's reason remains clear. He can sagely deprecate the act of revenge, as Clermont does:

> All worthy men should ever bring their blood
> To bear an ill, not to be wreak'd with good:
> Do ill for ill; never private cause
> Should take on it the part of public laws.
>
> [3.2.113–16]

But in Chapman's revenge tragedy this leads to a curious and paradoxical situation. Revenge is clearly viewed as a wrong by the hero, his passions are absolutely under the control of his will, external events conspire to assist him in avoiding the duel—and yet he still goes ahead and commits the action. Tourneur renders Charlemont's delay more compatible with experience by separating him completely from the "mad" act of revenge. D'Amville receives his punishment directly from Heaven.

The madness dispensed with, there is certainly no call for those motifs growing out of it—the play-within-the-play, the excess, and the death of the avenger. Both playwrights rightfully omit the play and the brutal violence of the multiple murders; whatever deaths do occur beyond the one that marks the original offense are not caused by the release of an uncontrollable passion into the world. But the two playwrights differ in the handling of the revenger's death. Chapman seems at first the more faithful to the original configuration; he allows Clermont to commit suicide. Tourneur, on the contrary, saves his revenger by a naïvely unconvincing device: D'Amville, the offender, is miraculously killed by his own weapon while attempting to execute Charlemont. There would appear to be little defense for this crude *deus ex machina*. Yet here again Tourneur's use of the configuration derives from the action required by the experience. Although the death scene is gauchely handled, it is aesthetically justifiable (in intention at least). Chapman's, its foundation being chiefly in the author's concept of nobility, strikes us as arbitrary.

Chapman has used every tool at his disposal to present an act of revenge purged of degrading qualities. He has distinguished his revenger from such distraught figures as Hieronimo and Antonio by his unshakeable objectivity and rationality.[10] He has focused upon his hero's courage rather than his doubts, engaging him in an affair of honor approved of by a large part of the community and carried out according to formal and recognized patterns of behavior. He has eliminated excessive violence from the duel scene through the ultimate conversion of the villain as a consequence of his meeting with the honorable Clermont (Montsurry dies "noble and Christian," forgiving Clermont, praising his valor, and commending his victory). By transforming the Ghost into a spokesman for Providence, he has bestowed upon his revenger the very authority that frees the agent of justice from personal guilt for his act. There would appear to be no reason for the revenger to die.

Chapman acknowledges as much by so structuring the action

that Clermont's suicide occurs as a result of events in the major
plot, *not* in response to the death of Montsurry. Subsequent to
the duel, Clermont receives news that Henry has executed the
Guise. Where Bussy's death had not moved him, this one does.
He contemplates revenge, but decides that "there's no disputing
with the acts of kings, / Revenge is impious on their sacred persons" (5.5.151–52). The alternative is to follow the Guise, for the
world, such as it is, offers no other meaningful course of action.
Clermont would not be "left negligent, / To all the horrors of the
vicious time" (5.5.185–86), nor "here live, ready every hour / To
feed thieves, beasts, and be the slave of power" (5.5.191–92).
With a nihilism worthy of Jean Genet, Clermont shakes off the
burden of life. Unfortunately, the alteration destroys the sense
of inevitability which is so integral a part of the death-of-the--
avenger motif. Our attitude toward Clermont's death is influenced by our involvement in the revenge plot and in that context
it strikes us as unnecessary. The suicide impresses us as having
been designed chiefly to end the play.

Chapman's defenders counter, quite reasonably, that the
death grows directly out of the intrigue plot which occupies the
central acts of the play. Lordi, who cautions against readings that
force the protagonist into confining molds like "Stoic" or "Revenger," finds the suicide an inevitable end in terms of the playwright's more ambitious attempts to define justice, honor, and
true nobility through the conduct of his hero. For Chapman,
says Lordi, "death is the test and measure of the moral integrity
of the truly noble man." Therefore, Clermont "must face death
with equanimity; and his death must be freely determined by
inner directives, not by external circumstances. . . . [Since] the
way one dies is the 'proof and crown / To all the skill and worth we
truly own,' " Chapman is compelled to conclude his play with this
final proof of Clermont's manhood. This insight seems a valid
one. Fred Fetrow adds still another useful level of interpretation.
He points out that Clermont "intends to create in Guise an agent
for the reform of a corrupt society," hoping that the Guise can
educate the King and that the King's example will set the tone for
the Balignys, they for the Maillards, and so on down through the
lowest orders of society. King Henry proves intractable, of
course, and by executing the Guise brings home to Clermont the
futility of his dream. "The tragedy," concludes Fetrow, "is not just

the death of virtue; the real tragedy is that stoic virtue has little or no effect upon humanity in general. Thus the tragedy is of a society rather than of an individual. The deaths of Clermont and Guise do not change the world from which they depart. Their deaths are ultimately as futile as their lives."[11]

No doubt both of these notions were in Chapman's mind as he wrote. Unfortunately, however, neither is sufficiently realized in terms of dramatic action to engage our feelings. Intellectually the reader can assent to the arguments of Lordi and Fetrow. Emotionally, he finds more accuracy in Millar MacLure's analysis of Clermont's suicide. Quoting the hero's farewell speech to his cherished Guise, MacLure quips, "As for the Senecal man, it is not always observed that *his* dying speech is almost entirely an act of devotion to his patron. . . . Hardly the last gesture of the self-sufficient man who is one with the All, but the passionate rejection of a world empty without his love."[12] Chapman's didactic approach to tragedy creates a divorce between his intentions and his achievements in the form. Noble as his goals were, he has not convinced us that his revenger deserved to die.

Tourneur's alteration of the tradition again seems the better solution—the revenger is allowed to live. His faith in Providence is vindicated. Although D'Amville is struck down a bit too patly and the moralizing becomes somewhat heavy, the motif, as adapted, is compatible with both the author's vision and the configuration as he uses it. In *The Atheist's Tragedy* the motifs hold together as a unit, despite the changes wrought in the configuration, as they do not in *The Revenge of Bussy D'Ambois*. Chapman's use of the motifs provides irrefutable testimony to the fact that the conventions were recognized as essential elements of the revenge tragedy as much by the seventeenth-century dramatists as by twentieth-century critics, but it also reveals how hollow the motifs can become when a playwright fails to respect their integrity.

If Chapman was interested in the Stoical man, he was not interested in an examination of the psychology of revenge. As a result, his treatment of the revenge plot, the portion of the play we are interested in here, has an abstract and moralistic quality to it. True, Chapman chose to and did write a revenge tragedy. But he did so, apparently, for the wrong reasons. Ironically, his reasons, and the cause for his failure in the field of revenge

tragedy, are the reasons many critics attach to all dramatists' use
of the revenge form. They were catering, the argument goes, to
the Elizabethan audience's insatiable appetite for violence.
There is no denying the popularity of the revenge play or that
writers like Chettle tried to capitalize on it. Reluctantly we must
also characterize Chapman's foray into revenge tragedy as an
attempt to exploit the popularity of the form. In fairness to
Chapman we should distinguish between his goals and the crass
commercialism of Chettle. Doubtless Chapman felt he was pressing the form into the service of a higher truth than it had
hitherto been exposed to. The crucial point is, however, that it is
immediately recognizable when the integrity of the form is being
violated, no matter what the purpose of the exploitation.

Both Chapman's and Tourneur's plays are wise and
frequently have penetrating, even piercing insights. In criticiz-
ing these plays one is certainly not accusing the authors of lacking intelligence or imagination but, rather, of failing to realize
these qualities in their dramas. While the reader knows he is in
the presence of a strong mind he is, in a sense, too conscious of
it. In *Hamlet*, one is conscious of the quality of Hamlet's mind. In
Antonio's Revenge, one senses that Antonio's mind is trembling on
the brink. In both *The Revenge of Bussy D'Ambois* and *The Atheist's
Tragedy*, one feels the force of the author's mind directly.
Whereas in the essay this is appropriate, in a fictive art like
drama, it is not. The fiction and its elements should strike us as
powerful.

III We shall move now from plays that belong to the genre
of revenge tragedy to those that are outside the genre
but indebted to it. In these works there are obvious signs that
their authors had some knowledge of and experience with revenge tragedy. Obviously indebtedness varies in degree, from
slight echoes in the phrasing of the dialogue to wholesale
importation of scenes, plots, and characters. When indebtedness
reaches monumental proportions, finely tuned critical judgments are required to decide whether the work is actually part of
the genre or simply heavily influenced by it. No attempt will be

made on these pages to construct a hierarchy of indebtedness among the many plays linked to revenge tragedy. But we shall offer a distinction between two kinds of indebtedness which might shed some light on the different types of relationships that develop.

The simplest kind of indebtedness occurs when an author borrows elements from the genre without regard for their purpose and function. Middleton, for example, slips a revenger into *The Changeling:* Tomasso, the brother of Alonzo, is clearly the distraught hero of a revenge tragedy. But Middleton's play is about Beatrice-Joanna. Tomasso is curiously out of place in it. He roams about like an actor who has strayed onto the right stage on the wrong night. Plays indebted through *borrowing,* then, are those which contain recognizable elements from the genre but make no thematic use of them.

Another kind of indebtedness must be described in terms of *influences.* Plays revealing the influence of revenge tragedy usually also contain borrowings, but the borrowings have, as in the genre itself, been adapted to and blended with the personal vision. But here again the vision is no longer centered upon revenge. Ultimately more important than vestigial borrowings, influences are more elusive: they are harder to recognize and harder still to prove. Influences involve indefinable echoes of tone or theme where there is nothing concrete to put a finger on. Whereas borrowings, by their nature, are generally objectively verifiable, influences are not, and in this mine field, even the most judicious must proceed with caution. Determining that one work has been influenced by another is largely a matter of conjecture based on one's experience and developed taste. One becomes sensitive to similarities in tone or theme. One's ear catches echoes. Perhaps without consciously intending to, one is relating the experience of this work to experiences known through other works. Whatever the causes, the process remains highly personal. Informing others that one sees an influence can be as hazardous as telling them one sees ghosts.

The difference is the difference between Middleton's use of revenge tragedy motifs in *The Changeling,* which has its revenger, its ghost, and its touches of madness, and Ford's use of them in *The Broken Heart.* In *The Changeling,* one is aware of several elements in the play that are easily traced directly to revenge tragedy; nonetheless, nothing about *The Changeling* transports one into the world of the revenger. In *The Broken Heart* the borrowed motifs are far less obvious, yet as the relationship between Orgilus, Penthea, and Ithocles develops, constant and subtle reverberations inform us that Ford had absorbed the lessons of the revenge configuration, that Orgilus's suffering takes the form of the revenger's madness. So it is with Webster's *The Duchess of Malfi*. While *The Duchess*, too, has obvious borrowings, it has something more central to it than any of the elements imported bodily from the genre which reminds one of the world of revenge tragedy.

There is something in the tone of *The Duchess* that links it to the revenge plays more strongly than borrowings alone ever could. Webster's multidimensional use of madness has a good deal to do with this similarity. Although it is a commonplace of criticism to point to the madness in *The Duchess* as a borrowing from the revenge plays, the difference in application is more striking than the likeness. As Harold Jenkins suggests, "Webster is using the idiom of the revenge play when his imagination is really engaged by something else."[13] Webster nowhere uses madness—at the level of the plot—in the same way madness is used in the revenge plot. To imply that Webster borrowed the madness in *The Duchess* from the revenge plays solely on the grounds that there is madness in each is to ignore the multitude of other possible sources. Besides, hunting for a literary source for the madness in Webster's play is like looking for the literary source for Shakespeare's vision of young love in *Romeo and Juliet*. The plot of *The Duchess of Malfi*, and the position of madness within it, is far removed from its usual position in the plots of revenge tragedy. Still, there is a similarity of vision in the handling of the madness that links this play to the genre.

But let us take the play as it develops. The first likeness we discover between *The Duchess of Malfi* and revenge tragedy is that the protagonists of both begin in innocence. Since this play concerns itself with the effects of evil upon innocence, it seems important to challenge those commentators who find the heroine willful or, worse, lustful. At the opening of the play the Duchess is not so much a willful woman as an innocent and inexperienced one. She does not take into account the malevolent natures of her brothers when she acts. It is enough for her that her actions are honorable and that she means to do no one an injury—why, then, should anyone set his will against her? In this regard she is innocent in another sense of the word, not entirely separable from the first: she is naïve. She is acting without taking into account the presence of evil in the world.

Today, pointing out that a character is innocent lays one open to the charge of sentimentalizing.[14] It should not be forgotten, however, that the Elizabethans and Jacobeans placed a greater value on innocence, particularly in women, than we do. To deny this, or overlook it because we are uncomfortable with it, is to do violence to a vision of life not wholly compatible with our own. True, the Duchess of Malfi was condemned for her actions in the sources Webster had available to him. But the play itself is purged of any suggestion that the Duchess is lustful. Critics misuse the sources when they argue that the audience, knowing that the historical Duchess was condemned for lust, would have brought this attitude toward her to the playhouse. Such a use of the sources makes for some odd applications. By this rule we might then say that because the audience knew Prince Hal was really only half the age of Hotspur, it would have seen Hal's killing of Hotspur as very unchivalrous indeed, since Hotspur was old enough to be his father.

Although the Duchess is neither a lustful woman nor a particularly willful one, she is innocent, and has much to learn about both the world and herself. We are introduced to her as a young woman eager for love and marriage and filled with the expectation that happiness will follow:

> Awake, awake, man!
> I do here put off all vain ceremony,
> And only do appear to you a young widow
> That claims you for her husband, and like a widow,
> I use but half a blush in't.[15]

Everything about her is such that we wish her the happiness she seeks. She is herself filled with a radiant joy of life and wherever she goes she spreads joy. She approaches everyone in an open, forthright manner, whether it is her husband, children, or friends, never using or manipulating them, so that all who know her love her—all except her brothers, though they have no more reason to hate her than anyone else does.

In her innocence, the Duchess resembles the revenger and, like him, she suffers a head-on collision with evil. A good deal of ink has been spilled over the possible motivation of the two brothers who abuse her, particularly that of Ferdinand. Nor is it surprising, in this post-Freudian era, that the motivation most favored by critics is Ferdinand's incestuous desire for his sister.[16] Yet since no one speculates that this is the Cardinal's motivation—in fact, few bother to speculate on the Cardinal's motives at all—the incest theme as the causal factor in the destruction of the Duchess is hardly what logicians would call a sufficient cause. At best it only covers one of the participants. That incest cannot be entirely ruled out as one of the possible causes for Ferdinand's actions means, primarily, that Webster has been deliberately vague in attributing any direct cause to the actions of the brothers. Had he wanted to, he could have made their motives quite clear. If he could not invent any himself, the sources certainly offered enough to fill the need. But without turning the play into an allegory, Webster wished to convey the capricious nature of evil. So he left the motives intentionally vague. The important thing is that for no reason—none rising out of the actions of the Duchess nor any growing out of the characters of the brothers—she is subjected to the cruelest and most barbarous treatment.

Truly her world has gone mad. That of course is the symbolic meaning of the series of mad scenes she is forced to encounter. Most scholars and critics have looked for the meaning of these madhouse scenes in the character of Ferdinand. True, they originate with him. But if we are following the action, our attention at this juncture should be riveted on the Duchess and Bosola (Ferdinand and his madness become central only after the death of the Duchess). We are not wondering who initiated the madness or why. Our main concern is, how will the Duchess hold up? And that is true both at the realistic and the symbolic levels. There is little question about what is actually going on at the realistic level, and it has nowhere been more astutely analyzed than by J. R. Mulryne.[17] But while many see that the symbolic nature of Webster's language and the violently disjointed and broken action of his plays point beyond realism, few have speculated on the symbolic function of the madness in *The Duchess of Malfi* as it relates to the character of the Duchess herself. In this area a heavy influence from the revenge plays was working on Webster's imagination.

Part of the difficulty here is the unusual relationship between the character of the Duchess and her role as tragic hero.[18] The tragic hero is supposed to learn something through his suffering. Therefore, there ought to be a change in him wrought by the suffering. The revenger's suffering drives him mad. But the Duchess does not change. In fact, both she and Webster are emphatic about the point: "I am Duchess of Malfi still" (4.2.142). Obviously the operative word is *still*. She is *still* what she has been all along. Now unchanging characters—characters who do not learn from their experience—make for static drama; they also defeat the whole purpose of tragedy. Yet static or nontragic are hardly charges normally hurled at *The Duchess of Malfi*. Paradoxically, the drama is not static *because* the Duchess refuses to change.

Webster makes the Duchess innocent not to add to her already considerable charm; rather, her innocence tells us that so far life has treated her kindly. Her frank and open nature wells up from her own goodness; it is not, however, a sign of her inner strength, because as yet she has been untried. Webster has given us a most unusual tragic protagonist, one who has reached a certain stage of perfection so that the dramatic question of the play need not be, can the protagonist perceive his error from the action? In a strange way the Duchess does not need new knowledge: the challenge will not be to her philosophical or ethical views. It will be to her strength. The dramatic question is, will she be able to maintain her goodness when confronted by the wanton destruction, the caprice, and the sheer madness of the world?

In many ways her drama parallels that of the Christian saint who must pass through the fires of this world before he is proven to be of the true gold. In this sense the Duchess resembles Celia in *Volpone* more than Hamlet or Vindice. But the dramaturgical and symbolic use of madness to develop the character of the Duchess was apparently learned by Webster from the revenge plays.

The drama of *The Duchess* is similar to that of *Hamlet* in that both are dramas of initiation. The question asked in *Hamlet* is, once the hero has seen the vulgar quality of the evil that is so much a part of life, will he be able to find an order beyond it that will make life meaningful? In contrast, we do not expect a new philosophical commitment from the Duchess. The test she must pass is whether she will remain the woman she was, once she sees what the world is. Bosola is betting that she will change, because if she does not she is a living refutation of his cynical view that everyone is as bad as he is. The more she withstands his pressures, the harder he pushes her by lowering her deeper and deeper into the madness that is the world. Ironically, it is Bosola who changes. In spite of himself he begins to admire her tenacity. His admiration grows, and as it grows it thrusts him into the paradoxical situation of wanting her to prove him wrong. He wants her to prove through her steadfastness that there is dignity and honor in life. But beyond a point, merely intensifying the pressure offers no further proof. Ultimately he realizes that the only real proof will be that she does not crack at the point of death. He must kill her to prove he is wrong. She must die to prove life is worth living. Her affirmation of life will only have validity for him if she is willing to die. Thus it is essential that the Duchess does not change.

Bosola tests the Duchess by staging a series of grotesque mad scenes. True, these scenes are nominally the creation of the nominal revenger of the play, Ferdinand, but that is beside the point. The point is that the Duchess, an innocent, is good because she has never had to come to terms with the reality of what the world is. For Webster this reality is that the world is a madhouse. That may be a severe view but Webster is not unique in holding it. Many a satirist before and after him have said as much.[19] All the revenge heroes are confronted by a similar world. Long before any of them constructs his own mad world he discovers that he is a denizen in a world that strongly resembles a madhouse. It is because he is surrounded by madness that he must descend into himself to find order.

This brings us to another series of similarities and contrasts between *The Duchess of Malfi* and the revenge tradition. In chapter 5, discussing the hero-revenger in relation to Eric Voegelin's analysis of tragedy, we spoke of the hero's tragic descent into himself. Voegelin does not simply state that the hero "goes within" himself, or that he "turns inward," for he wants to convey the sense of movement and direction that this interior journey takes.[20] The decision (frequently made at a subconscious level) to turn one's back on the external order because it is in some way unsatisfactory also requires turning one's back on the ordering principles of one's own life. Consequently, the most graphic way of describing this initial phase of the voyage of self-discovery is to speak of it as a *journey downward*. Since one has abandoned both the order of one's own life and the order of the external world, one enters a spiritual area with no guide-posts, no bench marks, no moorings. It is Lear's night on the heath, Hamlet's "to be or not to be." It is the dark night of the soul.

The Duchess makes such a journey. All the ordering principles in her world prove false. Webster has cleverly embodied in the two brothers all the elements that should give stability to the Duchess—the family, the state, and the church. And all turn on her. Beyond that, she is separated from the husband she loves and betrayed by the servant she has trusted. It is not so much that she has turned from the world as that the world has turned its back on her. Where formerly the world had indulged the Duchess and led her to believe it beneficent, it now turns its mad side toward her and laughs at the innocence and vulnerability it fostered.

So though the Duchess does not go mad, as the revenger does, she must also turn inward and pass through madness. Here the contrast is quite striking. Ordinarily the challenge to the tragic hero is to discover a new order through the journey into the depths of himself. Bosola's challenge to the Duchess is just the opposite. Can she maintain her faith, thus cut off from all external supports and cast into the world as madhouse? When one views *The Duchess of Malfi* in this light, one can see that Webster has wrought a new twist on the kind of tragic hero envisioned by Chapman and Tourneur, succeeding where they had failed because of what he had learned from Kyd and Shakespeare—that tragedy can be moving only if the tragic experience is truly rendered. It is a critical commonplace to call the Duchess *passive*. But while the word *passive* might do for Clermont or for Charlemont, it seems inadequate when applied to the Duchess, unless one wants to say that the prisoner who refuses to break under torture is passive, or that the person dying of cancer and refusing to allow the pain to alter his personality is passive. The

Duchess is like a beacon against which the tempests of the world crash, wave after wave, in a vain effort to extinguish her light.

While dwelling on common critical errors, we should also note that the strength that pulls the Duchess through these hard times is not simply a form of psychic strength. What saves the Duchess is more than what some seem to claim, that her inner strength came from an indomitable ego, that she believed strongly in herself. That, too, is missing the point, the point which Bosola does not fail to grasp. Although her strength is an inner strength, it comes to her from an external source. It is her faith that sustains her, her faith that though the world may turn upside down and inside out, as hers has, there is an order in the universe that is unalterable. Do as men will, right will remain right and wrong, wrong. Webster's Vittoria Corombona is the heroine of the tough ego. That Vittoria can defy church, state, and the moral order itself says little about the nature of reality but speaks volumes about the nature of the psyche. Despite the superficial similarities *The Duchess of Malfi* is an entirely different kind of drama than *The White Devil*. Whereas *The White Devil* concerns itself with the workings of twisted psyches, *The Duchess of Malfi* is a far more metaphysical play. After all, if what Bosola saw in the Duchess was an indomitable will, then what he is converted to at the end of the play is the worship of the self. This looks strangely like where he was at the beginning of the play. No, *The Duchess of Malfi* goes beyond psychology to metaphysics. Bosola sees the Duchess as one whose life points beyond itself to the permanence of the virtues he scoffed at.

But Webster was not writing another *Book of Martyrs*. He is writing of a woman whose claim is not to sanctity but to goodness and faith in the face of adversity. Yet the Duchess has been transfigured. She has passed through the madness unscathed, which is something quite different from being passive. When she says that she is "Duchess of Malfi still," she has earned the right to wave that *still* like a banner. Webster is here, as Shakespeare was with King Lear, precariously near the point where tragic hero shades into Christian saint, primarily because his basic vision in *The Duchess of Malfi* involves a truth that is equally applicable to either—that one's character is not a given but the result of how one conducts oneself in the process of living. It therefore follows that inevitably it takes a long time for a person to find his true nature (a fact succinctly expressed in the saying that God gives us one face and by the time we reach forty we make ourselves another). A corollary Webster works with is that if one does not fight a trouble through, one will not find the truth behind it.

There is yet another and very direct way in which the Duchess contrasts with the revenge heroes, one sufficiently important to remove *The Duchess of Malfi* permanently from any list of revenge tragedies. No doubt the Duchess's situation parallels that of the hero-revengers. Like Hieronimo, Hamlet, and Antonio—even more, perhaps, like Charlemont—she suffers from the activities of a villain-revenger. But unlike them she never herself contemplates revenge. Quite the opposite—she is the patient sufferer. But patience requires one of two things. It requires either the loss of all hope, as with Clermont, in which case failure to take revenge stems from a belief that all action is meaningless. In truth, this state is not quite the same thing as patience. Or, it requires belief. Patience of the Duchess's caliber can only emanate from a belief in a symbolism that teaches a hidden transcendent order. The Duchess must live through this test of her faith. She must neither go mad for revenge nor go mad out of despair. But the important point here is that, far from being a revenger, the Duchess is just the opposite.

As everyone knows, however, there is a revenger in *The Duchess of Malfi*, the brother Ferdinand. Whatever the validity of the other motives attributed to him, there is no doubt that Ferdinand is consumed by the desire for revenge:

Ferdinand. [to Bosola]   Antonio
Lurks about Milan; thou shalt shortly thither
To feed a fire, as great as my revenge,
Which ne'er will slack till it have spent his fuel:
Intemperate agues make physicians cruel.
[4.1.138–42]

With what degree of justification is another matter. But Ferdinand's presence in the play, either as villain-revenger or otherwise, does not render the play a revenge tragedy.

Ferdinand's madness is the play's strongest tie with revenge tragedy, but it is not the madness of the revenger. His madness does begin in passion. Before Ferdinand ever contracts his final lunacy, he is first carried away with excessive anger. The Cardinal tells us as much:

Cardinal.	You fly beyond your reason.
Ferdinand.	[To the absent Duchess] Go to, mistress!
	'Tis not your whore's milk that shall quench
	my wild-fire,
	But your whore's blood.
Cardinal.	How idly shows this rage! which carries you,
	As men convey'd by witches through the air,
	On violent whirlwinds—this intemperate noise
	Fitly resembles deaf men's shrill discourse,
	Who talk aloud, thinking all other men
	To have their imperfection.
Ferdinand.	Have not you
	My palsy?
Cardinal.	Yes—I can be angry
	Without this rupture: there is not in nature
	A thing that makes man so deform'd, so beastly,
	As doth intemperate anger:—chide yourself.
	You have divers men who never yet express'd
	Their strong desire of rest, but by unrest,
	By vexing of themselves:—come, put yourself
	In tune. . . . Are you stark mad?

$$[2.5.46-66]$$

The Cardinal himself is no touchstone. Webster makes him the perverted Stoic, only ironically a churchman and typically symbolizing the corruption of the Catholic faith. He is a testimony to an abuse of the reason that is as violent as Ferdinand's misuse of passion and, taken together, the two illustrate the barbarism of the times, both on the individual and the social levels. Nevertheless, the Cardinal's comment upon Ferdinand's passion is conventional enough to be valid. The usual signs of the disordered soul are evident in this portrait of passion—violent movement, noise, and musical discord—and the Cardinal, quite naturally, thinks of such intemperance, such vexation, such unrest, in terms of madness.

This madness of passion also culminates in a play-within-the-play in which this revenger hauls his victim into his world and acts out his fantasies of horror under the influence of the madness. But here the resemblances end. Ferdinand is hardly effecting justice when he tortures his sister. Nor does any ghost "legitimize" the passion by authorizing the torments that Ferdinand, by himself and through Bosola, imposes upon the

Duchess. Nowhere else in revenge tragedy is it so blatantly obvious that the offense is manufactured in the imagination. Webster has transferred the madness from the hero-revenger to the villain and makes it serve his personal vision in a new way.

Insofar as Webster structured his study of Ferdinand's madness partially in terms of the revenge tragedy configuration, the motifs have been instrumental in assisting him to bring to the surface a truth about the psychology of revenge that is never consciously dealt with in other plays of the genre. Webster saw that in the human mind there exists a kind of free-floating rage—a mysterious dissatisfaction stemming from the frustrations of life which are constant and inescapable that gives rise to an urge to strike out violently. He understood that when this floating rage manages to lock itself onto an object, however innocent (as it does in Ferdinand), this irrational urge to "hurt back" will break out with a grotesque ferocity that is apt to breed greater violence than even the most legitimate desire for justice.

And this is just the point—there is no legitimate desire for justice in Ferdinand's madness. Webster used the madness of inordinate passion entirely to suggest self-indulgence. Ferdinand makes no descent into the self. His descent is headlong, down the chain of being. Having had the "wolf of hatred snarling in his breast," he is significantly inflicted with lycanthropy (5.2.4–6). Bosola tells us how to take the new development: "a fatal judgement," he says, "hath fall'n upon this Ferdinand" (5.2.85–86). Webster presents it as the inevitable outcome of and simultaneously a punishment for Ferdinand's whirlwind passion.

The madness here is still clearly symbolic. If we attempt to view it literally, looking for accuracy in the presentation of symptoms, we get nowhere. As Reed admits, the disease, as presented, is merely a compound of "several contemporary concepts of symptomatic behavior" patched together to form a convincing picture of a mind falling apart.[21] Nor does it help to prescribe a modern-day cure (as John Bucknill does for Lady Macbeth).[22] We have a clear statement from Webster himself, through Bosola, that the wolf-madness is meant to be seen as a projection of the interior reality of the character:

> Man stands amaz'd to see his deformity
> In any other creature but himself.

But in our own flesh, though we bear diseases
Which have their true names only ta'en from beasts,
As the most ulcerous wolf, and swinish measle;

.   .   .   .

We delight
To hide it in rich tissue.

[2.1.50–58]

The disease which incapacitates Ferdinand at the end of the play
and renders him a most ulcerous wolf is a deformity that had
been there all along hidden beneath the rich tissue of his seemingly human nature. The enraged Ferdinand who presents a
dead man's hand to the Duchess (4.1.43.1) is little different from
the crazed Ferdinand who is discovered coming from a graveyard with a dead man's leg upon his shoulder (5.2.12–15). As
Bosola's speech warns us, the playwright's interest is not in the
lycanthropy itself but in its power to reflect upon the ultimate
meaning of the deeds and choices of the Duke's life.

When accepted as a symbol, the lycanthropy becomes far
more effective than it is as a case study, for its suggestiveness is
far-reaching. Its tie with the lupine species calls attention not
only to the savage and predatory qualities that Ferdinand shares
with the wolf itself but to the basic animality of the irrational
nature.[23] In this regard, it is a "fatal" judgment because it shapes
Ferdinand into the mold he had styled for himself. The general
state of insanity, as opposed to the specific form it takes, points
in addition to the chaotic state of Ferdinand's psyche, which,
beset by passion, could neither "examine well the cause" of this
fury nor control it. Finally, the lunacy serves to underscore the
effects of conscience upon Ferdinand who, though purged of his
intemperate rage by the death of the victim upon whom he had
sought revenge (4.2.273–91), is maddened by the knowledge of
what he had wrought in the throes of his passion. In this sense,
too, the madness is a "fatal judgment," for the act of murder
necessitates a tormented conscience. By providing this extended
visual picture of mental disintegration, then, Webster encom-
passes in one climactic dramatic image the totality of
Ferdinand's life.

In transferring the madness to the villain-revenger, Webster
makes no attempt to incorporate those aspects of it that are
peculiar to the hero-revenger. Within the genre, the madness

carries with it a luminosity. In his distraught state the revenger can see things others cannot. He is capable of piercing the illusions of the world. The madness of Ferdinand, on the other hand, is mere lunacy. He sees nothing but himself.

Here again it should be stated that whereas Ferdinand is not in the revenge tradition and his madness is not totally identifiable with the madness of the revenger, there has undeniably been an influence. While this influence has been overemphasized recently, it should not be ignored. The very way in which Ferdinand's madness contrasts with that of the revenger is proof of an influence working on Webster.

The indebtedness in *The Duchess of Malfi* goes beyond probable influences to unequivocal borrowing. Bosola's role as tool-villain is one we have met with before in the revenge tragedies. The tool-villain is cat's paw to the villain of the piece, the man who does all the dirty work. Lorenzo has his Serberine and his Pedringano, Piero his Strotzo, Claudius his Laertes. Hoffman has Lorrique and D'Amville Borachio. The role increases in importance after Marston in *The Malcontent* merges the tool-villain with the malcontent figure. The revenger Vindice seeks opportunities for revenge by getting employment as the tool-villain, Piato. Certainly the list of tool-villains would not be complete without Webster's own Flamineo.[24]

Before Malevole and *The Malcontent*, the tool-villain functioned primarily as a plot device that helped establish the true character of the villain. The tool-villain was first manipulated and then destroyed by the villain, who thereby exposed his callousness and identified himself with the hated Machiavellianism. But after Malevole, the tool-villain takes on new significance. Webster follows Marston and Tourneur in bringing the figure forward and fleshing him out into a full-fledged dramatic character. But he is the first to make the tool-villain a cynic.

Not that cynicism is any more a theme in Webster than revenge. The cynic does fascinate him as a type. And Webster's interest in the cynic goes beyond his usefulness as a stock character type, a droll fellow with an acid tongue ready to believe the worst of others. He obviously relished the cynic for these traits, for it is largely through them he could give to his plays that quality and tone that led Eliot to say that Webster was "directed toward chaos."[25] It is a wonderful phrase, and aptly

descriptive of Webster's cynics and the world they inhabit. But it
ought not to be applied to Webster himself except insofar as he
had a keen awareness of the chaos within his fellow man.
The charge is wholly unwarranted. When we read either *The
Duchess of Malfi* or *The White Devil* we are not struck by the chaos
in the mind that created these worlds, but by the penetration
and rugged integrity of vision that drove Webster to experience
and to render so hostile a world without himself becoming cynical. It is the world of the plays and not the author of the plays
that is oriented toward chaos. To create this realm of chaos—
and succeed so admirably that many have mistakenly taken it for
his world—Webster had to look long and hard at his cynics.
Cynicism was to be for him a textural element woven throughout the fabric of the drama to render that particular tone we call
Websterian.

Webster was not interested in probing what made one man
turn cynic and another not. Nor was he particularly interested in
what motivated them in their peculiar actions once their minds
are cast in the cynical mold. Webster is not so much interested in
investigating cynicism as observing and depicting it. For an almost clinical examination of cynicism from its genesis to its self-
destruction, we will have to wait for Thomas Middleton. Yet
Webster's is not a superficial glance, nor is he satisfied with re-
cording the ticks and mannerisms of the type. With Flamineo
and with Bosola he has caught something essential in the nature
of the cynic.

With Flamineo, Webster has pierced beyond the cynic's obvious contempt for others, so frequently taken as the cynic's
hallmark, to the truth that underlies it—the abyss of self-loathing that is at the core of the cynic's character. Once we are
conscious of how highly symbolic a dramatist Webster is, what
other interpretation are we to put on his making Flamineo the
brother of the woman he panders into adultery? Whoring his
sister is a kind of violation of himself. Webster's insight as represented in the character of Flamineo is that the cynic deliberately presents himself as a man whose disillusion with the world
stems from the fact that he has seen through the levels of hypocrisy that disguise the true grubbiness of men's actions. But the
real source of his disillusion is a deep-seated and secret disgust

with himself, which manifests itself under the cover of a witty, world-weary sophistication. The truth is, to live with himself he must destroy or render contemptible everything in his world that challenges his self-justification that he is no better or worse than the world has made him, only more honest than those who would pretend to be otherwise. What better way to symbolize both the cynic's contempt for himself and the world than to make him the callous destroyer of his entire family.

With Bosola, Webster has fixed his glance on another but closely related flaw located at the core of the cynic's character. While all that we have said of Flamineo is generally true of the cynic, there is an ironic twist to the cynic's character which is equally as true as Flamineo's self-loathing. Paradoxically, while the cynic is busily at work attempting to prove everything human loathesome and life itself a meaningless, cruel joke, there is within him, so long as the spark of human decency remains alive, a level at which he desires to be proved wrong. Until the individual reaches the absolute depths of cynicism where he becomes locked within the terms of his own negativism, this paradoxical state continues to exist. When it no longer does, the transformation experienced by Bosola is impossible:

> What would I do, were this to do again?
> I would not change my peace of conscience
> For all the wealth of Europe:—she stirs; here's life:
> Return, fair soul, from darkness, and lead mine
> Out of this sensible hell.
>
> · · · · · · · · · · · ·
> Her eye opes,
> And heaven in it seems to ope, that late was shut,
> To take me up to mercy.
>
> [4.2.339–49]

Flamineo and Bosola are both tool-villains and as such are in part at least borrowings from the revenge tragedy tradition. But though such shadows of revenge tragedy do play in the corners of Webster's drama as traceable borrowings and are also present in a very central way influencing the actual tone of the whole, yet the theme of revenge is itself nowhere present. Webster's great plays, as much as they call to mind the plays of the revenge tradition, are not themselves of it.

IV Both Middleton's *Women Beware Women* and *The Changeling* have from time to time been linked to the revenge tragedy tradition. But what has been said of Webster's relation to that tradition is largely true of Middleton's. Perhaps the most fruitful place to take up the discussion of Middleton's relation to the revenge tradition is where we left off speaking of Webster's, with the tool-villain. Like Webster, Middleton includes tool-villains in each of his major plays—Livia in *Women Beware Women* and DeFlores in *The Changeling*. Like Webster's tool-villains, Middleton's have undergone a sea change since their birth in the revenge tradition. They, too, have become characters in their own right. And, not coincidentally, cynics. But where Webster leaves off, Middleton begins. Webster was content to character-ize the cynic in the person of the tool-villain. For Middleton, the cynical tool-villain is only the narrow end of the wedge into the investigation of the cynical personality which is the chief the-matic subject of his major plays. His tool-villains are hardly more complex than Webster's. When we meet Livia and DeFlores, they, like Flamineo and Bosola, are full-blown cynics, and we are given no clearer idea of how they got that way than we were in Webster. But in Middleton we are also invited to witness the making of a cynic.

The process is somewhat similar in each play and in both there is a good deal of talk about revenge. Just about everyone in *Women Beware Women* longs to revenge himself on someone else. Nevertheless, revenge is clearly not a theme in the play. There is a masque-within-the-play and multiple murders, but these are not developed in terms of the usual configuration. Leantio, the most likely candidate for the part of hero-revenger, never as-sumes the role. In short, we need hardly belabor the obvious.[26] With *The Changeling*, however, the matter is quite different. We have several borrowings from the genre. We do have a revenger, Tomasso, the brother of Beatrice-Joanna's dead fiancé Alonzo, whom DeFlores has murdered at her behest. We have the ghost of the murdered man and, with a little ingenuity, we could ferret out delays, madnesses, disguises, and at least one play-within-the-play. But is *The Changeling* a revenge tragedy? Not in the least. As in Webster, none of the thematic concerns of the play have anything to do with revenge.

There is a striking parallel between the heroines of *The Duchess of Malfi* and *The Changeling* when we first meet them which makes the sharp divergence of their subsequent histories all the more revealing. We are introduced to Beatrice when, like the Duchess, she is still quite innocent, particularly of how one's actions will be used by the world as the foundation for one's character. She too acts without taking the world into account. But there the similarity ends. Where the Duchess had within her the inner strength and determination that could bring her through a crisis, Beatrice was a mediocre person with no inner resources and no standards. Where the Duchess's innocence was that of an openhearted, generous spirit, Beatrice-Joanna's was the innocence of a willful young woman accustomed to getting her own way. It little mattered whether her desire was just or unjust, right or wrong; that it was her desire was sufficient. Up to the time of the play we are to understand that this willfulness has had little more consequence than to form Beatrice-Joanna's character, her desires till now having limited themselves to the self-indulgences of an aristocratic young lady. But a character has been formed; the woman we meet is a romantic, with little regard for the notion that actions have consequences. Almost immediately upon the opening of the play she is congratulating herself on the ingenuity of her scheme to be rid of an unwanted fiancé and a troublesome servant at one stroke by hiring one to kill the other, then sending the survivor away handsomely financed to start a new life elsewhere.

Here is the center of Middleton's play, from which he develops the two themes that characterize *The Changeling*. The first is the theme which locates it in the tragic tradition because it is the theme underlying all tragedy, that is, the continuity of life. With most tragedies, the fact that actions have consequences is so fundamental a concept that it is taken for granted and not developed as a theme. In *The Changeling* as in *Macbeth* this assumption is itself investigated. In both plays, the protagonist acts as if it were not true, or as if, whether true or not, one may safely ignore it. Beatrice-Joanna, like Macbeth, makes the mistake of thinking that one decisive act, in her case as in his a murder, will clear her way. She learns, as does he, that one is not separable from what one does. Commit a murder and "You are the deed's creature"; you become a murderer. Nor can you leap over that fact and continue your life as if it were not true.

This theme of the continuity of life underlies the second theme of *The Changeling*. We said that cynicism was no more a theme in the drama of Webster than revenge was. This is not true of Middleton. Although revenge is not a theme in Middleton, cynicism definitely is. What seems to fascinate Middleton most is the way people become cynics.

As the central characteristic of the cynic is a refusal to feel the normal human emotions, the natural question to ask is, how did he get hardened against life? Middleton's profoundest insight was in just this area, the making of a cynic. He seems to have asked the question, what kind of person, under what type of pressure, would turn his back on life and harden himself against feeling? He came up with Bianca and Beatrice-Joanna, at first glance two of the least likely cynics one could imagine. If anything, they are, in fact, just the opposite of cynics; they are gushing romantics. However, since cynics are not born but make themselves, Middleton's instinct was right. Who is more likely to stop feeling and expecting than those whose feelings and expectations are so divorced from reality that the feelings will inevitably be trampled and the expectations thwarted, in other words, the romantics.

This, then, the making of the cynic, is the theme of *The Changeling*, and revenge plays no part in it. Beatrice-Joanna is fertile ground for the seeds of cynicism—a thoroughly commonplace but a thoroughly romantic young woman, filled with unrealizable expectations. She heedlessly commits a murder, only to find it has completely altered her life. Instead of clearing the obstacles to her happiness, she has created new ones. The murder has put her in the position where she must either face the fact of what she is or succumb to DeFlores's blackmail, buying his silence by becoming his whore. But Beatrice lacks the strength of character necessary for the first course of action. She chooses the latter, and by doing so begins the transition from romantic to cynic. She started her scheme with the intention that once her fiancé was murdered she would become the virgin bride of Alsemero and could forget the step she had to take to get there. That is no longer possible, but DeFlores offers her a way in which it is almost possible. If she will adjust her expectations downward, she can still be Alsemero's bride and with a little deception convince him she is his virgin bride. So now she is entering into a conspiracy with a man she formerly loathed as a devil, to deceive the man she loved enough to murder for. She becomes DeFlores's whore because to defy him would be to risk exposure. That would have required an act of heroism. How much easier to merely trim one's expectations to the situation—particularly when the other course required her to take responsibility for her actions.

The pattern of tragic action is *do, suffer,* and *know.* The person who can accept the implications of his actions and suffer their consequences through to the point of knowledge is justly regarded as a hero. It is an exacting task not within the capabilities of everyman. Most of us are never directly confronted by a situation in which we must make the momentous decision of the tragic hero. Life is seldom that exacting, and we are allowed to live our contradictory lives free from the severe judgment the tragic hero is subjected to. Yet we all know that if we see a man drowning, we are obliged to go to his aid and that on a sinking ship women and children have the first places in the lifeboats. In other words, if we are not called upon to be heroes, we do know what heroism and cowardice are. Should fortune decree that it is our lot to choose between being a hero or a coward we have no recourse but to choose, and that choice will make all the difference.

Confronted by the fact that she is a murderer and that everyone else will know it if she does not also become a whore, Beatrice-Joanna, as an act of will, chooses to add to her disgrace in a cowardly failure to rise to the demands of the situation. In embracing DeFlores, she not only acknowledges that she is one with him in the murder; their fornication also links them as spiritual equals. She begins to be what he is, a cynic. One who, to simply survive, has killed his feelings. She has refused to be a tragic hero by refusing to suffer her situation through to the tragic knowledge contained in it.

The contrast with *Macbeth* on this point is quite telling. To Macbeth it is of singular importance that his first crime is murder. The knowledge that he is a murderer haunts and eventually destroys Macbeth. Try as he may he cannot train his conscience to take that hurdle with ease. For Beatrice-Joanna, the fact that her initial crime is murder is incidental to her subsequent actions. It never troubles her conscience that she has caused a man to be murdered. She temporarily regrets having been so indiscreet as to place herself in the hands of a blackmailer. But even that she gets over quickly enough, once she finds what a dependable fellow DeFlores is. Shakespeare is writing about the torments of a murderer, Middleton about the calcification of the soul of the cynic so that no experience, not even murder, can touch it.[27]

Since the murder of Alonzo plays so small a role in *The Changeling*, the play hardly qualifies as a revenge play. The avenging brother Tomasso, a very minor figure in the plot, is a poor reflection of the traditional revenger. He never goes mad. He himself does not discover who the murderers are, nor does he destroy them. In fact, the crime of murder is not the undoing of Beatrice-Joanna; adultery is. She even boasts of being a murderess in a desperate attempt to deceive her husband about her adultery.

In short, there is nothing about *The Changeling* that justifies regarding it as a play written in the revenge tragedy tradition. Nor do we feel an influence from the revenge tragedies in this play. Nothing about either the tone or the handling of the theme reminds us of the world of revenge tragedy. The mad scenes of the subplot have an entirely different dramatic ancestry. *The Changeling* simply borrows various revenge elements, and these stand out in the play as odd anachronisms.

Let us not, then, in the future, lump together in one genre every play that contains a revenger or borrows motifs from revenge tragedy. The honor should be reserved for works which use the motifs in a given relationship, with the play structured around the efforts of a hero-revenger to confront evil head on in the attempt to comprehend its existence in a world supposedly presided over by a just God. Those plays, like *The Changeling* and *Women Beware Women*, which borrow the motifs but not the themes of revenge tragedy, should be seen as only distantly related through these borrowings, whereas others, like *The Malcontent, The Duchess of Malfi,* and *The Broken Heart,* in which the borrowings retain important traces of their original meaning though in new thematic contexts, occupy an intermediate position as plays heavily influenced by the genre but not of it.

Notes

Introduction

1. Fredson Bowers, *Elizabethan Revenge Tragedy,* pp. 20, 110; G. K. Hunter, Introduction to *Antonio's Revenge,* by John Marston, p. xiv; J. M. R. Margeson, *The Origins of English Tragedy,* pp. 169–71.

2. Studying the literary history of the genre are John Addington Symonds, *Shakspere's Predecessors in the English Drama,* pp. 387–98; A. H. Thorndike, "The Relations of *Hamlet* to Contemporary Revenge Plays," *PMLA* 17 (1902): 125–220; Percy Simpson, *"The Theme of Revenge in Elizabethan Tragedy," Proceedings of the British Academy,* vol. 21; Howard Baker, "Ghosts and Guides: Kyd's *Spanish Tragedy* and the Medieval Tragedy," *Modern Philology* 33 (1935–36): 27–35; L. G. Salingar, *"The Revenger's Tragedy* and the Morality Tradition," *Scrutiny* 6 (1938): 402–24; Bowers, *Elizabethan Revenge Tragedy,* pp. 62–258; Bernard Spivack, *Shakespeare and the Allegory of Evil,* pp. 353–61; Harrison, *Shakespeare's Tragedies,* pp. 89–93; Clifford Leech, *"The Atheist's Tragedy* as a Dramatic Comment on Chapman's *Bussy* Plays," *JEGP* 52 (1953): 525–30; Alvin Kernan, *The Cankered Muse,* pp. 211–32; Clarence V. Boyer, *The Villain as Hero in Elizabethan Tragedy,* pp. 99–164; Douglas Cole, "The Comic Accomplice in Elizabethan Revenge Tragedy," *Renaissance Drama* 9 (1966): 125–39; Geoffrey D. Aggeler, "Stoicism and Revenge in Marston," *English Studies* 51 (1970): 507–17; A. L. and M. K. Kistner, "The Senecan Background of Despair in *The Spanish Tragedy* and *Titus Andronicus," Shakespeare Studies* 7 (1974): 1–9.

3. Elizabethan attitudes toward revenge are studied by Lily Campbell, "Theories of Revenge in Renaissance England," *Modern Philology* 28 (1931): 281–98; Bowers, *Elizabethan Revenge Tragedy,* pp. 3–61; Philip Edwards, Introduction to *The Spanish Tragedy,* by Thomas Kyd, pp. lv–lxi; Ernst de Chickera, "Divine Justice and Private Revenge in *The Spanish Tragedy," Modern Language Review* 57 (1962): 228–32; V. H. Strandberg, "The Revenger's Tragedy: Hamlet's Costly Code," *South Atlantic Quarterly* 65 (1966): 95–103; Eleanor Prosser, *Hamlet and Revenge,* pp. 3–35; Elinor Bevan, "Revenge, Forgiveness and the Gentleman,"

Review of English Literature 8 (1967): 55–69; John Sibly, "The Duty of Revenge in Tudor and Stuart Drama," *Review of English Literature* 8 (1967): 46–54; Harold Skulsky, "Revenge, Honor and Conscience in *Hamlet*," *PMLA* 85 (1970): 78–87; Philip J. Ayres, "Degrees of Heresy: Justified Revenge and Elizabethan Narratives," *Studies in Philology* 69 (1972): 461–74.

1: The Ghost and Its Call to Excess

1. *A Warning for Fair Women*, ed. Charles Dale Cannon, Induction, ll. 54–59.

2. Robert H. West, "King Hamlet's Ambiguous Ghost," *PMLA* 70 (1955): 1114. Cf. also F. W. Moorman's comment that "in the plays of [Shakespeare's] predecessors, the ghost was a mere machine, a voice mouthing vengeance" ("Shakespeare's Ghosts," *Modern Language Review* 1 [1906]: 192) and J. Dover Wilson's that "the stock apparition of the Elizabethan theatre was a classical puppet, borrowed from Seneca, a kind of Jack-in-the-box, popping up from Tartarus at appropriate moments," "a ranting roistering abstraction" *(What Happens in "Hamlet,"* pp. 55, 57). Moorman did the pioneering study of the vengeful ghost in "The Pre-Shakespearean Ghost," *Modern Language Review* 1 (1906): 85–95.

3. These ghosts arise in *The Misfortunes of Arthur* (Gorlois), *The Battle of Alcazar* (Abdelmunen), *Locrine* (Albanact and Corineus), *The Spanish Tragedy* (Andrea), *Antonio's Revenge* (Andrugio), *The Tragedy of Orestes* (Agamemnon), and (of course) *Hamlet.*

4. *The Tragedy of Locrine 1595*, ed. Ronald B. McKerrow, 5.5.1998–2002.

5. Jane Harrison, *Prolegomena to the Study of Greek Religion*, pp. 214–15.

6. George Peele, *The Battle of Alcazar*, ed. W. W. Greg. The pertinent passages are 1.1.1–67 and 2.1.306–39. A significant portion of the latter is quoted as the epigraph of this chapter.

7. Thomas Kyd, *The Spanish Tragedy*, ed. Andrew S. Cairncross, 2.6.2 (all subsequent citations are to this edition).

8. Ronald Broude, "Time, Truth and Right in *The Spanish Tragedy*," *Studies in Philology* 68 (1971): 142.

9. Andrew S. Cairncross, Introduction to *The Spanish Tragedy*, by Thomas Kyd, p. xxvi.

10. G. K. Hunter, "Ironies of Justice in *The Spanish Tragedy*," *Renaissance Drama* 8 (1965): 104.

11. At 3.2.12–21, Hieronimo fights off the "direful visions" of hell that "fear my heart." At 3.12.6–19, the urgency to muster the forces of hell becomes stronger but is still put down ("I'll none of that. / This way I'll

take"). By 3.12.75–78, after the king's rebuff, Hieronimo is ready to surrender up his marshalship to "go marshal up the fiends in hell / To be avenged on you all for this." In his next soliloquy, he rejects heavenly justice and makes an irrevocable decision ("I will revenge his death" [3.13.20]).

12. Cf., for example, Pierre de la Primaudaye, *The French Academie, First Part*, p. 360: "We see no man upon earth of so base estate, no woman so feeble and weake, no living creature so little, but if they be striken, they will revenge themselves verie willingly as well as they can. How greatlie then ought this vertue to be accounted of, *which forceth this naturall lust of revenge, bred in all living creatures,* and how noble must the mind of that man needs be, which is able to master such a violent passion, *so common to all men,* thereby procuring to it selfe the name of a mild and gratious spirit, and readie to forgive, *which is proper and peculiar to the divine nature?*" (our italics).

13. John Marston, *Antonio's Revenge*, ed. G. K. Hunter, 3.1.44–51 (all subsequent citations are to this edition). In the Revels edition, W. Reavley Gair offers Keltie's translation of the passage from Seneca's *Thyestes* quoted by the Ghost: "You do not avenge crimes unless you conquer" (John Marston, *Antonio's Revenge*, p. 105 n. 51). Hunter has wisely glossed the Latin with Cunliffe's "Injuries are not revenged except where they are exceeded," which is closer to the meaning given the passage in other revenge tragedies. Cf. Thomas Goffe's *The Tragedy of Orestes* 3.6.93: "Reuenge is lost, vnlesse we doe exceed."

14. Lawrence J. Ross, Introduction to *The Revenger's Tragedy*, by Cyril Tourneur, p. xxi.

15. Philip J. Ayres, "Marston's *Antonio's Revenge:* The Morality of the Revenging Hero," *Studies in English Literature* 12 (1972): 370. Most critics argue that reality would have been better served had the violence committed by the revengers led, with a certain sense of inevitability, to their own demise.

16. Cyril Tourneur, *The Atheist's Tragedy, or, The Honest Man's Revenge,* ed. Irving Ribner, 2.6.20–23.

17. Mark Rose, "*Hamlet* and the Shape of Revenge," *English Literary Renaissance* 1 (1971): 134; Maynard Mack, Jr., *Killing the King*, p. 79.

18. The strokes used by Shakespeare to depict that character have given rise to a protracted debate on the theological affiliations of the Ghost. See Wilson, *What Happens in "Hamlet,"* pp. 51–86; John E. Hankins, *The Character of Hamlet*, pp. 131–71; Roy W. Battenhouse, "The Ghost in *Hamlet:* A Catholic 'Linchpin'?" *Studies in Philology* 48 (1951): 161–92; I. J. Semper, "The Ghost in *Hamlet:* Pagan or Christian?" *The Month*, n.s. 9 (1953): 222–34; West, "King Hamlet's Ambiguous Ghost," pp. 1107–17; Sister Miriam Joseph, "Discerning the Ghost in *Hamlet,*"

PMLA 76 (1961): 493–502, with comments thereupon by Paul N. Siegel in *PMLA* 78 (1963): 148–49; Eleanor Prosser, *Hamlet and Revenge,* pp. 97–142; Michael C. Andrews, "Professor Prosser and the Ghost," *Renaissance Papers 1974,* pp. 19–29.

19. William Shakespeare, *The Riverside Shakespeare,* ed. G. Blakemore Evans, *Hamlet* 1.5.22–25. Subsequent citations to Shakespeare in this chapter are from this edition. In quoting we have accepted editor's emendations and have silently omitted editorial brackets.

20. Wilson, *What Happens in "Hamlet,"* pp. 59–60; Hankins, *Character of Hamlet,* p. 132.

21. Prosser, *Hamlet and Revenge,* p. 138; Sister Miriam Joseph, "Discerning the Ghost," pp. 499–501.

22. Battenhouse, "The Ghost in *Hamlet,*" pp. 165–68.

23. A. P. Rossiter, *English Drama from Early Times to the Elizabethans,* p. 175.

2: Madness as Dramatic Symbol

1. Robert R. Reed, *Bedlam on the Jacobean Stage,* pp. 5–6.

2. See, for example, Edgar A. Peers, *Elizabethan Drama and Its Mad Folk,* p. 54. Peers's book nevertheless provides a detailed examination of the categories, causes, and treatments of madness and is useful as a general orientation to the subject.

3. Reed, *Bedlam,* p. 6.

4. Louis B. Wright, "Madmen as Vaudeville Performers on the Elizabethan Stage," *JEGP* 30 (1931): 54, 51, 52.

5. G. B. Harrison, *Shakespeare's Tragedies,* p. 93.

6. Thomas Dekker, *The Dramatic Works of Thomas Dekker,* ed. Fredson Bowers, vol. 2, *The Honest Whore, Part 1,* 5.2.155–56.

7. The twentieth century prefers to describe any state between absolute normality and actual psychopathy with the neutral term of "irrationality." The irrational, so temporary and so commonplace, is easily excused. Eric Voegelin argues, in fact, that the impassioned state is now considered the norm (*From Enlightenment to Revolution,* p. 50). For a discussion of this point in relation to modern literature, see Joseph Wood Krutch, *Modernism in Modern Drama,* pp. 21–22.

8. August Strindberg, *Six Plays of Strindberg,* trans. Elizabeth Sprigge, *The Father,* act 3, p. 47.

9. Eleanor Prosser, *Hamlet and Revenge,* p. 148 (our italics). Prosser can perhaps be pardoned when even Peers, in discussing the causes of insanity recognized in Elizabethan drama, passes over the madness of passion in one sentence, clearly oblivious to its importance. "We need not stay long," says Peers, "over the *numerous* characters *who speak of anger as*

leading to madness" (Elizabethan Mad Folk, p. 15 [our italics]). Joseph T. McCullen, in "Madness and the Isolation of Characters in Elizabethan and Early Stuart Drama," *Studies in Philology* 48 (1951): 206–18, shows even less awareness of this form of madness.

10. Scholars whose work had led them to a familiarity with Elizabethan psychological treatises are, of course, well aware of the fact that passion and madness were equated. The point was made long ago by Ruth Leila Anderson, *Elizabethan Psychology and Shakespeare's Plays* (see epigraph of this chapter). J. B. Bamborough in *The Little World of Man* and Lily Campbell in *Shakespeare's Tragic Heroes*, to give only two examples, also touch upon the topic. The problem is that their work has made little impact on revenge tragedy criticism, as Prosser's ignorance of it indicates.

11. Thomas Hobbes, *Leviathan*, ed. Michael Oakeshott, p. 63. Note that it is *excessive* passion and not passion per se to which the age objected; indeed, the passions were considered necessary in that, as the "motions" of the soul, they enabled man to take action upon the decisions made by his apprehending faculties. Pierre de la Primaudaye, for example, points out that anger, properly directed, was essential to acts of courage *(The French Academie, Second Part*, p. 307). To condemn passion altogether, as Shakespeare's Angelo does, or to attempt to suppress it when it is called for, as Marston's Pandulpho tries to do, is to be unnatural.

12. Aristotle, *The Basic Works of Aristotle*, ed. Richard McKeon, p. 1041; *Ethics* 7. 3. (1) (c).

13. John Hall, *The Court of Virtue*, ed. Russell A. Fraser, p. 259.

14. Robert Tofte, *The Blazon of Jealousie* (1615), pp. 59–60; quoted in Fredson Bowers, *Elizabethan Revenge Tragedy*, p. 21.

15. Richard Corbet, *The Times' Whistle*, ed. Joseph M. Cowper, p. 94; *Satire* 7, 2979–3009.

16. Joseph Hall, "Holy Observations," in *The Works of the Right Reverend Joseph Hall D.D.*, ed. Philip Wynter, 7:541.

17. John Ford, *The Dramatic Works of John Ford*, ed. W. Gifford, vol. 1, and *The Broken Heart*, ed. Donald K. Anderson, Jr.; Thomas Kyd, *The Spanish Tragedy*, ed. Andrew S. Cairncross; John Marston, *Antonio's Revenge*, ed. G. K. Hunter; William Shakespeare, *The Riverside Shakespeare*, ed. G. Blakemore Evans (subsequent quotations from Shakespeare in this chapter are taken from this edition).

18. Douglas Bush, *"Paradise Lost" in Our Time*, p. 37.

19. John Hall, *The Court of Virtue*, p. 272.

20. Robert Hoopes, *Right Reason in the English Renaissance*, p. 5.

21. Sir John Davies, *Nosce Teipsum*, in *Silver Poets of the Sixteenth Century*, ed. G. Bullett, p. 385.

22. Ibid., p. 379.

23. Joseph Hall, *Works,* 7:542 (our italics).

24. John Marston, *The Plays of John Marston,* ed. H. Harvey Wood, vol. 3. Cyril Tourneur, *The Revenger's Tragedy,* ed. Lawrence J. Ross.

25. Thomas Middleton, *The Works of Thomas Middleton,* ed. A. H. Bullen, vol. 1, *The Phoenix* 1.4.113–48.

26. Philip Massinger, *The Plays and Poems of Philip Massinger,* ed. Philip Edwards and Colin Gibson, vol. 2.

27. Peers has no more to say about "the introduction of Bedlam into a romance such as *The Pilgrim*" than that it is made "merely for the sake of giving some cheap amusement to the groundlings" (*Elizabethan Mad Folk,* p. 48). Wright, too, feels that the madhouse scenes have "slight motivation" and are "without dramatic justification" ("Vaudeville Performers," pp. 52–53). Reed is more perceptive. He actually notes that the sane Alphonso is "all but mad himself, his 'madness' is basically the result of reversals, but his mental stability is also impaired by an excess of choler." However, Reed fails to see the connection between Alphonso's distraction and the later madhouse scenes, for he views the forest as a *cure* rather than as a reflection of Alphonso's mental derangement (*Bedlam,* pp. 122–23).

28. John Fletcher, *The Works of Francis Beaumont and John Fletcher,* ed. Arnold Glover and A. R. Waller, vol. 5, *The Pilgrim* 2.1.175.

29. Reed, *Bedlam,* p. 54.

30. As William Empson points out in *Some Versions of Pastoral,* p. 51.

31. George Williams, Introduction to *The Changeling,* by Thomas Middleton and William Rowley, pp. xxii (citations in the text are to this edition).

32. Maynard Mack, "The Jacobean Shakespeare: Some Observations on the Construction of the Tragedies," in *Jacobean Theatre,* pp. 24–32.

3: Renaissance Psychological Theory

1. William Shakespeare, *The Riverside Shakespeare,* ed. G. Blakemore Evans (subsequent quotations from Shakespeare in this chapter are taken from this edition).

2. G. B. Harrison, *Shakespeare's Tragedies,* p. 93.

3. But see Carroll Camden, "On Ophelia's Madness," *Shakespeare Quarterly* 15 (1964): 247–55.

4. The most commonly consulted source books on this subject are Bartholomaeus Anglicus, *On the Properties of Things* (Book 3); Timothy Bright, *A Treatise of Melancholie;* Pierre Charron, *Of Wisdom;* Nicholas Coeffeteau, *A Table of Humane Passions;* Juan Huarte, *The Examination of Men's Wits;* Pierre de la Primaudaye, *The French Academie; Edward Reynolds, A Treatise of the Passions and Faculties of the Soule of Man;* and Thomas

Wright, *The Passions of the Minde in Generall.* Useful also are modern accounts of Renaissance psychology such as those by J. B. Bamborough, *The Little World of Man;* Ruth Leila Anderson, *Elizabethan Psychology and Shakespeare's Plays;* and William Rossky, "Imagination in the English Renaissance: Psychology and Poetic," *Studies in the Renaissance* 5 (1958): 49–73. Francis R. Johnson discusses the critical application of these theories to the drama in "Elizabethan Drama and the Elizabethan Science of Psychology" in *English Studies Today.* See also Louise C. Turner Forest, "A Caveat for Critics Against Invoking Elizabethan Psychology," *PMLA* 61 (1946): 651–72.

5. Renaissance psychologists, because they often describe the process of perception in terms of love, normally speak of an "object" which is perceived by the senses—man's eyes are dazzled by the sight of a beautiful woman. The "object," in terms of the revenge passion, would more properly be the murder; thus, it seems wiser to indicate the sensual impression that initiates the learning process by substituting the terms *event, injury,* or *offense* throughout this discussion.

6. Sir John Davies, *Nosce Teipsum,* in *Silver Poets of the Sixteenth Century,* ed. G. Bullett, p. 380.

7. La Primaudaye, *The French Academie, Second Part,* pp. 326–27.

8. See Anthonie Copley, *A Fig for Fortune,* pp. 11–19, whose Revenge plies Elizan Man with the arguments in this paragraph. An often-quoted argument of this type is given by Cutwolfe, the Italianate revenger in Thomas Nashe's *The Unfortunate Traveller:* "Reuenge is the glorie of armes, & the highest performance of valure: reuenge is whatsoeuer we call law or iustice. The farther we wade in reuenge, the neerer come we to the throne of the almightie. To his scepter it is properly ascribed; his scepter he lends vnto man, when he lets one man scourge an other. All true Italians imitate me in reuenging constantly and dying valiantly. Hangman, to thy taske, for I am readie for the vtmost of thy rigor." The argument is not popular with Cutwolfe's public: "Herewith all the people (outrageously incensed) with one conioyned outcrie yelled mainely, Awaie with him, away with him. Executioner, torture him, teare him." *The Works of Thomas Nashe,* ed. R. B. McKerrow, 2:326–27. Catherine Belsey explores this subject at length in "The Case of Hamlet's Conscience," *Studies in Philology* 76 (1979): 127–48.

9. John Ford, *The Broken Heart,* ed. Donald K. Anderson, Jr., 3.1.27–50.

10. Joseph Hall, "Characters of Virtues and Vices," *The Works of the Right Reverend Joseph Hall D.D.,* ed. Philip Wynter, 6:96–97.

11. John Marston, *Antonio's Revenge,* ed. G. K. Hunter, 1.2.267–68.

12. Thomas Kyd, *The Spanish Tragedy,* ed. Andrew S. Cairncross, 3.2.3–4.

13. Shakespeare, *Hamlet* 1.2.135–37.

14. Thomas Wright, *Passions of the Minde,* p. 45.

15. Ibid., p. 56.

16. La Primaudaye, *The French Academie, Second Part,* p. 325.

17. Envy, while it comes into play where villainous revengers are concerned (Piero envies Andrugio and D'Amville, Charlemont) has little to do with a Hamlet or a Hieronimo, and indignation is, of course, a variety of anger.

18. Francis Bacon, "Of Revenge" in *The Essays . . . of Francis Bacon,* ed. A. S. Gaye, p. 28.

19. Thomas Goffe, *The Tragedy of Orestes,* 4.7.54–58.

20. Cyril Tourneur, *The Revenger's Tragedy,* ed. Lawrence J. Ross.

21. The phrase is T. S. Eliot's. See "Cyril Tourneur" (1930) in *Selected Essays,* p. 166: "The cynicism, the loathing and disgust of humanity, expressed consummately in *The Revenger's Tragedy,* are immature in the respect that they exceed the object. Their objective equivalents are characters practising the grossest vices; characters which seem merely to be spectres projected from the poet's inner world of nightmare, some horror beyond words. So the play is a document on humanity chiefly because it is a document on one human being, Tourneur; its motive is truly the death-motive, for it is the loathing and horror of life itself." Cf. also the fine essay by B. J. Layman, "Tourneur's Artificial Noon: The Design of *The Revenger's Tragedy,*" *Modern Language Quarterly* 34 (1973): 20–35.

22. Robert Tofte, *The Blazon of Jealousie* (1615), quoted in Fredson Bowers, *Elizabethan Revenge Tragedy,* p. 21.

23. La Primaudaye, *The French Academie, Second Part,* p. 326.

4: **The Other Motifs**

1. For a fuller analysis of *Hoffman,* see Fredson Bowers, *Elizabethan Revenge Tragedy,* pp. 125–30.

2. The reader of revenge tragedy must be aware of subtle psychological insights. J. J. Lawlor testifies to the sensitivity required in analyzing the delay when he writes that "the Revenge matter, properly handled, offers great possibilities. It makes possible the presentation of a doomed man, one bidden by inescapable authority to certain acts. The intensity this offers is incalculable if the hero is bidden against his own conviction—more, against all desire and longing, if his very nature is revolted by what he must none the less perform. Conceive a man commanded to do what he has no assurance is right, and you have a situation of pure tragedy. But in the presentation it is of the highest importance that the hero shall not *openly* call in question the ethics or the efficacy of Revenge. Do that, and the thematic unity is broken; we pass from tragic intensity to controversial ardour. The true solution is to make the hero

question all things under the sun *except* the duty that is enjoined upon him, for from that he cannot escape. This, I submit, is the tragic conflict in *Hamlet*: the hero averse from the deed that is required of him, seeking endlessly the cause of that aversion, calling it by any name but its own, and failing to know it for what it is" ("The Tragic Conflict in *Hamlet*," *Review of English Studies*, n.s. 1 [1950] : 109).

3. See John Scott Colley, "*The Spanish Tragedy* and the Theatre of God's Judgments," *Papers on Language and Literature* 10 (1974): 241–53, for a perceptive analysis of the various plays within this play.

4. Citations are to Thomas Kyd, *The Spanish Tragedy*, ed. Andrew S. Cairncross; John Marston, *Antonio's Revenge*, ed. G. K. Hunter; Cyril Tourneur, *The Revenger's Tragedy*, ed. Lawrence J. Ross; Thomas Goffe, *The Tragedy of Orestes.*

5. Hamlet varies from the norm but the changes occur because of the necessity to modify the motif to fit with the character Shakespeare has given to his revenger. The variations will be discussed in chapter 8.

6. See 4.1.1–70 where Antonio defends his disguise. Marston draws upon the various ambiguities residing in the commonplace that the fool is the wisest of men to reveal his hero's ability to see beyond the communal fantasy.

7. See George L. Geckle, "*Antonio's Revenge*: 'Never more woe in lesser plot was found,'" *Comparative Drama* 6 (1972–73): 326–30; Maurice Charney, "The Persuasiveness of Violence in Elizabethan Plays," *Renaissance Drama*, n.s. 2 (1969): 59–70.

5: The Revenge Experience as Tragedy

1. William Shakespeare, *The Riverside Shakespeare*, ed. G. Blakemore Evans, *Hamlet* 1.1.47–49.

2. Eric Voegelin, *Order and History*, vol. 2, *The World of the Polis*, pp. 2, 1. We are indebted to the chapter on "Mankind and History" in this volume for the approach to the relationship of history and order developed here. The reader is encouraged to read the entire chapter, which is pertinent to this argument.

3. Ibid., p. 247.

4. Eric Voegelin, *Order and History*, vol. 3, *Plato and Aristotle*, p. 84. For another description of the descent, see Charles A. Hallett and Kenneth E. Frost, "Poetry and Reality: The Zetema and its Significance for Poetics," *International Philosophical Quarterly* 17 (1977): 430–35.

6: The Spanish Tragedy

1. For different views of the justice theme, see G. K. Hunter, "Ironies of Justice in *The Spanish Tragedy*," *Renaissance Drama* 8 (1965): 89–104;

Ejner J. Jensen, "Kyd's *Spanish Tragedy*: The Play Explains Itself," *JEGP* 64 (1965): 7–16; and J. R. Mulryne, Introduction to *The Spanish Tragedy*, by Thomas Kyd, pp. xix–xxvi.

2. Pierre de la Primaudaye, *The French Academie, Second Part*, pp. 326–27.

3. Cf., for example, Ronald Broude, "Time, Truth and Right in *The Spanish Tragedy*," *Studies in Philology* 68 (1971): 135—"Hieronimo's tragedy lies in the suffering he undergoes as circumstances combine to try his faith in Divine Justice of which he, as Knight Marshal, is earthly agent."

4. Thomas Kyd, *The Spanish Tragedy*, ed. Andrew S. Cairncross, 3.13.52–54 (citations throughout this chapter are to this edition).

5. G. K. Hunter, "Ironies of Justice," p. 73; Broude, "Time, Truth and Right," p. 142; Andrew S. Cairncross, Introduction to *The Spanish Tragedy*, by Thomas Kyd, p. xxvi.

6. Fredson Bowers, *Elizabethan Revenge Tragedy*, p. 68.

7. See above, p. 20.

8. "When Bel-imperia upbraids him for his apparent reconciliation with Hieronimo's murderers, he knows that the time has come and that he is Heaven's 'scourge and minister.' . . . the 'practices' that he devises so quickly, as if by inspiration, pat upon the entrance of the murderers, imitate those of the heavens themselves." S. F. Johnson, "*The Spanish Tragedy*, or Babylon Revisited," in *Essays on Shakespeare and Elizabethan Drama in Honor of Hardin Craig*, p. 28.

9. The analysis of the madness is based, of course, on a consideration of the text as it existed before the famous "additions" were appended. Many modern editors include the additions in the text itself rather than in an appendix, thus making it nearly impossible for the student to experience the play in its purer form.

10. The fact that the madness is sometimes momentary and marked by a return to sanity is erroneously used to argue the point that the revenger is not mad.

11. This linear movement of the revenge plot is examined in greater detail on pp. 24–28.

12. Anne Righter, *Shakespeare and the Idea of the Play*, pp. 73–74.

13. Arthur Brown, "The Play within a Play: An Elizabethan Dramatic Device," *Essays and Studies*, n. s. 13 (1960): 43.

14. A. L. and M. K. Kistner discuss the relationship between suicide, despair, and madness in "The Senecan Background of Despair in *The Spanish Tragedy* and *Titus Andronicus*," *Shakespeare Studies* 7 (1974): 1–9.

7: *Antonio's Revenge*

1. See John Marston, *Antonio's Revenge*, ed. G. K. Hunter, 5.3.116–86 (citations in the text are to this edition).

2. John Peter, *Complaint and Satire in Early English Literature*, pp. 224.

3. H. Harvey Wood, Introduction to *The Plays of John Marston*, 1:xxxv.

4. T. F. Wharton, "Old Marston or New Marston: The *Antonio Plays*," *Essays in Criticism* 25 (1975): 367–68. Wharton's essay contains an excellent analysis of the technical flaws in this play—for example, Marston's failure to control the imagery attached to villain and hero.

5. Fredson Bowers, *Elizabethan Revenge Tragedy*, p. 124; Samuel Schoenbaum, "The Precarious Balance of John Marston," *PMLA* 67 (1952): 1072; R. A. Foakes, "John Marston's Fantastical Plays: *Antonio and Mellida* and *Antonio's Revenge*," *Philological Quarterly* 41 (1962): 235. Foakes receives qualified support from Philip J. Ayres in "Marston's *Antonio's Revenge*: The Morality of the Revenging Hero," *Studies in English Literature* 12 (1972): 359–74. Wharton's refutation (cited above) is one of many but the most convincing.

6. Among the examples of the villain-hero form listed by Clarence V. Boyer in *The Villain as Hero in Elizabethan Tragedy* are *The Jew of Malta; Orlando Furioso; Selimus; Alaham; The True Tragedy of Richard III;* Shakespeare's *Richard III;* portions of *Titus Andronicus, Othello,* and *Antonio's Revenge; Lust's Dominion; Hoffman; The Revenger's Tragedy; The Duchess of Malfi; The Atheist's Tragedy; Sejanus;* and *Macbeth.* It is our feeling that Marston's inspiration for the villain-hero aspects of his tragedy come from (1) *Titus Andronicus*, in which he found a precedent for the juxtaposition of the villain-revenger with the hero-revenger and (2) *Richard III*, which emphasizes elements of retribution that become standard in later villain-hero plays (cf. *The Revenger's Tragedy, The Atheist's Tragedy,* and *Macbeth*). Because the term *retribution play* is often used synonymously with the term *villain-hero play* (see, for instance, Richard Levin's *The Multiple Plot in English Renaissance Drama*, pp. 38, 76), and because Marston has so obviously designed the tyrant's role with retribution in mind, we have chosen to use Levin's term rather than Boyer's throughout this chapter. It focuses more clearly on the specific problems of Marston's ending.

7. We use *pity* here as it is defined by J. V. Cunningham in *Woe or Wonder: The Emotional Effect of Shakespearean Tragedy*, pp. 16–23. Cf. also Lawrence N. Danson, "The Device of Wonder: *Titus Andronicus* and Revenge Tragedies," *Texas Studies in Literature and Language* 16 (1974): 27–42; and George L. Geckle, "*Antonio's Revenge*: 'Never more woe in lesser plot was found,'" *Comparative Drama* 6 (1972–73): 331–33. (Geckle's important essay is also the first to call attention to the relationship between the ghost and the theme of excess in the revenge action of Marston's play.)

8. Bowers, *Elizabethan Revenge Tragedy*, p. 123.

9. When Thomas Goffe appropriates the Julio scene for his revenge

tragedy, *Orestes,* he moves the incident to its proper place in the configuration. It immediately preceeds the deaths of Agamemnon and Clytemnestra as part of their final torture.

10. G. K. Hunter, Introduction to *Antonio's Revenge,* by John Marston, p. xv.

11. Marston takes pains to detail the thoughts that pass through Antonio's mind as he murders Julio:

> Howl not, thou pury mold, groan not ye graves,
> Be dumb, all breath. Here stands Andrugio's son,
> Worthy his father. So: I feel no breath;
> His jaws are fall'n, his dislodg'd soul is fled,
> And now there's nothing but Piero left;
> He is all Piero, father all; this blood,
> This breast, this heart, Piero all,
> Whom thus I mangle. Sprite of Julio,
> Forget this was thy trunk. I live thy friend.
> Mayst thou be twined with the soft'st embrace
> Of clear eternity; but thy father's blood
> I thus make incense of, to Vengeance.
> [3.1.195–206]

The logical processes Marston is depicting here closely resemble those he calls attention to in *The Dutch Courtesan,* 2.2.199–204, where Malheureux plots to kill Freevill. Malheureux, however, comes to a realization of "how easy 'tis to err / When passion will not give us leave to think!"

12. This point is elaborated upon by Geoffrey D. Aggeler, "Stoicism and Revenge in Marston," *English Studies* 51 (1970): 511.

13. Eugene M. Waith, *The Herculean Hero in Marlowe, Chapman, Shakespeare, and Dryden,* p. 48. Marston associates Antonio with the demigod Hercules through Galeatzo's comment, "Thou art another Hercules to us / In ridding huge pollution from our state" (5.3.129–30). Waith's summary of Renaissance humanist attitudes toward Hercules is therefore helpful in understanding Marston's thought. Hercules, comments Waith, "is both the great individual and the selfless benefactor. He is pitted against a cruel world, whose monsters he is obliged to combat, yet in fighting for himself he also saves the world. . . . The myth readily supports a concept of heroism in which the heroic act is first of all a vindication of individual integrity" (p. 43). For an interesting approach to Marston's view of the civilizational crisis in *Antonio's Revenge,* see William Babula, "The Avenger and the Satirist: John Marston's Malevole," *The Elizabethan Theatre 6* (1975): 48–50.

14. Wharton, "Old Marston or New Marston," p. 366.

8: *Hamlet*

1. William Shakespeare, *The Riverside Shakespeare,* ed. G. Blakemore Evans, *Hamlet* 3.1.78 (all subsequent citations to Hamlet in this chapter are to this edition).

2. John Addington Symonds, *Shakspere's Predecessors in the English Drama,* pp. 192–93. Cf. also Percy Simpson, "The Theme of Revenge in Elizabethan Tragedy," *Proceedings of the British Academy,* vol. 21 (1935), p. 14.

3. The phrase is F. W. Moorman's. See "Shakespeare's Ghosts," *Modern Language Review* 1 (1906):192.

4. These eschatological details obviously also have a thematic function, in that what we see of the Ghost's attitude toward the afterlife ("I could a tale unfold whose lightest word / Would harrow up thy soul, freeze thy young blood" [1.5.15–16]) is designed to condition our responses to the thoughts Hamlet expresses when he contemplates suicide. The horrors described by the Ghost give validity to Hamlet's fear of the nightmare-land of life after death. This is not to suggest that Hamlet obtains a glimpse through the Ghost's eyes and is therefore afraid; only that the audience is provided in advance with a picture which sets up a referent and reinforcement for something Hamlet will later be thinking about.

5. Robert H. West, "King Hamlet's Ambiguous Ghost," *PMLA* 70 (1955): 1115. West is responding to the arguments of Dover Wilson and Roy Battenhouse (see chap. 1, n. 12).

6. W. W. Greg's argument that the Ghost is "Hamlet's Hallucination" *(Modern Language Review* 12 [1917]:393–421) is, of course, untenable, for Shakespeare assures us in the reversal sequence in which Bernardo and Marcellus convince the skeptical Horatio of the Ghost's reality that this is no projection of Hamlet's own mind.

7. Moorman, "Shakespeare's Ghosts," p. 192; Sister Miriam Joseph, "Discerning the Ghost in *Hamlet,*" *PMLA* 76 (1961): 192; Lily Campbell, *Shakespeare's Tragic Heroes,* p. 147 n. 1.

8. For an important aspect of the antic disposition not discussed here, see Charles R. Forker, "Shakespeare's Theatrical Symbolism and Its Function in *Hamlet,*" *Shakespeare Quarterly* 14 (1963): 215–29.

9. Eleanor Prosser, *Hamlet and Revenge,* p. 234.

10. C. S. Lewis, "Hamlet: The Prince or the Poem?" *Proceedings of the British Academy,* vol. 28 (1942), p. 16.

11. Anne Righter, *Shakespeare and the Idea of the Play,* p. 160.

12. The play element is understated in *Titus Andronicus,* yet there is a ritualistic aspect to the banquet, primarily achieved by Titus's desire to stage and arrange events in preparation for his reception and murder of

Tamora. The suggestion of a staged action is increased by the fact that various characters arrive in costume—Tamora appears as Revenge and Titus "plays the cook."

13. Righter, *Shakespeare and the Play,* p. 81.

14. Note the similar conclusion reached from a comparison of these two playlets by Robert J. Nelson in *Play within a Play,* pp. 29–30: "Leave it to Hieronimo of Kyd's *Spanish Tragedie* to merge the real and the unreal and so leave us totally without perspective in a world of chaos. Hamlet is a subtler esthetician and a better metaphysician. He realizes that his action must be more circumscribed. . . . The free manipulation of reality is the essence of comedy and for it we must not look to the Prince of Denmark." Hamlet, says Nelson, "cannot create reality, he can work only on the given."

15. See the excellent analysis of this speech by Maurice Charney in "The 'Now Could I Drink Hot Blood' Soliloquy and the Middle of *Hamlet,*" *Mosaic* 10 (1977): 77–86.

16. Emrys Jones, *Scenic Form in Shakespeare,* pp. 66–88.

17. This point is well argued by Fredson Bowers in "Dramatic Structure and Criticism: Plot in *Hamlet,*" *Shakespeare Quarterly* 15 (1964): 207–18.

18. Nelson, *Play within a Play,* p. 27.

19. Lewis, "The Prince or the Poem?" p. 13.

9: *The Revenger's Tragedy*

1. John Marston, *Antonio's Revenge,* ed. G. K. Hunter; William Shakespeare, *The Riverside Shakespeare,* ed. G. Blakemore Evans.

2. Leslie Sanders, "*The Revenger's Tragedy:* A Play on the Revenge Play," *Renaissance and Reformation* 10 (1974): 26. On this subject see also Lillian Wilds, "The Revenger as Dramatist: A Study of the Character-as-Dramatist in *The Revenger's Tragedy,*" *Rocky Mountain Review* 30 (1976): 113–22.

3. Larry Champion, "Tourneur's *The Revenger's Tragedy* and the Jacobean Tragic Perspective," *Studies in Philology* 72 (1975): 311–12.

4. Muriel Bradbrook feels that *The Revenger's Tragedy* is built around "an enlarged series of peripeteia" (twenty-two in number, according to her count). These episodes are assumed to be united by the fact that each is somehow concerned with a scheme for revenge and that all of the reversals are effected through irony. See *Themes and Conventions of Elizabethan Tragedy,* p. 165.

5. G. K. Chesterton, *St. Francis of Assisi,* pp. 40–41.

6. Quotations from *The Revenger's Tragedy* are taken from Cyril Tourneur, *The Revenger's Tragedy,* ed. Lawrence J. Ross; 1.2.177–91.

7. Bradbrook, *Themes and Conventions*, p. 165.

8. One suspects not so much that Tourneur means to deny the order of nature as that he is not keenly interested in where the authority comes from. He is playing off the tradition of the ghost but, owing to his particular vision, the skull reverberates with suggestions of the Last Judgment rather than of natural law at its most primitive.

9. This approach probably originates with Clarence V. Boyer's study of Vindice in *The Villain as Hero in Elizabethan Tragedy*, pp. 146–50. There are, however, hints of this position in Fredson Bowers, *Elizabethan Revenge Tragedy*, pp. 132–34.

10. A perceptive exploration of this subject is made by Jonas A. Barish (see "The True and False Families of *The Revenger's Tragedy*, in *English Renaissance Drama*, pp. 142–54).

11. Alvin Kernan, *The Cankered Muse*, pp. 219–20.

12. Maynard Mack writes that the madness of the Jacobean hero was like that of Cassandra, in that it "contains both punishment and insight. She is doomed to know, by a consciousness that moves to measures outside our normal space and time; she is doomed never to be believed, because those to whom she speaks can hear only the opposing voice" ("The Jacobean Shakespeare: Some Observations on the Construction of the Tragedies" in *Jacobean Theatre*, p. 40). And Kernan: "Vindice also has the satirist's usual double nature, for he is at once the inspired prophet who sees that the depraved palace world is no more than a charnel house, and at the same time the very spirit of death itself " *The Cankered Muse*, pp. 230–31).

13. Ibid., p. 228.

14. The third plot of the play, that in which the Youngest Son rapes Antonio's wife, serves a similar function; it provides an even more specific example of the horror of the original offense. It differs, however, in that it hints that such offenses are punished by Providence, without the need for the action of a revenger.

15. Sanders, *"The Revenger's Tragedy,"* p. 35.

16. We are not convinced that Middleton wrote *The Revenger's Tragedy*, though he obviously had a strong influence on the man who did. To avoid becoming needlessly involved in this controversy, we have chosen to follow tradition and call the author "Cyril Tourneur."

10: The Derivative Play

1. The play was first printed in 1633 by Richard Meighen, a friend of the author, and was reissued in 1656 (along with two other plays by Goffe, *The Raging Turke, or Baiazet the Second* and *The Couragious Turke, or Amurath the First*) in a collection entitled *Three Excellent Tragaedies. Orestes*

is available in microprint in the series *Three Centuries of Drama: English 1512–1641,* edited by Henry Willis Wells, but since 1656 it has not been reprinted or anthologized in book form. All quotations in this chapter are taken from the Meighen quarto of 1633.

2. Compare Aeschylus's *Oresteia,* Sophocles' *Electra,* and Euripides' *Electra* and *Orestes.*

3. For recent analyses of Pikeryng's *Horestes* in the light of the revenge tradition, see Willard Farnham, *The Medieval Heritage of Elizabethan Tragedy,* pp. 258–63; Eleanor Prosser, *Hamlet and Revenge,* pp. 41–44; Robert S. Knapp, "*Horestes:* The Uses of Revenge," *ELH* 40 (1973): 205–20; Ronald Broude, "*Vindicta filia temporis:* Three English Forerunners of the Elizabethan Revenge Play," *JEGP* 72 (1973): 494–97. The play is also analyzed by P. Happé, "Tragic Themes in Three Tudor Moralities," *Studies in English Literature* 5 (1965): 207–27.

4. See John Gower, *The English Works of John Gower,* ed. G. C. Macaulay, 1: 277–86, and William Caxton, trans., *The Recuyell of the Historyes of Troye,* by Raoul Lefevre, ed. H. Oskar Sommer, 2:680–87. These tellings of the story follow models that derive from the fourth-century translation of Dictys that was so popular during the Middle Ages. Cf. *The Trojan War: The Chronicles of Dictys of Crete and Dares the Phrygian,* trans. R. M. Frazer, Jr.

5. David M. Bevington, *From Mankind to Marlowe: Growth of Structure in the Popular Drama of Tudor England,* p. 182.

6. This is the division suggested in the edition cited throughout this chapter: John Pikeryng, *The Interlude of Vice (Horestes) 1567,* ed. Daniel Seltzer. Doubtful readings pointed out by the editor have been silently corrected and abbreviations expanded.

7. "As we trace his career through the hybrid plays we discover in the latest of them the inevitable effect of his new environment upon the Vice. He was originally conceived and subsequently developed as a native of a metaphorical world which supported in all its parts the subjective logic of his role. But as he moves onto a new stage filled with human individuals and the diverse events of history or fable—a stage, moreover, rapidly transferring its allegiance from a homiletic to an aesthetic purpose—his original significance is compromised by his new surroundings, and his activity, though his energy is unimpaired, undergoes an important transformation. His traditional behavior is bent and twisted to accommodate him to events and persons too confirmed in history or fable to be accommodated to him, and too self-sufficient in their own concreteness to have any real use for his metaphorical presence among them. In the four plays we are about to consider the Vice is so clearly an imposition that his presence would be inexplicable without our awareness of the homiletic tradition still within these plays and of his peculiar hold on the stage as

the most durable feature of that tradition. But his presence remains possible for another reason: in a dramatic world that is no longer a metaphor he himself ceases to be metaphorical" (Bernard Spivack, *Shakespeare and the Allegory of Evil*, pp. 278–79).

8. Gower, *English Works, Confessio Amantis*, 3.2010–15. Cf. Caxton, *Recuyell*, 2:685, ll. 23–30.

9. Bevington, *From Mankind to Marlowe*, p. 182.

10. This moral has prompted critics to relate Pikeryng's Clytemnestra and Egistus to Mary Stuart and Lord Bothwell. See James E. Phillips, "A Revaluation of *Horestes* (1567)," *Huntington Library Quarterly* 18 (1955): 227–44.

11. One should mention that Goffe probably also knew two other English plays written about Orestes. What he learned from Thomas Dekker's *Orestes Furies* (or *Furens?*), a lost play of 1599 possibly identical with the lost *Agamemnon* by Chettle and Dekker performed in that year, cannot be determined. However, he makes little use of the dramatized version of the Orestes story in *The Second Part of the Iron Age* (1612–13), which ends Thomas Heywood's cycle of plays on Greek legend.

12. The reply tells us Orestes has read his *Hamlet:*

> Thinke on me, and reuenge: yes, those two words
> Shall serue as burthen vnto all my acts,
> I will reuenge, and then I'll thinke on thee:
> I'll thinke on thee, and then againe reuenge
> And stab, and wound, and still I'll thinke on thee.
> [4.7.54–58]

11: **Delimiting the Genre**

1. See chapter 10, note 3.

2. References are to George Chapman, *The Plays and Poems of George Chapman*, vol. 1, *The Tragedies*, ed. Thomas Marc Parrott.

3. Robert J. Lordi, Introduction to *The Revenge of Bussy D'Ambois*, by George Chapman, pp. 24–25 (the line numbers in this passage refer to Lordi's own edition). See pp. 26–30 of that edition for a further analysis of the injustice radiating out from the throne of King Henry into his realm.

4. Chapman's interest in Stoicism has been studied by Janet Spens, "Chapman's Ethical Thought," *Essays and Studies* 11 (1925): 145–69; John William Wieler, *George Chapman–The Effect of Stoicism upon His Tragedies;* Ennis Rees, *The Tragedies of George Chapman: Renaissance Ethics in Action;* Michael H. Higgins, "Chapman's 'Senecal Man': A Study in Jacobean Psychology," *Review of English Studies* 21 (1945): 183–91; Allen Bergson, "The Worldly Stoicism of George Chapman's *The Revenge of Bussy*

D'Ambois and *The Tragedy of Chabot, Admiral of France,"* *Philological Quarterly* 55 (1976): 43–64; Patricia Demers, "Chapman's *The Revenge of Bussy D'Ambois:* Fixity and the Absolute Man," *Renaissance and Reformation* 12 (1976): 12–20; Ronald Broude, "George Chapman's Stoic-Christian Revenger," *Studies in Philology* 70 (1973): 51–61; Peter Bement, "The Stoicism of Chapman's Clermont D'Ambois," *Studies in English Literature* 12 (1972): 345–57. See also Richard H. Perkinson, "Nature and the Tragic Hero in Chapman's *Bussy* Plays," *Modern Language Quarterly* 3 (1942): 263–85.

5. Chapman, *Plays and Poems,* 1:77.

6. Henry Hitch Adams, "Cyril Tourneur on Revenge," *JEGP* 48 (1949): 72–87; Clifford Leech, *"The Atheist's Tragedy* as a Dramatic Comment on Chapman's *Bussy* Plays," *JEGP* 52 (1953): 525–30. For the form, however, Tourneur has gone back to *Antonio's Revenge* and borrowed Marston's combination of the retribution plot and revenge tragedy, again juxtaposing tyrant and revenger but suggesting that the true hero will withhold action and let Heaven take its course.

7. The themes of *The Atheist's Tragedy* are so creditably analyzed in Richard Levin's *The Multiple Plot in English Renaissance Drama,* pp. 75–85, that there is no need to treat of the personal vision here. See also Robert Ornstein, *"The Atheist's Tragedy* and Renaissance Naturalism," *Studies in Philology* 51 (1954): 194–207; E. A. Strathmann, "Elizabethan Meanings of 'Atheism' " in *Sir Walter Ralegh: A Study in Elizabethan Skepticism,* pp. 61–97; George Truett Buckley, *Atheism in the English Renaissance.*

8. The ghost motif in *The Atheist's Tragedy* is discussed in chapter 1, Section III.

9. Cyril Tourneur, *The Atheist's Tragedy or, The Honest Man's Revenge,* ed. Irving Ribner, 3.2.28–36.

10. Chapman also distinguishes Clermont from the impassioned characters in his own play, Tamyra and Charlotte. Tamyra, for example, offers herself as a channel through which the spirit of vengeance could return to earth (1.2.1–10). But both Clermont and the Ghost of Bussy disclaim her.

11. Lordi, Introduction to *The Revenge of Bussy D'Ambois,* pp. 35–36; Fred M. Fetrow, "Chapman's Stoic Hero in *The Revenge of Bussy D'Ambois,"* *Studies in English Literature* 19 (1979): 236–37. Both of these essays exemplify the latest trend in criticism of Chapman's *Revenge,* the attempt to refute the long-standing judgment that Chapman never managed to translate his ideas into drama. Lordi and Fetrow are reacting against a stand taken by Spens, "Chapman's Ethical Thought," p. 150; James Smith, "George Chapman," part 2 in *Scrutiny* 4 (1935–36): 61; Ornstein, *Moral Vision,* pp. 74–75; Irving Ribner, *Jacobean Tragedy: The Quest for Moral Order,* p. 22. But neither fully understands the dramatic

medium. They seem unaware that drama develops in terms of builds, climaxes, reversals, suspense, and clashing desires which create recipro-cal action between characters within a scene.

12. Millar MacLure, *George Chapman: A Critical Study,* p. 131.

13. For a sensitive analysis of the different uses of the revenge tragedy structure in *Hamlet* and *The Duchess,* see Harold Jenkins, "The Tragedy of Revenge in Shakespeare and Webster," *Shakespeare Survey* 14 (1961): 45–55.

14. See Bernard McElroy, "Recent Studies in Elizabethan and Jaco-bean Drama," *Studies in English Literature* 19 (1979): 342–43; Joyce E. Peterson, *Curs'd Example: "The Duchess of Malfi" and Commonweal Tragedy,* pp. 56–68. Peterson goes far astray in her discussion of the opening situation of *The Duchess.* Statecraft has nothing to do with the Duchess's tragedy.

15. John Webster, *The Duchess of Malfi,* ed. John Russell Brown, 1.1.455–59.

16. The most fervent advocate of this theory is Elizabeth M. Brennan, "The Relationship between Brother and Sister in the Plays of John Webster," *Modern Language Review* 58 (1963): 488–94.

17. J. R. Mulryne, "*The White Devil* and *The Duchess of Malfi,*" in *Jaco-bean Theatre,* ed. John Russell Brown and Bernard Harris, pp. 201–25.

18. For various opinions on this subject, see Travis Bogard, *The Tragic Satire of John Webster,* pp. 63–81; Jane Marie Luecke, "*The Duchess of Malfi:* Comic and Satiric Confusion in a Tragedy," *Studies in English Literature* 4 (1964): 275–90; Alexander W. Allison, "Ethical Themes in *The Duchess of Malfi,*" *Studies in English Literature* 4 (1964): 263–73; James P. Driscoll, "Integrity of Life in *The Duchess of Malfi,*" *Drama Survey* 6 (1967): 43–53; Louis D. Gianneti, "A Contemporary View of *The Duchess of Malfi,*" *Comparative Drama* 3 (1969): 297–307; Charles R. Forker, "Love, Death, and Fame: The Grotesque Tragedy of John Webster," *Anglia* 91 (1973): 194–218; Joan M. Lord, "*The Duchess of Malfi:* 'The Spirit of Greatness' and 'of Woman,' " *Studies in English Literature* 16 (1976): 305–17.

19. On the world as madhouse, see chap. 2, Section IV.

20. Eric Voegelin, "Tragedy," in *Order and History,* vol. 2, *The World of the Polis,* pp. 243–66.

21. Robert R. Reed, *Bedlam on the Jacobean Stage,* p. 88.

22. Being a physician himself, John Bucknill wonders at "the want of reliance which the Doctor expressed in the resources of his art" and speculates that "in those early times the leech and the mediciner had not learnt to combine the moral influences which are the natural means of ministering to a mind diseased after the manner of Lady Macbeth's, with those sleep-producing oblivious antidotes which at present form the remedies of melancholia." He then proceeds to describe the steps the

doctor should have taken to cure the patient. "The treatment of such a
case as that of Lady Macbeth would be, to remove her from all scenes
suggesting unhappy thoughts, to attract her attention to new objects of
interest, and to find, if possible, some stimulus to healthy emotion. If she
had been thrown from her high estate, and compelled to labour for her
daily bread, the tangible evils of such a condition would have been most
likely to have rooted out those of the imagination and of memory. The
judicious physician, moreover, would not in such a case have neglected
the medicinal remedies at his command . . . he would have given the
juice of poppy, or some 'drowsy syrup,' to prevent thick-coming fancies
depriving her of her rest" *(The Mad Folk of Shakespeare: Psychological
Essays,* pp. 42–43).

23. Shakespeare's Gratiano, in remarking upon the wolvish nature of
Shylock's passion, provides another interesting gloss to Ferdinand's
anger:

> Thou almost mak'st me waver in my faith
> To hold opinion with Pythagoras,
> That souls of animals infuse themselves
> Into the trunks of men. Thy currish spirit
> Govern'd a wolf, who hang'd for human slaughter,
> Even from the gallows did his fell soul fleet,
> And whilst thou layest in thy unhallowed dam,
> Infus'd itself in thee; for thy desires
> Are wolvish, bloody, starv'd, and ravenous.

(William Shakespeare, *The Riverside Shakespeare,* ed. G. Blakemore Evans,
The Merchant of Venice 4.1.130–38.) The wolf of desire was appropriated
by poets and moralists throughout the seventeenth century. Edward
Reynolds, for example, calls upon the analogy to help him explain the
irascible appetites: the angry man who cannot obtain access to his
enemies will "vex and boyle with the more burning chafe," like a fierce
wolf who "barks at his absent prey with the more Ire: / when rag'd and
deceiv'd Hunger doth him tyre" *(A Treatise of the Passions and Faculties of
the Soule of Man,* p. 330).

24. See Douglas Cole, "The Comic Accomplice in Elizabethan Revenge Tragedy," *Renaissance Drama* 9 (1966): 125–39, for a history of this
character type.

25. T. S. Eliot, "Four Elizabethan Dramatists," in *Selected Essays,* p. 98.

26. For interpretations of *Women Beware Women,* see Edward Engelberg, "Tragic Blindness in *The Changeling* and *Women Beware Women,*"
Modern Language Quarterly, 23 (1962): 20–28; Inga-Stina Ewbank,
"Realism and Morality in *Women Beware Women,*" *Essays and Studies* 22
(1969): 57–70; Charles A. Hallett, "The Psychological Drama of *Women*

Beware Women," Studies in English Literature 12 (1972): 375–89; Larry S. Champion, "Tragic Vision in Middleton's *Women Beware Women," English Studies* 57 (1976): 410–24.

27. For a fuller study of cynicism in Middleton, see Charles A. Hallett, *Middleton's Cynics: A Study of Middleton's Insight into the Moral Psychology of the Mediocre Mind.* For other views of *The Changeling,* see Richard Hindry Barker, *Thomas Middleton,* pp. 121–31; Samuel Schoenbaum, *Middleton's Tragedies,* pp. 132–49; Helen Gardner, "Milton's 'Satan' and the Theme of Damnation in Elizabethan Tragedy," *Essays and Studies,* n.s. 1 (1948):46–66; Christopher Ricks, "The Moral and Poetic Structure of *The Changeling," Essays in Criticism* 10 (1960): 290–306.

Selected Bibliography

The following is essentially a list of works cited; however, for the convenience of the reader we have also included bibliographical information on other books and essays that have particular relevance to revenge tragedy or have played an influential role in revenge tragedy criticism. In listing important primary sources, we have tried to inform the reader of reprint editions that make the rarer texts easier to obtain and, for the plays given special emphasis in this book, we have noted the most recent critical editions.

Primary Sources

PLAYS

Chapman, George. *Bussy D'Ambois and The Revenge of Bussy D'Ambois.* Edited by Frederick S. Boas. The Belles-Lettres Boston: D. C. Heath & Co., 1905.

———. *The Plays and Poems of George Chapman.* Vol. 1, *The Tragedies.* Edited by Thomas Marc Parrott. London: George Routledge & Sons, 1910.

———. *The Revenge of Bussy D'Ambois.* Edited by Robert J. Lordi. Jacobean Drama Studies, no. 75. Salzburg: University of Salzburg, 1977.

Chettle, Henry. *The Tragedy of Hoffman.* Edited by Harold Jenkins. Malone Society Reprints, 1950.

Dekker, Thomas. *The Dramatic Works of Thomas Dekker.* Edited by Fredson Bowers. 4 vols. Cambridge: At the University Press, 1953–61.

Fletcher, John, and Beaumont, Francis. *The Works of Francis Beaumont and John Fletcher.* Edited by Arnold Glover and A. R. Waller. 10 vols. Cambridge: At the University Press, 1905–12.

Ford, John. *The Broken Heart.* Edited by Donald K. Anderson, Jr. Regents Renaissance Drama Series. Lincoln: University of Nebraska Press, 1968.

————. *The Dramatic Works of John Ford.* Edited by W. Gifford. 2 vols. London: John Murray, 1827.

Goffe, Thomas. *The Tragedy of Orestes.* London, 1633.

————. *The Tragedy of Orestes.* In *Three Centuries of Drama: English 1512–1641.* Edited by Henry Willis Wells. New York: Readex Microprint, 1953.

————. " 'The Tragedy of Orestes' by Thomas Goffe: A Critical Edition." Edited by Frank Norbert O'Donnell. Ph.D. dissertation, Ohio State University, 1950.

Heywood, Thomas. *The Dramatic Works of Thomas Heywood . . . in Six Volumes.* London: John Pearson, 1874. See 3:296–431 [*The Second Part of The Iron Age,* acts 4 and 5] for Heywood's dramatization of the Orestes story.

Hughes, Thomas. *The Misfortunes of Arthur.* In *Early English Classical Tragedies.* Edited by John W. Cunliffe, Oxford: Clarendon Press, 1912.

Kyd, Thomas. *The Spanish Tragedy.* Edited by Philip Edwards. The Revels Plays. Cambridge, Mass.: Harvard University Press, 1959.

————. *The Spanish Tragedy.* Edited by Andrew S. Cairncross. Regents Renaissance Drama Series. Lincoln: University of Nebraska Press, 1967.

————. *The Spanish Tragedy.* Edited by Thomas Ross. Fountainwell Drama Series, 6. Los Angeles: University of California Press, 1968.

————. *The Spanish Tragedy.* Edited by J. R. Mulryne. New Mermaids. New York: Hill & Wang, 1970.

————. *The Works of Thomas Kyd.* Edited by F.S. Boas. Oxford: Clarendon Press, 1901.

Locrine. See *Tragedy of Locrine, The.*

Marston, John. *Antonio's Revenge.* Edited by G. K. Hunter. Regents Renaissance Drama Series. Lincoln: University of Nebraska Press, 1965.

————. *Antonio's Revenge.* Edited by W. Reavley Gair. The Revels Plays. Manchester: Manchester University Press, 1978.

————. *The Dutch Courtesan.* Edited by M. L. Wine. Regents Renaissance Drama Series. Lincoln: University of Nebraska Press, 1965.

————. *The Malcontent.* Edited by M. L. Wine. Regents Renaissance Drama Series. Lincoln: University of Nebraska Press, 1964.

————. *The Plays of John Marston.* Edited by A. H. Bullen. 3 vols. Boston: Houghton Mifflin Co., 1887.

————. *The Plays of John Marston.* Edited by H. Harvey Wood. 3 vols. Edinburgh: Oliver & Boyd, 1934–39.

Massinger, Philip. *The Plays and Poems of Philip Massinger.* Edited by Philip Edwards and Colin Gibson. 5 vols. Oxford: Clarendon Press, 1976.

Middleton, Thomas. *The Works of Thomas Middleton*. Edited by A. H. Bullen. 8 vols. Boston: Houghton Mifflin & Co., 1885–86.

——— and Rowley, William. *The Changeling*. Edited by N. W. Bawcutt. The Revels Plays. London: Methuen & Co., 1958.

———. *The Changeling*. Edited by Patricia Thomson. New Mermaids. London: Ernest Benn, 1964.

———. *The Changeling*. Edited by George Williams. Regents Renaissance Drama Series. Lincoln: University of Nebraska Press, 1966.

Norton, Thomas, and Sackville, Thomas. *Gorbuduc; or, Ferrex and Porrex*. Edited by Irby B. Bauthen, Jr. Regents Renaissance Drama Series. Lincoln: University of Nebraska Press, 1970.

Peele, George. *The Battle of Alcazar 1597*. Edited by W. W. Greg. Malone Society Reprints, 1907.

Pikeryng, John. *The Interlude of Vice (Horestes) 1567*. Edited by Daniel Seltzer. Malone Society Reprints, 1962.

Seneca, Lucius Annaeus. *Seneca His Tenne Tragedies. Translated into English*. Edited by Thomas Newton. 1581. The Tudor Translations, Second Series 11 and 12. 2 vols. 1927. Reprint edition. Bloomington: Indiana University Press, 1966. Also available as *Seneca His Tenne Tragedies*. The English Experience No. 131. New York: Da Capo Press, 1969.

Shakespeare, William. *Hamlet*. Edited by J. Dover Wilson. Cambridge: At the University Press, 1934.

———. *Hamlet*. Edited by Horace Howard Furness. New Variorum Edition of Shakespeare. 1877. Republication of 10th edition. 2 vols. New York: Dover Publications, 1963.

———. *Hamlet*. Edited by Cyrus Hoy. Norton Critical Editions. New York: W. W. Norton & Co., 1963.

———. *The Riverside Shakespeare*. Edited by G. Blakemore Evans. Boston: Houghton Mifflin Co., 1974.

———. *Titus Andronicus*. Edited by J. C. Maxwell. Arden Shakespeare Series. 3rd edition. 1961. New York: Barnes & Noble, 1968.

———. *The Tragedy of "Hamlet": A Critical Edition of the Second Quarto, 1604, with Introduction and Textual Notes*. Edited by Thomas Marc Parrott and Hardin Craig. Princeton: Princeton University Press, 1938.

———. *The Tragedy of Hamlet, Prince of Denmark*. Edited by Jack Randall Crawford. The Yale Shakespeare. 1917. Revised by C. F. Tucker Brooke. New Haven: Yale University Press, 1954.

Strindberg, August. *Six Plays of Strindberg*. Translated by Elizabeth Sprigge. Garden City, N.Y.: Doubleday & Co., Anchor Books, 1955.

Three Centuries of Drama: English 1512–1641. Edited by Henry Willis Wells. New York: Readex Microprint, 1952–63.

Tourneur, Cyril. *The Atheist's Tragedy, or The Honest Man's Revenge.* Edited by Irving Ribner. The Revels Plays. Cambridge: Harvard University Press, 1964.

————. *The Atheist's Tragedy.* Edited by Brian Morris and Roma Gill. New Mermaids. New York: W. W. Norton & Co., 1976.

————. *The Plays of Cyril Tourneur.* Edited by George Parfitt. Plays by Renaissance and Restoration Dramatists. Cambridge: At the University Press, 1978.

————. *The Revenger's Tragedy.* Edited by R. A. Foakes. The Revels Plays. Cambridge, Mass.: Harvard University Press, 1966.

————. *The Revenger's Tragedy.* Edited by Lawrence J. Ross. Regents Renaissance Drama Series. Lincoln: University of Nebraska Press, 1966.

————. *The Revenger's Tragedy.* Edited by Brian Gibbons. New Mermaids. New York: Hill & Wang, 1967.

————. *The Works of Cyril Tourneur.* Edited by Allardyce Nicoll. 1930. Reprint edition. New York: Russell & Russell, 1963.

The Tragedy of Locrine 1595. Edited by Ronald B. McKerrow. Malone Society Reprints. 1908.

A Warning for Fair Women: A Critical Edition. Edited by Charles Dale Cannon. The Hague: Mouton & Co., 1975.

Webster, John. *The Complete Works of John Webster.* Edited by F. L. Lucas. 4 vols. London: Chatto & Windus, 1928.

————. *The Duchess of Malfi.* Edited by John Russell Brown. The Revels Plays. London: Methuen & Co., 1964.

————. *The Duchess of Malfi.* Edited by Elizabeth M. Brennan. New Mermaids. New York: Hill & Wang, 1966.

————. *The Duchess of Malfi.* Edited by Clive Hart. Fountainwell Drama Series, 18. Los Angeles: University of California Press, 1972.

POETRY AND PROSE

Aquinas, Saint Thomas. *Basic Writings of St. Thomas Aquinas.* Edited by Anton C. Pegis. 2 vols. New York: Random House, 1945.

Aristotle. *The Basic Works of Aristotle.* Edited by Richard McKeon. New York: Random House, 1941.

Bacon, Francis. *The Essays or Counsels Civil and Moral of Francis Bacon, Lord Verulam, Viscount St. Albans.* Edited by A. S. Gaye. Oxford: Clarendon Press, 1921.

Bartholomaeus Anglicus. *On the Properties of Things.* Translated by John Trevisa. Edited by M. C. Seymour. 2 vols. Oxford: Clarendon Press, 1975.

Bright, Timothy. *A Treatise of Melancholie,* 1586. Reprint edition. The

English Experience, no. 212. New York: DaCapo Press, 1969.

Caxton, William, trans. *The Recuyell of the Historyes of Troye.* By Raoul Lefevre. Edited by H. Oskar Sommer. 2 vols. London: David Nutt, 1894.

Charron, Pierre. *Of Wisdome, 3 books.* 1612. Reprint edition. The English Experience, no. 315. Norwood, N.J.: Walter J. Johnson, 1971. Also available as *The "wisdom" of Pierre Charron; an original and orthodox code of morality.* Studies in Romance Languages and Literature. Chapel Hill: University of North Carolina Press, 1961.

Coeffeteau, Nicholas. *A Table of Humane Passions.* Translated by E. Grimeston. London, 1621.

Copley, Anthonie. *A Fig for Fortune.* London, 1596.

Corbet, Richard. *The Times' Whistle.* Edited by Joseph M. Cowper. Early English Text Society, no. 48. London: N. Trübner & Co., 1871.

Davies, Sir John. *Nosce Teipsum.* In *Silver Poets of the Sixteenth Century.* Edited by G. Bullett. London: J. M. Dent & Sons, 1947.

Dictys of Crete. *The Trojan War: The Chronicles of Dictys of Crete and Dares the Phrygian.* Translated by R. M. Frazer, Jr. Bloomington: Indiana University Press, 1966.

Gower, John. *The English Works of John Gower.* Edited by G. C. Macaulay. Early English Text Society, nos. 81–82. 2 vols. London: Kegan Paul, Trench, Trübner & Co., 1900.

Hall, John. *The Court of Virtue (1565).* Edited by Russell A. Fraser. New Brunswick, N.J.: Rutgers University Press, 1961.

Hall, Joseph. *The Works of the Right Reverend Joseph Hall, D.D.* Edited by Philip Wynter. 10 vols. Oxford: Oxford University Press, 1863.

Hobbes, Thomas. *Leviathan.* Edited by Michael Oakeshott. New York: Crowell-Collier Publishing Company, Collier Books, 1962.

Huarte de San Juan, Juan. *The Examination of Men's Wits.* Translated by M. Camillo Camilli and Richard Carew. 1594. Reprint edition. Gainesville, Fla.: Scholars' Facsimiles & Reprints, 1959. Also available as *The Examination of Men's Wits.* The English Experience, no. 126. New York: DaCapo Press, 1969.

La Primaudaye, Pierre de. *The French Academie.* Translated by T[homas] B[owes]. London, 1594.

Lefevre, Raoul. *The Recuyell of the Historyes of Troye.* See Caxton, William.

Nashe, Thomas. *The Works of Thomas Nashe.* Edited by R. B. McKerrow. 5 vols. 1910. Reprint edition. Revised by F. P. Wilson. Oxford: Basil Blackwell, 1958.

Reynolds, Edward. *A Treatise of the Passions and Faculties of the Soule of Man.* Edited by Margaret Lee Wiley. 1640. Reprint edition. Gainesville, Fla.: Scholars' Facsimiles & Reprints, 1971.

Wither, George. *Abuses Stript, and Whipt: or Satyricall Essayes.* In *Juvenilia.*

1622. Reprint edition. Spenser Society, no. 9. Manchester: Charles S. Simms, 1871. See "Of Revenge" and "Of Choller."

Wright, Thomas. *The Passions of the Minde in Generall.* 1604. Reprint edition. Urbana: University of Illinois Press, 1971.

Secondary Sources

Adams, Henry Hitch. "Cyril Tourneur on Revenge." *JEGP* 48 (1949): 72–87.

Aggeler, Geoffrey D. "Stoicism and Revenge in Marston." *English Studies* 51 (1970): 507–17.

Allison, Alexander W. "Ethical Themes in *The Duchess of Malfi.*" *Studies in English Literature* 4 (1964): 263–73.

Anderson, Ruth Leila. *Elizabethan Psychology and Shakespeare's Plays.* University of Iowa Humanistic Studies, vol. 3, no. 4. Iowa City: University of Iowa Press, 1927.

Andrews, Michael C. "*Hamlet:* Revenge and the Critical Mirror." *English Literary Renaissance* 8 (1978): 9–23.

———. "Professor Prosser and the Ghost." In *Renaissance Papers 1974.* Edited by D. G. Donovan and A. L. Deneef. The Southeastern Renaissance Conference, 1975. Pp. 19–29.

Ayres, Philip J. "Degrees of Heresy: Justified Revenge and Elizabethan Narratives." *Studies in Philology* 69 (1972): 461–74.

———. "Marston's *Antonio's Revenge:* The Morality of the Revenging Hero." *Studies in English Literature* 12 (1972): 359–74.

———. "Parallel Action and Reductive Technique in *The Revenger's Tragedy.*" *English Language Notes* 8 (1970): 103–7.

———. *Tourneur: "The Revenger's Tragedy."* London: Edward Arnold, 1977.

Babb, Lawrence. *The Elizabethan Malady: A Study of Melancholia in English Literature from 1580 to 1642.* East Lansing: Michigan State College Press, 1951.

Babula, William. "The Avenger and the Satirist: John Marston's Malevole." *The Elizabethan Theatre 6* Edited by G. R. Hibbard. Hamden, Conn.: Shoe String Press, 1975.

Baker, Howard. "Ghosts and Guides: Kyd's *Spanish Tragedy* and the Medieval Tragedy." *Modern Philology* 33 (1935–36): 27–35.

———. *Induction to Tragedy: A Study in the Development of Form in "Gorbuduc," "The Spanish Tragedy," and "Titus Andronicus."* University, La.: Louisiana State University Press, 1939.

Bamborough, J. B. *The Little World of Man.* 1952. Reprint edition. Folcroft, Pa.: Folcroft Library Editions, 1972.

Barish, Jonas. "*The Spanish Tragedy,* or the Pleasures and Perils of Rhetoric." In *Elizabethan Theatre.* Edited by John Russell Brown and

Bernard Harris. Stratford-upon-Avon Studies, 9. London: Edward Arnold, 1966.

———. "The True and False Families of *The Revenger's Tragedy.*" In *English Renaissance Drama: Essays in Honor of Madeleine Doran and Mark Eccles.* Edited by Standish Henning, Robert Kimbrough, and Richard Knowles. Carbondale: Southern Illinois University, 1976.

Barker, Richard Hindry. *Thomas Middleton.* New York: Columbia University Press, 1958.

Battenhouse, Roy W. "The Ghost in *Hamlet:* A Catholic 'Linchpin'?" *Studies in Philology* 48 (1951):161–92.

Belsey, Catherine. "The Case of Hamlet's Conscience." *Studies in Philology* 76 (1979):127–48.

Bement, Peter. "The Stoicism of Chapman's Clermont D'Ambois." *Studies in English Literature* 12 (1972):345–57.

Bergson, Allen. "The Ironic Tragedies of Marston and Chapman: Notes on Jacobean Tragic Form." *JEGP* 69 (1970):613–30.

———. "The Worldly Stoicism of George Chapman's *The Revenge of Bussy D'Ambois* and *The Tragedy of Chabot, Admiral of France.*" *Philological Quarterly* 55 (1976): 43–64.

Bevan, Elinor. "Revenge, Forgiveness, and the Gentleman." *Review of English Literature* 8 (1967): 55–69.

Bevington, David M. *From Mankind to Marlowe: Growth of Structure in the Popular Drama of Tudor England.* Cambridge, Mass.: Harvard University Press, 1962.

Boas, F. S. "The Play Within the Play." *The Shakespeare Association Papers, 1925–26* 5 (1927):134–56.

Bogard, Travis. *The Tragic Satire of John Webster.* 1955. Reprint edition. New York: Russell & Russell, 1965.

Boklund, Gunnar." *The Duchess of Malfi": Sources, Themes, Characters.* Cambridge; Mass.: Harvard University Press, 1962.

Bowers, Fredson. "The Audience and the Revenger of Elizabethan Tragedy." *Studies in Philology* 31 (1934):160–75.

———. "The Death of Hamlet: A Study in Plot and Character." In *Studies in the English Renaissance Drama in Memory of Karl Julius Holzknecht.* Edited by Josephine W. Bennett, Oscar Cargill, and Vernon Hall, Jr. New York: New York University Press, 1959.

———. "Dramatic Structure and Criticism: Plot in *Hamlet.*" *Shakespeare Quarterly* 15 (1964):207–18.

———. *Elizabethan Revenge Tragedy 1587–1642.* Princeton: Princeton University Press, 1940.

———. "Hamlet as Minister and Scourge." *PMLA* 70 (1955):740–49.

Boyer, Clarence V. *The Villain as Hero in Elizabethan Tragedy.* 1914. Reprint edition. New York: Russell & Russell, 1964.

Bradbrook, Muriel. *Themes and Conventions of Elizabethan Tragedy.* 1935. Reprint edition. Cambridge: At the University Press, 1966.

Bradley, A. C. *Shakespearean Tragedy.* 1904. Reprint edition. New York: Fawcett Publications, 1968.

Brennan, Elizabeth M. "The Relationship between Brother and Sister in the Plays of John Webster." *Modern Language Review* 58 (1963): 488–94.

Broude, Ronald. "George Chapman's Stoic-Christian Revenger." *Studies in Philology* 70 (1973): 51–61.

———. "Revenge and Revenge Tragedy in Renaissance England." *Renaissance Quarterly* 28 (1975): 38–58.

———. "Time, Truth, and Right in *The Spanish Tragedy.*" *Studies in Philology* 68 (1971): 130–45.

———. "*Vindicta filia temporis:* Three English Forerunners of the Elizabethan Revenge Play." *JEGP* 72 (1973): 489–502.

Brown, Arthur. "The Play within a Play: An Elizabethan Dramatic Device." *Essays and Studies,* n.s. 13 (1960): 36–48.

Buckley, George Truett. *Atheism in the English Renaissance.* Chicago: University of Chicago Press, 1932.

Bucknill, John. *The Mad Folk of Shakespeare: Psychological Essays.* 2nd ed. 1867. Reprint edition. New York: Burt Franklin, 1969.

Bush, Douglas. *"Paradise Lost" in Our Time.* Ithaca: Cornell University Press, 1945.

Cairncross, Andrew S. Introduction to *The Spanish Tragedy.* See Primary Sources (Plays): Kyd, Thomas.

Caldwell, Mark L. "Hamlet and the Senses." *Modern Language Quarterly* 40 (1979): 135–54.

Camden, Carroll. "On Ophelia's Madness." *Shakespeare Quarterly* 15 (1964): 247–55.

Campbell, Lily. *Shakespeare's Tragic Heroes: Slaves of Passion.* 1930. Reprint edition. New York: Barnes & Noble, 1970.

———. "Theories of Revenge in Renaissance England." *Modern Philology* 28 (1931): 281–98.

Campbell, Oscar J. "What's the Matter with Hamlet?" *Yale Review* 32 (1942): 309–22.

Caputi, Anthony. *John Marston, Satirist.* Ithaca: Cornell University Press, 1961.

Champion, Larry. "Tourneur's *The Revenger's Tragedy* and the Jacobean Tragic Perspective." *Studies in Philology* 72 (1975): 229–321.

———. "Tragic Vision in Middleton's *Women Beware Women.*" *English Studies* 57 (1976): 410–24.

Chang, Joseph. " 'Of Mighty Opposites': Stoicism and Machiavellianism." *Renaissance Drama* 9 (1966): 37–58.

Chang, Ta-tsung. "Implausible and Plausible Causes of Hamlet's Delay in Exacting Revenge." *Tamkang Journal* 13 (1975):285–353.

Charney, Maurice. "The 'Now Could I Drink Hot Blood' Soliloquy and the Middle of *Hamlet.*" *Mosaic* 10 (1977):77–86.

————. "The Persuasiveness of Violence in Elizabethan Plays." *Renaissance Drama*, n.s. 2 (1969):59–70.

————. *Style in "Hamlet."* Princeton: Princeton University Press, 1969.

Chesterton, G. K. *St. Francis of Assisi.* New York: George H. Doran Co., 1924.

Cole, Douglas. "The Comic Accomplice in Elizabethan Revenge Tragedy." *Renaissance Drama* 9 (1966):125–39.

Colley, John Scott. "*The Spanish Tragedy* and the Theatre of God's Judgments." *Papers on Language and Literature* 10 (1974):241–53.

Conrad, Bernard R. "Hamlet's Delay—A Restatement of the Problem." *PMLA* 41 (1926):680–87.

Coursen, Herbert R., Jr. "That Within: Hamlet and Revenge." *Bucknell Review* 11 (May 1963):19–34.

————. "The Unity of *The Spanish Tragedy.*" *Studies in Philology* 65 (1968):768–82.

Cox, Lee Sheridan. *Figurative Design in "Hamlet": The Significance of the Dumb Show.* Columbus: Ohio State University Press, 1973.

Cunliffe, John W. *The Influence of Seneca on Elizabethan Tragedy.* London: Macmillan & Co., 1893.

Cunningham, J. V. *Woe or Wonder: The Emotional Effect of Shakespearean Tragedy.* Denver: University of Denver Press, 1951.

Cutts, John P. "Shadow and Substance: Structural Unity in *Titus Andronicus.*" *Comparative Drama* 2 (1968):161–72.

Danson, Lawrence N. "The Device of Wonder: *Titus Andronicus* and Revenge Tragedies." *Texas Studies in Literature and Language* 16 (1974):27–43.

de Chickera, Ernst. "Divine Justice and Private Revenge in *The Spanish Tragedy.*" *Modern Language Review* 57 (1962): 228–32.

————. "Palaces of Pleasure: The Theme of Revenge in Elizabethan Translations of Novelle." *Review of English Studies*, n.s. 11 (1960):1–7.

Demers, Patricia. "Chapman's *The Revenge of Bussy D'Ambois:* Fixity and the Absolute Man." *Renaissance and Reformation* 12 (1976):12–20.

Doebler, John. "The Play Within the Play: The *Muscipula Diaboli* in *Hamlet.*" *Shakespeare Quarterly* 23 (1972):161–69.

Doran, Madeleine. *Endeavors of Art: A Study of Form in Elizabethan Drama.* Madison: University of Wisconsin Press, 1954.

Driscoll, James P. "Integrity of Life in *The Duchess of Malfi.*" *Drama Survey* 6 (1967): 42–53.

Dunfey, Sister Francesca. " 'Mighty Showes': Masque Elements in Jacobean and Caroline Drama." *Shakespeare Studies* 6 (1967–68):122–46.

Edwards, Philip. Introduction to *The Spanish Tragedy.* See Primary
    Sources (Plays): Kyd, Thomas.
————. *Thomas Kyd and Early Elizabethan Tragedy.* London: Longmans,
    Green & Co., 1966.
Ekeblad, Inga-Stina. See Ewbank, Inga-Stina [Ekeblad].
Eliot, T. S. *Selected Essays.* New edition. New York: Harcourt, Brace &
    Co., 1950.
Elliott, G. R. *Scourge and Minister: A Study of "Hamlet" as Tragedy of
    Revengefulness and Justice.* Durham, N.C.: Duke University Press, 1951.
Empson, William. *Some Versions of Pastoral.* 1935. Reprint edition. Nor-
    folk, Conn.: James Laughlin, 1952.
Engelberg, Edward. "Tragic Blindness in *The Changeling* and *Women
    Beware Women.*" *Modern Language Quarterly* 23 (1962):20–28.
Everett, Barbara. "*Hamlet:* A Time to Die." *Shakespeare Survey* 30
    (1977):117–23.
Ewbank, Inga-Stina [Ekeblad]. "An Approach to Tourneur's Imagery."
    Modern Language Review 54 (1959):489–98.
————. "The 'Impure Art' of John Webster." *Review of English Studies* 9
    (1958):253–67.
————. "Realism and Morality in *Women Beware Women.*" *Essays and
    Studies* 22 (1969): 57–70.
————. " 'These Pretty Devices': A Study of Masques in Plays." In *A Book
    of Masques in Honour of Allardyce Nicoll.* Edited by T. J. B. Spencer and
    Stanley Wells. Cambridge: At the University Press, 1967.
Faber, M. D., and Skinner, Colin. "*The Spanish Tragedy,* Act IV." *Philolo-
    gical Quarterly* 49 (1970):444–59.
Farnham, Willard. *The Medieval Heritage of Elizabethan Tragedy.* Berkeley:
    University of California Press, 1936.
Farr, Dorothy M. *Thomas Middleton and the Drama of Realism: A Study of
    Some Representative Plays.* New York: Barnes & Noble, 1973.
Fergusson, Francis. *The Idea of a Theater, A Study of Ten Plays: The Art of
    Drama in Changing Perspective.* Princeton: Princeton University Press,
    1949.
Fetrow, Fred M. "Chapman's Stoic Hero in *The Revenge of Bussy D'Am-
    bois.*" *Studies in English Literature* 19 (1979): 229–37.
Fieler, Frank B. "The Eight Madmen in *The Duchess of Malfi.*" *Studies in
    English Literature* 7 (1967):343–50.
Finkelpearl, Philip J. *John Marston of the Middle Temple: An Elizabethan
    Dramatist in his Social Setting.* Cambridge, Mass.: Harvard University
    Press, 1969.
Foakes, R. A. "The Art of Cruelty: Hamlet and Vindici." *Shakespeare
    Survey* 26 (1973):21–31.
————. "John Marston's Fantastical Plays: *Antonio and Mellida* and

Antonio's Revenge." Philological Quarterly 41 (1962):229–39.

———. *Marston and Tourneur.* London: Longmans, 1978.

———. "On Marston, *The Malcontent,* and *The Revenger's Tragedy." The Elizabethan Theatre 6.* Edited by G. R. Hibbard. Hamden, Conn.: Shoe String Press, 1975.

Forest, Louise C. Turner."A Caveat for Critics Against Invoking Elizabethan Psychology." *PMLA* 61 (1946):651–72.

Forker, Charles R. "Love, Death, and Fame: The Grotesque Tragedy of John Webster." *Anglia* 91 (1973):194–218.

———. "Shakespeare's Theatrical Symbolism and Its Function in *Hamlet." Shakespeare Quarterly* 14 (1963):215–29.

Freeman, Arthur. *Thomas Kyd, Facts and Problems.* Oxford: Clarendon Press, 1967.

Gardner, Helen. *The Business of Criticism.* Oxford: Oxford University Press, 1959.

———. "Milton's 'Satan' and the Theme of Damnation in Elizabethan Tragedy." *Essays and Studies,* n.s. 1 (1948):46–66.

Geckle, George L. "*Antonio's Revenge:* 'Never more woe in lesser plot was found.' " *Comparative Drama* 6 (1972–73): 323–35.

Gianneti, Louis D. "A Contemporary View of *The Duchess of Malfi." Comparative Drama* 3 (1969):297–307.

Golding, M. R. "Variations in the Use of the Masque in English Revenge Tragedy." *Yearbook of English Studies* 3 (1973):44–54.

Gottschalk, Paul. "Hamlet and the Scanning of Revenge." *Shakespeare Quarterly* 24 (1973):155–70.

Granville-Barker, Harley. *Prefaces to Shakespeare.* Vol. 1, *Hamlet.* 1937. Reprint edition. Princeton: Princeton University Press, 1946.

Grebanier, Bernard. *The Heart of "Hamlet": The Play Shakespeare Wrote.* New York: Thomas Y. Crowell Co., 1960.

Greg, W. W. "Hamlet's Hallucination." *Modern Language Review* 12 (1917):393–421.

Hallett, Charles A. *Middleton's Cynics: A Study of Middleton's Insight into the Moral Psychology of the Mediocre Mind.* Jacobean Drama Studies, no. 47. Salzburg: University of Salzburg, 1975.

———. "The Psychological Drama of *Women Beware Women." Studies in English Literature* 12 (1972):375–89.

———. "The Retrospective Technique and its Implications for Tragedy." *Comparative Drama* 12 (1978):3–22.

——— and Frost, Kenneth E. "Poetry and Reality: The Zetema and its Significance for Poetics." *International Philosophical Quarterly* 17 (1977):415–43.

Hamilton, A. C. "*Titus Andronicus:* The Form of Shakespearean Tragedy." *Shakespeare Quarterly* 14 (1963):201–13.

Hankins, John E. *The Character of Hamlet.* Chapel Hill: University of North Carolina Press, 1941.

Hapgood, Robert. "*Hamlet* Nearly Absurd: The Dramaturgy of Delay." *Tulane Drama Review* 9 (Summer 1965):132–45.

Happé, P. "Tragic Themes in Three Tudor Moralities." *Studies in English Literature* 5 (1965):207–27.

Harrison, G. B. *Shakespeare's Tragedies.* London: Routledge and Kegan Paul, 1951.

Harrison, Jane. *Prolegomena to the Study of Greek Religion.* Cambridge: At the University Press, 1903.

Hart, A. "Once more the Mouse-Trap." *Review of English Studies* 17 (1941):11–20.

Hartford, G. F. "Once More Delay." *English Studies in Africa* 20 (1977):1–9.

Havely, Cicely. "The Play-Scene in *Hamlet.*" *Essays in Criticism* 23 (1973):217–35.

Herndl, George C. *The High Design: English Renaissance Tragedy and the Natural Law.* Lexington: University of Kentucky Press, 1970.

Higgins, Michael H. "Chapman's 'Senecal Man': A Study in Jacobean Psychology." *Review of English Studies* 21 (1945):183–91.

———. "The Convention of the Stoic Hero as Handled by Marston." *Modern Language Review* 39 (1944):338–46.

———. "The Development of the 'Senecal Man': Chapman's *Bussy d'Ambois* and Some Precursors." *Review of English Studies* 23 (1947):24–33.

Hoopes, Robert. *Right Reason in the English Renaissance.* Cambridge, Mass.: Harvard University Press, 1962.

Hughes, Geoffrey. "The Tragedy of a Revenger's Loss of Conscience: A Study of *Hamlet.*" *English Studies* 57 (1976):395–409.

Hunter, G. K. "English Folly and Italian Vice: The Moral Landscape of John Marston." In *Jacobean Theatre.* Edited by John Russell Brown and Bernard Harris. Stratford-upon-Avon Studies, 1. London: Edward Arnold, 1960.

———. "The Heroism of Hamlet." In *Hamlet.* Edited by John Russell Brown and Bernard Harris. Stratford-upon-Avon Studies, 5. London: Edward Arnold, 1963.

———. Introduction to *Antonio's Revenge.* See Primary Sources (Plays); Marston, John.

———. "Ironies of Justice in *The Spanish Tragedy.*" *Renaissance Drama* 8 (1965):89–104.

———. "Seneca and the Elizabethans: A Case-Study in 'Influence.' " *Shakespeare Survey* 20 (1967):17–26.

Ingram, R. W. *John Marston.* Boston: Twayne Publishers, 1978.

Jacobsen, Daniel J. " 'There It Goes'—or Does It?: Thunder in *The Revenger's Tragedy.*" *English Language Notes* 13 (1975):6–10.

James, D. G. "Moral and Metaphysical Uncertainty in *Hamlet.*" In *The Dream of Learning: An Essay on "The Advancement of Learning," "Hamlet" and "King Lear.*" Oxford: Clarendon Press, 1951.

Jenkins, Harold. "The Tragedy of Revenge in Shakespeare and Webster." *Shakespeare Survey* 14 (1961):45–55.

Jensen, Ejner J. "Kyd's *Spanish Tragedy:* The Play Explains Itself." *JEGP* 64 (1965):7–16.

Johnson, Francis R. "Elizabethan Drama and the Elizabethan Science of Psychology." In *English Studies Today.* Edited by C. L. Wrenn and G. Bullough. London: Oxford University Press, 1951.

Johnson, S. F. "The Regeneration of Hamlet." *Shakespeare Quarterly* 3 (1952):187–207.

———. *"The Spanish Tragedy,* or Babylon Revisited." In *Essays on Shakespeare and Elizabethan Drama in Honor of Hardin Craig.* Edited by Richard Hosley. Columbia: University of Missouri Press, 1962.

Jones, Emrys. *Scenic Form in Shakespeare.* Oxford: Clarendon Press, 1971.

Jones, Robert C. "Italian Settings and the 'World' of Elizabethan Tragedy." *Studies in English Literature* 10 (1970):251–68.

Joseph, Bertram. *Conscience of the King: A Study of "Hamlet."* London: Chatto & Windus, 1953.

Joseph, Sister Miriam. "Discerning the Ghost in *Hamlet.*" *PMLA* 76 (1961):493–502.

Kiefer, Frederick, "Seneca's Influence on Elizabethan Tragedy: An Annotated Bibliography." *Research Opportunities in Renaissance Drama* 21 (1978):17–34.

Kernan, Alvin. *The Cankered Muse: Satire of the English Renaissance.* New Haven: Yale University Press, 1959.

Kistner, A. L. and M. K. "Morality and Inevitability in *The Revenger's Tragedy.*" *JEGP* 71 (1972):36–46.

———. "The Senecan Background of Despair in *The Spanish Tragedy* and *Titus Andronicus.*" *Shakespeare Studies* 7 (1974):1–9.

Knapp, Robert S. *"Horestes:* The Uses of Revenge." *ELH* 40 (1973):205–20.

Kitto, H. D. F. *Form and Meaning in Drama: A Study of Six Greek Plays and of "Hamlet.*" London: Methuen & Co., 1956.

Knights, L. C. *An Approach to "Hamlet."* London: Chatto & Windus, 1960.

Krutch, Joseph Wood. *Modernism in Modern Drama: A Definition and an Estimate.* 1953. Reprint edition. Ithaca: Cornell University Press, Cornell Paperbacks, 1966.

Laird, David. "Hieronimo's Dilemma." *Studies in Philology* 62 (1965):137–46.

Lawlor, J. J. "The Tragic Conflict in *Hamlet.*" *Review of English Studies*, n.s. 1 (1950):97–113.

Lawrence, W. W. "Hamlet and the Mouse-Trap." *PMLA* 54 (1939):709–35.

———. "The Play Scene in *Hamlet.*" *JEGP* 18 (1919):1–22.

Layman, B. J. "Tourneur's Artificial Noon: The Design of *The Revenger's Tragedy.*" *Modern Language Quarterly* 34 (1973):20–35.

Leech, Clifford. "*The Atheist's Tragedy* as a Dramatic Comment on Chapman's *Bussy* Plays." *JEGP* 52 (1953):525–30.

Lever, J. W. *The Tragedy of State*. London: Methuen & Co., 1971.

Levin, Harry. *The Question of Hamlet*. New York: Oxford University Press, 1959.

Levin, Michael Henry. "'Vindicta mihi!': Meaning, Morality, and Motivation in *The Spanish Tragedy.*" *Studies in English Literature* 4 (1964):307–24.

Levin, Richard. *The Multiple Plot in English Renaissance Drama*. Chicago: University of Chicago Press, 1971.

Lewis, C. S. "Hamlet: The Prince or the Poem?" *Proceedings of the British Academy*, vol. 28. London: Humphrey Milford, 1942.

Lisca, Peter. "*The Revenger's Tragedy:* A Study in Irony." *Philological Quarterly* 38 (1959):242–51.

Lord, Joan M. "*The Duchess of Malfi:* 'the Spirit of Greatness' and 'of Woman.'" *Studies in English Literature* 16 (1976):305–17.

Lordi, Robert J. Introduction to *The Revenge of Bussy D'Ambois*. See Primary Sources (Plays): Chapman, George.

Lucas, F. L. *Seneca and Elizabethan Tragedy*. Cambridge: At the University Press, 1922.

Luecke, Jane Marie. "*The Duchess of Malfi:* Comic and Satiric Confusion in a Tragedy." *Studies in English Literature* 4 (1964):275–90.

McCullen, Joseph T. "Madness and the Isolation of Characters in Elizabethan and Early Stuart Drama." *Studies in Philology* 48 (1951):206–18.

McElroy, Bernard. "Recent Studies in Elizabethan and Jacobean Drama." *Studies in English Literature* 19 (1979):342–43.

Mack, Maynard. "The Jacobean Shakespeare: Some Observations on the Construction of the Tragedies." In *Jacobean Theatre*. Edited by John Russell Brown and Bernard Harris. Stratford-upon-Avon Studies, 1. London: Edward Arnold, 1960.

———. "The World of *Hamlet.*" *Yale Review* 41 (1951–52):502–23.

Mack, Maynard, Jr. *Killing the King: Three Studies in Shakespeare's Tragic Structure*. Yale Studies in English, no. 180. New Haven: Yale University Press, 1973.

MacLure, Millar. *George Chapman: A Critical Study*. Toronto: University of Toronto Press, 1966.

Margeson, J. M. R. *The Origins of English Tragedy*. Oxford: Clarendon Press, 1967.

Mehl, Dieter. *The Elizabethan Dumb Show: The History of a Dramatic Convention*. 1964. Reprinted in English. Cambridge, Mass.: Harvard University Press, 1966.

———. "Forms and Functions of the Play within a Play." *Renaissance Drama* 8 (1965):41–61.

Moorman, F. W. "The Pre-Shakespearean Ghost." *Modern Language Review* 1 (1906):85–95.

———. "Shakespeare's Ghosts." *Modern Language Review* 1 (1906):192–201.

Mroz, Sister Mary Bonaventure. *Divine Vengeance: A Study in the Philosophical Background of the Revenge Motif as It Appears in Shakespeare's Chronicle History Plays*. 1941. Reprint edition. New York: Haskell House Publishers, 1971.

Muir, Kenneth. *Shakespeare: "Hamlet."* London: Edward Arnold, 1963.

Mulryne, J. R. Introduction to *The Spanish Tragedy*. See Primary Sources (Plays): Kyd, Thomas.

———. "*The White Devil* and *The Duchess of Malfi.*" In *Jacobean Theatre*. Edited by John Russell Brown and Bernard Harris. Stratford-upon-Avon Studies, 1. London: Edward Arnold, 1960.

Murray, Peter B. *A Study of Cyril Tourneur*. Philadelphia: University of Pennsylvania Press, 1964.

———. *Thomas Kyd*. New York: Twayne Publishers, 1969.

Nelson, Robert J. *Play within a Play: The Dramatist's Conception of His Art, Shakespeare to Anouilh*. New Haven: Yale University Press, 1958.

Nicoll, Allardyce. "*The Revenger's Tragedy* and the Virtue of Anonymity." In *Essays on Shakespeare and Elizabethan Drama in Honor of Hardin Craig*. Edited by Richard Hosley. Columbia: University of Missouri Press, 1962.

Nosworthy, J. M. "A Reading of the Play-Scene in *Hamlet.*" *English Studies* 22 (1940):161–70.

Ornstein, Robert. "*The Atheist's Tragedy* and Renaissance Naturalism." *Studies in Philology* 51 (1954):194–207.

———. *The Moral Vision of Jacobean Tragedy*. Madison: University of Wisconsin Press, 1960.

Orange, Linwood E. "Hamlet's Mad Soliloquy." *South Atlantic Quarterly* 64 (1965):60–71.

Palmer, D. J. "The Unspeakable in Pursuit of the Uneatable: Language and Action in *Titus Andronicus.*" *Critical Quarterly* 14 (1972):320–39.

Pearce, Howard. "Virtù and Poesis in *The Revenger's Tragedy.*" *ELH* 43 (Spring 1976): 19–37.

Pearn, B. R. "Dumb-Show in Elizabethan Drama." *Review of English*

Studies 11 (1935):385–405.

Peers, Edgar A. *Elizabethan Drama and Its Mad Folk.* Cambridge: W. Heffner & Sons, 1914.

Perkinson, Richard H. "Nature and the Tragic Hero in Chapman's *Bussy* Plays." *Modern Language Quarterly* 3 (1942):263–85.

Peter, John. *Complaint and Satire in Early English Literature.* Oxford: Clarendon Press, 1956.

Peterson, Joyce E. *Curs'd Example: "The Duchess of Malfi" and Commonweal Tragedy.* Columbia: University of Missouri Press, 1978.

Phillips, J. E. "A Revaluation of *Horestes* (1567)." *Huntington Library Quarterly* 18 (1955):227–44.

Prior, Moody E. "The Play Scene in *Hamlet.*" *ELH* 9 (1942):188–97.

Prosser, Eleanor. *Hamlet and Revenge.* Stanford: Stanford University Press, 1967.

Ratliff, John D. "Hieronimo Explains Himself." *Studies in Philology* 54 (1957):112–18.

Reed, Robert R. *Bedlam on the Jacobean Stage.* Cambridge, Mass.: Harvard University Press, 1952.

———. "Hamlet, the Pseudo-Procrastinator." *Shakespeare Quarterly* 9 (1958):177–86.

Rees, Ennis. *The Tragedies of George Chapman: Renaissance Ethics in Action.* Cambridge, Mass.: Harvard University Press, 1954.

Reese, Jack E. "The Formalization of Horror in *Titus Andronicus.*" *Shakespeare Quarterly* 21 (1970):77–84.

Reither, James Allen. "Thomas Goffe, Dramatist." Ph.D. dissertation, University of Oregon, 1972.

Replogle, Carol. "Not Parody, Not Burlesque: The Play Within the Play in *Hamlet.*" *Modern Philology* 65 (1969):150–59.

Ribner, Irving. *Jacobean Tragedy: The Quest for Moral Order.* New York: Barnes & Noble, 1962.

Rice, Eugene F. *The Renaissance Idea of Wisdom.* Cambridge, Mass.: Harvard University Press, 1958.

Ricks, Christopher. "The Moral and Poetic Structure of *The Changeling.*" *Essays in Criticism* 10 (1960):290–306.

Righter, Anne. *Shakespeare and the Idea of the Play.* London: Chatto & Windus, 1962.

Rose, Mark. "*Hamlet* and the Shape of Revenge." *English Literary Renaissance* 1 (1971):132–43.

Ross, Lawrence J. Introduction to *The Revenger's Tragedy.* See Primary Sources (Plays): Tourneur, Cyril.

Rossiter, A. P. *English Drama from Early Times to the Elizabethans: Its Background, Origins, and Developments.* 1950. Reprint edition. New York: Barnes & Noble, 1967.

Rossky, William. "Imagination in the English Renaissance: Psychology and Poetic." *Studies in the Renaissance* 5 (1958):49–73.

Salingar, Leo G. "*The Changeling* and the Drama of Domestic Life." *Essays and Studies* 32 (1979):80–96.

―――. "*The Revenger's Tragedy* and the Morality Tradition." *Scrutiny* 6 (1938):402–24.

―――. "Tourneur and the Tragedy of Revenge." In *The Age of Shakespeare.* Edited by Boris Ford. Vol. 2, *The Pelican Guide to English Literature.* London: [Harmondsworth, Middlesex]: Penguin Books, 1955.

Sanders, Leslie. "*The Revenger's Tragedy:* A Play on the Revenge Play." *Renaissance and Reformation* 10 (1974):25–36.

Schoenbaum, Samuel. *Middleton's Tragedies: A Critical Study.* New York: Columbia University Press, 1955.

―――. "The Precarious Balance of John Marston." *PMLA* 67 (1952): 1069–78.

―――. "*The Revenger's Tragedy:* Jacobean Dance of Death." *Modern Language Quarterly* 15 (1954):201–7.

Schücking, Levin L. *The Meaning in "Hamlet."* 1937. Reprint edition. New York: Barnes & Noble, 1966.

Schuman, Samuel. *Cyril Tourneur.* Boston: Twayne Publishers, 1977.

Scott, Michael. *John Marston's Plays: Theme, Structure, Performance.* New York: Barnes & Noble, 1978.

Semper, I. J. "The Ghost in *Hamlet:* Pagan or Christian?" *The Month,* n.s. 9 (1953):222–34.

Sibly, John. "The Duty of Revenge in Tudor and Stuart Drama." *Review of English Literature* 8 (1967):46–54.

Siegel, Paul N. Reply to "Discerning the Ghost in *Hamlet.*" *PMLA* 78 (1963):148–49.

―――. *Shakespearean Tragedy and the Elizabethan Compromise.* New York: New York University Press, 1957.

Siemon, James Edward. "Disguise in Marston and Shakespeare." *Huntington Library Quarterly* 38 (1975):105–23.

Simpson, Percy. "The Theme of Revenge in Elizabethan Tragedy." In *Proceedings of the British Academy,* vol. 21. London: Humphrey Milford, 1935.

Sisson, C. J. "The Mouse-Trap Again." *Review of English Studies* 16 (1940):129–36.

Skulsky, Harold. " 'I Know My Course': Hamlet's Confidence." *PMLA* 89 (1974):477–86.

―――. "Revenge, Honor, and Conscience in *Hamlet.*" *PMLA* 85 (1970): 78–87.

Smith, James. "George Chapman." Part 1 in *Scrutiny* 3 (1934–

35):339-50; Part 2 in *Scrutiny* 4 (1935-36):45-61.

Soellner, Rolf. "The Madness of Hercules and the Elizabethans." *Comparative Literature* 10 (1958):309-24.

Sommers, Alan. " 'Wilderness of Tigers': Structure and Symbolism in *Titus Andronicus.*" *Essays in Criticism* 10 (1960):275-89.

Spens, Janet. "Chapman's Ethical Thought." *Essays and Studies* 11 (1925): 145-69.

Spivack, Bernard. *Shakespeare and the Allegory of Evil: The History of a Metaphor in Relation to His Major Villains.* New York: Columbia University Press, 1958.

Stabler, A. P. "Melancholy, Ambition, and Revenge in Belleforest's *Hamlet.*" *PMLA* 81 (1966):207-13.

Stagg, Louis C. "Figurative Imagery in Revenge Tragedies by Three Seventeenth-Century Contemporaries of Shakespeare." *South Central Bulletin* 26, no. 4 (1966): 43-50.

Strandberg, V. H. "The Revenger's Tragedy: Hamlet's Costly Code." *South Atlantic Quarterly* 65 (1966): 95-103.

Strathmann, E. A. "Elizabethan Meanings of 'Atheism.' " In *Sir Walter Ralegh: A Study in Elizabethan Skepticism.* New York: Columbia University Press, 1951.

Symonds, John Addington. *Shakspere's Predecessors in the English Drama.* 1884. New edition. London: Smith, Elder & Co., 1900.

Thorndike, A. H. "The Relations of *Hamlet* to Contemporary Revenge Plays." *PMLA* 17 (1902):125-220.

Tomlinson, T. M. "The Morality of Revenge: Tourneur's Critics." *Essays in Criticism* 10 (1960):134-47.

———. *A Study of Elizabethan and Jacobean Tragedy.* Cambridge: At the University Press, 1964.

Tricomi, Albert H. "The Aesthetics of Mutilation in *Titus Andronicus.*" *Shakespeare Survey* 27 (1974):11-19.

Ure, Peter. "On Some Differences Between Senecan and Elizabethan Tragedy." 1948. Reprinted in *Elizabethan and Jacobean Drama: Critical Essays by Peter Ure.* Edited by J. C. Maxwell. English Texts and Studies. New York: Barnes & Noble, 1974.

Vyvyan, John. *The Shakespearean Ethic.* London: Chatto & Windus, 1959.

Voegelin, Eric. *From Enlightenment to Revolution.* Edited by John H. Hallowell. Durham, N.C.: Duke University Press, 1975.

———. *Order and History.* 4 vols. Baton Rouge: Louisiana State University Press, 1956-1975.

Waith, Eugene M. *The Herculean Hero in Marlowe, Chapman, Shakespeare, and Dryden.* New York: Columbia University Press, 1962.

———. "The Metamorphosis of Violence in *Titus Andronicus.*" *Shakespeare Survey* 10 (1957):39-49.

Walker, Alice. " 'Miching Malicho' and the Play Scene in *Hamlet.*" *Modern Language Review* 31 (1936):513–17.

Watson, Curtis Brown. *Shakespeare and the Renaissance Concept of Honor.* Princeton: Princeton University Press, 1960.

West, Robert H. "Ghosts." In *The Invisible World: A Study of Pneumatology in Elizabethan Drama.* Athens, Ga.: University of Georgia Press, 1939.

———. "King Hamlet's Ambiguous Ghost." *PMLA* 70 (1955): 1107–17.

Wharton, T. F. *"The Malcontent* and 'Dreams, Visions, Fantasies.' " *Essays in Criticism* 24 (1974):261–74.

———. "Old Marston or New Marston: The *Antonio* Plays." *Essays in Criticism* 25 (1975):357–69.

Wieler, John William. *George Chapman—The Effect of Stoicism upon His Tragedies.* 1949. Reprint edition. New York: Octagon Books, 1969.

Wilds, Lillian. "The Revenger as Dramatist: A Study of the Character-as-Dramatist in *The Revenger's Tragedy.*" *Rocky Mountain Review* 30 (1976): 113–22.

Wilds, Nancy G. " 'Of Rare Fire Compact': Image and Rhetoric in The Revenger's Tragedy." Texas Studies in Literature and Language 17 (1975):61–74.

Williams, George. Introduction to *The Changeling.* See Primary Sources (Plays): Middleton, Thomas and Rowley, William.

Willson, Robert F., Jr. *"Hamlet:* The Muddled Mouse-Trap." *CLA Journal* 22 (1978):160–66.

Wilson, J. Dover. *What Happens in "Hamlet."* 1935. 3rd edition. Cambridge: At the University Press, 1967.

Wood, H. Harvey. Introduction to *The Plays of John Marston.* See Primary Sources (Plays): Marston, John.

Wright, Louis B. "Madmen as Vaudeville Performers on the Elizabethan Stage." *JEGP* 30 (1931):48–54.

Index

343

Dante, 234
Death of avenger: analyzed, 11, 97–
100, 164. In: *Antonio's Revenge*,
161–62, 179–80, 242; *Atheist's
Tragedy*, 277, 279; *Hamlet*, 11, 99,
158, 217–21; *Horestes*, 251, 262;
Orestes, 262–64; *Revenge of Bussy
D'Ambois*, 277–79; *Revenger's Tragedy*,
99, 241–42; *Spanish Tragedy*, 158–59,
160
Dekker, Thomas: *The Honest Whore I*,
42; *Orestes Furies (Furens)*, 317 n.11
Delay: defined, 10, 84–89, 274; effect
of omission of, 85; motives for,
87–88; as plot device, 86–87; related
to madness, 86, 89, 148; theatricality
of, 12. In: *Atheist's Tragedy*, 274,
275–77; *Antonio's Revenge*, 166, 172,
173; *Hamlet*, 87–89, 199–200, 206,
212–17; *Hoffman*, 85–86; *Horestes*,
249; *Orestes*, 87, 255–56; *Revenge of
Bussy D'Ambois*, 274–77; *Revenger's
Tragedy*, 231–32
Derivative play, 254, 256–57, 261, 264
Descent into self, 123–24, 176, 229; of
Duchess of Malfi, 286–89; of Hamlet, 196; of Hieronimo, 147; of Vindice, 229
Dictys, 254, 316 n.4
Didactic approach to revenge, 271–72
Disguise, 93–95; Antonio's, 94, 95, 309
n.6; Hamlet's, 95, 190–94, 200, 258,
313 n.8; Hieronimo's, 93–94;
Orestes', 255; Revenge's (in *Horestes*),
248–49; Vindice's, 94, 238–40, 242
Double (Pandulpho and Antonio),
166–68, 172–73, 174

Eliot, T. S., 125, 293, 308 n.21
Excess. *See* Multiple murders

Farnham, Willard, 316 n.3
Fetrow, Fred, 278, 318 n.11
Fletcher, John, *The Pilgrim:* 42, 44,
53–54, 55–56
Foakes, R. A., 162
Ford, John: and passion as madness,
45–46, 47–48; *Broken Heart*, 47–48,
58, 65, 282, 300

Forker, Charles R., 313 n.8, 319 n.8
Free-floating rage, 6–7, 11, 291
Frost, Kenneth E., 309 n.4
Gair, W. Reavley, 303 n.13
Geckle, George, 309 n.7, 311 n.7
Ghost, 8–9, 17–40, 96, 229–30; as ex-
position, 183–84; list of, 302 n.3; re-
lation of to Furies, 20–21, 105; Senecan traits of, 17, 18–21; skull as,
228–31; theatricality of, 12, 18–19.
In: *Antonio's Revenge*, 19, 28–35, 96,
168–70, 176–77, 183, 185, 231;
Atheist's Tragedy, 33, 276; *Hamlet*,
35–39, 182–90, 194, 207–10 passim,
214, 231, 303 n.18, 313 n.4; *Orestes*,
246, 258–59, 260–61; *Revenge of
Bussy D'Ambois*, 277; *Revenger's
Tragedy*, 228–30, 231; *Spanish
Tragedy*, 21–28, 34–35, 140, 141–45,
155, 158, 160, 183, 186, 231
Goffe, Thomas, *The Tragedy of Orestes:*
87, 91, 244–46, 254–64, 303 n.13,
315 n.1, 317 nn.11 and 12
Gower, John, 247, 252, 253, 316 n.4
Greg, W. W., 313 n.6
Hall, John, 44
Hall, Joseph, 45, 50, 65
Hankins, John E., 37
Happé, J. P., 316 n.3
Harrison, G. B.: on Ophelia, 3, 42, 61
Harrison, Jane, 20
Hero: believability of, 114–16, 117–18,
124–26; Elizabethan concepts of,
116–18, 122–25; Chapman's concepts of, 269–71, 272; Marlowe's
concepts of, 114–16; Marston's concepts of, 174; concepts of in revenge
tragedy, 118–19, 119–27, 202; importance of to civilization, 109–10,
116–18; of retribution and revenge
plots compared, 163–65, 178–79;
saints as, 110. *See also* Hero, tragic
Hero, tragic: inadequacy of Elizabethan psychology to explain,
101–2; revenger as, 32, 98, 113–14,
119–27, 202; Antonio as, 161–62,
174; Beatrice as, 299–300; Charle-